Africa Writing Europe

C|ross
ᴜltures

Readings in the Post / Colonial

Literatures in English

105

Series Editors

Gordon Collier
(Giessen)

†Hena Maes–Jelinek
(Liège)

Geoffrey Davis
(Aachen)

Africa Writing Europe

Opposition, Juxtaposition, Entanglement

Edited by
Maria Olaussen and Christina Angelfors

Amsterdam - New York, NY 2009

Cover image: Gordon Collier

Cover design: Pier Post

The paper on which this book is printed meets the requirements of "ISO 9706:1994, Information and documentation - Paper for documents - Requirements for permanence".

ISBN: 978-90-420-2593-6
© Editions Rodopi B.V., Amsterdam – New York, NY 2009
Printed in The Netherlands

Table of Contents

Acknowledgements

———— ⟨⟩ ————

S TUDYING THE IMAGE OF EUROPE in African literature is an
idea that was born out of collaboration between researchers in English and French literature at the School of Humanities, Växjö University, Sweden. Africanists from several European countries, from Africa,
Australia, and the USA were later attached to the project. Some of the
essays in this volume are reworked versions of lectures delivered at the
School of Oriental and African Studies in London 2005. This was the
venue for "The First European Conference of African Studies," organized
by AEGIS (Africa–Europe Group for Interdisciplinary Studies). The
"Africa Writing Europe" project arranged a panel at that conference. The
research project ended with a symposium held at Växjö University in June
2006.

We hope that the new way of viewing the relationship between Europe
and Africa which is presented in this volume will contribute to an increased
understanding of the complex interaction between the two continents, with
Europe, for once, occupying the place of the Other.

We wish to thank all seminar participants for sharing their ideas and
contributing to the development of the project. Special thanks go to Thomas
Brückner for planning and organising the initial project proposal, the
seminars and the Summer School during his stay as guest researcher at
Växjö University. We would like to thank the contributors for their dedication to this project, their enthusiastic and diligent work during our workshops sessions, and, most of all, for their patience. The readers who peer-
reviewed the contributions responded promptly and we wish to thank them
for their valuable feedback on our work. We are grateful to Geoffrey Davis

for his careful reading of the manuscript and to Anders Forsberg for invaluable technical assistance.

We also thank STINT (the Swedish Foundation for International Cooperation in Research and Higher Education), without whose financial support over several years the project could not have been run. Many thanks also to the Bank of Sweden Tercentenary Foundation for supporting the project in its initial phase.

◄►

Africa Writing Europe
– ‹› – An Introduction

MARIA OLAUSSEN

I

T HIS STUDY OF THE IDEA OF EUROPE in African literature
charts the development and significance of what has conventionally been seen as an opposition, but which in this book is seen
as a complex and changing juxtaposition. In our understanding, the two
geographical spaces and concepts are interdependent and intertwined rather
than clear-cut and separate. The focus on Europe involves a shift from a
study of African literature as expressions of the specific concerns of African societies only, to readings which point to the importance of this literature for global concerns in general but also particularly for a new
understanding of the relations between Africa and Europe. *Africa Writing
Europe* aims at questioning this binary by studying how Europe is implicated in the definition of Africa and Africa in the definition of Europe.

Achille Mbembe's study *On the Postcolony* focuses on the discursive
production of Africa as one of the "imaginary significations" that have
become necessary for Europe to constitute itself.[1] He sees the difficulty in
"speaking rationally about Africa" as a specifically European problem
emanating from the opposition between self and other which has come to
characterize European encounters with Africa.[2] Africa thus stands for ab-

---

[1] Achille Mbembe, *On the Postcolony* (*De la postcolonie, essai sur l'imagination
politique dans l'Afrique contemporaine*, 2000; Berkeley: U of California P, 2001): 2.
[2] Mbembe, *On the Postcolony*, 2.

solute otherness and challenges the European philosophical tradition which, according to Mbembe, encounters "virtually insurmountable difficulties" when it comes to dealing with the experience of the other.[3] The development of modernity is, according to Mbembe, the key to understanding the development and legacy of the binary between Europe and Africa. The challenge is here encompassed by the fact that Europe was constituted through modernity where ideals of rationalism and universality are central, whereas "Africa was born to modernity" through the slave trade and colonialism.[4] Mbembe's most urgent question concerns "the possibilities of accomplishing in reality the promises of universality contained in the ideals of the *Aufklärung.*"[5]

Dipesh Chakrabarty's *Provincializing Europe* similarly engages with Europe as an "imaginary figure" which determines the context of all debates concerning political modernity.[6] The importance of this imaginary figure of Europe lies, according to Chakrabarty, in the fact that concepts such as "citizenship, the state, civil society, public sphere, human rights, equality before the law, the individual, distinctions between public and private, the idea of the subject, democracy, popular sovereignty, social justice, scientific rationality, and so on all bear the burden of European thought and history" and at the same time form the basis of an "indispensable [...] universal and secular vision of the human."[7] Chakrabarty's concern with this legacy is similar to that of Mbembe, in that he points to the importance of this vision as a global force for social justice even as it carries the impact of the history of European expansion. As Chakrabarty puts it, "The European colonizer of the nineteenth century both preached this Enlightenment humanism at the colonized and at the same time denied it in practice."[8] Europe is thus constituted on the basis of the refusal to admit the colonized subject into universality and of appropriating the idea of the human for a specific racially determined, class-bound, and gendered figure. This appropriation of the universal for the European lies at the basis of the Europe–Africa opposition.

---

[3] Mbembe, *On the Postcolony*, 2.

[4] *On the Postcolony*, 13.

[5] *On the Postcolony*, 11.

[6] Dipesh Chakrabarty, *Provincializing Europe: Postcolonial Thought and Historical Difference* (Princeton NJ: Princeton UP, 2000): 4.

[7] Chakrabarty, *Provincializing Europe*, 4.

[8] *Provincializing Europe*, 4.

When African literature speaks about Europe, it returns to the origin of the opposition – both to the ideals of universality and to the betrayal of these ideals. In modernity, the African subject, constituted through structures of oppression and exploitation, articulates Europe in a way that challenges the very basis of the Africa–Europe opposition. While the subject as shaped by literature escapes any easy identification with the subject as shaped by and in social space, there are intricate connections between literature and material reality. The literary text can be seen as a transformative site of possibilities for articulating new subject-positions. The novelist Carlos Fuentes, in his speech at the International Literature Festival in Berlin in 2005, saw the power of fiction as residing in invention. "Fiction invents what the world lacks, what the world has forgotten, what it hopes to attain and perhaps can never reach."[9] He also saw the task of the critical imagination as that of "responding to the passage of history with the passion of literature."[10] The paradoxical result of looking for the idea of Europe in African literature is that it takes us back to the historical context of the colonial encounter, thereby revealing the fragility of the oppositions underpinning colonialism.

The present study is part of a shift of focus within postcolonial studies.[11] This adjusted focus is influenced by a similar turn towards masculinity within gender studies, the increasing interest in whiteness within studies of ethnic identities, and the study of heteronormative structures in queer studies.[12] What these shifts of focus have in common is both an awareness

---

[9] Carlos Fuentes, "In Praise of the Novel," *Critical Inquiry* 32 (Summer 2006): 614.

[10] Fuentes, "In Praise of the Novel," 615.

[11] See, for instance, *Africa and Europe: En/Countering Myths: Essays on Literature and Cultural Politics,* ed. Carlotta von Maltzan (Frankfurt am Main: Peter Lang, 2003), *Occidentalism: Images of the West,* ed. James G. Carrier (Oxford: Clarendon, 1995), *Africa, Europe and (Post)colonialism,* ed. Susan Arndt & Marek Spitczok von Brisinski (Bayreuth African Studies, 2006), Graham Huggan, *The Postcolonial Exotic: Marketing the Margins* (London & New York: Routledge, 2001), John McLeod, *Postcolonial London: Rewriting the Metropolis* (London & New York: Routledge, 2004), *Encounter Images in the Meetings between Africa and Europe,* ed. Mai Palmberg (Uppsala: Nordic Africa Institute, 2001).

[12] Judith Butler's *Gender Trouble* from 1990 has led to an interest in performativity and destabilization of categories beyond that of queer studies. Other important contributions to this shift in focus are, for instance, Eve Kosofsky Sedgwick, *Epistemology of the Closet* (Berkeley & Los Angeles: U of California P, 1990), Chrys Ingraham, "The Heterosexual Imaginary: Feminist Sociology and Theories of Gender" (1994), in *Queer*

of the predominance of European, male, white, and heteronormative perspectives and an interest in revealing power-structures. What further unites these perspectives is a focus on the interdependence of the oppositions within the binaries and a move towards destabilizing categories. 'Europe' comes into existence through 'Africa' in much the same way as masculinity is created in a binary where femininity is of crucial importance, whiteness gains significance only by maintaining its difference from blackness, and the heterosexual norm is established by marginalizing other sexualities. What has hitherto been a dominant but invisible perspective is therefore placed under scrutiny. While this shift in focus has to do with revealing power-structures that work through their invisibility, there is often a concern, especially within critical whiteness studies, that this attention will in fact have the opposite effect: i.e. of reifying rather than dismantling opposites. In an essay on the phenomenology of whiteness, Sara Ahmed sees "any project that aims to dismantle or challenge the categories that are made invisible through privilege [as] bound to participate in the object of its critique."[13] Addressing the images of Europe in African literature with the aim of questioning the binary itself is one such project.

The essays in this volume address literary texts from a variety of geographical locations and are here presented in an order that forms a movement from South Africa to West Africa, through North Africa, to texts that are primarily concerned with the immigrant experience in Europe. This order is

---

Theory/Sociology, ed. Steven Seidman (Malden MA: Blackwell, 1996): 203–19, Stevi Jackson, *Heterosexuality in Question* (London: Sage, 1995), Jonathan Ned Katz, *The Invention of Heterosexuality* (New York: Plume, 1995), and Judith Halberstam, *Female Masculinity* (Durham NC & London: Duke UP, 1998). For discussions of whiteness, see Vron Ware, *Beyond the Pale: White Women, Racism and History* (London & New York: Verso, 1992), Ruth Frankenberg, *White Women, Race Matters: The Social Construction of Whiteness* (Minneapolis: U of Minnesota P, 1993), *Displacing Whiteness: Essays in Social and Cultural Criticism*, ed. Ruth Frankenberg (Durham NC: Duke UP, 1997), and Richard Dyer, *White: Essays on Race and Culture* (London: Routledge, 1997). Frantz Fanon's discussions of masculinity and race in *Black Skin, White Masks* have led to several feminist readings. For studies of masculinity from a postcolonial perspective, see also Ashis Nandy, *The Intimate Enemy: Loss and Recovery of Self under Colonialism* (New Delhi: Oxford UP, 1983), and *African Masculinities: Men in Africa from the Late Nineteenth Century to the Present*, ed. Lahoucine Ouzgane & Robert Morrell (New York: Palgrave Macmillan, 2005).

[13] Sara Ahmed, "A Phenomenology of Whiteness," *Feminist Theory* 8.2 (2007): 149–42.

intended to draw attention to the Cape-to-Cairo sweep in colonial history and to look at how these literary texts articulate the possibility of imagining anew the relation between Africa and Europe. The Cape-to-Cairo image serves as a reminder of the persistence of a colonial fantasy of the African continent in relation to Europe. This fantasy, most famously imagined by Cecil John Rhodes, still produces the continent as part of a totalizing vision for European adventurers and travellers. Most importantly, this image also leads to a definition of Africa which excludes both North and South Africa on the grounds that these areas are somehow not part of Africa proper.[14] This historicist and exceptionalist notion can be traced to a Hegelian definition of Africa that identifies northern Africa with Asia and sees Africa as "still involved in the conditions of mere nature," thus existing only "on the threshold of the World's History."[15] As Peter Merrington argues, the Cape-to-Cairo image was central in the forging of colonial South Africa as linked to European culture and civilization by evoking similarities in climate and culture with the Mediterranean and inventing an historical affinity between Ancient Egypt and southern Africa.[16] This imagined connection was particularly important at the time of the Union of South Africa and, as Merrington shows, it existed as part of a neo-Hegelian ideology aimed at separating southern Africa from the rest of the continent in order to claim for it a place among what was perceived to be 'civilized' nations and what was defined as history proper. Defining Africa as the entire continent challenges this neo-Hegelian idea whereby particular geographical areas and ethnicities are seen as exceptional and non-African. It also allows for a radical reinterpretation of genealogies, in the sense that Africa is at times allowed to merge with Europe and is defined both within and in opposition to historical traces of exchange.

---

[14] Hegel divides Africa into three parts: North Africa, which he calls "European Africa"; the Nile delta, which he sees in connection to Asia; and sub-Saharan Africa, which he terms "Africa proper" and which he describes as "the land of childhood, which, lying beyond the day of self-conscious history, is enveloped in the dark mantle of Night." Georg Friedrich Wilhelm Hegel, *Lectures on the Philosophy of History*, tr. J. Sibree (*Vorlesungen über die Philosophie der Geschichte*, 1834; tr. Mineola NY: Dover, 2004): 91.

[15] Hegel, *Lectures on the Philosophy of History*, 99.

[16] Peter Merrington, "A Staggered Orientalism: The Cape-to-Cairo Imaginary," in *South Africa in the Global Imaginary*, ed. Leon de Kock, Louise Bethlehem & Sonja Laden (Pretoria: U of South Africa P, 2004): 57–93.

Defining Europe within this opposition evolves around the colonial encounter. For the purposes of this study, we have analysed literary texts written in English or French, and the main focus will therefore be on the specific contexts assumed or projected by these texts. This does not mean that Europe is defined exclusively as the colonial metropolis or that Africa would be expressed in these languages only, but it does carry an understanding of Europe as marked by French and British colonial history even when the texts under discussion deal with other parts of Europe. The relation between Europe and Africa is, of course, far more complex than this focus would allow. Increasing attention is now paid to the colonial past of other European nations as well as to African migrant literature in European languages other than English and French.[17] Chakrabarty's discussion of the function of historicism as part of colonial power-structures is important in this context:

> Historicism is what made modernity or capitalism look not simply global but rather as something that became global over time, by originating in one place (Europe) and then spreading outside it. This 'first in Europe, then elsewhere' structure of global historical time was historicist.[18]

The arrival of the settler intellectual at the metropolitan centre is often expressed in terms of an arrival at a place which is already familiar and where events take place without delay or displacement.[19]

Historicism is not restricted to the relation between various nations in Europe and their colonies. As Chakrabarty points out, this mechanism works through margins and centres in other parts of the world: "different non-Western nationalisms would later produce local versions of the same narrative, replacing 'Europe' by some locally constructed center."[20] While

---

[17] See, for instance, *Transcultural Modernities: Narrating Africa in Europe*, ed. Elizabeth Bekers, Sissy Helff & Daniela Merolla (Matatu 36; Amsterdam & New York: Rodopi, 2008). For a discussion of the idea of Europe in Zimbabwean literature written in Shona, see Kennedy C. Chinyowa, "Battling between Alienation and Desire: Images of 'European-ness/Western-ness' in Contemporary Zimbabwean Literature," in *Africa and Europe: En/Countering Myths: Essays on Literature and Cultural Politics*, ed. Carlotta von Maltzan (Frankfurt am Main: Peter Lang, 2003): 133–46.

[18] Chakrabarty, *Provincializing Europe*, 9.

[19] See, for instance, McLeod, *Postcolonial London*.

[20] Chakrabarty, *Provincializing Europe*, 7.

Chakrabarty refers to the fuzzy boundaries of Europe, there is no discussion of the process of historicism within Europe itself. Historicism is seen in the process of claiming certain events as European only, regardless of the difficulties of defining the exact boundaries of Europe and of the involvement and influence of non-Europeans in these events. This process of inclusion and exclusion within Europe itself, however, also needs to be studied in order to understand Europe in postcolonial terms. The need to belong to Europe structures the relations between margins and centres inside Europe within the same narrative that determines the relation between European colonial powers and their colonies.

Defining Europe thus involves a recognition of how the ideas of progress and development came to be identified with particular regions, national cultures, and languages rather than others and of the implications that changing power-relations within Europe had for marginalized areas. The history of scientific racism and the Holocaust shows that all ethnicities, both within and beyond of Europe, were objects of classification and that these scientific activities had far-reaching consequences.[21] For marginalized ethnicities, the need to align oneself both culturally and ethnically with the most powerful European nations was often an act of survival. The slavery, racism, and exploitation that European colonial powers perpetrated against Africans on the African continent form the basis of the wealth that all Europeans continue to enjoy through those mechanisms, which have come to define the European. While the development of national identities in all European countries needs to be placed within the context of European expansion within and exploitation of other parts of the world, it is also important to study how this interest in discovering a colonial past might reinforce rather than challenge the power-structures that define Europe. A focus on postcolonial Europe which aims only at excavating colonial practices among marginalized European nations allows these nations to identify with the colonial powers of the past rather than with their victims. Wholesale denial of participation in colonial history, on the other hand, could also be an expression of a need to identify with a particular definition of progress and development whereby only the most civilized nations have remained untouched by racism and colonialism. Development-aid discourse can similarly be seen as structuring the relations between donors and receivers in such a way as to participate in a definition and consolidation of a

---

[21] See Stephen Jay Gould, *The Mismeasure of Man* (Harmondsworth: Penguin, 1981).

European identity defined as able and superior.[22] Once the Africa–Europe opposition is undermined, these complex questions of complicity need to be addressed on an entirely new basis, one that allows for the fact that all identities have been shaped by and continue to express structures of power and exclusion.

The definitions of Europe and European used in this volume vary. This becomes particularly significant in the contributions discussing South African literature. Dorothy Driver and Gabeba Baderoon place their analyses within a definition of 'European' which, according to the second definition given in the *Oxford English Dictionary*, can mean "a person of European extraction who lives outside Europe." The apartheid categorizations established a usage in which a person could be both a South African and a European. Geoffrey V. Davis, conversely, reads Europe in the texts by Dan Jacobson as what was left behind in Lithuania by the European settlers who emigrated and became part of Africa. In Wumi Raji's contribution, Europe is defined in relation to the ideologies that inform a new rendering of the indigenous Yorùbá legend in Femi Osofisan's play *Morountodun*. In Ann–Sofie Persson's reading of Marie Cardinal's texts, the protagonist herself, as a French settler in Algeria, embodies both Europe and Africa. A similar duality of Europe is present in Jarmo Pikkujämsä's reading of Ken Bugul's autobiography, where the immigrant experience in Europe provides a new perspective on the Senegalese village. The immigrant experience is also present in the contributions by Alexandra Schultheis, myself, and Jopi Nyman; here Europe is defined as the location of exile from Africa.

The role of Islam in the literary representations of Africa and African tradition studied in this volume is primarily one of opposition to a European way of life or European identities. This stance is particularly evident in Tatamkulu Afrika's autobiography, discussed by Gabeba Baderoon, where the definitions of the apartheid state facilitate the use of an Islamic identity as first and foremost African. It is also present in the literary texts discussed by Ann–Sofie Persson, Jarmo Pikkujämsä, and Alexandra Schultheis. The representation of Islam as part of the expression of an African identity must be understood within the context of an orientalist discourse which continues to identify Islam in opposition to Europe and the West. In

---

[22] For a study focusing on the identity of development aid workers see Maria Baaz Eriksson, *The Paternalism of Partnership: A Postcolonial Reading of Identity in Development Aid* (New York & London: Zed, 2005).

his final preface to *Orientalism*, written in 2003, Edward Said wishes to remind his readers of his main argument: namely, that "neither the term Orient nor the concept of the West has any ontological stability; each is made up of human effort, partly affirmation, partly identification of the Other."[23] He goes on to point out that these "supreme fictions" are nevertheless used in an increasing polarization of Islam from the West, where both are described in reductionist and totalizing terms. Said defines critical thought specifically concerned with the interpretation of literature as opposed to this polarization. He sees it as a "slow working together of cultures that overlap, borrow from each other, and live together in far more interesting ways than any abridged or inauthentic mode of understanding can allow."[24] *Africa Writing Europe* aims at understanding precisely this working-together of cultures in the face of the increasing tendency towards simplification and polarization.

The question of gender is a central aspect of most essays in this volume. As several feminist scholars have shown, the colonial encounter which brought about African modernity and created the opposition between Africa and Europe is a gendered process.[25] The production of tradition vs. modernity remains caught up in a gendered opposition between the public and the private in which authenticity and cultural self-determination are located in practices that primarily determine the lived experience of women.[26] Colonial discourse on African village life sets the latter in opposition to Europe, either as a site of oppressive practices where European intervention is needed or as preserves of an important and superior cultural heritage. Uma Narayan argues that the gendering of concepts such as tradition and culture was an inherent part of both colonial and anticolonial discourse. Narayan writes specifically about India but her analysis of the term 'west-

---

[23] Edward W. Said, "Preface to the Twenty-fifth Anniversary Edition," *Orientalism* (New York: Vintage, 2003): xvii.

[24] Said, "Preface to the Twenty-fifth Anniversary Edition," xxix.

[25] See, for instance, Uma Narayan, *Dislocating Cultures: Identities, Traditions and Third World Feminism* (New York & London: Routledge, 1997).

[26] Eric Hobsbawn and Terrence Ranger argue that African tradition is produced through the tradition – modernity opposition and that invented traditions formed an important part of the policy of indirect rule. *The Invention of Tradition*, ed. Eric Hobsbawm & Terrence O. Ranger (Cambridge: Cambridge U P, 1983). See also Partha Chatterjee, *Nationalist Thought and the Colonial World: A Derivative Discourse?* (London: Zed, 1986).

ernization' is useful for the way in which Europe functions in African literature in relation to female experience.

> the term 'westernization' functions in colonial and postcolonial
> Third World contexts primarily as a sort of rhetorical term, and that
> the term is often deployed in inconsistent as well as problematic
> ways [...] This 'selective labelling' of certain changes and not
> others as symptoms of 'westernization' reflects underlying political
> agendas.[27]

The production of Europe, as many of the essays in this volume show, is
caught up in this use of the term 'westernization' as specifically concerned
with changes in the life situation of women. What is perceived as Europe
and a European way of life gains its meaning from the perceived authenticity of African village life. The complexities of this stance are brought out
in the essays by Jarmo Pikkujämsä and Alexandra Schultheis. Another significant aspect of the gendered Africa–Europe dichotomy is the experience
of girls growing up in colonial societies. Ann–Sofie Persson's reading of
Marie Cardinal's autobiographical work shows how the restrictions placed
on the adolescent girl become synonymous with a European way of life,
whereas Algeria is connected with the freedom of childhood.

European modernity saw the rise of scientific enquiry, and it was
through science that Europe came to be defined and described in opposition
to Africa. The primary aim of the pseudo-science of phrenology and other
forms of scientific racism was to establish a hierarchy of human races
based on both physical attributes and moral, social, and intellectual capaci-
ties associated with these attributes.[28] The bodies of African women were
important sites of investigation for European male scientists determined to
establish the superiority of European races. The European body became the
visible sign of moral superiority, involving Victorian ideals of female subordination, sexual restraint in men, and an absence of sexual desire in women. These ideals were seen as universally valid and attainable for all races
but as most clearly associated with the peoples of Western Europe. The
African 'difference' was established within a discourse of inferiority and
shame in which sexual promiscuity and female licentiousness were seen as

---

[27] Narayan, *Dislocating Cultures: Identities, Traditions and Third World Feminism*, 22.
[28] Stephen Jay Gould, *The Mismeasure of Man*.

the defining characteristics of inferiority.[29] When European feminist movements challenged these ideals of femininity and demanded sexual fulfilment for women as well, they articulated a resistance to a form of oppression apparently experienced by white women only. In the colonial context,
where female chastity was seen as one of the most important defining characteristics of civilization, a focus on sexuality and the female body could
not be articulated without reinforcing old ideas of racial inferiority.[30] The
transvaluation achieved by feminism in Europe, where women advocate
and identify with sexual freedom, did not lead to a similar transvaluation in
racial terms. Instead, the perceived superiority of Europe remains intact,
while African societies and social groups that advocate ideals of domesticity and sexual control are seen as outdated and, once again, in need of European expertise in order to develop. African feminist movements, in their
work for gender equality in various domains, negotiate the legacies of colonial images of African women as well as the complex ways in which
feminist and colonialist histories converge.[31] Gwendolyn Mikell, for

---

[29] Sander Gilman's analysis of nineteenth-century ideas of sexuality in Europe
through the Saartjie Baartman case (the 'Hottentot Venus') shows the production of
female sexuality as chiefly connected to blackness and as pathological and dangerous.
Gilman, *Sexuality: An Illustrated History* (New York: John Wiley & Sons, 1989), and
"Black Bodies, White Bodies: Towards an Iconography of Female Sexuality in Late
Nineteenth Century Art, Medicine and Literature," *Critical Inquiry* 12.1 (1985): 204–42.
See also Yvette Abrahams, "The Great Long National Insult: 'Science', Sexuality and
the Khoisan in the 18th and early 19th Century," *Agenda* 32 (1997): 34–48.

[30] Literary representations of the body and sexuality in African literatures are discus-
sed in several essays in *Body, Sexuality and Gender: Versions and Subversions in Afri-
can Literatures*, vol. 1, ed. Flora Veit–Wild & Dirk Naguschewski (*Matatu* 29–30;
Amsterdam & New York: Rodopi, 2005). On the question of silence about sexuality in
African feminist discourse, see Desiree Lewis, "Against the Grain: Black Women and
Sexuality," *Agenda* 63 (2005): 11–24, Signe Arnfred, "African Sexuality/Sexuality in
Africa: Tales and Silences," in *Rethinking Sexualities in Africa*, ed. Signe Arnfred
(Uppsala: Nordic Africa Institute, 2004): 59–76.

[31] For discussions of African feminism see, for example, Mary Kolawole, *Womanism
and African Consciousness* (Trenton NJ: Africa World Press, 1997), Molara Ogundipe–
Leslie, *Recreating Ourselves: African Women and Critical Transformation* (Trenton
NJ: Africa World Press, 1994), *The Politics of (M)othering: Womanhood, Identity, and
Resistance in African Literature*, ed. Obioma Nnaemeka (London: Routledge, 1997),
African Women and Feminism: Reflecting on the Politics of Sisterhood, ed. Oyeronke
Oyewumi (Trenton NJ: Africa World Press, 2003), and Susan Arndt, *The Dynamics of
African Feminism: Defining and Classifying African-Feminist Literatures*, tr. Isabel
Cole (*Feminismus im Widerstreit*, 2000; tr. Trenton NJ: Africa World Press, 2002).

instance, defines African feminism directly in opposition to the movements
that developed in Europe and the USA as "distinctly heterosexual, pro-
natal, and concerned with many 'bread, butter, culture and power' issues."[32] These definitions of a specifically African feminism are at times
expressed in such a way that they tend to take the statements and concerns
of European feminist movements and the theoretical achievements within
queer studies as expressions of the views of European women in general.[33]
Such a tendency must be understood in the context of what Chandra Talpade Mohanty, in her highly influential essay "Under Western Eyes," describes as the opposition between "Western feminist self-presentation and
Western feminist re-presentation of women in the third world."[34] In this
discursive context, European women are presented as "secular, liberated,
and having control over their own lives" as against the material reality
which demands continued feminist struggle in all parts of the world.[35] The
gendered representations of Europe in African literature can often be traced
to this discursive opposition and, as many of the contributions in this
volume show, they also move beyond and challenge such assumptions.

II

Dorothy Driver addresses the question of Europe through a reading of Nja-
bulo Ndebele's novel *The Cry of Winnie Mandela*.[36] Driver argues that
Europe enters this novel as white domination, most brutally in the figure of
Winnie Mandela's torturer but also the myth of the waiting woman in the
Greek myth of Penelope and Odysseus. The recasting of this myth in the

---

[32] Gwendolyn Mikell, "Introduction" to *African Feminism: The Politics of Survival in Sub-Saharan Africa*, ed. Mikell (Philadelphia: U of Pennsylvania P, 1997): 4.

[33] For a discussion of literary representations of feminism and whiteness in African women's texts, see Susan Arndt, "Boundless Whiteness? Feminism and White Women in the Mirror of African Feminist Writing," in *Body, Sexuality and Gender: Versions and Subversions in African Literatures*, vol. 1, ed. Flora Veit–Wild & Dirk Naguschewski (*Matatu* 29–30; Amsterdam & New York: Rodopi, 2005): 157–72.

[34] Chandra Talpade Mohanty, "Under Western Eyes: Feminist Scholarship and Colonial Discourses," in *Third World Women and the Politics of Feminism*, ed. Chandra Talpade Mohanty, Ann Russo & Lourdes Torres (Bloomington: Indiana UP, 1986): 74.

[35] Mohanty, "Under Western Eyes," 74.

[36] Njabulo Ndebele, *The Cry of Winnie Mandela* (Claremont, Cape Town: David Philip, 2003).

novel represents, according to Driver, a new relation between Africa and Europe, and a redefinition of both. Driver shows how Africa, approached through the figure of Winnie Mandela, is moved beyond a reified Africa–Europe opposition to an acknowledgement of the implications that both have in the social constitution of the other. The call for Africa's return, through the figure of Winnie Mandela, complicates the idea of Africa as a traditional, precolonial society. Ndebele's novel deals with the connections between the domestic and the political through the stories of four fictional South African women who address themselves to Winnie Mandela, and who are finally joined by Penelope in the form of a woman travelling on her own through South Africa. Each of the four women tells a story of abandonment in which the reasons for the husband's departure can be traced to the changes in South African societies brought about by colonialism and apartheid.

Driver's reading emphasizes an analogy she finds in Ndebele's novel between European domination, in the form of apartheid, and male domination in the dysfunctional families that these women finally leave. Driver shows how a new understanding of Africa and Europe emerges in the novel's rearrangement of familial relations. The importance of the myth of Penelope in this novel lies, according to Driver, in its structuring influence on how the four women fulfil the patriarchal demands placed on them as waiting women. Driver shows how the call to Winnie Mandela functions as a point of departure from Western ideals of domesticity because of the way she broke Penelope's law. The possibility for change is offered to the returning men if they participate with the women in changing gender relations. The Africa–Europe dichotomy is similarly challenged in a process of political transformation in which Europe is invited to visit Africa in a manner different from that of the original colonial encounter.

The opposition between Africa and Europe generally focuses on the colonial relationship, with Africa as the colonized and Europe as the colonial powers of Western Europe. The experience of Eastern European immigrants to South Africa challenges this opposition, with, as Geoffrey V. Davis shows in his reading of Dan Jacobson, particular relevance in the history of Jewish migration from Europe to South Africa. Jacobson's account of his family history and visit to Lithuania in *Heshel's Kingdom*[37] shows a reversal of the established oppositions between Africa and Europe. The his-

---

[37] Dan Jacobson, *Heshel's Kingdom* (London: Hamish Hamilton, 1998).

tory of Europe here reveals itself as the history of Lithuania through South
African eyes, but it also approaches South Africa from the perspective of an
expatriate life in England. Most importantly, this family history writes
Europe as the experience of the Holocaust. Davis shows how Jacobson's
writing traces the movement from Lithuania to South Africa in the depiction of his family history, but, at the same time, also encompasses the opposite trajectory as a story of discovery of how Jacobson's South African
background determined his idea of Lithuania.

The Eastern European background is, in this reading, revealed to constitute the reversal of the Europe–Africa dichotomy. Davis shows how Lithuania, in Jacobson's reworking of his childhood memories, emerges as a
paradox. Lithuania is 'Nowhere' and stands for deprivation, backwardness,
limitations, and superstition, whereas South Africa represents modernity
and progress, and promises opportunities, freedom, and personal autonomy.
In the exploration of his family history, however, Jacobson encounters
other aspects of Lithuania. The importance of religion and the history of the
pogroms and the Holocaust are revealed as part of the European heritage
which Jacobson struggles to understand through his family history. Davis
shows how this re-evaluation of the importance of religion, Lithuania, and
the Eastern European heritage is established against the background of a
South African landscape. An important dimension of Europe emerges here,
as a point of departure for those who faced poverty and persecution, and
who were promised new beginnings elsewhere. Davis's reading also shows
that the freedom, prosperity, and autonomy promised by emigration come
at a cost. When Jacobson's grandfather makes the decision to return to
Lithuania after World War I, rather than to stay on in the USA, he does so
for religious reasons. The decision to return to Lithuania and adhere to the
old religious ways, rather than expose his family to what he sees as a corruption of their faith, ends with the Holocaust. As Davis points out in his
reading, Europe thus also equals death, misery, and horror from the sur-
vivors' point of view. It is only through Jacobson's reworking of family
history that the grandfather's view of Europe emerges in opposition to
those who survived by emigrating.

Gabeba Baderoon's contribution uses the idea of Islam to examine the
relation between what is defined as African and European in the South
African context, and the way the tensions between these terms developed
during colonialism and apartheid. By focusing on the word 'kaffir', a term
of abuse that developed and gained its currency from the need to establish

South Africa as 'European', Baderoon traces the tensions between Africa and Europe in South African terminology to the denial of the presence of Islam and the meaning of colouredness. This denial is extended to the intimate and private realm, what Baderoon calls "the silent, the shameful, the untranslatable and the unsayable." It is also extended to the presence of the Indian Ocean connection, with a cultural heritage of Swahili, Arabic, and Portuguese, as well as of an Islamic religious tradition. These denials work together in the formation of Europe in South Africa as identical to an Enlightenment heritage of progress, freedom, and prosperity, rather than as slavery, suffering, and unreason. The European Enlightenment heritage is approached through a reading of the poetry collection *Castaway* by Yvette Christiansë,[38] where the Atlantic slave trade is what most signifies the presence of Europe. *Castaway* tells the story of St Helena, an island which served as a place of punishment and exile for Europeans, but also as a source of slaves. Baderoon shows how the history of the island works as a point of origin in *Castaway* by telling the story of Christiansë's grandmother, a child of slaves. What signifies distance from Europe thus comes to represent, from another perspective, both origin and longing. Baderoon points to a further rewriting of Europe in her analysis of Tatamkhulu Afrika's autobiography *Mr Chameleon*.[39] Although born in Egypt and raised as a white person in apartheid South Africa, Tatamkhulu Afrika joins the resistance and claims an African identity on the basis of his actions and recognition by others. Baderoon shows how the life story of Afrika reverses the colonial Cape-to-Cairo trajectory and shapes the story of a hard-earned self-definition as African. The literary representations of Europe in these texts, according to Baderoon, refigure colonial and apartheid definitions which establish a clear separation between Africa and Europe.

Wumi Raji's reading of Femi Osofisan's play *Morountodun*[40] is placed within a context which questions the opposition between Europe and Africa. Following Paulin Hountondji and his theory of cultural mutation, the European influence is here seen not as fundamentally opposed to indigenous African traditions but, rather, as another aspect of the plurality inherent in all cultures. The confrontation between Africa and Europe is not considered as being of a different order from that of any other confronta-

---

[38] Yvette Christiansë, *Castaway* (Durham NC & London: Duke UP, 1999).
[39] Tatamkhulu Afrika, *Mr Chameleon* (Johannesburg: Jacana Media, 2005).
[40] Femi Osofisan, *Morountodun and Other Plays* (Lagos: Longman, 1982).

tion, renewal or upheaval that characterized these societies. Raji argues that Osofisan's transformation of the Yorùbá legend of Moremi within the historical context of the peasant uprising in Western Nigeria in the late 1960s involves a radical questioning of the legend. This reworking displaces the dominant character and reveals the patriarchal basis of previous reinterpretations of the legend where the female aristocratic heroine is seen as acting on behalf of the people rather than as one of them. Wumi Raji identifies the Marxist and feminist influence in Osofisan's dialogic relation to the traditional material he uses in his plays. Ordinary people replace the aristocracy and the female character takes on a radically different role. Osofisan's encounter with Marxist and feminist thought took place in a European context but, according to Wumi Raji, Osofisan engages dialogically with structures of thought derived from both a European context and from African indigenous traditions. This open engagement with a variety of traditions is, according to Wumi Raji's reading of *Morountodun,* an example of how cultural mutation works in the meeting of African and European texts. The idea of female sacrifice as part of political liberation is questioned in *Morountodun* and transformed within the context of a feminist reinterpretation. This idea of female sacrifice or the waiting woman is, however (as the contributions by Dorothy Driver and myself in this volume show), strongly present in Greek mythology and has undergone a great many literary transformations. Africa writes Europe in the case of *Morountodun* also as part of these ongoing reinterpretations of expressions concerning political agency in relation to female sacrifice.

The question of return to Africa is discussed in the essays of Jarmo Pikkujämsä, Ann–Sofie Persson, and Alexandra Schultheis. Pikkujämsä's reading of the autobiographical texts by Ken Bugul[41] is another example of the questioning of the opposition between Africa and Europe. The depiction of a return to the African village and the exploration of the gender dynamics of traditional village life emerge as a reaction to the idealization of the *evoluée* and of life in Europe. The focus on the returnee and her choice to enter into a polygamous marriage in the Senegalese village forms the framework for the conceptualization of Europe. The idea of the African

---

[41] Ken Bugul, *Cendres et braises* (Paris: L'Harmattan, 1994), *Riwan ou le chemin de sable* (Paris & Dakar: Présence Africaine, 1999), *The Abandoned Baobab: The Autobiography of a Senegalese Woman,* tr. Marjolijn de Jager (*Le Baobab fou,* Dakar: NEA, 1984; tr. New York: Lawrence Hill, 1991).

village as radically different from the European metropolis is placed at centre stage in the narrative, but this idea is undermined through the fact that it is the exilic experience of the protagonist in Europe that determines the meaning of the African village. The fact that traditional Africa is presented as a solution to an individual sense of dislocation shows that it is in areas perceived as belonging to a private sphere that the traditional is allowed to develop in opposition to European modernity. The notion of return is central in the autobiographies, and Pikkujämsä argues that it is in the narratives of return to Africa that the meaning of Europe emerges. Thus the practises of the Islamic brotherhood, for instance, which severely circumscribe women's freedom to choose, are not represented in a context where the life situations of Senegalese men would be compared to those of Senegalese women. These practices gain their meaning exclusively from the opposition to the exile experience in Europe. It is significant that Europe here comes to stand for sexual promiscuity and decadence, accusations which formed the basis of colonial European denigration of African societies. Islam, defined as non-Western, denies the European origin of the values that are now used to define the African village.

The experience of exile and return in Marie Cardinal's *Au pays de mes racines*[42] reflects the changing meaning of the Africa–Europe opposition in the life of a French girl growing up in a settler family in colonial Algeria. Ann–Sofie Persson reads the narrative as, in some cases, speaking both for Algeria and France, and, in other cases, as reflecting an exclusion from both. Europe becomes synonymous with France and Paris and is further identified with culture and the history of civilization, whereas Algeria is seen primarily as rural. Belonging and exclusion gain a gendered meaning when the narrator identifies Algeria rather than France as the true mother. France is the motherland in a negative sense. This identification is connected to the mother–daughter relationship in which metropolitan Europe stands for a cold and absent mother and Algeria for the nurturing mother. A further dimension is added with adolescence. At this stage, the freedom of childhood is exchanged for the strict discipline of a Catholic upbringing aimed chiefly at controlling the female body. The movement from childhood to adolescence encompasses a movement from freedom to restriction and prohibition which, in the mind of the young girl, is identified as the loss

---

[42] Marie Cardinal, *Au pays de mes racines, suivi de Au pays de Moussia par Bénédicte Ronfard* (Paris: Grasset & Fasquelle, 1980).

of Algeria. Europe is thus produced as a site of conflict, restriction, lack, and prohibition.

The gendering of Europe is further discussed in Alexandra Schultheis's contribution. In her reading of Tayeb Salih's *Season of Migration to the North*[43] and Leila Aboulela's *The Translator*,[44] Schultheis focuses on the articulation of Europe through their common concern with the Sudanese postcolonial elite in relation to modernity and the European university. The immigrant man in Europe is, in Salih's novel, depicted within the context of colonialist and orientalist tropes which rely on the seduction, violation, and death of European women. By evoking *Season of Migration to the North*, Aboulela's novel could potentially offer a conclusion to the narrative of migrancy. This conclusion is, however, according to Schultheis, undermined by the use of the romance genre. Aboulela depicts the immigrant as a young Sudanese widow and constructs the romance plot around her relationship with a British man. The romance is here developed through a quest in which the necessary obstacles are seen as differences in culture and religion and where the happy ending through marriage suggests a successful 'translation'. Schultheis reads the novel against the gendered conventions of romantic fiction in order to find differently articulated modernities.

The narratives of modernity offered in these novels invest the university with the contradictory function (which can also be ascribed to ideas of Europe) of imprisoning the African student within an orientalist discourse while also offering possibilities for self-invention. Schultheis reads the university through Foucault's concept of heterotopia, as a counter-site which offers an imagined projection of power-relations in society at large. The heterotopic mirror is here seen to reflect Europe for the postcolonial elite, rather than the colonies for the Europeans as in Foucault's discussion. What is also significant in the rendering of Europe through the university in these novels is the transformation that occurs when the heterotopic space turns into home. The novels reject a narrative which places Europe in opposition to 'home' and where the return to Sudan with a university education is placed within a trajectory of development.

---

[43] Tayeb Salih, *Season of Migration to the North*, tr. Denys Johnson–Davies (Portsmouth NH: Heinemann, 1969).

[44] Leila Aboulela, *The Translator* (Edinburgh: Polygon, 1999).

Europe's relation to the refugee is also at the centre of my own essay on Abdulrazak Gurnah's *By the Sea*.[45] In this reading, I focus on how the novel expresses the idea of Europe as helper and the African as help-seeking stranger. These positions are gendered in a way that challenges conventional power-structures between men and women, European and African. The stranger gains admission to Europe only by occupying the position of someone in need of help, a position which closes off alternative ways of understanding the encounter. The Derridean concept of the *arrivant* is here used to discuss how the theme of exile and arrival in Europe can be used to redefine subjectivities in such a way that they move beyond the relation between Africa and Europe. This reading also stresses the literary text as a work of art which functions specifically to dismantle the assumptions whereby the subject of literature would necessarily reproduce the subject in social space. In order to develop this point, I discuss the *arrivant* through encounters which evoke other literary texts and where the Europe–Africa opposition is challenged rather than reproduced. *The Odyssey* and the character of the waiting woman are placed in a context where the stranger is revealed as someone familiar who returns. Dorothy Driver's discussion of *The Cry of Winnie Mandela* and the appearance of Penelope in that novel shows how Ndebele's re-reading of the myth functions as a new way of envisaging the gendered power-relations between Europe and Africa. By offering a new way of imagining womanhood in Africa and Europe, the myth, as used in *The Cry of Winnie Mandela*, also invites men to participate in this new vision. The myth functions in a similar way in *By the Sea* but is here primarily concerned with the meaning of masculinity. The immigrant man is recognized as someone who belongs and who is expected in Europe rather than as a help-seeking stranger. The definition of masculinity is further developed through the use of Herman Melville's short story "Bartleby the Scrivener" in the novel in relation to questions of agency and passivity. In this reading I focus on how the agency–passivity opposition was used in the creation and consolidation of colonial ideals of masculinity.

Europe as a place of refuge becomes most problematic in the writing specifically viewed and produced as refugee writing. Jopi Nyman discusses refugee writing as a genre and places it within the context of discussions of exilic writing. The distinction between literature of exile and refugee writing reiterates the distinction between the European as refugee and Europe

---

[45] Abdulrazak Gurnah, *By the Sea* (London: Bloomsbury 2002).

as a site of refuge for those who had to flee from other parts of the world. According to Nyman, the generic conventions and ideals surrounding the modernist exilic writer have reinforced this division between the exile and the refugee. This reading of texts written by African refugees living in Wales[46] focuses on the mapping of spaces that they come to inhabit during their forced migration. Although this writing deals with the experiences of the refugee, it inscribes Europe through a number of strategies. In his reading, Nyman shows that the racism which the refugees encounter in Europe dominates the image of Europe even when it is set against the backdrop of the experiences of oppression and torture which made them flee to Britain. Europe still emerges as a site on which the experience of difference is placed at the forefront. Writing Europe through the experience of arriving as a refugee in Europe turns the question of survival into one of identity. Nyman identifies a mockery of the instructional discourse in these poems as a way of commenting on European ideas of ignorance while revealing European ignorance about life in the places the refugees have left behind. Another strategy discussed by Nyman concerns the images of landscape in these poems. The Welsh mountains are described in the context of African images of home rather than as part of a specifically European landscape. Nyman's readings show that it is precisely in the form of the mountain and the sea that this connection between past and present turns into a connection between Africa and Europe and consequently challenges the difference through rewriting Europe.

A juxtaposition of Europe and Africa that focuses on the idea of Europe rather than on the idea of Africa thus opens up new possibilities of understanding the processes of exclusion and appropriation which underlie the binary. This juxtaposition reveals the mechanisms which produce the Enlightenment heritage as *European* history with the disregard for the global interdependence that brought about these historical events. The intervention of Africa points to the significance of including other aspects of European history and to acknowledgement of the ways in which Europe is implicated in Africa. This specific meaning of Europe is discussed by Jacques Derrida in terms of "what the word Europe means today." In this he includes "our

---

[46] *Between a Mountain and a Sea: Refugees Writing in Wales*, ed. Eric Ngalle Charles, Tom Cheesman & Sylvie Hoffmann (Swansea: Hafan, 2003); *Nobody's Perfect: Refugees Writing in Wales*, vol. 2, ed. Eric Ngalle Charles, Tom Cheesman & Sylvie Hoffmann (Swansea: Hafan, 2004); *Soft Touch: Refugees Writing in Wales*, vol. 3, ed. Eric Ngalle Charles, Tom Cheesman & Sylvie Hoffmann (Swansea: Hafan, 2005).

Enlightenment heritage" but also an awareness of "the totalitarian, geno-cidal and colonialist crimes of the past."[47] The challenge lies in holding on to the promises of this heritage while dismantling the dichotomies that inhibit its realization.

WORKS CITED

Aboulela, Leila. *The Translator* (Edinburgh: Polygon, 1999).
Abrahams, Yvette. "The Great Long National Insult: 'Science', Sexuality and the Khoisan in the 18th and early 19th Century," *Agenda* 32 (1997): 34–48.
Afrika, Tatamkhulu. *Mr Chameleon* (Johannesburg: Jacana Media, 2005).
Ahmed, Sara. "A Phenomenology of Whiteness." *Feminist Theory* 8.2 (2007): 149–67.
Alarcrón, Norma, Caren Kaplan & Minoo Moallem, ed. *Between Woman and Nation: Nationalisms, Transnational Feminisms, and the State* (Durham NC & London: Duke UP, 1999).
Arndt, Susan. "Boundless Whiteness? Feminism and White Women in the Mirror of African Feminist Writing." in *Body, Sexuality and Gender*, ed. Veit–Wild & Naguschewski, 157–72.
——. *The Dynamics of African Feminism: Defining and Classifying African-Feminist Literatures*, tr. Isabel Cole (*Feminismus im Widerstreit*, 2000; tr. Trenton NJ: Africa World Press, 2002).
——, & Marek Spitczok von Brisinski, ed. *Africa, Europe and (Post)colonialism: Racism, Migration and Diaspora* (Bayreuth: Bayreuth African Studies 77, 2006).
Arnfred, Signe, ed. *Re-Thinking Sexualities in Africa* (Uppsala: Nordic Africa Institute, 2004).
Bekers, Elisabeth, Sissy Helff & Daniela Merolla, ed. *Transcultural Modernities: Narrating Africa in Europe* (Matatu 36; Amsterdam & New York: Rodopi, 2008).
Bugul, Ken. *The Abandoned Baobab: The Autobiography of a Senegalese Woman*, tr. Marjolijn de Jager (*Le Baobab fou*; Dakar: NEA, 1984; tr. New York: Lawrence Hill, 1991).
——. *Cendres et braises* (Paris: L'Harmattan, 1994).
——. *Riwan ou le chemin de sable* (Paris & Dakar: Présence Africaine, 1999).
Butler, Judith. *Gender Trouble: Feminism and the Subversion of Identity* (London & New York: Routledge, 1990).

---

[47] Jacques Derrida, "Enlightenment past and to come," *Le Monde diplomatique: English Edition*, online: http://mondedipl.com/2004/11/06derrida

Cardinal, Marie. *Au pays de mes racines, suivi de Au pays de Moussia par Béné-dicte Ronfard* (Paris: Grasset & Fasquelle, 1980).

Carrier, James G., ed. *Occidentalism: Images of the West* (Oxford: Clarendon, 1995).

Chakrabarty, Dipesh. *Provincializing Europe: Postcolonial Thought and Historical Difference* (Princeton NJ: Princeton UP, 2000).

Charles, Eric Ngalle, Tom Cheesman & Sylvie Hoffmann, ed. *Between a Mountain and a Sea: Refugees Writing in Wales* (Swansea: Hafan, 2003).

——. *Nobody's Perfect: Refugees Writing in Wales 2* (Swansea: Hafan, 2004).

——. *Soft Touch: Refugees Writing in Wales 3* (Swansea: Hafan, 2005).

Chatterjee, Partha. *The Nation and Its Fragments: Colonial and Postcolonial Histories* (Princeton NJ: Princeton UP, 1993).

——. *Nationalist Thought and the Colonial World: A Derivative Discourse?* (London: Zed, 1986).

Chinyowa, Kennedy C. "Battling between Alienation and Desire: Images of 'European-ness / Western-ness' in Contemporary Zimbabwean Literature," in *Africa and Europe*, ed. von Maltzan, 133–46.

Christiansë, Yvette. *Castaway* (Durham NC & London: Duke UP, 1999).

Derrida, Jacques. "Enlightenment past and to come," *Le Monde diplomatique: English Edition*: online http://mondedipl.com/2004/11/06derrida

Dyer, Richard. *White: Essays on Race and Culture* (London: Routledge, 1997).

Eriksson Baaz, Maria. *The Paternalism of Partnership: A Postcolonial Reading of Identity in Development Aid* (New York & London: Zed, 2005).

Fanon, Frantz. *Black Skin, White Masks*, tr. Charles Lam Markmann (*Peau noire, masques blancs*, 1952; tr. New York: Grove, 1967).

Fuentes, Carlos. "In Praise of the Novel," *Critical Inquiry* 32 (Summer 2006): 610–17.

Gilman, Sander. "Black Bodies, White Bodies: Towards an Iconography of Female Sexuality in Late Nineteenth Century Art, Medicine and Literature," *Critical Inquiry* 12.1 (1985): 204–42.

——. *Sexuality: An Illustrated History* (New York: John Wiley & Sons, 1989).

Gould, Stephen Jay. *The Mismeasure of Man* (Harmondsworth: Penguin, 1981).

Gurnah, Abdulrazak. *By the Sea* (London: Bloomsbury 2002).

Halberstam, Judith. *Female Masculinity* (Durham NC & London: Duke UP, 1998).

Hegel, Georg Wilhelm Friedrich. *Readings in the Philosophy of History*, tr. J. Sibree (*Vorlesungen über die Philosophie der Geschichte*, 1834; tr. Mineola NY: Dover, 2004).

Hobsbawm, Eric, & Terrence O. Ranger. *The Invention of Tradition* (Cambridge: Cambridge UP, 1983).

Huggan, Graham. *The Postcolonial Exotic: Marketing the Margins* (London & New York: Routledge, 2001).

Ingraham, Chrys. "The Heterosexual Imaginary: Feminist Sociology and Theories of Gender" (1994), in *Queer Theory/Sociology*, ed. Steven Seidman (Malden MA: Blackwell, 1996): 203–19.

Jacobson, Dan. *Heshel's Kingdom* (London: Hamish Hamilton, 1998).

Jackson, Stevi. *Heterosexuality in Question* (London: Sage, 1995).

Katz, Jonathan Ned. *The Invention of Heterosexuality* (New York: Plume, 1995).

Kolawole, Mary. *Womanism and African Consciousness* (Trenton NJ: Africa World Press, 1997).

Lewis, Desiree. "Against the Grain: Black Women and Sexuality," *Agenda* 63 (2005): 11–24.

Maltzan, Carlotta von, ed. *Africa and Europe: En/Countering Myths: Essays on Literature and Cultural Politics* (Frankfurt am Main: Peter Lang, 2003).

Mbembe, Achille. *On the Postcolony* (*De la postcolonie, essai sur l'imagination politique dans l'Afrique contemporaine*, 2000; Berkeley: U of California P, 2001).

McLeod, John. *Postcolonial London: Rewriting the Metropolis* (London & New York: Routledge, 2004).

Merrington, Peter. "A Staggered Orientalism: The Cape-to-Cairo Imaginary," in *South Africa in the Global Imaginary*, ed. Leon de Kock, Louise Bethlehem & Sonja Laden (Pretoria: U of South Africa P, 2004): 57–93.

Mikell, Gwendolyn, ed. *African Feminism: The Politics of Survival in Sub-Saharan Africa* (Philadelphia: U of Pennsylvania P, 1997).

Mohanty, Chandra Talpade. "Under Western Eyes: Feminist Scholarship and Colonial Discourses," in *Third World Women and the Politics of Feminism*, ed. Chandra Talpade Mohanty, Ann Russo & Lourdes Torres (Bloomington: Indiana UP, 1986): 51–80.

Nandy, Ashis. *The Intimate Enemy: Loss and Recovery of Self under Colonialism* (New Delhi: Oxford UP, 1983).

Narayan, Uma. *Dislocating Cultures: Identities, Traditions, and Third World Feminism* (London & New York: Routledge, 1997).

Ndebele, Njabulo S. *The Cry of Winnie Mandela* (Claremont, Cape Town: David Philip, 2003).

Nnaemeka, Obioma, ed. *The Politics of (M)othering: Womanhood, Identity, and Resistance in African Literature* (London: Routledge, 1997).

Ogundipe–Leslie, Molara. *Recreating Ourselves: African Women and Critical Transformation* (Trenton NJ: Africa World Press, 1994).

Osofisan, Femi. *Morountodun and Other Plays* (Lagos: Longman, 1982).

Ouzgane, Lahoucine, & Robert Morrell, ed. *African Masculinities: Men in Africa from the Late Nineteenth Century to the Present* (New York: Palgrave Macmillan, 2005).

Oyewumi, Oyeronke, ed. *African Women and Feminism: Reflecting on the Politics of Sisterhood.* (Trenton NJ: Africa World Press, 2003).

Palmberg, Mai, ed. *Encounter Images in the Meetings between Africa and Europe.* (Uppsala: Nordic Africa Institute, 2001).

Said, Edward W. "Preface to the Twenty-Fifth Anniversary Edition," *Orientalism* (New York: Vintage, 2003): xv–xxx.

Salih, Tayeb. *Season of Migration to the North*, tr. Denys Johnson–Davies (Portsmouth NH: Heineman, 1969).

Sander, Gilman. "Black Bodies, White Bodies: Towards an Iconography of Female Sexuality in Late Nineteenth Century Art, Medicine and Literature," *Critical Inquiry* 12.1 (1985): 204–42.

Sedgwick, Eve Kosofsky. *Epistemology of the Closet* (Berkeley & Los Angeles: U of California P, 1990).

Spivak, Gayatri Chakravorty. "Three Women's Texts and a Critique of Imperialism," *Critical Inquiry* 12.1 (1985): 43–61.

Veit–Wild, Flora, & Dirk Naguschewski, ed. *Body, Sexuality and Gender: Versions and Subversions in African Literatures*, vol. 1 (Matatu 29–30; Amsterdam & New York: Rodopi, 2005).

Ware, Vron. *Beyond the Pale: White Women, Racism and History* (London & New York: Verso, 1992).

Young, Robert. *White Mythologies: Writing History and the West* (London & New York: Routledge, 1990).

◀▷

"On these premises I am the government"
– ‹›› – Njabulo Ndebele's *The Cry of Winnie Mandela* and the Reconstructions of Gender and Nation[1]

DOROTHY DRIVER

> If the whites do not want to change their attitudes, let the blacks advance and leave them behind; and when they have been left behind, let them be waited for on the day they realise the value of change.[2]

I

THE CALL "Mayibuye Afrika! Come back Africa!" echoes wordlessly through Njabulo Ndebele's recent novel *The Cry of Winnie Mandela*. It resounds not just with longing or demand but with a kind of pain – hence the word 'cry' – deflected through the figure of Winnie Mandela, who, in the terms posed by the novel, symbolizes the nearly unspeakable contradiction of the call for Africa's return. The novel blunts its immediate impact as a 'cry' through its narrative distance, its composi-

[1] Since this essay was written as part of the Africa Writing Europe research project, thanks are due to the directors of the project, Professors Maria Olaussen and Christina Angelfors of Växjö University, and to the various participants, for useful workshop discussions, as well as to the funders for making the workshops possible. My thanks too to the South African National Research Foundation for the financial resources that facilitated this research, and to the Centre for African Studies, University of Cape Town, for office space and technical support in 2008, when this essay was being revised.

[2] Njabulo Ndebele, "Black Development," in *Black Viewpoint*, ed. B.S. Biko (Durban: Spro-Cas, 1972): 28.

tional orderliness, and the measured tones of its desire for the restoration of
Africanness, and – avoiding (in a complicated way) an essential, precolonial African identity as the object of its quest – it ostensibly quite coolly acknowledges the influence of European modes of social behaviour in the
cultural formation of Africanness. Yet, not quite muffled by this apparent
control, and giving the novel an urgency that puts it among the foremost
post-apartheid fiction, is a cry imagined to be not just from and about South
Africa's most famous, or most notorious, woman – Who am I? Where are
my origins? What have I become? – but also from and about Africa itself.

It might at first glance strike readers as odd that a critic – in this case
myself – would pick on *The Cry of Winnie Mandela* in order to address
Africa's imagining of Europe. The novel does not explicitly formulate an
African position, although Ndebele's interest in an African sensibility and
aesthetic is everywhere to be found in this novel about a country that is on
the one hand "known by a cardinal point"[3] (the African continent bearing
the names of the three other points), and on the other by "a dot […] in the
world map" (113). Moreover, the novel does not actually represent Europe,
and the extended cry that constitutes it is a self-address, not an explicit
address to Europe (and, indeed, that Europe is not explicitly addressed is
part of the point of this post-protest novel). However, Europe is present in
the novel in the form of an historically complex and insidiously pervasive
white domination manifested as colonialism and apartheid: on the one
hand, a colonial civilizing mission that strove to introduce a bourgeois
domesticity to a select group of Africans in a masquerade of egalitarianism,
and, on the other, a set of legislation that disrupted home and family and
strove to put a halt to African modernization.

Europe also enters the novel through two specific figures: Penelope from
the classical European myth of Penelope and Odysseus, and Major Theunis
Swanepoel, Winnie Mandela's white torturer. (It is also instructive that for
the cover of his book Ndebele chose Willie Bester's sculpture of Sartjie
Baartman. The latter has become an iconic, if ambiguous, figure in South
Africa's new nation-building, especially given the return of her remains
from Europe to South Africa. Bester's sculpture is a construction from
scrap metal, one of whose parts is stamped "Made in England.") Like Penelope, Winnie Mandela is expected to wait chastely and patiently for her

---

[3] Njabulo Ndebele, *The Cry of Winnie Mandela* (Claremont, Cape Town: David
Philip, 2003): 114. Further page references are in the main text.

husband's release from prison and his return home, but Penelope's actual appearance in the novel in the form of a travelling woman helps mark the end of the myth of the waiting woman, and at least this form of European domination. Major Swanepoel undergoes no such fictional re-invention, and is only referred to rather than appearing as a character. Instead, Ndebele overturns the legacy of apartheid through a critique of various black South African responses to it. He has a key character recall the process of negotiation that black South Africans engaged in as they prepared for the country's first democratic elections, and in this way he proposes what he calls the "complexity, ambiguity, nuance and emergent order" (71) that need to replace the oppositional thinking that still lingers after apartheid. As with apartheid, so with colonialism: Ndebele's novel heralds the end of the kind of thinking that underpinned them both. And it does so in such a way as to place as provisional and fluid rather than as fixed and oppositional the very concepts 'Europe' and 'Africa' themselves. Penelope's welcome on African soil by a group of black South African women helps dispel the old distinctions of black and white, and signals a new relation between Europe and Africa, in which each is altered by the other's transformation.

Ndebele deploys a set of analogies based on varieties of waiting that work hard in the novel, not least because of the subtlety of their interaction. Women under apartheid are waiting for their husbands to come home; men are waiting to return to their homes or to the women who signify home; Winnie Mandela is – or was – waiting for her husband; her husband has also been waiting to leave prison for home. Black South Africans under apartheid are – or were – generally in a state of waiting. Waiting is imposed upon women by a patriarchal culture, on Winnie Mandela by a media-orchestrated public made up of both black and white South Africans, and on black South Africans by white or European domination. Africa – in South Africa – is waiting for its own return.

The novel is initially structured around four fictional South African women, each of whom has seen her husband leave home on account of one or other of what Ndebele calls "the powerful social forces" (4) that represent Europe's dominion over Africa: industrialization and migrant labour, political detention and exile, and the diasporic movement ordained by the need for a specialized education not available locally to black South Africans. Waiting for their husbands' return has changed the women's experience of time and space. Time – for the waiting women – is "measured in states of waiting" (7), and "blur[s] into oblivion" (12), so that their world becomes "a zone of absence without duration" (6, repeated 7). So, too, says the novel, has waiting for the end of apartheid changed time and space for all black South Africans. In a particularly powerful scene in the book, one of the four women, Marara Joyce Baloyi, speaks about how apartheid withheld from black South Africans what should have been the ordinary pleasures of travelling through a country no longer their own. The enjoyment of natural beauty that normally enlivens travel is replaced by anxiety and a sense of unbelonging, so that journeys are experienced as "psychological time without space" (69).

Ndebele's specific wording both here and earlier in the novel, on the rupture of the concrete experience of time and space, is reminiscent of Mikhail Bakhtin's commentary on the chronotope, and invites us to dwell for a moment on his relation to Bakhtin in order to develop the Africa–Europe theme of the present discussion. Bakhtin uses the concept of the chronotope (space–time) to distinguish between novelistic genres and varieties of novelistic discourses, as well as to suggest the fictional constitution of individual characters.[4] In literary realism, for instance, the individual is placed in a chronotopic relation to the physical world through being inscribed in a specific time and space, which means that time is materialized, and space historicized. With this come conditions conducive to the development of a fictional character capable of interacting with the world. But in what Bakhtin calls "the Greek romance" of the Hellenistic era, with its essentially alien and abstract space–time connections, chance or fate replaces the individual agency and historical causation that the depiction in realism of "one's own native world" would be able to dramatize; time in such alien circumstances, says Bakhtin, is no more than "an indefinitely prolonged present."[5]

Similarly, Ndebele represents as alien the world of apartheid inhabited by black South Africans, for they experience time and space as void and immobile, as do the black South African women who have to wait so patiently for their husbands' return. Hence the "psychological time without

---

[4] Mikhail Bakhtin, *The Dialogic Imagination*, tr. Caryl Emerson & Michael Holquist, ed. Michael Holquist (Austin & London: U of Texas P, 1981). The discussion that follows refers specifically to Bakhtin's chapter "Forms of Time and Chronotope in the Novel," 84–258.

[5] Bakhtin, *The Dialogic Imagination*, 101, 148. Bakhtin says that in the "abstract-alien" realm of a Greek romance, the world and the individual are essentially unchanging, showing "no potential for evolution, for growth, for change" (110).

space" for blacks travelling in apartheid South Africa, and the "zones of absence without duration" for the waiting women. Ndebele draws our attention not simply to a particular experience withheld from black South Africans in real life, but also to what he sees as the problems of black South African narrative under white domination. For one thing, he has said, black South African narrative came to a halt under apartheid;[6] for another, it has suffered from a focus on what he calls the "spectacular" rather than the "ordinary."[7] As my essay will show, *The Cry of Winnie Mandela* is about the capacity of the narrative of South Africa to move on as it ought, marking the return to black South Africans of their own world and their own history. Ndebele's novel offers itself, then, both as a dramatic presentation of characters freeing themselves from a spatially and historically disembodied existence, and as a model of a narrative that allows its characters, as he puts it, gradually "to emerge as fully-fledged beings" (35). The issue of representation is central to his text.

When, therefore, Ndebele's four women form an ibandla (*ibandla* is the Xhosa/Zulu term for a formal group) and resolve to invite Winnie to join

---

[6] Njabulo Ndebele, "Memory, Metaphor, and the Triumph of Narrative," in *Negotiating the Past*, ed. Sarah Nuttall & Carli Coetzee (Cape Town: Oxford UP, 1998): 27. Besides the way Ndebele describes his black characters' experience of time and space, another indication that Ndebele might have read Bakhtin before writing *The Cry of Winnie Mandela* is Bakhtin's interest in the novel of travel, where the "native country" is the "internal organizing center for seeing and depicting" (103) and the journey itself "imparts to the temporal sequence of the novel a real and essential organizing center" (104). When social contradictions start to surface in fiction, says Bakhtin, the world of narrative is on the move (129).

[7] Ndebele first used these terms in an address, "The Rediscovery of the Ordinary: Some New Writings in South Africa," delivered in London in 1984. The essay appears in his volume *The Rediscovery of the Ordinary* (1991), which was reprinted as *South African Literature and Culture: Rediscovery of the Ordinary*, intro. Graham Pechey (Manchester & New York: Manchester UP, 1994). His concept of the 'spectacle' bears some relation to its use in Guy Debord's *Society of the Spectacle* (Detroit MI: Black & Red, 1983) and perhaps also Jean Baudrillard's *Simulations*, tr. Paul Foss, Paul Patton & Philip Beitchman (New York: Semiotexte, 1983), where it functions as an ideological simulation of reality through superficial and deceptive images. For Ndebele, the 'spectacle' relates specifically to the 'spectacular' images normalized under apartheid and uncritically echoed in some of the resistance literature of the 1970s and 1980s. The concept of the 'ordinary' is designed to resist any literary tendency to focus on the 'spectacular' at the expense of the intricacies and intimacies of everyday life. His more specific definitions will be provided in due course.

them, they evoke her in part as the creature (like them) of an alien myth, and in part as a figure in another kind of story. (In this essay I use her full name for the historical representation, and her first name for the fictionalized figure.) The women want Winnie to explain to them the dashed hopes her appalling behaviour has caused: why, in the words of one of the women, Winnie failed "to live up to the dream of [Nelson Mandela's] return" (66). The cry of Winnie Mandela referred to in the book's title is, then, also a cry to Winnie Mandela. For many black South Africans, the novel implies, the reunion of these two iconic figures, Winnie and Nelson Mandela, would have symbolized the restoration of the African nation. However, by the end of the novel another kind of union has been envisaged, as Ndebele puts in place a new conception of family and home. Home functions in Ndebele's novel as the site of a new kind of gender relation and a metonym for a newly defined country and nation. The re-invention of an African home is crucial to the novel, or, as one of Ndebele's characters says, "The rebuilding of homes and communities may have become the most compelling factor in enabling us to sustain our nationhood" (72).

The formation of the nuclear family home was central to the colonial evangelism that saw itself as modernizing Africa, and to the creation of a consumer culture and bourgeois hegemony. The Western concept of home also facilitated the distinction between public and private so crucial to the modernized, industrialized, capitalist world. However, the home was simultaneously degraded under apartheid. In the historical moment created by the complex contradictions and collusions of capitalist industrialization, colonial evangelism, bourgeois modernization and then apartheid as well, with the different kinds of 'betterment' policies and varieties of resettlement under increasingly legislated social divisions, the nuclear family home was, on the one hand, proclaimed as a sign of modernity, a private space, and as women's (sole) domain, and, on the other, rendered inaccessible as such.

Moreover, the West's distinction between public and private was unfamiliar to those used to traditional rural life, and both the distinction itself and its gendering unsettled established practices.[8] "My home is not / My

---

[8] See Jacklyn Cock, *Maids and Madams: A Study in the Politics of Exploitation* (Johannesburg: Ravan Press, 1980); John & Jean Comaroff, "Home-Made Hegemony: Modernity, Domesticity, and Colonialism in South Africa," in *African Encounters with Domesticity*, ed. Karen Tranberg Hansen (New Brunswick NJ: Rutgers UP, 1992): 37–74; Elizabeth Elbourne, "Domesticity and Dispossession: The Ideologies of Domesticity and 'Home' and the British Construction of the Primitive from the Eighteenth to the

home!" as H.I.E. Dhlomo once wrote.[9] But Ndebele's portrayal also focuses on the abuse of the home by African men. Besides dominating women in compensation for their disempowerment under apartheid, modern African husbands took advantage of women's domestic responsibility, benefitting from but not reciprocating the unwaged housework, the selfless child-raising, the material and other support wives often gave husbands, and above all from women's compulsion to await – chastely – their return. Yet the unhomeliness of the home under apartheid has implications not simply of alienation – as in Dhlomo's response – or simply of inhuman demands, burdens, prohibitions and deprivations – as in the experience of Ndebele's female characters – but also of a strangeness induced in Winnie. Evoked as a 'real' presence by the four women, Winnie takes centre stage for the last third of the novel. This strangeness is suggested in Winnie's spirited diatribe against the kind of domestic order that mission education imposed on African women, what she sees as the rectangular grids of Western modernity so fundamental to civilizing control: "dimensions of order that get structured into the mind" (88), "one of the central features of whiteness" (89). Apartheid denied her any actualization of an ordered existence – "they emptied order out of me" (89) – and she became "the embodiment of disruption" instead (89).

The model of behaviour that Winnie Mandela's life put in place is ultimately rejected in Ndebele's novel, but it remains nonetheless as an historical model to be confronted, sympathized with, and understood. Her oppositional reaction – from order to disorder – is likened to that of the "lawless" figures (94) who reject out of hand the laws passed by an undemocratically elected South African government, whether or not these laws are worth keeping. However, it is not they who find a detailed place in his book: along with the four women, Winnie Mandela's particular history – her entry through marriage into the forefront of the anti-apartheid struggle, her bannings, detentions, and treatment in prison, her abuse by the media, and

---

Early Nineteenth Centuries," in *Deep HiStories: Gender and Colonialism in Southern Africa*, ed. Wendy Woodward, Patricia Hayes & Gary Minkley (Cross/Cultures 57; Amsterdam & New York: Rodopi, 2002): 27–54; Cherryl Walker, *Women and Resistance in South Africa* (Cape Town & Johannesburg: David Philip; New York: Monthly Review Press, 2nd ed. 1991); and Julia Wells, *We Now Demand! The History of Women's Resistance to Pass Laws in South Africa* (Johannesburg: Witwatersrand UP, 1993).

[9] H.I.E. Dhlomo, "Valley of a Thousand Hills," in *Collected Works*, ed. Nick Visser & Tim Couzens (Johannesburg: Ravan, 1985): 318.

other consequences of her political behaviour, as well as, simply, of her
race and gender position – all gives Ndebele the opportunity to investigate
a way out of what his novel conceptualizes as the oppositional culture
bequeathed by British colonization and apartheid. As the novel progresses,
both Winnie and Penelope's four 'descendants' show themselves as figures
of ambiguity, not least because they are considerably more than simply
waiting women.[10] And Winnie (by now on her way to becomng a more
fully fledged fictional character) comes to realize that she has lived in an
"in between space from which [her] serenities and terrors have emerged"
(87). Although the novel seems to retain some difference between herself
and the other women, she finally occupies – as they do – an intersection of
order and disorder, as indeed of waiting and not waiting, more complicated
and more nuanced than the oppositional structure the novel suggests was
brought in by an alien European colonial mind-set as it confronted what it
saw as darkest Africa.

Pertinent to this new representation is Ndebele's argument about the
need for South African writing to move from "a fixed and unhistorical
image" to a "fiercely energetic and complex dialectic in the progress of
human history."[11] White opinion tended to see Winnie Mandela as, on the
one hand, a famous wife, and, on the other, a political thug, making her the
creature not simply of the Penelope myth but also of media representation
("Miss Thing," 116). But as the novel unfolds, a nuanced understanding
emerges of the political and cultural pressures placed on Winnie – as on the
four other African women – who takes up, as it were, a position in a dialec-

---

[10] Femaleness and ambiguity have a long connection in South African culture. For
instance, referring to rural women in the campaign against carrying passes, Cherryl
Walker writes: "women in the reserves were in fact caught in the pincers of a policy
whose aims and results were in themselves contradictory. By trying to manipulate the
traditional, tribal, political and economic structures but manipulate them to their own
ends, the government was undermining them. Women's position in the resulting system
was ambiguous, their status and self-image ambivalent – subordinate, junior, yet burdened with responsibilities and a de fact authority not sanctioned by society" (235).

[11] Njabulo Ndebele, *South African Literature and Culture: Rediscovery of the Ordinary*, intro. Graham Pechey (Manchester & New York: Manchester UP, 1994): 160.
See also Ndebele, Interview, "Njabulo Ndebele," with Duncan Brown & Bruno van
Dyk, in *Exchanges: South African Writing in Transition*, ed. Duncan Brown & Bruno
van Dyk (Pietermaritzburg: U of Natal P, 1991): 49–57, where he speaks of an enduring indebtedness to "the dialectical approach to human society [...] (in spite of all
that's been said of the decline of the Eastern bloc)" (55).

tic, thus signifying considerably more than a static "embodiment of disruption." In this heavily symbolic novel, then, Winnie as well as Ndebele's other women characters are presented (albeit differently) as figures reflecting a "new universe" in which "new political meanings and values will emerge." "It is there," the text adds, "that we may find our new homes" (71).[12]

One of the women asks Winnie how she had "navigated through the terrors of a long journey from one state of being into another" (65), another sympathizes with her inability to "act out normalcy" (69) in the face of radical domestic upheaval, and another suggests that Winnie could have shared with Nelson "the travails of [their] separation" (52). The fourth woman advises that Winnie should have been able to await Nelson's warm response rather than submitting to the "emotional obligation to embrace him" (81). Indeed, the novel proclaims the priority of Nelson's reconciliation with Winnie over any reconciliation between black and white South Africans, thus contradicting the thrust of the South African Truth and Reconciliation Commission (TRC).[13] Instead, the novel's interest is in two other kinds of reconciliation: self-reconciliation, and a self–other reconciliation within the African group. Far from being "an instrument for validating the politics of reconciliation" (113), Winnie is an instrument in a dialectic that takes into account the variety of historical forces at work in black South Africa: the complex history of gender formation as represented in the women's stories, and also of class and ethnic formation, as will later emerge. It is only on a dialectical basis that the Africa–Europe relation can be reformed.

Gender relations are therefore at stake on both a personal and a national level. When the last of the four women calling to Winnie tells her that she should have demanded a different approach from Nelson when he came out of prison and into her home, she is arguing that the man should enter the

---

[12] In an essay entitled "A Home for Intimacy," *Mail and Guardian* 12.17 (Johannesburg; 26 April–2 May 1996): 29, written about his own return to South Africa after twenty years' absence, Ndebele gives the term "intimacy" to what his novel calls a "new universe." The essay reappears almost verbatim in his novel, with some significant adjustments.

[13] For an interesting analysis of Ndebele's novel in the context of the TRC, see Yianna Liatsos, "Truth, Confession and the Post-Apartheid Black Consciousness in Njabulo Ndebele's *The Cry of Winnie Mandela*," in *Modern Confessional Writing: New Critical Essays*, ed. Jo Gill (London & New York: Routledge, 2006): 115–36.

woman's life history rather than the woman entering the man's, for the latter would be at the expense of her independence. Says 'Mannete Mofolo:

> "You gave away your moment, girl. When your Nelson came back into the world map of your dots, you were not there to show him how to read the map. You gave away the opportunity to show him your world and for him to decide to live with it or not. You should have affirmed your world, girl, with all its green valleys and rolling deserts." (84)

This advice recalls the courageous remark used as the title for this essay: "On these premises I am the government." It was made by a woman who appeared before the TRC to bear witness to the invasion of her home space.[14] The woman's words evoke the courage of many other black women who bore witness in the TRC.[15] Such womanly self-assertion challenged the brutalities of both apartheid and male domination, however vulnerable women's homes and bodies may in the end be to physical onslaught. Ndebele's novel expands on this kind of assertion by embedding it in a narrative part of whose point is simply to assume that the words be heard by those to whom they are spoken. The transformation of gender may ultimately depend on the transformation of men in response to women's transformation, but the major interest is in women's affirmation and transformation.[16] In this multi-layered, analogical text, the female affirmation is at the same time an African affirmation, made to men in the one case, and to Europe in the other. As has already been implied in this essay, and as

---

[14] *Truth and Reconciliation Commission of South Africa Report* (Cape Town: Truth and Reconciliation Commission, 1998–2003), vol. 4: 291. The words are Nonceba Zokwe's, spoken to a security-force policeman threatening to come into her home. They are transcribed and translated in two different ways in TRC documentation. In the transcripts of the Human Rights Violations Hearings, Special Hearing on Women, Case EC0018/96, East London, 17 April 1996), they appear as follows: "I am the government here on these premises, I am the leader."

[15] See Fiona Ross, *Bearing Witness: Women and the Truth and Reconciliation Commission in South Africa* (London: Pluto Press, 2003).

[16] See Dorothy Driver, "Truth, Reconciliation, Gender: The South African Truth and Reconciliation Commission and Black Women's Intellectual History," *Australian Feminist Studies* 20/47 (2005): 219–29, where I argue that although the TRC aimed at a shared memory, it reproduced fundamentally oppositional gender distinctions, and created a realm of limited reciprocity between women and men in its failure to provide a platform for men to hear women.

will continue to develop in due course, Ndebele's analogical procedure involves analogies both shifting and asymmetrical.[17]

When we are told that "in Lesotho the vagina is fondly known as *lesotho*" (50), and that men should "come in and linger" rather than enter "thrusting and pumping" (50), we hear not only African women's suggestion to men – or their returning husbands – but also a suggestion that Europe might have entered Africa differently, rather than invading the "primal country" in the manner of "rape" (50). The "green valleys and rolling deserts" in 'Mannete Mofolo's advice to Winnie function as both metaphor and metonym, signifying both women's bodies and the country as a whole. 'Mannete Mofolo's advice to Winnie to affirm her world thus also refers to an African affirmation to Europe.

The analogy between European domination and male domination functions not to equate the very different kinds of atrocity and neglect and so on, but to focus on a mode of liberation from the two. The novel implies that Nelson's – and the public's – expectations about Winnie are to be understood in the context of an ideology that placed impossible burdens and demands on women while at the same time – through the manner of European and male domination – making impossibly difficult any human fulfilment of these expectations. It also implies that British colonialism invented in Africa a version of patriarchalism reminiscent of what it felt to be a European tradition, as in Terrence Ranger's argument about the invention of tradition.[18] Locating in the ideology of domesticity the nexus of patriarchal domination and European intrusion into Africa (colonialism, modernization, apartheid), the novel identifies the domestic as the site of transformation, not in any opposition (disorder) but in the rearrangement of domesticity as a modern African formation. Domesticity is thus to become the space of both women and men, in a new dialectical moment of gender equality. To this end, Ndebele evokes and redirects elements claimed to be traditionally African – women's endurance, fortitude and courage, their use of the ibandla as psychological or spiritual resource and as the domain of

---

[17] See Ndebele's essay "Of Lions and Rabbits: Thoughts on Democracy and Reconciliation," *Pretexts* 8.2 (1999): 147–58, for discussion of what he calls the "constant ebb and flow of shifting identities in South African history which constantly subvert any tendency towards simplification" (149).

[18] See Terrence Ranger's chapter, "The Invention of Tradition in Colonial Africa," in *The Invention of Tradition*, ed. Eric Hobsbawm & Terrence O. Ranger (Cambridge: Cambridge U P, 1983): 211–60.

ubuntu, and the practice of hospitality, conventionally associated with
ubuntu. Evoking and redirecting these various elements, the novel re-writes
the African home, the Africa–Europe encounter, and the African novel as
well.

II

'Ubuntu' is an originally Xhosa and Zulu term that entered official South
African discourse through the TRC, and is generally associated with African humanism and African socialism. Desmond Tutu glosses it in the following terms – "our [i.e. African] humanness, caring, hospitality, our sense
of connectedness, our sense that my humanity is bound up in your humanity" – adding that it needs to be regained by the black South African community.[19] Hence Ndebele's creative engagement.[20]

Ndebele dramatizes the process of ubuntu in his techniques of characterization, as if to the letter of its standard formulation: "a person is a person
because of and through other people."[21] In other words, his main fictional
characters perform a complex human interaction that follows the spirit of
ubuntu. The structure of his novel and its characterization assure the
autonomy of each of his women characters – each one worthy of being
"admired in her own right" (4) – but place them within the defining context
of the group. Moreover, as developing fictional characters, the women also

---

[19] Desmond Tutu, *Sunday Times* (26 May 1991): 2; quoted in *A Dictionary of South
African English on Historical Principles* (Oxford: Oxford UP/Dictionary Unit for
South African English, 1996): 749. Some of the quotations used in this essay in relation
to ubuntu and hospitality are repeated from my 2005 essay, "Truth, Reconciliation,
Gender." For invaluable discussion of ubuntu, see Mark Sanders' *Complicities: The
Intellectual and Apartheid* (Durham NC & London: Duke UP, 2002): 119–21, 124–30
and passim.

[20] Ellen Kuzwayo, among others, also registers the importance of ubuntu as an enabling myth: "I have no intention of creating an impression that black people are in any
way special; in terms of their attitudes of interaction with other groups; of their regard
for sharing with others, be it knowledge, land or wealth; of their concern with their
neighbours in times of common need and serious crisis. However, I am convinced that
the impact of the philosophy of 'ubuntu' has played a major role." Ellen Kuzwayo, "My
Life Is My Neighbours," *Monitor: The Journal of the Human Rights Trust* (Special Issue
on Human Rights in South Africa, 1988): 133.

[21] I use here the formulation translated from the Xhosa by Noni Jabavu, *The Ochre
People* (Johannesburg: Ravan, 1963): 69.

take on creative power, forging a sociality alternative to that imposed on Africa by Europe. His techniques thus promote a nuanced rather than oppositional understanding of the relation between self and other that dismisses the individualism black South Africans conventionally associate with European culture. In these two ways, Ndebele portrays his characters in an African mode – or, to put it differently, he creates a mode of characterization doubly appropriate to a novel that asserts its Africanness: individuals in community, and individuals as mutually transformative. To demonstrate these claims requires some teasing-out of the detail.

The novel falls into two parts, and the introductory section to each part is presented via a self-conscious authorial narrator who stresses the fictional status of the characters and the mediation involved. The four women are presented first in four separate accounts and then, in Part Two of the novel, in four further accounts. The accounts in Part One represent an outsider's view: three of them emanate from a third-person perspective, while the one in the first person is told by a woman alienated from herself. Then, in Part Two, the women speak either largely or altogether in their own voices (whether in dialogue or quoted monologue, or letter, or first-person narrative), and reveal themselves through their memories of what they were actually like as opposed to what they were meant to be like. Although in both Part One and Part Two the figure of faithful Penelope remains a "stick used to beat other women with," as Margaret Atwood says in her very different fictional reconstruction of Penelope,[22] each of the African women's lives tells increasingly fully in what ways they submitted to the myth's precepts, and in what ways they did not.

From within the ibandla, which provides them with the safe space for reflection that Winnie has hitherto been deprived of, the four women evoke Winnie through both her similarity and her difference from them. Remembering their one-time admiration for her, but anguished by her recent behaviour (her ostentatious infidelity and its embarrassing public emergence, her shameless ability to behave as if she were above the law, her support for 'necklacing' and other violence) the women are fascinated by and drawn to Winnie as the self they have not stooped to be, as well as the self they have not dared to be. The contrast illuminates what they feel (variously, for the accounts differ from one another) to be their own timidity, passivity, or acquiescence to social norms, and also their moral decency and private

---

[22] Margaret Atwood, *The Penelopiad* (Melbourne: Text Publishing, 2005): 2.

courage (although they know they were not tested as she was), but above all their capacity to reflect on themselves. Revealing themselves as in many ways more akin to and certainly more drawn to Winnie than to Penelope, they nonetheless use Winnie as a means by which to reflect on themselves. In other words, the four women become other to themselves when they evoke Winnie as their 'other'.

This process comes to play a part in Winnie's character development. In her response to them, which makes up most of the rest of Part Two of the novel, Winnie separates herself into two, as in a dialogue between self and soul. She becomes, in effect, the self-reflexive human being that stands as Ndebele's ethical and aesthetic model, here as elsewhere.[23] In sum, the four women re-create Winnie as she re-creates them. They give her the occasion, impetus, and safe space for self-questioning that the ibandla has helped give them, and her presence in their lives expands their own self-questioning and redefinition. After Winnie physically joins the ibandla, the five women turn to the whole country as their new home, their transformation into travelling women standing for a new human state.

It is also a crucial aspect of Ndebele's characterization in both Part One and Part Two that the women's two states – of waiting and not waiting – are simultaneously held in place, despite the overall shift in focus from waiting to travelling. Although their communities expect chastity and patience from them, and although they internalize these expectations, the women in many ways do not in fact wait passively. Nor can they be seen simply as the creatures of a myth imposed by Europe, given the novel's focus on both their own and the community's agency. In Ndebele's understanding, the European myth readily rooted itself in Africa, given the way colonialism redirected aspects of Africa's traditionally patriarchal culture in order to reorganize the African family and home. But in Ndebele's novel the myth does not account entirely for the lives of women, nor does it remain unambiguously a European paradigm. Moreover, the act of waiting is not necessarily to be seen as negative, as later discussion of Penelope will show. The women's fictional embodiment increasingly reveals the paucity of the standard rhetorical oppositions through which human beings and situations are described and assessed, including the moral oppositions brought into play in judging Winnie. 'Opposition' is replaced by 'nuance' in Ndebele's thinking, for 'opposition' is at the same time a close relation,

---

[23] See Ndebele's essay "Memory, Metaphor and the Triumph of Narrative."

both self-contesting and mutually defining. This is why it is possible to say that with their evocation of Winnie as 'other' the travelling women become both more and less like her, and she in turn becomes both more and less like them. In constructing a new social imaginary, Ndebele's focus is on the productive, mutual, and shifting relations between terms. This is a dialectical relation, not one that ends in closure.

The novel's unfolding from waiting to travelling is part and parcel of the shifts from the 'spectacular' to the 'ordinary', and from the outsider's to the insider's view, that have so concerned Ndebele in his critical writing.[24] In the novel, too, his interest in the representation of the "ordinary" is partly in its capacity for complexity and self-confrontation. Responding to the intimacy the four women offer, Winnie gives an account of herself that abandons political posturing and turns instead to self-reflection and self-doubt. The 'spectacular' historical figure, a figure once distorted by myth and stereotype but then later conjured up by four female compatriots in an ibandla, now becomes a more fully fledged fictional self, a figure who inhabits and is inhabited by the 'ordinary'. At the same time, the novel retains the paradoxical and ambiguous relation it has set up between the representation of historical figures, on the one hand, fictional constructedness, on the other hand, and the apparent independence of life-like characters, on yet another hand. Ndebele has noted, after all, that his four women are instances of "thought turning into desire" (35).

---

[24] For the concept of the spectacular, see *inter alia* the opening paragraph: "The history of black South African literature has largely been the history of the representation of the spectacle" from the "monstrous war machine developed over the years" to "high commodity consumption" (*South African Literature and Culture*, 41). For the concept of the ordinary, see especially Ndebele's analysis of three short stories which show, for example, "new possibilities of understanding and action" (52), "the discovery of complexity in a seemingly ordinary and faceless worker" (53), "the piling up of detail, the brilliant flashes of philosophical revelation" (54), "the honesty of the self in confrontation with itself" (55), the validity of an experience in an "imaginative cultural context" that has nothing to do with any "surrounding 'superior' civilization" (56), the way that "the ordinary daily lives of people […] constitute the very content of the struggle, for the struggle involves people not abstractions," and a "newness" based on "a range of complex ethical issues" in a variety of relationships (57). He also says: "By rediscovering the ordinary, [we are reminded] that the problems of the South African social formation are complex and all-embracing; that they cannot be reduced to a single, simple formulation" (57).

Besides the novel's focus on the new-found capacity to tell one's own story, to question one's self-construction, and to engage with the other as an aspect of the self (all of which Ndebele refers to in his commentary on the 'ordinary'), Ndebele's criticism has referred, too, to the capacity of the 'ordinary' to incorporate the ethical complexities of the variety of human relationships in modern society. While his interest in the 'ordinary' dovetails with his interest in ubuntu through their common investment in the interrelational, both also dovetail with his use of Bakhtin, most notably in the fictional journey the novel makes, further and further from myth and further and further into Bakhtin's 'native' representation. Not only is the dialectical or interrelational established in the novel as a mode of African human-becoming, but it is also established at a level of abstraction relating to the standard opposition between Europe and Africa.[25] Specifically, then, the discursive opposition can no longer capture the nuance Ndebele is putting in place, for this discursive opposition turns instead into a dialectical relation. The nuance and ambiguity associated with the dialectical are suggested partly by the collusion of the African women and their community in the imposition of the Penelope myth, partly by the reappearance of Penelope in the novel, and partly by the characteristics of African modernity as Ndebele represents them. It remains to deal with the latter two points.

III

At the end of the novel, the five travelling women (Winnie among them) pick up another 'other', a white female hitchhiker, the mythic Penelope come to life once again on the newly travelled South African roads. "For more than two thousand years," she says, "I have been on a pilgrimage of reconciliation" (119). They have already asserted their liberation from the mythic Penelope's symbolic control; that is, they have both recognized and distanced themselves from their social constitution under what was once unquestionedly a European sign. Important also is the strength of their self-assertion as the five African women welcome Penelope into their car and into South Africa itself. They now make themselves hospitable to Penelope

---

[25] Ndebele links the dialectical and the interrelational in his interview in *Exchanges* in 1991, where – after discussing his persistent indebtedness to the dialectical as an explanatory model – he says that the role of literature in the future "will be to make us conscious of the multiplicity and complexity of human experience," partly through indicating via language "the way we can interact with one another" (56).

in her new form. Acting as her host, offering a seat in their car to this white female stranger (who is also not a stranger, since so much has been shared), is to offer her a place where she, too, can be human (which is also to say, fictional as well as 'ordinary') in the way they are. After joining the women in an acknowledgement of their shared history and mutual liberation, as women and as human beings, Penelope continues on her own journey of human consciousness, what Judith Butler calls "identity as movement in the promising sense."[26] This is much the kind of movement undertaken also by Winnie in her own acts of self-reflection, and by the other four women.

Ndebele's interest in the interrelational combines here with his multi-layered and sometimes asymmetrical analogical procedure: the scenic presentation symbolically refers to Africans welcoming the European stranger as guest, but also calls up the analogy of wives welcoming estranged husbands, an analogy well flagged in the novel through the reference to the "green valleys and rolling deserts" (84). For these five travelling women together, this African world of valleys and deserts has by now already been affirmed, and it is only on that basis that a welcome may be so freely and hospitably given to the visiting or returning European. To pursue Ndebele's analogy in the context of the dialectical or interrelational procedure set up in the novel, it is in these transformed conditions of female self-assertion that the men may properly come home, with their own corresponding transformation thus facilitating further the women's transformation; and it is in these conditions that Africa can be transformed into home and become (like the ibandla) a transformative site for all those who live in it.

Before resuming the commentary on the Africa–Europe connection, it is worth adding a note about Ndebele's take on hospitality. Hospitality forms the basis of the dialectical or interrelational exchange dramatized in the novel, where transformed figures reconstitute others as they themselves are reconstituted in the exchange.

Through Penelope's mode of arrival and welcome onto African soil Ndebele re-invents the Africa–Europe connection. This re-invention involves a subtle and unspoken engagement with Jacques Derrida's theorizations

---

[26] Judith Butler, "Collected and Fractured: Response to *Identities*," in *Identities*, ed. Kwame Anthony Appiah & Henry Louis Gates, Jr. (Chicago & London, U of Chicago P, 1995): 447.

of hospitality[27] (our sense of an allusion is strengthened, I think, by the title
of the novel's final chapter, "The Stranger"). For Derrida, hospitality is
fundamentally contradictory in subscribing to "the laws of hospitality," on
the one hand, and "the law of hospitality," on the other.[28] For the sake of
simplicity, we might, rather, call these the two aspects of hospitality. In the
one, the host has sovereignty over the house opened to the stranger, but in
the other the host needs to relinquish that sovereignty in welcoming the
unwelcome guest. Ndebele's focus is on the former aspect of hospitality as
a model of behaviour, He also takes on board the gendering of hospitality,
where – to put it bluntly – there may be two 'masters', wife as well as husband, in the same house.[29] In discussions of the African homestead with its
codes of hospitality, women have a degree of power in relation to men,[30]
although men remain the head of the household. This ambiguity often extended into the modern bourgeois African home. In Ndebele's formulation,
it is the husband who returns and who should, in some respect, remain the

---

[27] See Jacques Derrida, *Of Hospitality: Anne Durfourmantelle invites Jacques Derrida to Respond*, tr. Rachel Bowlby (Stanford CA: Stanford UP, 2000), and "Hostipitality," tr. Barry Stocker, *Angelaki* 5.3 (2000): 3–18.

[28] Hospitality in the classic sense, that is, according to "the laws" of hospitality, cannot exist, as Derrida claims, "without sovereignty of oneself over one's home" (*Of Hospitality*, 55); yet in its absolute sense as "the law" of hospitality it depends at the same
time on the renunciation of that sovereignty in the offer of "an unconditional welcome"
(*Of Hospitality*, 77). These two meanings of hospitality are indivisible: "It wouldn't
effectively be unconditional, the law, if it didn't have to become effective, concrete,
determined, if that were not its being as having-to-be. It would risk being abstract,
utopian, illusory, and so turning over into its opposite. In order to be what it is, the law
thus needs the laws" (*Of Hospitality*, 79). His essay "Hostipitality" returns to this aporia,
and also notes that in "folding the foreign other into the internal law of the host," hospitality "tends to begin by dictating the law of its language and its own acceptation of the
sense of words, which is to say, its own concepts as well ("Hostipitality," 7).

[29] Of the host's gender, Derrida says, for instance: "The host [...] must be the master
in his house, he (male in the first instance) must be assured of his sovereignty over the
space and good he offers or opens to the other as the stranger" ("Hostipitality," 14).

[30] In his Xhosa novel *Ityala Lamawele* (1914), Krune Mqhayi shows the mother of the
homestead opening the homestead to people in need and teaching the young girls that
"womanhood means looking after and caring for even those unknown strangers"; quoted
in his own translation by Peter Mtuze in his "A Feminist Critique of the Image of
Woman in the Prose Works of Selected Xhosa Writers (1909–1980)" (doctoral dissertation, University of Cape Town, 1990): 31. In the same novel, good girls reject men
who lack ubuntu as insufficiently morally elevated to be marriageable (30).

stranger or guest, acceding to the woman's sovereignty ("to come into my life, he would have to walk into my house first," 80). In the context of the two aspects of hospitality, and with the guest's recognition of the host's self-assertion, the stranger or guest or social other might be welcomed into the house without danger to the host.

In the welcoming of Penelope by the five women, Ndebele's engagement with questions of hospitality alludes to both women's reception of men and – following the analogical model – to the colonial encounter. But a key complexity emerges in the silent claim the novel makes about the corruption through myth or ideology of Homer's Penelope figure. It is quite possible to read Homer's Penelope as a resourceful woman, fending off unwanted suitors through guile and trickery. Self-reliant and true to herself, she was as much a part of a Greek story about heroic behaviour as Odysseus was, and crucial to that story was her noble status as a woman who could not be taken by force, only persistently importuned.[31] Her chastity, represented in the *Odyssey* as her own choice, was of a piece with the complexity of her character. That this story of Penelope was popularly altered in Christian times into a myth of the patiently waiting and essentially subordinated woman stands for the reduction of a complex aspect of European culture of the Heroic or Bronze Age to a consumable, 'spectacular' image. (Identifying this reduction helps explain the tonal distance of – particularly – the novel's opening pages.) In the degraded Christian myth, as opposed to the Homeric legend, Penelope is an allegorical figure of patience and fidelity rather than an historical agent. The legendary human being has been traduced in the myth; she has become the locus of others' projections: on

---

[31] More might be said about the use Ndebele makes of Homer's *Odyssey*, an epic tale about the return to home, the infractions of hospitality, and the complexities of the human heart. See Homer, *The Odyssey*, tr. Robert Fagles, intro. & notes Bernard Knox (New York: Viking, 1996). In his introduction (3–64), Knox refers interestingly to changing interpretations of the *Odyssey*: in contrast to revenge, some critics have found in the *Odyssey* an "ethical transformation" connected in part with the assumption of personal responsibility; Knox is here quoting from Alfred Heubeck's introduction to the Oxford Commentary on the *Odyssey* (Introduction to Homer, *The Odyssey*, 41). The intricate similarities between *The Cry of Winnie Mandela* and *The Odyssey* help point to the nuances and asymmetry of the novel's analogy: Nelson might on one reading be likened to Odysseus, in a one-to-one correspondence supported by Athena's description of Odysseus as Penelope's "dear, departed husband" (Homer, *The Odyssey*, Book 15, line 25, page 320), but this correspondence extends into analogy with Ndebele's reference to the "dear departed white man" (94).

the one hand, a masculinist demand that all women passively and submis-
sively wait for their men; on the other, a Western feminist claim that women are nothing more than the victims of men. And it is this Penelope, the
Penelope of myth, this figure who has been used as a stick "to beat other
women with," that Ndebele initially uses in the novel in order to evoke the
European attempt to redefine an African femininity and thus to represent
Europe in its moment of overbearing colonial contact with Africa. Winnie
Mandela is comparably represented as a creature of myth, a figure rescrip-
ted to suit others' agendas. It is the business of the novel to restore to these
figures their nature as 'ordinary' women, which – to return to Bakhtin – involves seeing them in a novelistic rather than mythic chronotope.

    Ndebele's discussion of American practices of greeting and naming is
pertinent here, since he thereby creates the simple, albeit provocative, contrast he needs. African conventions of greeting and naming are shown as
quite different from the conventions spread by Americans wherever they
go. Ndebele characterizes the American mode through its use of first
names, and the African mode through its concern with genealogy and its
formal use of titles and last names. The former produces superficial famil-
iarities and a shallow pseudo-democracy, whereas, in the latter, "Everyone
is accorded initial respect and recognition" (55).

    An older European practice associated with feudalism would retain the
kind of formality Ndebele associates with Africa, and the pertinence of his
reference to American practice is that it evokes a process of commodification that has gradually taken over older cultures, whether European or
African. Ndebele's new opposition – not African vs. European but African
vs. American – lends resonance to the contrast he creates between living
human figures (or their proper fictional representation) and their commodification. Commodification occurs in mythification, which – like certain acts
of naming – detaches human beings from the 'ordinary', which is to say,
from their full, social and familial context. Ndebele calls this "the ritualistic
suppression of origins" (55). The reference to naming by first names also
draws the reader's attention to the way South African Europeans rename
Africans for their own convenience, and thus to the poverty of ordinary
human relations in apartheid South Africa.

    The link here may at first sight seem tenuous, but Ndebele's contrast
between a code of behaviour that accords "recognition and equality," on the
one hand, and a facile practice that only pretends to, on the other, provides
further grounds on which to understand the novel's ongoing argument

about the difference between a figure in an embodied and grounded narrative and the paltry figure created through "imposed convention" (54). Imposed conventions, whether in naming practices or mythification, mediate 'ordinary' historical reality and 'ordinary' human beings in such a way as to reduce them to 'spectacle', and at the same time impoverish the kinds of human social relations associated with ubuntu. Rather than making the argument, his novel enacts it: it creates a set of figures who become more and more fully fledged characters, as if they might at any moment break free of abstraction and enter a fully realized world.

The Europe symbolized by the Penelope myth is, then, an americanized Europe, where americanization stands in Ndebele's thinking for the falsifying simplification of historical reality. In contrast, the Europe that Ndebele's novel now starts to recall is the Europe of an altogether different history, a Europe not (as Europe in fact was) produced through its own acts of colonization, but instead a Europe that finds its likeness in Africa. Reappearing on African soil, in the form of a travelling woman, Penelope is represented as coming from a world other than the Christian English-speaking culture imposed on Africans by British colonizers: "She has a strange accent. Certainly not British or American" (118). Through this glimpse of Penelope's Greece, Ndebele asks us to imagine the persistence of a pre-Christian heroic age, a world that for good or ill is able to live out for itself an autonomous and organic cultural existence without being diverted by a 'superior' commercial civilization. Pre-Christian Greece is, like Africa, a world of ritual: Odysseus undergoes "cleansing rituals" in order "to forestall possible civil strife following his brutal slaying" of Penelope's suitors (120), and – at her own initiative – Penelope embarks on a "cleansing pilgrimage" (120). These cultural practices belong to a sociality far more complex than the degraded Penelope myth can suggest.

Ndebele makes no representation here of utter social harmony; indeed, he suggests the opposite with regard to gender relations, for – in her response to a question from Winnie – Penelope remarks that Odysseus' rituals should have acknowledged other responsibilities, too: "My Odysseus had no idea he had to reconcile himself with me as well" (120).[32] Yet the Penelope Ndebele's novel has by now retrieved is not the long-term victim of an

---

[32] As Olive Schreiner's Rebekah reminds us in *From Man to Man* (1926; London: Virago, 1982), "Even the Greeks had gathered their learning from Asia and Africa" (431).

enforced waiting but is instead capable of dealing with her husband's failure in a culturally organic manner.[33] Moreover, she has long been waiting for this African encounter: "As soon as you decided on this trip, I had to meet you" (119). In becoming less like the kind of European woman that Western civilization brought to Africa and that Africans have associated with modernity, and more like an African woman with her cleansing rituals (she is also a "white woman with a heavy tan on her face, neck and arms," 117), she allows us to re-imagine the colonial encounter. Penelope, it should also be said, may well function, at least momentarily at the start of the novel, as an allegorical figure for black South Africa under European or white domination: "she waited through an absence without duration [in an] indeterminate condition made bearable only by faith, the one device that makes infinity endurable" (1). Following this line, we might also find in Penelope an Africa waiting for its own return.

Penelope's emergence on African soil thus functions as the actualization of an event that might have been historically possible if circumstances had been different, and that has now been made possible in the moment of history Ndebele projects: a new human encounter that accords recognition to this other woman, hence this other Africa, "as an essential ingredient in the definition of human freedom" (120).

In contrast, negative interaction between Europe and Africa is concretized through the relation between Winnie and the white torturer, Ndebele's other figure for Europe. Ndebele describes Major Swanepoel's treatment of Winnie as penetration and invasion; "in the inner recesses" of his victim, Swanepoel found "for himself a permanent home" (100). In this and other wording, Ndebele echoes terminology from Homi Bhabha's *The Location of Culture*, and thus drives home the divided and disoriented state of the tortured individual.[34] The perverse intrusion sparks off in Winnie a political reaction she herself names as raping and maiming (113) and which she sees as a direct inheritance from Swanepoel's brutality towards her and her fellow prisoners: "Did I become your daughter, Major Swanepoel?" (99).

---

[33] In *Fantastic Metamorphoses, Other Worlds: Ways of Telling the Self* (Oxford & New York: Oxford UP, 2002), Marina Warner writes that "episodes of rape and insemination lie at the foundation of cultures and nations in Greek and Roman thought" (11).

[34] *The Location of Culture* (London & New York: Routledge, 1994) reads: "The recesses of the domestic space become sites for history's most intricate invasions" (9). Other similar terms in Ndebele's novel are "shattered intimacy," "invasions" (90) or "systematic invasion" (88), and "inner recesses" (100).

But where Bhabha might have used his term "uncanny" for Winnie's transgression of the gendered boundary between public and private so crucial to the civil State,[35] Ndebele's effort is to bring to consciousness the contradictions Winnie represents, for her behaviour is a crucial part of the complex dialectic his novel projects. Ndebele concurs with a now conventional understanding of the roots of mindless violence in the anti-apartheid struggle[36] but shifts the discussion to the self-recognition and assumption of responsibility (rather than blind justification) that a dialectical process involves. Ndebele's implication is not simply that a different originary relation between black and white, female and male, Europe and Africa would have produced a different reaction but, rather, that these very terms and the relation between them need to be re-thought.

Under these different forms of European domination (the suggestion is), South Africa becomes a country where the possibility of certain kinds of interpersonal relations is obliterated, and a violent disjuncture between self and other put in their place. In particular, it becomes a place where the absence of an "enabling environment" within which a "sense of personal capability" can develop derails black South Africans from the destiny they would otherwise have had, or from what Ndebele calls their "giftedness" (113). 'Ordinary' human histories are repressed (whether in reality or in representations that focus only on the 'spectacular'), and so is the discursive capacity for self-questioning.

Although a major interest for Ndebele is the re-invention of Africa as the home it might have been, Europe is also being re-invented as a site of a female self-assertion that could not be realized in the Africa–Europe encounter. Ndebele's premise – as suggested earlier in this essay – is that through colonization and apartheid, European and African patriarchal cul-

---

[35] Bhabha, *The Location of Culture*, 10. But for discussion of Winnie Mandela as uncanny, see Dirk Klopper, "Narrative Time and the Space of the Image: The Truth of the Lie in Winnie Madikizela–Mandela's Testimony Before the Truth and Reconciliation Commission," *Poetics Today* 22.2 (2001): 453–74, and Meg Samuelson, *Remembering the Nation, Dismembering Women? Stories of the South African Transition* (Scottsville: U of KwaZulu–Natal P, 2007): 195–230.

[36] As a recent commentator puts it, "It should [...] come as no surprise that such patterns of violence and coercion had spread into the resistance movements themselves after years of experience at the hands of the South African authorities." Helena Pohlandt–McCormick, "Controlling Woman: Winnie Mandela and the 1976 Soweto Uprising," *International Journal of African Historical Studies* 33.3 (2000): 614.

tures combined not to create an organic society based on the gentle coming together of time-tried conventions about human interaction and mutual respect but instead a society of oppositional reactions. South African society froze into a reactionary gender formation which redirected – to different degrees – the patriarchal power formations conventional to each culture into an excessive and abusive masculinism and a damaging individualism in which established human responsibilities and social decencies were all too easily forgotten. Recalling a legendary Penelope who is more like an African than a modern European woman, Ndebele reminds us of the cost of the Europe–Africa encounter. Ndebele's implication is that if we understand how both Europe and Africa were invented, or invented themselves, in the manner of that original mis-encounter, we can also understand how to make an epistemological escape from the oppositional cultural and discursive model that colonization put in place. Winnie, after all, says at one point: "*You*, all of you, have to reconcile not with me, but with the meaning of me" (113; emphasis in original).

With further regard to what Winnie Mandela 'means', we need to consider some of the symbolism generated in the latter part of the novel. First, the symbolism of the white Volkswagen Caravelle in which the women travel the newly claimed national roads: the vehicle (the vehicle itself, and the vehicle of the metaphor) is the new carrier, as it were, of the newly signifying sign 'woman', a sign which has by now left behind, as sole signified, the trappings of a submissive femininity, and of any conventional Western understanding of the woman-at-home. Albeit in a light way, the vehicle and the Venter trailer that carries their luggage stress the complexity of the women's race–gender–class positions. For one thing, the names, Volkswagen Caravelle and Venter, suggest in their etymologies (German, French, and Dutch-Afrikaans) some of the hybridizations that make up an African modernity. For another, the car and trailer invite us to recall what Ndebele once named as "the glitter of apartheid,"[37] as does Winnie's pair of designer glasses (116, 117). Material values have become more important in African modernity than in, let's say, the Africa to which the poet Mazisi Kunene beckons in his poem "A Note to All Surviving Africans":

---

[37] "Just as [black South Africans] had no option but to accept the conditions of life imposed on them, […] they may have no option but to fit into the available business and civil service culture and rise through the ranks," where "the glitter of apartheid: building, banks, etc., previously an index of the oppressed's powerlessness, now represent, disturbingly, the possibility of fulfillment" (Ndebele, *South African Literature and Culture*, 153).

We are not the driftwood of distant oceans.
Our kinsmen are a thousand centuries old.
Only a few nations begat a civilization
Not of gold, not of things, but of people.[38]

And what of the fact that the women are in charge, instead of being those (we imagine) trudging along the roadside as smart cars pass them by? Ndebele claims that the four women are representative of "millions of other women" (117), presumably including the unemployed; and, indeed, his selection of the four descendants does show some economic and geographical range. In focusing on the women's air of economic privilege, Ndebele acknowledges the class discrepancies of a modernized African society but in representing their position as provisional – they have simply hired the vehicle and its driver for a while – he suggests their position is current rather than lasting. There are other indications that the journey has just started. Ndebele's is, of course, a story about black and white, Africa and Europe, where black South Africans are represented only by characters with African-language names. But the metaphor of the journey intersects with that of the home when one of his characters speaks of "a house with so many rooms, so many brothers and sisters and relatives," that they risk being forgotten in any effort of "reconciling extremes" (71). Embedded in this story is the direction to be taken by yet another story, a story about those who are left out in the business of "reconciling extremes." Any simple reconciliation of extremes does not offer this novel the home it is striving to re-invent: this, too, is what is meant by Winnie's "the meaning of me." Class as it intersects with ethnicity and race is also part of the novel's dialectic.

The white Volkswagen Caravelle is certainly an ambiguous signifier, but for Ndebele it is no more a mark of inauthenticity than is the Blue Train "snaking its way through the vineyards" in the "first rays of the sun" (106). The train is a "marvel" of "awakening" (107) as it enters the world of orange and green which, like the "green and brown" (118) landscape, is so deeply symbolic of the new nation. Ndebele takes care to distance the desired Africanness from other signs of rank materialism. The travelling women are sharply distinguished from a figure called "Topsy-girl," "a member of the board of several companies in the new South Africa," a "familiar figure

---

[38] Mazisi Kunene, "A Note to All Surviving Africans," in *The Lava of This Land*, ed. Denis Hirson (Evanston IL: Northwestern UP, 1997): 94.

on the social pages of glossy magazines," a woman whose heart "is a glass
of Chardonnay, misty with chilled freshness" (28).[39] Topsy has, although
in a different way from Winnie, been penetrated by whiteness. Ndebele's
other foregrounded signs of African corruption are those he associates with
a reactionary "lawlessness," figures who "still think safety [i.e. driving
safely] is something you do for the white man" (94). In a passage that
echoes the trope of travelling so crucial to the novel, as well as the trope of
driving one's own car, Ndebele refers to speeding motorists who "have yet
to begin to live their own lives; to drive their own cars according to laws
made and confirmed by their own legislature. [...] They continue to hand
over their lives to the dear departed white man" (94). Winnie sees this behaviour as comparable to her own "embodiment of disruption" (89): "one's
very life is raging against an imposed order" (94), given that South African
laws were not passed democratically.

    In contrast, to be differently African in Ndebele's novel is to incorporate
what is liked, or needed, of the European without giving up one's own
position. The extensive descriptions in the novel of the rituals of tea-drinking so obsessively observed by the women in the ibandla suggest a different
kind of enfoldment of Europe within Africa.[40] Whatever the gentle mockery of the descriptions, these African women have turned tea-drinking into
something other than it was in Europe, just as – to take a well-known
example of African–European hybridization – the African Zionist churches
rearranged Protestant church practice. The name stays the same and the
referent changes: the term 'un-African' would not obtain. The useful concept here to oppose the reactive behaviour of the speeding motorists is not
assimilation (which would imply that the dominating culture had absorbed
the assimilating subjects), but what we may provisionally call a hybridizing
hospitality, or a hospitable hybridity, for the subjects themselves, from their

---

[39] In *Uncle Tom's Cabin; or, Life among the Lowly*, ed. John A. Woods (1852; New
York: Oxford UP, 1965) by Harriet Beecher Stowe, Topsy is a young slave girl who, on
being asked about who made her in the context of a discussion about God, replies:
"Nobody, as I knows on ... I spect I grow'd" (277). Ndebele's reference may equally be
to the Topsy-girl dolls marketed after the success of Stowe's publication, or indeed
simply to a marketable blackness, for the name is used by young dark-skinned women
advertising their bodies on the internet.
[40] For the idea of enfoldment, although not the precise term, see Sanders' *Complicities*, which speaks (after Derrida) of "the basic folded-together-ness of being, of
human-being, of self and other" (11).

own self-assertive position, are able to absorb a new culture without being absorbed by it, and able also to give it out anew, in a process of dialectical interaction between self and other. The self is transformed as it transforms the other, whose transformation (as self) has a corresponding transformative effect on the self (as other).

Whereas he might have written a novel about two ideals or essences either smoothly or contradictorily conjoined (African womanhood and European womanhood, for instance, on the model – let's say – of what feminist critics once suggested was a conjoining of masculinity and femininity into a state of androgyny), Ndebele instead investigates a more complex process of interconnection in character construction. In calling the four women "Penelope's South African descendants" (14), the novel points via the term "descendant" not to a genealogical lineage that might have been more important – or differently important – regarding African conceptions of self and community in a less patriarchal environment but to the disruption of that lineage. The four women are not, for instance, said to be descended from Nandi, Shaka's spirited mother, nor from the feared warrior Mantisi, nor – to go further afield – from the Zimbabwean spirit-medium Nehanda, who protected fighters in the First and Second Chimurenga, nor from any other of the many royal or prominent women of Southern African history (Winnie's own behaviour may in certain ways be seen as more reminiscent of these famous African women than of the European figure). Our invitation is not to search for an alternative myth; instead, we are invited to focus on the complex intersection of distorted myths and redirected desires, now brought to light.

In a speech called "Iph' Indlela" (literally: show me the road) delivered nearly three years before the publication of *The Cry of Winnie Mandela*, Ndebele passed judgment on the evils being revealed in the TRC: "Suddenly, 'the heart of darkness' is no longer the exclusive preserve of 'blackness'; it seems to have become the very condition of 'whiteness' at the Southern corner of the African continent."[41] Given this comment, what do we make of the following words in the novel, "Mees Winnie – she dead" (104, 112), quoted as if they have floated into the text from Joseph Conrad's novella about the colonial conquest of the Congo, over a hundred

---

[41] Njabulo Ndebele, "Iph' Indlela: Finding Our Way into the Future," Steve Biko Memorial Lecture at the University of Cape Town (as September 2000), unpublished paper, 5.

years earlier? "Iph' Indlela" sharply reverses what Ndebele takes to be Conrad's terms. There is a good deal of difference in Ndebele's allusion to
Conrad's novella three years later in *The Cry of Winnie Mandela*. That the
later text likens Winnie herself to Kurtz brings to our full attention the intensely complicated nature of her cry, a cry not about a confrontation of
Europe and Africa so blatant and crude that the relations might one day
with some ease be unravelled, but about the corrupted and confused mani-
festations of self and other at the point of their unwilling and unwelcome
yet also (sometimes) accepted or welcomed or even intensely desired intersection: for instance, about the intrusion into 'blackness' of so heinous a
'whiteness' that African human-centred ideals are altogether replaced with
violent political strategy and grand political posturing. Whereas Ndebele's
earlier statement in "Iph' Indlela" reveals a more optimistic view of the
'Southern corner' as the very last bastion in the African continent of the
now publicly unmasked European, the novel recognizes the history of complex (con)fusions, intrusions, and intersections that have forged an African
modernity and whose recognition is crucial to Ndebele's concern with "the
recovery of epistemological agency,"[42] and with freeing discursive and
creative processes from old epistemologies.

Whereas Ndebele associates the quest for nuance with the "endless human
search for the right thing to do," he on one occasion early in the novel succumbs to the temptation to give a glimpse of a more precisely defined end-
point to this journey besides, simply, the "Africa" that is both "direction"
and "destination" (114). The "product of ambiguous journeys," his character Delisiwe says, is "mellowness" (51). Mellowness, represented in this
novel by a generic African woman with an enduring gaze ("the gaze of an
eye that penetrates with a soft enduring softness," 7) stands as a relatively
comforting postcolonial African response to the suffering, pain, and anguish
inflicted both from elsewhere and from one's own self-recognition. Yet,
after Winnie herself imagines the "mellowness" she does not in the end
achieve (110), she reminds her audience once again of her capacity to harm
(and for *her capacity* we also hear that of the nation itself)[43] – "I am all of

---

[42] David Attwell, *Rewriting Modernity: Studies in Black South African Literary History* (Scottsville: U of KwaZulu–Natal P, 2005): 182.

[43] In his autobiographical essay "A Home for Intimacy," written and published in
1996, Ndebele uses the pronoun "we" for statements similar to Winnie's "I am all of you
who maim and rape." In the essay he writes: "We have continued in the last two years in
fits of violence, to wipe out our families and whole communities; we have abandoned

you who maim and rape" (113) – and her narrative ends with a hardly senti-
mentalized reminder of "the delicate point of convergence between dream
and desolation" (113). Africa has acknowledged its complex parentage: the
women are "no longer orphans" (113). While any "mellow fruitfulness"
wafting-over from Keats's "Ode to Autumn" (to combine with the vernacu-
lar use of the word "mellow," particularly in African American culture)
helps retrieve for Ndebele's new world an atmosphere associated with the
pleasure of "unending seasons" (41), the overall tone is sober, its focus on
"responsibility" (114).

I V

Ndebele has throughout his critical career been interested in writing as a
means to black redefinition. "Poetry should not only shock us into a fresh
recognition of familiar situations, but should force us to consider dismantling oppressive structures. [...] Our poetry should [...] go beyond [...] the
confirmation of oppression to reveal the black man's attempt to re-create
himself."[44] One of the oppressive structures is the hierarchical and categori-
cal distinction between Africa and Europe; another is that between men and
women. These two structures, as I have indicated throughout this essay, are
connected as ideas (analogically), as well as through historical process.

In his earliest prose fiction, Ndebele's creative engagement with gender
reconstruction was at first invested most visibly in male re-empowerment
as part of new nation-building. This was standard in literature written under
apartheid, and especially in the black-consciousness era from the mid-
1970s into the early 1990s. Less standard were fictional invitations to see
masculinity as a performance played out in the face of powerful women. In
Fools and Other Stories, the nuances of masculinity provide much of the
substance and drama of the writing: masculinity sometimes functions as a

---

patients to their deaths in hospitals because we are on strike; we humiliate and hold university officials hostage, and trash campuses; we block highways; we burn people suspected of being witches; we abuse our children and rape our women; we engage in
brutal taxi wars from which, if passengers miraculously escape being killed, they will
surely die once the minibuses of death, in a display of recklessness, charge down the
highway in a frenzy of speed" (29). In the novel, a passage similar to that in the essay is
spoken by one of the four women rather than Winnie (70).

[44] Ndebele, "Artistic and Political Mirage: Mtshali's *Sounds of a Cowhide Drum*," in
Soweto Poetry, ed. Michael Chapman (Johannesburg: Heinemann, 1982): 193.

self-conscious and even anxious invitation to the feminine, and sometimes as an effort to ward off its power. In "The Prophetess," the young protagonist distinguishes himself from boys who boast about the exploits of the penis. Choosing instead to become a man in a manner that does not repress sexual difference nor abject the feminine, the young boy hears within him his mother's voice, and creates or finds within himself "the power of the prophetess," which is the power of healing, specifically of healing his mother.[45]

In this short story, Ndebele's argument about gender could be said to rehearse in small one of the arguments in *The Cry of Winnie Mandela*. (Ndebele's story "Death of a Son," published after *Fools*, offers a comparable hint about the power of women.) The novel, however, gives over to women the power of gender redefinition. Another difference is that the novel lends a national impact to the women's invitation to men to redefine their masculinity. When one of the novel's characters says, "Rape is the invasion of the primal country. It is the first form of violence and brutality" (50), she speaks in the voice of both woman and land. Besides functioning as a reference to the colonial encounter, as suggested earlier, her call to men to "come in and linger" instead of "thrusting and pumping" (50) is a call to all those who re-enter home (whether as returning husbands or returning exiles) to participate in the creation of a different kind of world for both women and men. In a different relation to women, men can help produce both themselves and the whole country anew.

Although Ndebele's critical writing does not refer, as his creative writing does, to the need for masculinity to take on attributes associated with the feminine, or to the feminine as a demand to be heard, his much-quoted critical argument about "the closed epistemological structures of South African oppression" certainly makes space for redefinitions of gender, focusing as it does on the discovery of "new worlds" and a new "process and movement" hitherto hidden from view.[46] Here Ndebele stands, to speak generally, with other contemporary African thinkers – in the south, figures such as

---

[45] Ndebele, *Fools and Other Stories* (Johannesburg: Ravan, 1983): 47. For a different conclusion, see Stefan Helgesson, *Writing in Crisis: Ethics and History in Gordimer, Ndebele and Coetzee* (Scottsville: U of Kwazulu–Natal P, 2004): 93.

[46] Ndebele, "'Beyond Protest': New Directions in South African Literature," in *Criticism and Ideology: Second African Writers' Conference, Stockholm 1986*, ed. Kirsten Holst Petersen (Uppsala, Sweden: Scandinavian Institute of African Studies, 1988): 211, 216.

Chabani Manganyi, Chirevo Kwenda, Zine Magubane, and Abnerson Majeke – who in their different ways engage with the profound difference between Europe and Africa, and sometimes also the corruption of Africa by European thought. A generation ago, Manganyi writes of being black "in a social world created by white people primarily for their own ends," where the experience of being black was deeply affected by the social fact that only the white body signified "wholesomeness."[47] More recently, Majeke and Kwenda have stressed the forms of social division and inhuman behaviour that entered Africa with the European presence. Majeke addresses the imposition of Roman-Dutch law on an indigenous system: "Roman Law by definition entrenches private property, individual ownership and the right to kill in defence of property," and its philosophical foundations "tolerated one of the worst forms of slavery in human memory." Moreover, says Majeke, combined with Dutch, or Germanic, law, Roman law relegated women to the status of legal minors, and was responsible for the curtailment not only of European but also of African women's voices.[48] Most pertinently to Ndebele's thinking in *The Cry of Winnie Mandela*, Kwenda argues in his essay "Beyond Patronage: Giving and Receiving in the Construction of Civil Society" that the patronage of colonialism involved "a kind of giving which refuses to receive but takes what it wants by force or guile." The alternative is the capacity "to receive with honour."[49] This line of argument about Europe's failure to see Africans as equally human or as capable of offering an ethical vision is borne out by Zine Magubane in her book *Bringing the Empire Home*, which argues that the European settlers to the Cape would not have survived had it not been for African generosity,

---

[47] The two quotations are from N. Chabani Manganyi, "Preface" to *Mashangu's Reverie, and Other Essays* (Johannesburg: Ravan, 1977): [i]; and *Being-Black-in-the-World* (Johannesburg: Spro-Cas/Ravan, 1973): 6.

[48] A.M.S. Majeke, "Towards a Culture-Based Foundation for Indigenous Knowledge Systems in the Field of Custom and Law," in *Indigenous Knowledge and the Integration of Knowledge Systems: Towards a Philosophy of Articulation*, ed. Catherine A. Odara Hoppers (Claremont: New Africa, 2002): 146.

[49] Chirevo V. Kwenda, "Beyond Patronage: Giving and Receiving in the Construction of Civil Society," *Journal of Theology for Southern Africa* 101 (1998): 1, 10. Kwenda's essay has been reprinted under the same title in *Sameness and Difference: Problems and Potentials in South African Civil Society*, ed. James R. Cochrane & Bastienne Klein (Washington DC: Council for Research in Values and Philosophy, 2000): 243–68.

but that there was no place in their "revised narratives of self for acknowledgment of social intimacy with or dependence on Africans."[50]

In the same kind of spirit as Kwenda, in particular, Ndebele's book challenges Europeans to receive from Africa a new understanding of African–
European relations and a mode of conduct distinguished from an aggressive
masculinism. Hints of a newly africanized conduct appear in *July's People*,
Nadine Gordimer's novel of "historical transfer,"[51] where the entrance of
the white children into an African mode of being is marked by their receiving food with cupped hands and softened knees, an African gesture of
acceptance, thanks, and respect. *Ex Africa semper aliquid novi*, as Livy
said, speaking for the European. In the context of the European military
masculinism that drove colonization, such a gesture is readily associated
with the feminine, and readily rejected for being something all too new, to
return to the quotation from Livy.

Characteristic of European and African patriarchal cultures at the point
of their hostile contact was a reactionary gender formation. To make crude-
ly explicit the argument implied by Ndebele, European colonization and
African resistance lacked the feminine. In an Africa whose response to
Europe could have been – or could now be – differently conceived, on the
basis of Europe's different mode of entry, masculinism would have been –
or could now be – kept in check by the feminine, which retains forms of
power.[52] Learning the woman's map is tantamount to men's learning a new

---

[50] Zine Magubane, *Bringing the Empire Home: Race, Class, and Gender in Britain
and Colonial South Africa* (Chicago: U of Chicago P, 2004): 137.

[51] Stephen Clingman uses the term "historical transfer" to refer to the transfer of cultural and political authority from white to black. He applies the term to *The Conser-
vationist*, but it has particular aptness also as regards *July's People*. Stephen Clingman,
The Novels of Nadine Gordimer: History from the Inside (London: Bloomsbury, 2nd ed.
1993): 141.

[52] Anthropologists give a picture of precolonial Africa that may seem similar to the
one Ndebele is proposing. For example: "Many precolonial African cosmologies, like
many of their indigenous American counterparts, relied upon a model of gender relations that was dualistic in nature. That is, unlike in Western theories of origin and social
order, women were not perceived to be defective or deficient men. Certainly they were
regarded as lacking in certain male characteristics, but men, similarly, were understood
to be lacking in certain female aspects; this situation made it necessary to combine male
with female elements to ensure that the world worked as it was designed to." Susan
Kingsley Kent, "Gender Rules: Law and Politics," in *The Companion to Gender History*

way of being-black-in-the-world, to use (somewhat anachronistically) Manganyi's book title. So, too, by analogical extension, do Europeans need to
re-learn the map of Africa, or, like Penelope, wait at the roadside to hitch a
ride.

As suggested at the start of this essay, *The Cry of Winnie Mandela* does
not make an explicit address to Europe or even to South African whites.
However, Ndebele's critical writing speaks more clearly than his novel
does of "the need to alter perceptions" among whites,[53] and his interest in
redressing the conventional focus on white society is instructively inclusive:

> Now, when we focus our attention on the black majority, we should
> not be thought to be exercising an arbitrary and reflex alternative
> choice, but we want to study and evaluate its structural situation
> within the total national context as a way towards focusing on the
> entire national entity. When we do that, we invest in a total national
> concern.[54]

It is because of this kind of statement that Anthony O'Brien is able to make
the interesting claim that "black freedom and change become a condition of
white – a revolutionary reversal of the entire history of South Africa."[55] A
crucial aspect of any such reversal is that it is at the same time not a reversal: Europe and Africa, black and white, male and female, self and other
are no longer polarized "extremes" (71) but part of a dialectical process,
whether represented as elements of fictional realism or as discursive concepts in a theoretical argument about epistemological change.

This essay has argued that Ndebele's novel invests in the consciousness
of a group of women with a new sense of their own cultural and historical

---

(Oxford: Blackwell, 2004): 92. However, this dualistic and additive model lacks the
interaction or dialectic Ndebele seems to be striving for.

[53] Ndebele, "Life-Sustaining Poetry of a Fighting People," *Staffrider* 5.3 (1983): 44.

[54] Ndebele, "The Challenges of the Written Word: A Reflection on Prose," in *Culture
in Another South Africa*, ed. Willem Campschreur & Joost Divendal (New York: Olive
Branch, 1989): 18–19. As early as 1972, in "Black Development," *Black Viewpoint*, ed.
B.S. Biko (Durban: Spro-Cas, 1972), Ndebele was speaking of the national group as an
interaction of racial groups, and of this interaction as "the most important agent for
social dynamism" (13).

[55] Anthony O'Brien, *Against Normalization: Writing Radical Democracy in South
Africa* (Durham NC: Duke UP, 2001): 50.

construction, their independence from men and their self-reliance, and an
ethical responsibility involving interconnectedness with others and mutual
adaptation. Their capacity to claim and to live out their discovery – the
novel suggests – will redefine their relations with men, and, more generally, heterosexual relations and heterosexuality itself (assuming that men will
rise to the challenge by accepting women's autonomy and acknowledging
their difficult histories), and will thereby put in place a new understanding
of what it is to be African, a newly re-africanized South African nation, and
new relations between Africa and Europe. Ndebele's investment in an
African consciousness with a capacity to claim and live out the implications
of its cultural and historical construction puts in place a new understanding
of what it is to be 'African' or 'European' or, indeed, both.

   Bakhtin speaks of the nineteenth-century realist novel bringing forth a
"new element [...] on European soil" (86) as it departs from the homo-
genizing power of myth in order to delineate the concrete connections of
time and space in their historical and geographical specificities. In a comparable manner, Ndebele's novel forges a new element on African soil. His
fictional trope of travelling restores to the representation of black South
Africa the movement and flux of a reality that British colonialism had mis-
takenly seen as static and unchanging, and that South African apartheid had
also tried, in its way, to freeze.There is much more to say – in a subsequent
essay – about the way in which Ndebele's novel brings into being a black
South African narrative realism that functions simultaneously as a meta-
fiction interrogating the two opposing chronotopes Bakhtin calls the 'alien'
and the 'native.' Of importance in the present discussion has been Ndebele's interest in the dialectical relation between these two chronotopes. In
the former, the individual is governed by myths and laws not of her or his
own making, and in the latter the individual strives to fulfil the personal
destiny which Ndebele calls "giftedness." For black South Africans,
according to Ndebele, the relation between the two – the 'alien' and the
'native' – is an occasion for considerable self-reflection. His novel impli-
cates Europe in that African self-reflection, and also functions as a quiet but
forthright retort to Europe about its own need for self-interrogation. His re-
invention of Africa is thus a re-invention of Europe as well.

WORKS CITED

Attwell, David. *Rewriting Modernity: Studies in Black South African Literary History* (Scottsville: U of KwaZulu–Natal P, 2005).

Atwood, Margaret. *The Penelopiad* (Melbourne: Text Publishing, 2005).

Bakhtin, Mikhail. *The Dialogic Imagination*, tr. Caryl Emerson & Michael Holquist, ed. Michael Holquist (Austin & London: U of Texas P, 1981).

Baudrillard, Jean. *Simulations*, tr. Paul Foss, Paul Patton & Philip Beitchman (New York: Semiotexte, 1983).

Bhabha, Homi K. *The Location of Culture* (London & New York: Routledge, 1994).

Butler, Judith. "Collected and Fractured: Response to *Identities*," in *Identities*, ed. Homi Bhabha, Henry Louis Gates, Jr. & Kwame Anthony Appiah (Special issue of *Critical Inquiry*; Chicago & London: U of Chicago P, 1995).

Clingman, Stephen. *The Novels of Nadine Gordimer: History from the Inside* (1986; London: Bloomsbury, 2nd ed. 1993).

Cock, Jacklyn. *Maids and Madams: A Study in the Politics of Exploitation* (Johannesburg: Ravan Press, 1980).

Comaroff, John, & Jean Comaroff. "Home-Made Hegemony: Modernity, Domesticity, and Colonialism in South Africa," in *African Encounters with Domesticity*, ed. Karen Tranberg Hansen (New Brunswick NJ: Rutgers UP, 1992): 37–74.

Debord, Guy. *Society of the Spectacle* (Detroit MI: Black & Red, 1983).

Derrida, Jacques. "Hostipitality," tr. Barry Stocker, *Angelaki* 5.3 (2000): 3–18.

——. *Of Hospitality: Anne Dufourmantelle Invites Jacques Derrida to Respond*, tr. Rachel Bowlby (Stanford CA: Stanford UP, 2000).

Dhlomo, H.I.E. "Valley of a Thousand Hills," in Dhlomo, *Collected Works*, ed. Nick Visser & Tim Couzens (Johannesburg: Ravan, 1985): 295–320.

A Dictionary of South African English on Historical Principles (Oxford: Oxford UP/Dictionary Unit for South African English, 1996).

Driver, Dorothy. "Truth, Reconciliation, Gender: the South African Truth and Reconciliation Commission and Black Women's Intellectual History," *Australian Feminist Studies* 20.47 (2005): 219–29.

Elbourne, Elizabeth. "Domesticity and Dispossession: The Ideologies of Domesticity and 'Home' and the British Construction of the Primitive from the Eighteenth to the Early Nineteenth Centuries," in *Deep Histories: Gender and Colonialism in Southern Africa*, ed. Wendy Woodward, Patricia Hayes & Gary Minkley (Cross/Cultures 57; Amsterdam & New York: Rodopi, 2002): 27–54.

Helgesson, Stefan. *Writing in Crisis: Ethics and History in Gordimer, Ndebele and Coetzee* (Scottsville: U of Kwazulu–Natal P, 2004).

Homer. *The Odyssey*, tr. Robert Fagles, intro. & notes Bernard Knox (New York: Viking, 1996).

Jabavu, Noni. *The Ochre People* (Johannesburg: Ravan, 1963).

Kent, Susan Kingsley. "Gender Rules: Law and Politics," in *The Companion to Gender History* (Oxford: Blackwell, 2004): 86–109.

Klopper, Dirk. "Narrative Time and the Space of the Image: The Truth of the Lie in Winnie Madikizela–Mandela's Testimony Before the Truth and Reconciliation Commission," *Poetics Today* 22.2 (2001): 453–74.

Kunene, Mazisi. "A Note to All Surviving Africans," in *The Lava of This Land*, ed. Denis Hirson (Evanston IL: Northwestern UP, 1997): 94.

Knox, Bernard. "Introduction" (1996) to Homer, *The Odyssey*, tr. Fagles, 3–64.

Kuzwayo, Ellen. "'My Life Is My Neighbours'," *Monitor: The Journal of the Human Rights Trust* (Special Issue on Human Rights in South Africa, 1988): 131–33.

Kwenda, Chirevo. "Beyond Patronage: Giving and Receiving in the Construction of Civil Society," *Journal of Theology for Southern Africa* 101 (1998): 1–10. Repr. in *Sameness and Difference: Problems and Potentials in South African Civil Society*, ed. James R. Cochrane & Bastienne Klein (Washington DC: Council for Research in Values and Philosophy, 2000): 243–68.

Liatsos, Yianna. "Truth, Confession and the Post-Apartheid Black Consciousness in Njabulo Ndebele's *The Cry of Winnie Mandela*," in *Modern Confessional Writing: New Critical Essays*, ed. Jo Gill (London & New York: Routledge, 2006): 115–36.

Manganyi, N. Chabani. "Preface" to Manganyi, *Mashangu's Reverie, and Other Essays* (Johannesburg: Ravan, 1977): [i–v].

——. *Being-Black-in-the-World* (Johannesburg: Spro-Cas / Ravan, 1973).

Magubane, Zine. *Bringing the Empire Home: Race, Class, and Gender in Britain and Colonial South Africa* (Chicago: U of Chicago P, 2004).

Majeke, A.M.S. "Towards a Culture-Based Foundation for Indigenous Knowledge Systems in the Field of Custom and Law," in *Indigenous Knowledge and the Integration of Knowledge Systems: Towards a Philosophy of Articulation*, ed. Catherine A. Odara Hoppers (Claremont: New Africa, 2002): 141–57.

Mtuze, Peter. "A Feminist Critique of the Image of Woman in the Prose Works of Selected Xhosa Writers (1909–1980)" (doctoral dissertation, University of Cape Town. 1990).

Ndebele, Njabulo S. "Artistic and Political Mirage: Mtshali's *Sounds of a Cowhide Drum*," in *Soweto Poetry*, ed. Michael Chapman (Johannesburg: Heinemann, 1982): 190–93.

——. "'Beyond Protest': New Directions in South African Literature," in *Criticism and Ideology: Second African Writers' Conference, Stockholm 1986*, ed. Kirsten Holst Petersen (Uppsala, Sweden: Scandinavian Institute of African Studies, 1988): 205–18.

——. "Black Development," in *Black Viewpoint*, ed. B.S. Biko (Durban: Spro-Cas, 1972): 13–28.

——. *The Cry of Winnie Mandela* (Claremont: David Philip, 2003).

——. "The Challenges of the Written Word: A Reflection on Prose," in *Culture in Another South Africa*, ed. Willem Campschreur & Joost Divendal (New York: Olive Branch, 1989): 18–31.

——. *Fools and Other Stories* (Johannesburg: Ravan, 1983).

——. "A Home for Intimacy," *Mail and Guardian* 12.17 (Johannesburg; 26 April–2 May 1996): 28–29.

——. "Iph' Indlela: Finding Our Way into the Future," Steve Biko Memorial Lecture at the University of Cape Town (12 September 2000).

——. Interview. "Njabulo Ndebele," with Duncan Brown & Bruno van Dyk, in *Exchanges: South African Writing in Transition*, ed. Brown & van Dyk (Pietermaritzburg: U of Natal P, 1991): 49–57.

——. "Life-Sustaining Poetry of a Fighting People," *Staffrider* 5.3 (1983): 44–45.

——. "Memory, Metaphor, and the Triumph of Narrative," in *Negotiating the Past*, ed. Sarah Nuttall & Carli Coetzee (Cape Town: Oxford UP, 1998): 19–28.

——. "Of Lions and Rabbits: Thoughts on Democracy and Reconciliation," *Pretexts* 8.2 (1999): 147–58.

——. *South African Literature and Culture: Rediscovery of the Ordinary* (Manchester & New York: Manchester UP, 1994).

O'Brien, Anthony. *Against Normalization: Writing Radical Democracy in South Africa* (Durham NC: Duke UP, 2001).

Pechey, Graham. "Introduction" to Njabulo S. Ndebele, *South African Literature and Culture: Rediscovery of the Ordinary*, 1–16.

Pohlandt–McCormick, Helena. "Controlling Woman: Winnie Mandela and the 1976 Soweto Uprising," *International Journal of African Historical Studies* 33.3 (2000): 585–614.

Ranger, Terrence O. "The Invention of Tradition in Colonial Africa," in *The Invention of Tradition*, ed. Eric Hobsbawm & Terrence O. Ranger (Cambridge: Cambridge UP, 1983): 211–60.

Ross, Fiona. *Bearing Witness: Women and the Truth and Reconciliation Commission in South Africa* (London: Pluto Press, 2003).

Samuelson, Meg. *Remembering the Nation, Dismembering Women? Stories of the South African Transition* (Scottsville: U of KwaZulu–Natal P, 2007).

Sanders, Mark. *Complicities: The Intellectual and Apartheid* (Durham NC & London: Duke UP, 2002).

Schreiner, Olive. *From Man to Man* (1926; London: Virago, 1982).

Stowe, Harriet Beecher. *Uncle Tom's Cabin; or, Life among the Lowly*, ed. John A. Woods (1852; New York: Oxford UP, 1965).

Truth and Reconciliation Commission of South Africa Report, 7 vols. (Cape Town: Truth and Reconciliation Commission, 1998–2003).

Walker, Cherryl. *Women and Resistance in South Africa* (Cape Town & Johannesburg: David Philip; New York: Monthly Review Press, 2nd ed. 1991).

Warner, Marina. *Fantastic Metamorphoses, Other Worlds: Ways of Telling the Self*
(Oxford & New York: Oxford UP, 2002).
Wells, Julia. *We Now Demand! The History of Women's Resistance to Pass Laws in
South Africa* (Johannesburg: Witwatersrand UP, 1993).

❖

"A deeper silence"
– ❧ – Dan Jacobson's Lithuania[1]

GEOFFREY V. DAVIS

I

THE COMMON AIM of the researchers involved in the *Africa Writing Europe* project is to study the representation of Europe in African literatures written in English and French. Our focus thus lies on an idea of Europe defined in terms of the relationship between the independent states of Africa and those European nations which were their former colonial masters, one of whose major legacies to Africa has been their languages. This is logical enough, for insofar as they have addressed European matters at all African writers have tended to do so through representations of aspects of the colonial or postcolonial axis.

It is, however, the case that by focusing on a notion of Europe proceeding largely from the erstwhile colonial relationship, one is necessarily reducing African writers' perception of Europe to the Western European metropolitan centres of England and France, and thereby depriving their idea of Europe of an important dimension; for, as I hope to show in this contribution, there is also an Eastern European connection to which we

For visiting fellowships which supported my research in preparing this essay I am greatly indebted to the Harry Ransom Humanities Research Center of the University of Texas at Austin and to Prof. Maria Olaussen of Växjö University, Sweden. I should also like to acknowledge the encouragement of Prof. Bernth Lindfors of the University of Texas, who first suggested that I look at the work of Dan Jacobson.

[1] The phrase "a deeper silence" is taken from the Prologue to Jacobson's *Heshel's Kingdom* (London: Hamish Hamilton, 1998): xi.

should pay some attention. It is true that Eastern Europe did not play a particularly significant role in the history of most of the territories Europe colonized in Africa.[2] Yet when we turn to the case of the settler colony of South Africa things look rather different – among the successive waves of European immigrants who settled in that country were many thousands from Eastern Europe. When they or their descendants chose to 'write Europe', their prime focus of attention might well have fallen, and indeed in some cases does sometimes still fall, not on Britain or France but on Lithuania or Latvia, their very different places of origin.

II

The majority of people of Eastern European origin who migrated to South Africa were Jews, some 40,000 of whom arrived over the years 1880–1910. By the time the Union of South Africa was established in 1910 they made up 3.7 percent of the white population of the country.[3] Of those, the greatest number came from Lithuania. Indeed, as Gideon Shimoni informs us, the South African Jewish community was sometimes referred to as "a colony of Lithuanian Jewry."[4] The figures bear this out. Government statistics show that by 1924 Lithuanians comprised 70 percent of the total Jewish population.[5] Most came from the province of Kovno.[6]

Between the second half of the nineteenth century and the beginning of the twentieth, some 400,000 Lithuanians emigrated.[7] Most of them opted for the USA, some chose Palestine. South Africa ranked second in popularity after America. There were a host of reasons for their leaving, among them persecution by the Czarist regime, deportations of population, the obligation to perform military service, and widespread poverty, starvation, and disease. There was also extreme overcrowding because the Jewish

---

[2] Except, of course, through their support of many liberation movements.

[3] Gideon Shimoni, *Jews and Zionism: The South African Experience (1910–1967)* (Cape Town: Oxford U P, 1980): 5.

[4] Shimoni, *Jews and Zionism*, 5.

[5] Shimoni, *Jews and Zionism*, 6. Of the rest 10 percent came from Poland, 8 percent from Latvia, and 12 percent from Russia.

[6] Kovno (Ковно) is the Russian name for the pre-1917 Czarist Russian province. In German it is spelled Kowno. The Lithuanian name, which I use throughout, is Kaunas.

[7] Saulius Žukas, ed. *Lithuania. Past, Culture, Present* (Vilnius: Baltos lankos, 1999): 68.

population of Russia had since 1791 been confined to only four percent of Western Russia (which became known as the Pale of Settlement) and 94 percent of the Jews were actually living there by 1880.[8] There was also the pressure of the pogroms, which, after the assassination of Czar Alexander II in 1881, occurred particularly in the south of Russia, Kiev, Odessa, and Warsaw, as well as in Nizhni–Novgorod (1884). Lithuanian Jews were well aware of the threat they posed.

Suggestions have been made for why so many Eastern European Jews should have chosen to migrate to South Africa. For Shimoni, the process was "a chance by-product of immigration to England or transitory passage through England."[9] Some who had intended to make for the USA found themselves delayed in England, where they heard about the many economic opportunities available in South Africa resulting particularly from the exploitation of the Kimberley diamond fields after 1867. Jews from Lithuania also had before them the shining examples of people like Samuel Marks and Isaac Lewis who had left their home country, set up small businesses in England, and then moved on to South Africa, where they achieved phenomenal success and were soon numbered amongst the richest men in the country. When such news was reported back to Lithuania or when, for instance, Marks and Lewis contributed a fabulous sum to the restoration of the synagogue in their home town of Neustadt–Sugind, many more were encouraged to follow them out in search of similar good fortune. Not surprisingly, Sammy Marks in particular was regarded by many as "the pioneer of Lithuanian Jewish migration to South Africa."[10]

III

Those who emigrated escaped the terrible fate of those who remained behind.

The First World War and its aftermath saw Lithuania become the victim of a bewildering sequence of foreign occupations. It seemed to be the country's fate to be caught up in the political and territorial ambitions of stronger foreign neighbours. Nevertheless, the country was able in 1918 to

---

[8] Chaim Gershater, "From Lithuania to South Africa," in *The Jews in South Africa*, ed. Gustav Saron & Louis Hotz (Cape Town: Oxford UP, 1955): 62.

[9] Shimoni, *Jews and Zionism*, 7.

[10] Chaim Gershater, "From Lithuania to South Africa," 69.

regain its independence, albeit without the capital Vilnius, which between
1915 and 1920 was occupied first by the Germans, then by the Bolsheviks,
and finally by the Poles. One historian has commented: "Between 1919 and
1920 administrations changed in Vilnius so many times that it is easy to
become confused trying to remember them all."[11] The outcome of the
vicissitudes in the country's fortunes was that Vilnius ultimately fell into
Polish hands and remained separated from the rest of Lithuania until 1940,
when it was occupied by the Russians. During the interwar years, Kaunas
functioned as the country's temporary capital.

On 24 June 1941 the German army entered Vilnius and Kaunas, and by
27 June the whole of the country had been occupied. Many Lithuanians, in
the erroneous belief that they were being 'liberated' from Soviet control,
welcomed them. Then the Holocaust began.

It has been estimated that before the Second World War there were some
240,000 Jews in Lithuania, which was about eight percent of the popula-
tion. About 60,000 of them lived in Vilnius and about 40,000 in Kaunas.
This means that every third person in the major towns of Lithuania was a
Jew. By 1970, according to the census of that year, there were only 23,600
Jews left in the country.[12] Tomas Venclova, a Lithuanian professor at Yale
University, has recorded what happened to those the statistics do not
account for. He writes:

> During the war hundreds of thousands of people were killed in the
> Paneriai woods near Vilnius, in the Ninth Fort casemates in Kaunas,
> in the Vilnius and Vilijampolé ghettos, in the towns of Lithuania.
> They were exterminated not only by Germans but by Lithuanians as
> well. […] It is thought that 3,800 died in Kaunas on June 25–26,
> 1941.[13]

Before the catastrophe of the war Vilnius had been a major centre of Jewish
culture and learning, often described as the "Jerusalem of Lithuania."[14] It

---

[11] *Lithuania: Past, Culture, Present*, ed. Žukas, 161.

[12] See the extract from Tomas Venclova's 1975 article "Jews and Lithuanians," repr.
in *Lithuania: Past, Culture, Present*, ed. Žukas, 88–90.

[13] Venclova, "Jews and Lithuanians," in *Lithuania: Past, Culture, Present*, ed.
Žukas, 88.

[14] The reader is referred here to the major study by the French scholar Henri Minczeles, *Vilna, Wilno, Vilnius: La Jérusalem de Lituanie* (Paris: Éditions La Découverte,
2000).

boasted a large Jewish community of some 55–60,000 people; it had many libraries and schools, ninety-six synagogues, a Jewish national theatre, and a lively Hebrew press. When the Second World War broke out, Lithuania fell under the control first of the Soviet Union and then of Nazi Germany. Under Russian control there were many deportations and executions; under Nazi control, the Jewish population of Vilnius was forced into ghettoes and later systematically executed. Both the Jewish community of Vilnius and their culture were virtually wiped out.[15]

The fact that Lithuanians collaborated in the slaughter has been a source of contention and embarrassment in the country itself ever since. The authors of *Lithuania. Past, Culture, Present* seek to comprehend the matter, first, by suggesting that although the Lithuanian and Jewish communities had lived side by side for centuries the Jews had always been regarded as "an exotic insert with no spiritual connection to us,"[16] no serious attempt having been made to understand them, which they dub "a serious mistake,"[17] and, secondly, by referring to the resentment felt towards Jews who, on account of their communist political sympathies, were associated in the popular mind with the deportations during the period of Soviet occupation in 1940–41, even though many Jews were themselves deported by the Soviets. Nevertheless, the authors frankly acknowledge that there remain serious questions for Lithuanians to answer:

> can the nation be held responsible for those Lithuanians who took part in the Jewish genocide? Was it possible to do more to help the Jews persecuted by the Nazis, and if so, why was this not done? Why was the percentage of Jews murdered in Lithuania one of the highest in Europe?[18]

IV

Here is not the place to discuss in any great detail the history of Jewish immigration to South Africa from Lithuania or to record the process of

---

[15] See Tomas Venclova, *Vilnius: City Guide* (Vilnius: R. Paknio Leidykla, 3rd ed. 2001), for details.

[16] Venclova, "Jews and Lithuanians," in *Lithuania: Past, Culture, Present*, ed. Žukas, 90.

[17] Venclova, "Jews and Lithuanians," 90.

[18] *Lithuania: Past, Culture, Present*, ed. Žukas, 196.

settlement which ultimately led to their "finding their way to every corner of South Africa," as James Campbell puts it.[19] We should, however, note that the period of their arrival in the country coincided with the beginnings of industrialization after the discovery of diamonds at Kimberley in 1867 and with the rise of the Witwatersrand as an industrial and commercial centre after the discovery of gold there in 1886. These two developments not only set in train the transformation of the country – and heralded a turbulent phase in its history – they also provided immigrants with all manner of opportunities to make their fortunes. Dan Jacobson, whose own father came out in 1903, has captured the course of their dispersion and the variety of their new-found activities very well:

> [...] many of them made their way to the gold- or diamond-fields; many remained in the well-established ports like Cape Town and Durban which served the rapidly growing cities of the interior. In addition to these, however, a quite remarkable number spread out in all directions along the rapidly expanding railway lines, and beyond them, across the length and breadth of the country: a pattern of movement strikingly unlike that of their cousins who had gone to the United States, say, or to England. These newcomers set themselves up in business as itinerant merchants (*smouse*) or village shopkeepers, or first as the one, then as the other; some became cattle speculators, farmers, hoteliers. As recently as the 1940s it sometimes seemed to me, when I travelled as a boy with my family on holiday journeys across the country, that there was no place as small and remote as to be without its Jewish family or families.[20]

The formation of a South African Jewish identity which differed in significant ways from the Eastern European was due in part to historical circumstances. As Shimoni points out, these Jews had arrived in a country to which they had been preceded by both Anglo-Jews and German Jews. Thus "by 1910 most of the characteristic communal institutions were al-

---

[19] James T. Campbell, "Beyond the Pale: Jewish Immigration and the South African Left," in *Memories, Realities and Dreams: Aspects of the South African Jewish Experience*, ed. Milton Shain & Richard Mendelssohn (Johannesburg & Cape Town: Jonathan Ball, 2000): 106.

[20] Dan Jacobson, "Foreword" to *From A Land Far Off. South African Yiddish Stories in English Translation*, ed. Joseph Sherman (Cape Town: Jewish Publications – South Africa, 1987): ix.

ready in existence and [...] they bore the input of the Anglo-Jewish form rather than those of the Lithuanian *shtetl*."[21] The result of this, he concludes, was that by the 1930s, "while the flavour of Jewish life in the community was deeply influenced by the *Litvak* background, the forms remained basically Anglo-Jewish."[22] Further, as Krut reminds us in an incisive article on the origins of the Jewish community in Johannesburg, the gradual assimilation of South African Jews into "the white, urban, English-speaking [...] middle class"[23] was furthered by the fact that the British had won the Boer War and, unlike the Afrikaners, were prepared to guarantee Jewish religious freedom and civil rights.[24]

There were also ideological and political influences which would prove of great significance for the future of the Jewish community in South Africa. The background of the Lithuanian Jews who emigrated to the country was quite complex. For one thing, Zionism was, as Shimoni puts it, "part of the spiritual baggage which Lithuanian Jews brought with them to South Africa."[25] Further, a number of them had been involved in the socialist workers' *Yiddischer Arbeiter Bund*[26] and thus had experience of radical left-wing politics. From this diverse community would emerge many who were destined to play important roles in the South African business world, in the country's politics, and in its literary culture.

V

One of the most remarkable things about Jewish involvement in South African political life which was much commented on at the time was the

---

[21] Shimoni puts the earlier Anglo-Jewish population at 7000 people and those who came from Germany at 3000 (see Shimoni, *Jews and Zionism: The South African Experience [1910–1967]*, 12).

[22] Shimoni, *Jews and Zionism: The South African Experience (1910–1967)*, 18.

[23] Riva Krut, "The Making of a South African Jewish Community in Johannesburg, 1880–1914," in *Class, Community and Conflict: South African Perspectives*, ed. Belinda Bozzoli (Johannesburg: Ravan, 1987): 153.

[24] Krut, "The Making of a South African Jewish Community in Johannesburg, 1880–1914," 141.

[25] Shimoni, *Jews and Zionism: The South African Experience (1910–1967)*, 19.

[26] See, among others, Marcia Leveson, "Insiders on Outsiders: Some South African Jewish Writers," in *Memories, Realities and Dreams: Aspects of the South African Jewish Experience*, ed. Shain & Mendelssohn, 65.

extent to which Jews involved themselves – often at very great personal risk – in the struggle against apartheid.[27] As Shimoni records,

> Throughout this period [of apartheid] Jewish names kept appearing in every facet of the struggle: amongst reformist liberals; in the radical Communist opposition; in the courts, whether as defendants or as counsel for the defence; in the lists of bannings and amongst those who fled the country to avoid arrest.[28]

The Jews were "massively overrepresented in the ranks of the opposition";[29] at a time when they constituted barely four percent of the white population of South Africa, they made up 40 percent of the political left.

When the Treason Trial took place in the years 1956–61, more than half of the twenty-three whites arrested were Jews; among them were some well-known names – Lionel Bernstein, Joe Slovo, Ruth First, and Lionel Forman. Since Jews were prominent not only in the opposition but also in the legal profession, it came about that the African National Congress (ANC) was represented at the trial by Israel Maisels, a senior lawyer and a Jew. When in 1963 the police captured the leadership of the underground armed wing of the ANC, *Umkhonto we Sizwe*, at Rivonia, all the whites arrested – Arthur Goldreich, Lionel Bernstein, Hilliard Festenstein, Dennis Goldberg, and Bob Hepple – were Jews. At the trial which followed – by a twist of irony – the state prosecutor, the then Deputy Attorney General of the Transvaal, Percy Yutar, was also a Jew.[30]

Two of the most important oppositional figures in South Africa, albeit positioned quite differently on the political spectrum – Joe Slovo and Helen Suzman – were Jews of Lithuanian origin. Slovo was born there in the

---

[27] Why this should have been so was the subject of much speculation, especially on the part of Afrikaners. Beinart mentions as possible reasons the non-racialism of the African National Congress (ANC) which meant that Jews were treated as equals; the fact that a number of them were communists; and their opposition to the isolation from the world community which the imposition of apartheid had brought about. See Peter Beinart, "The Jews of South Africa," *Transition* 71 (Fall 1996): 75–78.

[28] Shimoni, *Jews and Zionism: The South African Experience (1910–1967)*, 227.

[29] Campbell, "Beyond the Pale: Jewish Immigration and the South African Left," 98.

[30] On Yutar's involvement and career, see Glenn Frankel, "The Road to Rivonia: Jewish Radicals and the Cost of Conscience in South Africa," in *Memories, Realities and Dreams: Aspects of the South African Jewish Experience*, ed. Shain & Mendelssohn, 194–96.

village of Obelai (Obel) in 1926 and went out with his family at the age of nine to join his father in South Africa; Suzman's father came out from the village of Klykoliai near the Latvian border.

"However one casts him," Campbell concedes, "Slovo stands as one of the most important figures in twentieth-century South African politics."[31] He planned the guerrilla campaigns of *Umkhonto we Sizwe*; he became a leading member of the South African Communist Party; he was the first white ever to become a member of the ANC executive; and he was appointed Minister of Housing in Mandela's cabinet. When he died, some 40,000 people attended his funeral.[32]

In her autobiography, *In No Uncertain Terms*, Helen Suzman, for many long years the sole representative of liberal opposition in the South African parliament, describes how her father and his brother came out to South Africa "for the usual reasons," among which she numbers avoiding twenty-five years of military service in the Russian army, escaping the pogroms, and seeking a better life.[33] They went to the Witwatersrand, set up in business, made successful investments, and married sisters who had also emigrated from Eastern Europe. Suzman adds that people of her parents' generation who emigrated "were rarely able to revisit the families they left in Eastern Europe, and any remaining links were wiped out by the Holocaust."[34]

VI

In literature, too, Jews of Eastern European origin achieved considerable prominence. No reader of South African literature can long remain unaware of the significance writers such as Nadine Gordimer, Gillian Slovo, Rose

---

[31] Campbell, "Beyond the Pale: Jewish Immigration and the South African Left," 142.

[32] On Slovo, see Campbell, "Beyond the Pale: Jewish Immigration and the South African Left," 141–56; his own *Slovo: The Unfinished Autobiography* (Johannesburg: Ravan, 1995); the section devoted to him in Immanuel Suttner's *Cutting through the Mountain: Interviews with South African Jewish Activists* (London: Viking, 1997): 221–44; and his daughter Gillian Slovo's memoir, *Every Secret Thing* (London: Little, Brown, 1997).

[33] Helen Suzman, *In No Uncertain Terms* (London: Sinclair–Stevenson, 1993): 4. See also the interview with Suzman in Suttner's *Cutting Through the Mountain: Interviews with South African Jewish Activists* (London: Viking, 1997): 423–44.

[34] Suzman, *In No Uncertain Terms*, 17.

Zwi, and Dan Jacobson attach to their Eastern European, Lithuanian or, in the case of Gordimer, Russian roots. This is not to suggest that the question of origins, the memory of Lithuania, is a constant or even a major theme in their work; rather, it is something to which they choose variously to return, with greater or lesser emphasis, during different phases of their writing careers.

In a short story entitled "My Father Leaves Home," for instance, Nadine Gordimer evokes the history of Jewish migration to South Africa from Eastern Europe. She does so by fictionalizing the story of her own father's migration to South Africa. That the initial impulse for the story was auto-biographical Gordimer has revealed in interview. This is part of what she had to say:

> My father came from a typical little shtetl. You couldn't get a high school education so when you were about twelve you either learned to be a shoemaker or to mend watches. He mended watches. […] In a recent book of mine, a collection of stories called *Jump*, there is a story called "My Father Leaves Home" and this came about because I didn't know anything about him, and I have never been to Russia […] But a few years ago I was in Hungary and went to a small town on the Russian border. Travelling around in Hungary I could see the remains of what a shtetl was like. In Hungary certain incidents happened at a little railway station and I began to think that it must have been at a railway station like this that my father left home. Slowly a story came out of it. A kind of imaginative idea of what it must have been like for him.[35]

In the story, the narrator, a representative of a later generation participating in a hunting party in an unnamed Eastern European country whose language she does not speak and confronted with an unfamiliar environment of slatted wooden houses, horse-drawn carts, and old women wearing head scarves, imagines the circumstances under which her father, as a young 'man' of thirteen, trained as a watchmaker, would have departed to seek his fortune on the South African goldfields decades before. She recalls how he set up a business on the Rand repairing miners' watches and how he mar-

---

[35] Nadine Gordimer, "My Father Leaves Home," in: *Jump and Other Stories* (London: Bloomsbury, 1991): 57–66. The quotation is to be found in Immanuel Suttner's *Cutting Through the Mountain: Interviews with South African Jewish Activists*, 108, 110. At the time Gordimer is referring to, Lithuania was under Russian control.

ried an English-speaking woman rather than a 'home girl'. She describes, too, the stages in his complex process of identity-formation as a Jewish South African: his immediate sympathetic identification with the black miners, migrants like himself ("In this, their own country, they were migrants from their homes"[36]); the tensions in his marriage, his English wife constantly taunting him with his supposedly 'inferior' Eastern European background (and his response: "You speak to me as if I was a kaffir"[37]); and, finally, the child's memory of her father shouting at his black employee ("someone my father had made afraid of him"[38]). Critics have focused on the subtle way in which the story depicts the Jew as caught between whites and blacks, belonging to neither, and on the effect this had in turn on relations between Jews and Africans, with the narrator's father venting his frustration at his own situation on the blacks, himself becoming racist.[39] While recognizing that the implied statement of this story consists in a critique of Jewish attitudes to Africans under apartheid, it is worth noting in the present context the narrative skill and economy of means with which Gordimer is also able to render what she calls "a kind of imaginative idea" of the situation of the emigrant which so many experienced.

Gillian Slovo's 1989 novel *Ties of Blood* similarly explores the theme of the relationship of Jew and African, only at very much greater – indeed, epic – length, the novel being almost eight hundred pages long. It opens with a brief prologue bearing the designation "Lithuania: 1902," which conjures up a melodramatic scene in which the young Riva Cyn, standing before the body of her deceased mother, despairs over the curse with which her mother reacted to her decision to leave the country: "'Take your children to suffer in a world apart from us. Go – but without my blessing'."[40] In spite of her anguished reaction to this, the daughter remains determined to "leave this country, this place that delivered nothing but pain to her people"[41] and give her children a better life. In a fairly dismissive analysis of the novel as "the didactic illustration of a thesis," Marcia Leveson suggests that "it is the Jewish experience of emigrating from Lithuania which is

---

[36] Nadine Gordimer, "My Father Leaves Home," 62.

[37] Gordimer, "My Father Leaves Home," 64.

[38] "My Father Leaves Home," 66.

[39] See Marcia Leveson, "Insiders on Outsiders: Some South African Jewish Writers," 71.

[40] Gillian Slovo, *Ties of Blood* (London: Michael Joseph, 1989): 1.

[41] Slovo, *Ties of Blood*, 1–2.

paralleled with that of the blacks who came to the city from rural areas. Slovo suggests that the Jewish commitment to the struggle of the blacks against apartheid flows precisely from the Jews' own experience of discrimination and oppression."[42] The theme of the novel, traced through two interwoven Jewish and black family chronicles over several generations from 1906 to 1988, is the mutual commitment of Jews and blacks to the coming liberation of South Africa.

Rose Zwi's novel *Another Year in Africa* (1995) is set in the fictional town of Mayfontein on the Rand near Johannesburg during the late 1930s and early 1940s. It is a powerful and informative chronicle of exile, alienation, and assimilation centering on a Jewish community of Lithuanian origin. There is Berka Feldman, the cobbler, who first came out to South Africa in 1892; Leib Schwartzmann, the blacksmith, who had given up his legal studies for a trade under the influence of the workers' movement; Reb Hershl, the baker, who was once a Hebrew teacher; and Dovid Yehuda, the tailor, whose father had emigrated in 1912, only to return disillusioned to Lithuania, convinced that South Africa had no future. Set against the backdrop of world events, especially the increasing persecution of the Jews in Germany in the 1930s, the first years of the Second World War, and the rise of Nazi sympathies in South Africa itself in the shape of the Greyshirts, the novel confronts its protagonists with emotionally difficult questions of identity. Berka, who has come to love Johannesburg, is all in favour of assimilation to their new South African way of life; Hershl dreams of a future Jewish state and of moving to Palestine; Dovid, the socialist, longs to return to *der heim* of Lithuania and is convinced that the Soviet occupation of the country under the Nazi–Soviet Non-Aggression Pact heralds "a golden age."[43]

Pervading the novel are memories of Lithuania: "the half-forgotten songs and psalms of his childhood"[44] which Berka hums; the landscapes around their home village of Ragaza, "the broad sandy road with little wooden houses under shingled roofs, a horse and cart in the distance,"[45]

---

[42] Leveson, "Insiders on Outsiders: Some South African Jewish Writers," 68.

[43] Rose Zwi, *Another Year in Africa* (Johannesburg: Bateleur, 1980; Melbourne: Spinifex, 1995): 151. Both editions have the same pagination. There are also excerpts in Claudia Bathsheba Braude's *Contemporary Jewish Writing in South Africa: An Anthology* (Lincoln & London: U of Nebraska P, 2000): 1–22.

[44] Rose Zwi, *Another Year in Africa*, 7.

[45] Zwi, *Another Year in Africa*, 23.

preserved in the photographs adorning the walls of Berka's house; the love for Jewish traditions of *shul* and synagogue which they were brought up in and which Schwartzmann still observes; the Yiddish songs which David sings of the poverty of the workers and of the devastation of war. And at the heart of the novel is Ruth, Berka's six-year-old granddaughter, "burdened with a consciousness of tragedy and persecution, with memories that weren't even hers,"[46] plagued by recurring nightmares of the pogroms Berka has told her about which he experienced in his childhood and which, he reassures her, will never recur, little suspecting what is to come. This is a novel in which, Claudia Braude suggests, Rose Zwi "gave fictional form to memory of her childhood nightmares."[47]

VII

Dan Jacobson has in common with the other South African writers whose work I have briefly touched upon above the fact that his family origins lie in Eastern Europe. His novels, essays, and autobiographical writings are thus informed by a history of migration, by his identity as a South African, and, more recently, by a search for his Eastern European roots. As a secular Jew, he has made the Jewish diaspora a constant concern in his work, particularly in the novel *The Beginners* (1966), which is essentially a story of migration over three generations, based in part on his own family's migration from Lithuania to South Africa.[48] Some thirty years after writing that work, the author himself visited Lithuania with the aim of researching the history of his own family, especially the life of the grandfather he had never known, who had been a rabbi there. *Heshel's Kingdom* (1998), the account Jacobson wrote about his journey, is at once an autobiographical memoir, a family history, a study of migration and a travelogue. It is, as the critic Margaret Daymond has emphasized, "compelling but painful reading,"[49] for, in addressing his family's origins, Jacobson was confronting not only the history of Jewish emigration from Eastern Europe to South Africa

---

[46] *Another Year in Africa*, 11.

[47] Claudia Bathsehba Braude, "Introduction" to *Contemporary Jewish Writing in South Africa*, ed. Braude, lxii.

[48] Dan Jacobson, *The Beginners* (1966; Harmondsworth: Penguin, 1968).

[49] Margaret Daymond, "Imagining the Worst: Fictional Exploration and Autobiographical Record in Doris Lessing's *Walking in the Shade* and *Mara and Dann*, and in Dan Jacobson's *Heshel's Kingdom*," *English Academy Review* 16 (1999): 81.

but also the Holocaust as it was experienced in Lithuania. Against the background of that event, the work becomes, as one might expect from this author, at once a philosophical meditation on questions of memory, identity, and faith and a moving interrogation of his own past. In what follows, I want to offer some account of Jacobson's growing preoccupation with Lithuania, of the place it came to occupy in his literary work, and of the conclusions he drew from a visit to the country late in life.

Jacobson grew up in Kimberley but left South Africa in 1954 while still a young man to pursue in England a literary career that he felt would not be open to him at home. His reasons for leaving apartheid South Africa were thus artistic and cultural rather than primarily political. Since moving to Britain, he has produced a body of work of great range and interest; his is a prime example of a successful expatriate existence.

VIII

The novel *The Beginners*, while not his first work, was Jacobson's first truly ambitious project, running to almost five hundred pages and deploying a cast of some forty characters. It is essentially a family chronicle spanning four generations and set in the four countries *from* which or *to* which members of the family variously migrate: Lithuania, South Africa, Israel, and England. Over a vast canvas, it thus seeks to encompass the many wanderings and migrations of Jewish people in the first half of the twentieth century. It is a novel which portrays the recurring conflict of the generations, a novel very much of ideas, of the intellect, confronting its characters with complex moral choices, philosophical and religious problems, and political options. Like many authors' early works, it is in part autobiographically inspired – so much so that Jacobson himself conceded that in this novel "I can't distinguish now what is autobiographical and what isn't […] the edges of real life and fiction are hopelessly blurred."[50] Insofar as the work does have autobiographical roots, it recalls the migration of Jacobson's grandmother and her numerous children from Lithuania to South Africa; it reflects his own youthful, third-generation restlessness in the country and his subsequent move to Britain; and it draws on the time he spent working on a kibbutz in Israel.

---

[50] In an interview with Stephanie Nettell entitled "Continued Discontinuity," *Books and Bookmen* (June 1966).

As the first work of Jacobson's that deals with Lithuania in any detail, *The Beginners* focuses on two significant aspects of the Lithuanian experience, the first being the large-scale migration of Jews to South Africa and the second being the events which took place in the country during the Second World War. The chronicle Jacobson unfolds thus begins – briefly – with the generation that fled Czarist oppression in the Lithuania of the 1890s and then moves on to those who followed in the immediate aftermath of the First World War, depicting in greater detail their initial problems of acculturation, their difficult economic circumstances, and their gradual assimilation into comparative prosperity.

In the opening episode of the novel the now aged Avrom Glickman is seen making the journey back from South Africa to Lithuania to bring out his wife and their two youngest children, the money for the passage out having been saved in South Africa from the earnings of their sons. While waiting in Bremen for the train that will take him on to Lithuania, Avrom rashly succumbs to a charitable impulse and gives all his gold sovereigns to a tearful Jewish woman from Latvia stranded with her children, his act perhaps being prompted, it is suggested, by his envy of his sons, who are achieving the success in South Africa that remains denied to him. Arriving back in his Lithuanian village, he has to confront his wife, who has been waiting for four years for his return – and now in vain. They will have to wait a further four years before enough money can again be saved by their diligent sons in South Africa for them finally to make the journey out.

The second occasion on which Lithuania plays a role in the novel centres on the harrowing moment when the young Joel Glickman, now working on a kibbutz in Israel, discovers something of what had happened to the Jews of Lithuania during the war. Jacobson introduces into the narrative a young cousin of the Glickmanns by the name of Yitzchak Sklar who has witnessed the Holocaust in Lithuania. Through him, the author is able to acquaint the reader with the reality of the more recent terrible history of that country. Yitzchak's experiences, which he recounts at length to Joel in response to the latter's hesitant question about what had happened, are typical of the horrors that had befallen the country: "He had lived. The others had been killed."[51] When the Germans invaded and his family's Lithuanian neighbours immediately took advantage of the invasion to set upon them and kill them, he managed to escape into the woods, where he remained, sheltered

---

[51] Jacobson, *The Beginners*, 279.

by a peasant and his wife until they, in their turn, were killed by un-
identified soldiers. Returning years later to the *shtetl* of his birth to find no
one remaining, Yitzchak then made his way through Latvia and Poland,
Austria, and Italy to Israel.

IX

The migration of Lithuanian Jews to South Africa and the fate during the
Holocaust of those who remained behind become central themes in
Jacobson's non-fictional account of his visit to the country, *Heshel's King-
dom* (1998).

Jacobson describes his desire to make the journey to Lithuania, particularly after the death of his mother, as "an obligation, even a compulsion."[52] It was a project which would not be realized for many years,
however, since, under Soviet rule, the closing of the Baltic states to Western visitors restricted access to all but the privileged. Of South Africans, it
would seem that, thanks to his status as a leading member of the South
African Communist Party, only Joe Slovo belonged to that group – and
when he visited the country in 1981 there were few left in his home village
who remembered him. He briefly describes his visit in his autobiography:

> We strolled around the back paths chatting occasionally to old peo-
> ple (they all seemed to be women), trying to find someone who
> remembered the Slovo family and remembered us as children. The
> old ladies consulted the even older sisters, but we continued to draw
> a blank. "The synagogue?" "They burnt it to the ground." "The
> ritual bath house?" "That also." "The people, are there any Jews?"
> "Those that didn't run away were all slaughtered, even children."[53]

Able to trace only two second cousins, he described his trip as "a journey of
half-completed rediscoveries."[54] In some ways, the term might apply
equally well to Jacobson's experience.

---

[52] Dan Jacobson, *Heshel's Kingdom* (London: Hamish Hamilton, 1998): 94. Further
page references are in the main text.

[53] Quoted from Suttner, *Cutting through the Mountain: Interviews with South African
Jewish Activists*, 225.

[54] Quoted by Campbell, "Beyond the Pale: Jewish Immigration and the South African
Left," 143.

He was not able to go to Lithuania until the 1990s, when, as a result of the political changes that had taken place in Eastern Europe, the country had once again become independent and it was finally opened to people from the West. In visiting Lithuania, Dan Jacobson was, of course, not only researching the history of his own family – his father had emigrated from Eastern Europe to South Africa in 1903, his mother in 1920 – he was also taking on the whole history of Jewish emigration from Eastern Europe to South Africa. As we saw above, over the peak period of that migratory movement between 1880 and 1910 some 40,000 Jews left Lithuania for South Africa.

For Jews of Jacobson's generation Lithuania was identified not only as the source of such large-scale migration to South Africa but also as the site of some of the most appalling atrocities of the Second World War, which resulted in the liquidation of 95 percent of the country's Jewish population at the hands of invading Nazi forces, but all too frequently, too, as the victims of their own erstwhile Lithuanian neighbours and – later – of the Lithuanian militia. Thus, Dan Jacobson's task in tracing and seeking to come to terms with his own family history was, as we shall see, rendered much more complicated by events subsequent to their emigration to South Africa, by what he aptly calls "the gulf of an unspeakable history" (3).

Jacobson defines his purpose in going to the country quite specifically. He wishes, in contemplating the life and faith of his grandfather, the rabbi Heshel Melamed, who died at the age of fifty-three and did not himself emigrate to South Africa, to establish what he has inherited from him, "what" as he puts it, "we have in common and what we do not; how remote we are from one another and how close; in what terms it might be possible for me to put together all I already know about us both with everything I will never know" (5). He wishes, too, in contemplating his forthcoming visit, "to establish the physical reality of the country" (96) – not least because, before going, he concluded that this would probably be all he *could* achieve. And finally, in disclaiming (with a note added to the text in a later revision) that "this is not an autobiography" (73), he intends "to follow [of the many threads that run through my earliest years] only one: that of the connection I had, or did not have, to the distant part of the world my parents had come from" (73). All of this would constitute a challenging enough task at the best of times; in the light of the dreadful story which constitutes Lithuanian history in the first half of the last century it is rendered well-nigh impossible – for how do you establish connections, he asks, when, for example, "not a single member of [your] mother's family who was alive in Lithuania at the time of the German invasion [...] survived" (97). He did not and could not, therefore, entertain any hope of meeting anyone who had actually known his grandfather. On leaving the country later, he will be forced to the conclusion that "everything about Heshel Melamed as an individual that had been hidden from me before I went there remains hidden still, and always will do so" (99). In this sense at least, his journey is a failure, exemplified particularly by his breaking-off of the search for his grandfather's grave and the site of his *shul* at Varniai.

Of course, it goes without saying that Dan Jacobson was well aware of the difficulties of his undertaking. In the prologue to the book, he describes the difficulty of ever knowing the past in terms of an image drawn from the Kimberley of his childhood, a landscape dotted with the gaping pits of disused diamond mines, into which he would occasionally toss a stone. Imagine, he asks the reader, a stone falling into the pit of such a mine, but never reaching the bottom. Such an image of the past – "echoless and bottomless" – resonates through the text, as Jacobson wonders, for example, whether it is possible "to have 'roots' in such an abyss" (98). By which he means the catastrophe that befell Lithuania, or finally – when gazing on the site where once the synagogue stood in the small town where his grandfather had been rabbi and his mother was born – he rejects the imagery of "bottomless pits" and "soundless chambers" (208) as an appropriate means of evoking the past in favour of something more simple, the topography of contemporary Lithuania itself, which, he concludes, "will do just as well. These benches and that set of civic buildings; those trees and traffic signs; the curve of this empty road" (208–209).

There is, as the reader soon notices, a second, more tragic facet to Jacobson's recollections of the past lives of his grandfather and his generation in Lithuania. He constantly reiterates the thought that all of those decisions and actions of his grandfather, which are so difficult to assess and which in retrospect seem so unwise, were necessarily taken in ignorance of the future. Jacobson and subsequent generations who enjoy the benefit of hindsight know, as his grandfather could not, that there was much worse to come. As he confesses in reflecting on the family's flight before the Germans in the First World War: "I cannot get out of my mind what was to happen a generation later [...] when an entire people tried to flee and found their murderers waiting for them wherever they turned" (39).

The process by which Jacobson approaches dealing with the past is very much that of a novelist rather than a historian or social scientist. Unlike Rose Zwi in *Last Walk in Naryshkin Park*,[55] for instance, he does not scour the archives of Israel and the USA to explore the Jewish histories of the towns and villages he is to visit. Rather, he prepares the reader – and himself – for what lies ahead through the construction of family portraits: his grandfather, "a fateful absence" because never known, recollected through the little that has remained of him – a striking photograph taken just before his journey to America in 1912 and bearing "indubitable witness to the consciousness that was then his" (9), his spectacles, his address book; his wife, Jacobson's grandmother, recalled through memories of the many ways in which she asserted her will in an effort to "test the limits of her existence" (26) within the constraints of her marriage and of the time; and, finally, Jacobson's own mother, brought up speaking German, Russian, and Hebrew, the circumstances of her emigration to South Africa documented by Jacobson via her schoolgirl essays, somewhat sceptical in view of the great contrasts visible in South African society of the benefits of progress and of migration (55). Such well-observed character studies not only serve to ground Jacobson's enquiry firmly in the history of his own family, which provides the inspiration for his journey; that of his grandfather in particular provokes much of the intellectual debate within the book. The tenacity of his grandfather's orthodox faith prompts Jacobson to examine the religious divide between them and to define his own sceptical secularism. He does so in an effort to comprehend both what he regards as the "paradox" of his grandfather's tragically early death – which he sees as "the kindest thing he did for his wife and children" (4), since it was their resulting penury that motivated the migration to South Africa and spared them the later Holocaust – and what, with the ambivalent benefit of hindsight, he considers "the terrible mistakes of judgement he made" largely for religious reasons, when, just before the First World War, he failed to take up the opportunity of a position in the USA and returned to Lithuania, thus unknowingly exposing his family to the dreadful vicissitudes of life in Lithuania during and after that war. To Jacobson, this decision appeared "bizarre and incomprehensible, even mad" (75–76) – at least, that is, until he came to understand his grandfather and his world somewhat better.

---

[55] Rose Zwi, *Last Walk in Naryshkin Park* (Melbourne: Spinifex, 1997; Johannesburg: U of the Witwatersrand P, 1998).

The author's analysis of his own attitude to the idea of Lithuania is a fundamental aspect of *Heshel's Kingdom*. As Sheila Roberts points out, "it is from within a childhood and young adulthood lived in Kimberley, rather than any of the other places in which Jacobson has lived, that he [...] discovers the snags that tie him to an Eastern European family past."[56] Thus the impact of the book depends very much on the reader's appreciation of the evolution of his thinking about the place from that of the child unaware of the history, through that of the young man who has learnt what happened there during the war, to that of the older author who is now able to visit the country and can test his views against the reality – or, rather, what remains of it. As a child growing up on the other side of the world, his perception of the country was wholly negative: to him, Lithuania was a paradox, a place "where no one I knew had ever gone but whence so many of them had come" (35), "an unimaginable region" productive only of "fear, bewilderment, [...] something resembling pity" (73), and disbelief even at the idea of "finding [himself] linked so closely to a world so strange to [him]," a region responsible for all the problems attendant upon his family's being perceived in South Africa as "different" (73). It seemed, he tells us, "like a wound within him" (75), a place which held no appeal for him, associated in his childish mind only with pogroms, the practice of orthodox religion, and poverty, from all of which, by coming to South Africa, his mother had successfully escaped. No wonder that, as a child, he believed, as did others of his generation, that his parents effectively came from "Nowhere" – with a capital "N" (76). And, of course, at that time he never paused to entertain the notion that the places from which his parents had escaped – Vilnius and Kaunas, for instance – might actually have been "centres of a high civilisation" (76) or that, in their view, it might have been South Africa rather than Lithuania that was "Nowhere."

Youthful preconceptions of Lithuania as a place of "backwardness and deprivation" (92) pale into insignificance, however, as the truth about the extent of the tragedy that had befallen the country and the entirety of Jewish life during the war filters through, and Jacobson, too, becomes aware of it. By the end of the war he could think of Lithuania only as "a locus of terror, a hole in space and time from which no hope, light or reason could ever emerge" (92).

---

[56] Sheila Roberts, "A Way of Seeing: Dan Jacobson's *Heshel's Kingdom*," *Current Writing* 10.1 (1998): 57.

Accordingly, when, later in life, Jacobson does go to the country, the decision actually to visit the scene of so much devastation was a difficult, even a courageous one. Jacobson's text offers eloquent and forceful testimony to the impact the visit would have on his attitude to the place. Especially when he sees the exhibits at the Jewish Museum in Vilnius,[57] he realizes – as he puts it – "how little reconstructed since my childhood had been my view of the 'old country'" (123) and he is made aware of the "worth and importance" of the religious faith practised and the secular learning followed there, all of which causes him to recall – and revise – his earlier view of Lithuania as "that Nowhere of a place, that desolate Pale of prayer, pogroms and deprivation" (124). Humbled by the impact of the museum, he confesses that hitherto he had not appreciated "the full extent of the devastation" or the speed with which it had been carried out. It had taken actually going there to bring this home to him. He therefore insists on the awful statistics: "Only 5 percent of the Jews living there at the time of the German invasion were alive four years later"; or "one in twenty survived"; or "600 years of Jewish life were brought to an end over a period of ten weeks only" (125). And that, of course, also means that the past of his own family in Lithuania had been eradicated.

It goes without saying that Jacobson's depiction both of family history and of present-day Lithuania benefits greatly from his gifts as a novelist. The book abounds in finely drawn character studies: of his grandfather, for instance, his qualities deduced from the sole surviving photograph of him; of Vera the mathematics teacher, encountered in Varniai, apparently the last Jew living there; of Shlomo, his guide in Kaunas, describing himself, somewhat curiously, as "the ambassador to the Jewish people" (148); of his driver Albertis, admired for his judicious mixture of independence and deference. Jacobson has a fine eye for the visual details of rural activity – scattering seed, harrowing, scything – and can evoke a sense of place convincingly in a few lines. Nowhere more so than in the moving paragraphs with which he evokes his first sight of his grandparents' home town of

---

[57] The Vilna Gaon Jewish State Museum of Lithuania was established in 1989 "to keep alive the memory of the Litvak (Lithuanian-Jewish) history and culture, as well as to research and record the Jewish history of Lithuania." The introductory brochure further defines its aims as: "to develop the historical consciousness of Lithuanian society, distorted under Soviet rule. The absence of knowledge about the history, culture and annihilation of Lithuania's once largest minority – the Jewish people – has resulted in misleading stereotypes." The museum is located at Pamènkalnio 12, LT-2001 Vilnius.

Varniai with its two churches, its river bridge, its wooden houses with their vegetable gardens (183–85). Jacobson also displays, if infrequently, a joy in comic incident, as when his grandfather Heshel finds his wife reading Ernest Renan's *Vie de Jésus* and, rabbi that he is, hurls it out into the street, where it is left to soak in the mud.

His description of Lithuania is, as must be expected from what his account of the country's history tells us, a predominantly desolate one. Flying into the country in an almost empty plane, viewing from above landscapes empty of people, arriving at an almost empty airport, staying in one town after another in hotels where there seem hardly to be any other guests, he finally arrives in the town his family came from, that too a place "empty of traffic, empty of people" (183). It does not surprise us when he describes the strongest emotion he felt in the country as "sadness […] a stunned sadness of a kind I had never felt before" (140). On his visit, Jacobson journeys to the capital, Vilnius, to the second city and former capital, Kaunas, to the district capital, Rasenai, and to the small town of Varniai in the north-east of the country where his grandparents had lived and his mother had spent her youth. All of these places are sites of massacres, and Jacobson spares neither himself nor his readers the details: he views the records of the mass murder of the Jews in the Jewish Museum at Vilnius; he visits Fort IX outside Kaunas where 30,000 people were murdered between 1941 and 1944, a place which has, he concludes, seen "as much evil doing as any place on earth" (158); he lists the figures for the women and children shot at Rasenai by the *Einsatzkommandos* on a single day; and he is taken to the Jewish cemetery in Varniai, where he assumes his grandfather is buried, and there puzzles over the inscription on a memorial standing in front of it which describes it as the place where the Jewish cemetery "used to be" – until 1941, that is, after which there were no more Jews to bury there (189).

On two occasions – his visits to Fort IX and to the old Jewish cemetery at Kelme – Jacobson is made aware of the difficulty the Lithuanians themselves experience in facing up to the fact that the Nazis who murdered the Jews in the country were assisted by Lithuanian collaborators. At Fort IX, for example, we learn that although the memorial does now identify the dead as Jews, it fails to record the fact that the assistants of the Nazis were Lithuanians (163) and that this is because the authorities refused to allow the addition; likewise at Kelme, where the local authorities were equally reluctant to have anything like the actual numbers of those killed on the stone placed at the memorial site – presumably for the same reason (211).

I mentioned earlier that one facet of *Heshel's Kingdom* is Jacobson's persistent probing of his grandfather's religious faith and of his own understanding of it. In searching for what he and his grandfather have in common, he is constantly aware that between Heshel's faith and his lack of it there lies an immense gulf, one which it is ultimately impossible to bridge, since, as Jacobson puts it, "my scepticism is so profound [and] I am confronted or affronted by so many moral and intellectual difficulties" (31) as to render any belief in God inconceivable. In this the author is not alone: all nine of Heshel's children relinquished their faith. One reason for this, it would seem, was the wholesale infatuation with which they embraced the new-found opportunities South Africa represented. In emigrating, they had, as Jacobson puts it, "exchanged night for the promise of day, superstition for the promise of reason, limitation and frustration for a hitherto unimaginable degree of personal autonomy" (68). More than this, indeed, for, as the later history of the Holocaust would show, "they had exchanged an anonymous death at the hands of murderers for life itself" (68). In so doing, they had plainly rejected what their father had stood for and had abandoned "the old ways" (66). Ironically, they were in a sense re-enacting the abandonment of religious faith and practices by those Lithuanian Jews who had emigrated to America, whose example had so alienated their father and caused him to turn down the opportunity to stay in the USA.

In the course of the book one becomes aware of Jacobson's growing respect for his grandfather and for his motivation in returning from America to the poverty of a Lithuanian *shtetl*, and for the values for which he stood. He comes to understand that Heshel's essential purpose was to preserve his family from what he perceived as corruption (21), that he was opting for a life in security, a life of "prayer, study, preaching [and] teaching" (22) in preference to what America had to offer. As so often in this impressive book, Jacobson finds moving words to describe his feelings:

> Looking about me in Lithuania, searching for him in the midst of a devastating absence and emptiness, I was surprised to find myself grasping for the first time the full reality *to itself* of the obliterated community he had belonged to. Seeing him in the context of his vanished people, of the nation that now is not, I began to understand for the first time how it could once have seemed to him sufficient; as much as he needed; as much as a man like himself could expect to find on God's unredeemed earth. (99–100)

In the penultimate chapter of the book entitled "Now," Jacobson seeks to formulate some conclusions. Unlike the earlier parts of the book, the chapter is cast as a personal address to his grandfather; it is a compendium of reflections, prompted by his trip, on the current state of Jewry, on the subsequent history of the family, and on the human propensity to adapt to circumstances and act as though the past, however recent, had never happened.

The chapter opens with an apology in which the author speaks of his shame "at having lived so long and understood so little about us both." That use of "both" establishes the interconnectedness of the two of them, which, of course, it was Jacobson's original aim to gauge. He confesses that he has always borne a grudge against his grandfather because of his decision to turn down the offer of a position in Cleveland and return to Varniai. By returning, we should recall, his grandfather had potentially exposed his family to future danger which they would inevitably have suffered, had he not died first and they in consequence emigrated to South Africa. Even though he, of course, knows that his grandfather could have had no knowledge of what was to happen in Lithuania later on, Jacobson still subconsciously reproached him for his decision. One result of his own trip to Lithuania has been, however, that it has enabled him to see that his grandfather's return was "a principled one." Jacobson can now acknowledge the fact that "You put your faith first" (216).

In the light of his visit, Jacobson also revises the view he had held earlier that the Jewish religion had been "morally culpable [...] in that it had persuaded an entire people to keep themselves together, separate from all others," with what consequences we know. This argument he now dismisses as an "absurdity," since, as he has now realized, in Eastern Europe "there never had been a neutral, secular social space from which they had chosen to exclude themselves." They had always been "one among a multitude of competing groups" (218); there had been no separate way.

Faced with the enormity of the tally of one day's killings in Rasenai – four hundred and forty-six Jewish males, four hundred and forty women, one thousand and twenty children – Jacobson recognizes the gulf that separates those who fell victim to the catastrophe and those who survived. He suspects that his grandfather's faith would have been strengthened rather than undermined if he had lived to witness these events, although he confesses that he, as a person without religious belief, does not understand how this could be.

Recalling once again "history's iron law," by which he means that "we are all revealed to those who come after us to have been ignorant by necessity, solemn prophets who knew little or nothing of what lay ahead" (222), he devotes the latter part of the chapter to a number of observations on the current state of Jewry, recording developments his grandfather could never have imagined, many of them from subsequent family history: the dwindling numbers in the Jewish community in South Africa and else- where, for example; the number of Heshel's grandchildren who have mar- ried out, so much so that some of their offspring, including Jacobson's own, can in the strict sense no longer be regarded as Jews; the fact that one of his great-grandsons has become an orthodox Jew and is to enter a *yeshiva*; the growing influence of orthodoxy in Israel; and so on.

Throughout the book, to a greater or lesser extent, it has been apparent that, for all the decades of his expatriate life in England, Jacobson writes very much as a South African. Paul Gready has characterized him as "irreparably formed and conditioned by his initial years in South Africa."[58] Jacobson unwittingly confirms this himself, when he visits Vera in Varniai and, without thinking, introduces himself as someone from South Africa: "For some reason I did not answer 'England,' as I had said to people every- where else. South Africa, I said, *Dorem Afrika*" (191). It is a particularly moving moment, all the more so as she turns out to be the last Jew in Varniai and he is confirmed as the first visitor from South Africa. Quite early on in the book, Jacobson had stated that "the parched landscapes of Kimberley and the northern Cape gave me my deepest and most tenacious idea of what the world should look like" (71), and clearly, in *Heshel's King- dom*, it is the landscape of South Africa and his experience of growing up there[59] that condition his view of the world and provide the imagery with which he seeks to comprehend the past. It is the history of Jewish emigra- tion to South Africa that counterpoints his visit to Lithuania. As Sheila Roberts puts it, in this book "Jacobson looks at the history of Lithuania through his South African eyes, he also re-examines the country of his birth

---

[58] Paul Gready, "Dan Jacobson as Expatriate Writer: South Africa as Private Resource and Half-Code and the Literature of Multiple Exposure," *Research in African Litera- tures* 25.4 (1994): 21.

[59] See, in this connection, Jacobson's volume *Time and Time Again: Autobiographies* (London: André Deutsch, 1985) and his Cape Town lecture "Growing up Jewish," in *Memories, Realities and Dreams: Aspects of the South African Jewish Experience*, ed. Shain & Mendelssohn, 15–27.

in the light of that history."[60] This wholly absorbing dual perspective is the source of much of the fascination the book holds for the reader. And so it is perhaps appropriate that he ends with an ironic and rather bitter reflection on transition and change in South Africa. As a South African, he tells us, he was made aware early in life how humans organize themselves into groups which define themselves through internal bonds and the exclusion of others, through solidarity and its opposite, which he terms "oppugnancy." Likewise, he has observed how infinitely adaptable human beings can be, ever ready to accommodate to changing circumstances and what he calls "the demands of those placed in authority over us" (228). In contemporary South Africa – and he is referring here to the immediate post-apartheid era of the mid- to late 1990s – he has observed how whites have adapted to the abolition of racial legislation and the consequent undermining of their sense of superiority, carrying on with their lives in radically altered circumstances, as though the past dispensation had never been. But what, Jacobson wonders, would happen if there were to be a further radical change, a different government, another war? What then? And then, he concludes, finally turning once again to his grandfather: "Then... I am sure, Heshel Melamed, you know what I mean" (230).

It would be a somewhat bleak and pessimistic vision of the future on which to conclude – albeit one unfortunately borne out by history, particularly in Lithuania – were it not for the dream that Jacobson recounts on the final pages of the book, a dream Roberts has appositely termed "the profound response of his inner life to a misery and horror previously unimagined."[61] Now back in England, he dreams of Varniai, of his mother and her brothers and sisters, of the silent absence of his grandfather, and of his being led up into the family house he had never found, where "there was no Hitler, no years, no Holocaust, no loss, no migration, no sorrow, everything was as it had been and always would be" (235). It is only in the unreality of the dream that he can overcome what at the beginning of the book he had called "the gulf of an unspeakable history."

---

[60] Sheila Roberts, "A Way of Seeing," 69.
[61] Sheila Roberts, "A Way of Seeing," 59.

WORKS CITED

Beinart, Peter. "The Jews of South Africa," *Transition* 71 (Fall 1996): 60–79.

Bozzoli, Belinda, ed. *Class, Community and Conflict: South African Perspectives* (Johannesburg: Ravan, 1987).

Braude, Claudia Bathsheba, ed. *Contemporary Jewish Writing in South Africa. An Anthology* (Lincoln & London: U of Nebraska P, 2000).

Campbell, James T. "Beyond the Pale: Jewish Immigration and the South African Left," in *Memories, Realities and Dreams: Aspects of the South African Jewish Experience*, ed. Milton Shain & Richard Mendelssohn (Johannesburg & Cape Town: Jonathan Ball, 2000): 96–162.

Daymond, Margaret. "Imagining the Worst: Fictional Exploration and Autobiographical Record in Doris Lessing's *Walking in the Shade* and *Mara and Dann*, and in Dan Jacobson's *Heshel's Kingdom*," *English Academy Review* 16 (1999): 81–90.

Frankel, Glenn. "The Road to Rivonia: Jewish Radicals and the Cost of Conscience in South Africa," in *Memories, Realities and Dreams: Aspects of the South African Jewish Experience* (2000), ed. Shain & Mendelssohn, 187–98.

Gershater, Chaim. "From Lithuania to South Africa," in *The Jews in South Africa*, ed. Saron & Hotz, 59–84.

Gordimer, Nadine. "My Father Leaves Home," in *Jump and Other Stories* (London: Bloomsbury, 1991): 57–66.

Gready, Paul. "Dan Jacobson as Expatriate Writer: South Africa as Private Resource and Half-Code and the Literature of Multiple Exposure," *Research in African Literatures* 25.4 (1994): 17–32.

Jacobson, Dan. *The Beginners* (London: Weidenfeld & Nicolson, 1966; Harmondsworth: Penguin, 1968).

——. "Foreword," in *From A Land Far Off: South African Yiddish Stories in English Translation*, ed. Joseph Sherman (Cape Town: Jewish Publications – South Africa, 1987).

——. "Growing up Jewish," in *Memories, Realities and Dreams* (2000), ed. Shain & Mendelssohn, 15–27.

——. *Heshel's Kingdom* (London: Hamish Hamilton, 1998).

——. *Time and Time Again: Autobiographies* (London: André Deutsch, 1985).

Krut, Riva. "The Making of a South African Jewish Community in Johannesburg, 1880–1914," in *Class, Community and Conflict. South African Perspectives* (1987), ed. Bozzoli, 135–59.

Leveson, Marcia. "Insiders on Outsiders: Some South African Jewish Writers," in *Memories, Realities and Dreams* (2000), ed. Shain & Mendelssohn, 60–75.

Minczeles, Henri. *Vilna, wilno, vilnius: La jérusalem de lituanie* (Paris: Éditions La Découverte, 2000).

Nettell, Stephanie. "Continued Discontinuity," *Books and Bookmen* (June 1966).

Roberts, Sheila. "A Way of Seeing: Dan Jacobson's *Heshel's Kingdom*," *Current Writing* 10.1 (1998): 57–73.

Saron, Gustav, & Louis Hotz, ed. *The Jews in South Africa* (Cape Town: Oxford UP, 1955).

Shain, Milton, & Richard Mendelssohn, ed. *Memories, Realities and Dreams: Aspects of the South African Jewish Experience* (Johannesburg & Cape Town: Jonathan Ball, 2000).

Shimoni, Gideon. *Jews and Zionism: The South African Experience (1910–1967)* (Cape Town: Oxford UP, 1980).

Slovo, Gillian. *Every Secret Thing* (Boston MA & London: Little, Brown, 1997).

——. *Ties of Blood* (London: Michael Joseph, 1989).

Slovo, Joe. *Slovo: The Unfinished Autobiography* (Johannesburg: Ravan, 1995).

Suttner, Immanuel, ed. *Cutting through the Mountain: Interviews with South African Jewish Activists* (London: Viking, 1997).

Suzman, Helen. *In No Uncertain Terms* (London: Sinclair–Stevenson, 1993).

Venclova, Tomas. *Vilnius: City Guide* (Vilnius: R. Paknio Leidykla, 3rd ed. 2001).

——. "Jews and Lithuanians," repr. in *Lithuania. Past, Culture, Present* (1999), ed. Žukas, 88–90.

Žukas, Saulius, ed. *Lithuania: Past, Culture, Present* (Vilnius: Baltos lankos, 1999).

Zwi, Rose. *Another Year in Africa* (Johannesburg: Bateleur, 1980; Melbourne: Spinifex, 1995).

——. *Last Walk in Naryshkin Park* (Melbourne: Spinifex, 1997; Johannesburg: U of the Witwatersrand P, 1998).

❖

"A language to fit Africa"

– ◇ – 'Africanness' and 'Europeanness' in the South African Imagination[1]

GABEBA BADEROON

Native
5. A member of an indigenous ethnic group. Freq. with a suggestion of inferior status, culture, etc., and hence (esp. in modern usage) considered offensive.
a. A member of the indigenous ethnic group of a country or region, as distinguished from foreigners, esp. European colonists.
Native
c. Austral. and N.Z. A white person born in Australia or New Zealand, as distinguished from first-generation immigrants and Aborigines. Now disused.
African
n. a. A native or inhabitant of Africa; a Black African.
b. *spec.* Applied to a white resident of Africa.
European
2. A person of European extraction who lives outside Europe; hence, a white person, esp. in a country with a predominantly non-white population.
— *Oxford English Dictionary*, 2006.

---

[1] The section on the etymology of 'kaffir' has previously appeared in an essay titled "Ambiguous Visibility: Islam and the Making of a South African Landscape," *The Arab World Geographer* 8.1–2 (Spring–Summer 2005): 90–103. The quotation in the title is from J.M. Coetzee, *White Writing: On the Culture of Letters in South Africa* (New Haven CT & London: Yale UP, 1988): 7.

Native
n. and adj. Obsolescent, offensive. ... the word came to be used exclusively of black Africans [showing a] sense-change from 'indigenous' to
'black'
African
n. 1. A black person of African descent
2. Any person born or living in Africa
adj. Of or pertaining to Africa: applied to both black people (as in general
English) and, esp. in the past, to persons born or living in Africa, but of
European extraction
n. Afrikaner adj. Afrikaans
European
n. A white person
— *Dictionary of South African English on Historical Principles*, 1996

I

HISTORY MODULATES the meanings of words, and therefore it is possible to trace subsumed histories through changing etymologies. For instance, one can track how colonialism generated complex new meanings for words relating to identity and place. The word 'native' provides a compelling illustration of this effect. According to the *Oxford English Dictionary*, 'native' was first used in the fourteenth century to mean 'indigenous' and 'one originating in a particular place'. By 1806, the word came to refer both to the indigenous inhabitants of colonial territories settled by Europeans *and* to European settlers in colonial Australia and New Zealand. How did the word 'native' come to include such apparently contradictory meanings? This essay addresses the impact of colonial settlement on the meanings of the words 'European' and 'African' in South Africa into the twenty-first century, where these terms marked and crossed the dividing line of 'race', and the boundary between 'indigenous' and 'native'. The shifting trajectories of 'native' thus suggest a model for reading the etymologies of 'European' and 'African', words that signalled competing senses of identity and belonging in South Africa.

This essay focuses on the long accrual of meanings of 'African' and 'European' and their traces of relations in the South African colonies between European settlers, indigenous people, and slaves who had been brought from territories around the Indian Ocean. I argue that the effects of these relations lingered into the twentieth century and helped shape apartheid. Thus, to analyze the way in which Europeanness and Africanness have figured in the South African imagination engages with subsumed histories of imperialism, colonial settlement, genocide, and slavery. In this essay, I explore the meanings of the words through the etymology of the notorious word 'kaffir' and the analysis of two literary texts: *Mr Chameleon* (2005) by Tatamkhulu Afrika; and *Castaway* (1999) by Yvette Christiansë. *Mr Chameleon* and *Castaway* are both autobiographical works that allude to the place of Islam in colonial and apartheid South Africa. This will form a further area of focus in the essay. I will also examine strategies of belonging through which European settlers asserted a relationship to the African landscape, and the way in which a relationship with Africa and Africans wrote itself onto a 'European' identity in South Africa. The essay also addresses the relation of black South Africans to Europeanness through processes of naming and forgetting. Lastly, I will explore the possibility of a 'private' archive of memory and the body through which hidden elements of these histories become visible.

Because they were used as racial labels meaning 'white' and 'black' under apartheid ('separateness'), the system of racial hierarchy that governed South Africa from 1948 to 1994, the terms 'European' and 'African' are among the most heavily freighted in South Africa. At one time under apartheid, 'European' was the official term used for a white person, and the term 'Non-European' was used to refer to black people. 'African' was never used as an official term for black people by the apartheid state. Instead, it used the words 'Native', 'Bantu', and, lastly, 'Black'. As a result, each of them carries meanings ingrained by apartheid, and today both 'Native' and 'Bantu' remain offensive terms in South Africa. However, 'Black' and 'African' were rearticulated with positive connotations as part of the anti-apartheid resistance, an effect that has been heightened in the post-apartheid period through the proclamation of an 'African Renaissance' led by South Africa.[2]

The relation to Europe and Africa – along with the fantasy of a self-evident difference between Europeannness and Africanness – was central to both black and white identities in the South African colonies. In the course of the colonial encounter, 'European' and 'African' came to mean

---

[2] *A Dictionary of South African English on Historical Principles*, ed. Penny Silva, Wendy Dore, Dorothea Mantzel, Colin Muller & Madeleine Wright (Oxford: Oxford UP, 1996): 6.

respectively 'settler' and 'native', 'white' and 'black'. I argue that the texts
analyzed in this essay unsettle the assumption of a stable notion of Europeanness and Africanness. In fact, these texts rewrite the notion of African
and European identities in South Africa, to the extent of showing that
whiteness could be *indistinguishable* from blackness. As I will outline below, etymology and literature map the entanglements and contradictions
that subvert the certainties of racial labels.

II

In 1652, one hundred and seventy years after Portuguese sailors first
rounded the south of the African continent, the Dutch established a refresh-
ment station at the Cape, on the southern tip of Africa. The reason the
Dutch colonized the Cape was to provision their ships engaged in the trade
in spices and slaves from Asia to Europe. Facing resistance to forced labor
by the indigenous people of the Cape, the Khoisan, the Dutch resorted to
slave labour and brought slaves to the colony from East Africa, India, and
South-East Asia, many of whom were Muslim. Slaves at the Cape spoke
Behasa Melayu – a lingua franca in territories around the Indian Ocean –
and became known as 'Malays'.

In the era of Dutch control, slavery structured all social relations in the
colony, and had profound and lingering consequences for concepts of race
and sexuality at the Cape. Because white colonists were given sexual access to slave women's bodies under Dutch rule, the Cape Colony was
among the most racially heterogeneous territories in the world, and an extensive and complex set of relations developed around skin colour, citizenship, and social status.[3] Shifts in European imperial control had implications for the way slavery operated at the Cape. The British took control of
the Cape Colony from the Dutch from 1795 to 1803, and the Cape became
a permanent British colony from 1806 onwards. Under the Batavian Code
(also known as the Statutes of India) during Dutch rule, the visible practice
of Islam was punishable by death, but this changed in 1804 when freedom
of religious expression was granted to Muslims by the Dutch, who sought
Muslims' loyalty in the face of an impending British invasion.

---

[3] Cheryl Hendricks, "Ominous Liaisons: Tracing the Interface between 'Race' and
Sex at the Cape," in *Coloured by History, Shaped by Place: New Perspectives on Coloured Identities in Cape Town*, ed. Zimitri Erasmus (Cape Town: Kwela, 2001): 37.

Under British control, gradations of skin colour came to have increasingly restrictive legal meanings.[4] Such meanings became attached to racial labels that structured the rights to citizenship. In apartheid South Africa, the capacity of labels such as 'European' and 'African' to have ambiguous and even opposing meanings posed fundamental conceptual, legal, and ontological problems for the administration of a system of racial separateness.

In South Africa, the concepts of 'Europeanness' and 'Africanness' are both crucially related to and disarticulated from the actual territories of Europe and Africa. During the colonial period, the territories of Europe and Africa became figured as 'far' and 'near' respectively, and the identities 'European' and 'African' were shaped by a geography of desire and belonging. Among settlers, this was manifested in an ambiguous relationship of belonging to the African landscape, as I argue below in the section on 'kaffir'. The tension within the notion of a European identity in Africa is suggested by the name 'Afrikaner', the Afrikaans word for a settler but also a *white* identity, which literally means 'African'. The name 'Afrikaner' was almost never rendered in its translated form 'African'. It is only in the post-apartheid era that the Africanness of Afrikaner identity has become widely asserted in political and popular discourse. However, in the name 'Afrikaner', Africa is the intimate point of arrival, and Europe is made the distant point of origin, testifying to the complex geography at work in the relation of white settlers to the African landscape, overwritten by the racial labels 'European' and 'African'.

In *White Writing* (1988), his influential study of landscape in South African literature, J.M. Coetzee argued that European colonists held an ontologically tenuous grasp over the land. He observed that, for settlers in South Africa, the landscape refused to be blank and inscribable, denying a fantasy of a new Eden. Instead, the African landscape was riven with a stubbornly anterior indigenous presence that rendered colonists in South Africa *belated* arrivals – temporary, newcomers, passing.[5] "Africa was not a new world," Coetzee concluded.[6] As a consequence, the colonists were peculiarly "unsettled settlers."[7] Yet, by the end of the nineteenth century, history text-

---

[4] Timothy Keegan, *Colonial South Africa and the Origins of the Racial Order* (Charlottesville: UP of Virginia, 1996): 24.

[5] Coetzee, *White Writing*, 8.

[6] *White Writing*, 2.

[7] *White Writing*, 8.

books in the South African colonial territories articulated a different vision
of the land – that its history *began* in 1652 with the arrival of Jan van
Riebeeck, the Dutch commander of the provisioning outpost established at
the Cape.[8] This was a rhetorical declaration of settler belonging so profound that nothing *existed* before. How was it achieved?

I contend that, along with the brute power of war, displacement, and
genocide, this sense of belonging was realized through two discursive
mechanisms. First, through the relation of colonists to slaves and indigenous people. In the colonists' imagination, slaves played a critical part in a
triangular relationship to the land between colonists and the indigenous
Khoi and San. Responding to the anterior claim to belonging and ownership over the land by indigenous people, colonists portrayed Africans as
lazy and unreliable, and, by contrast, depicted slaves as compliant, skilled,
and law-abiding. The opposition of 'lazy' indigenous people to industrious
slaves working on behalf of the colonists facilitated a discourse through
which the latter asserted a right of legitimate ownership over the land. To
buttress this opposition, evidence of resistance by slaves was underplayed,
and colonists represented the conduct of slave-owners at the Cape as
"mild."[9] In fact, records in the Office of the Protector of Slaves show that
the exercise of control over slaves was often extremely violent. The presence of slaves crucially thus shaped colonists' conception of identity and
ownership over but, more importantly, of *belonging to* the land.

The second discursive mechanism through which colonists' sense of
belonging to the African landscape was secured was by naming the details
of the landscape and people who preceded European settlement as profoundly *other*, as lacking in fit and significance. This Adamic project of
naming, I contend, is recounted in the nine pages in the *Dictionary of South
African English on Historical Principles* (1996) that delineate the meanings
and usage of the most notorious word in South Africa, known most point-
edly from its licensing of violence towards black people during apartheid,
but used and elaborated during the colonial period. The word is 'kaffir'.

As the *Dictionary of South African English on Historical Principles*
(henceforth *DSAE*) conveys, 'kaffir' is a comprehensively abusive word
used to denote black people in South Africa, exemplary of the denial of

---

[8] Leslie Witz, "Beyond Van Riebeeck," in *Senses of Culture: South African Culture
Studies*, ed. Sarah Nuttall & C. Michael (Oxford & New York: Oxford U P, 2000): 324.

[9] Keegan, *Colonial South Africa*, 16.

black people's humanity under apartheid – and offensive to the extent of being unsayable today (in fact, its use constitutes a hate crime in South Africa); entries in the *DSAE* (342) show that even during the colonial period there was resistance to the use of the term by people about whom it was used. The word is unpardonably painful and violent, and I wish to give it neither currency nor recuperation here. However, because of the language from which it is derived and, as I show below, from which usage it has widely departed, the provenance of the word reveals a subsumed history of race, landscape, and belonging in South Africa.

The word 'kaffir' is derived from the Arabic word for non-believer or infidel, often rendered in English as 'kaffir'. In Islam, the root word of 'kaffir' means 'closed', denoting someone who is closed to Islam. With a Muslim presence dating from 1658 when the Dutch brought Muslims to the Cape as slaves and servants, it is reasonable to assume that Islam in South Africa delivered the word to the colonial lexicon. However, the use of the word to describe people in South Africa *predates* the arrival of Muslims in the colonial territories. According to the *DSAE*, the first recorded use of 'kaffir' applied to southern Africa (in the form 'caffre') appeared in Richard Hakluyt's *The Principal Navigations, Voyages, Traffiques and Discoveries of the English Nation*, the first volume of which was published in 1589. G. Theal indicates that European settlers in South Africa adopted the word from its use by East African Muslims for 'infidels' in the southern part of Africa (*DSAE*, 347). Henry Lichtenstein writes, in his *Travels in Southern Africa*: "being Mahommedans, they gave the general name of Cafer (Liar, Infidel) to all the inhabitants of the coasts of Southern Africa."[10]

What are the implications of the provenance of the word 'kaffir' in South Africa? One is that developments in the colonial period were essential to the terminology and ethos of apartheid South Africa. Secondly, before European settlement, Southern Africa was part of a geography (and cosmology) created by the connective tissue of the Indian Ocean. Before the word became associated with Dutch and British relations with Nguni polities in the Eastern Cape, the use of 'kaffir' applied to Southern Africa carried with it a history of relations with East Africa, India, and South East Asia, and with Swahili and Arabic-speaking traders. Thirdly, while today

---

[10] Henry Lichtenstein, *Travels in Southern Africa in the Years 1803, 1804, 1805, and 1806*, tr. Anne Plumtre (1812; Cape Town: Van Riebeeck Society, 1928): 241.

Muslims constitute less than two percent of South Africa's population, examining the history of Islam in South Africa engages with the core of the colonial racial order.

However, the role of Islam should be read obliquely here, as the later career of the word 'kaffir' in the South African colonies suggests: demonstrating its divergence from an original Islamic meaning, in South Africa, the word would also come to be applied *to* Muslims, as the name of slaves who performed the duties of policemen during the Dutch period.[11]

While its starkly declamatory use during apartheid was as a noun, my attention here is with the use of 'kaffir' as an adjective. During the colonial period, particularly the nineteenth century, as indicated in citations in the *DSAE*, settler society used this modifier to name indigenous fruit, birds, trees, paths, food, tools, what they perceived to be the behavior, mentality and sense of time of indigenous people – everything anterior to them. Both Dutch and British settlers used the term with a range of connotations, not all necessarily derogatory according to the *DSAE*, though that sense hovered near every use of the word. Crucially, whether or not the use of the word during the colonial era posed as a neutral designation, the adjective performed the function of disarticulating the naturalness of fit between those concepts and the place in which they occurred.

The nine pages of the *DSAE* listing the uses and elaboration of the word thus constitute an immense catalogue of renaming and re-placing 'nativeness' into 'otherness'. The use of the word 'kaffir'to name South African flora and fauna denotes 'indigenous' and 'wild' (*DSAE*, 343). Tied to the increasingly common derogatory meanings of 'kaffir', indigeneity itself, rather than conveying a sense of belonging and anteriority, became a concept. With the landscape designated 'barren' and 'wild', it could also be deemed 'empty'.[12] The notion that events that occurred 'previously' had no meaning or were 'uninscribed' occurred discursively through the word 'kaffir'.

Leslie Witz points out how thoroughly the word colluded with other elements of the colonial project to deny humanity to blacks. In school textbooks, the local inhabitants were not even designated as human. Van

---

[11] Nigel Worden, Elizabeth van Heyningen & Vivian Bickford–Smith, *Cape Town: The Making of a City* (Claremont: Verloren, 1998): 61.

[12] Witz, "Beyond Van Riebeeck," 324.

Riebeeck was called "the first human" to live in South Africa.[13] In the course of the colonial period, the use of 'kaffir' as an adjective proliferated into a multitude of terms, so much so that "the word became strongly associated with South Africa [itself]" (*DSAE*, 347). The meanings and uses of the word 'kaffir' listed in the *DSAE* have no prevalence outside of southern Africa.[14] If one tracks the divisions that the usage calls into existence, I argue that there are three main outcomes, each intimately linked with the others.

First, there is an ontological function. Settlers appear to name as 'kaffir' what must remain separate from them, clearing a space for a selfhood that is defined against the Other. As Edward Said argues in *Orientalism*, the creation of Otherness is a formula for the creation of the Self.[15] The alternative appears to be that indigeneity threatens to consume them, suggested by an insidious sense of time, such as a 'kaffir appointment', for which one need not be punctual, or becoming a 'kaffirboetie' (little brother) by feeling a contaminating sympathy for the despised group, or 'to go to the kaffirs', which means to deteriorate.

Secondly, 'kaffir' also functions to remake the landscape. In colonial South Africa, this denigratory modifier metastasizes into a vast naming that *forces* newness on a world that was not new. The landscape was named in a way that enabled it to be claimed: 'kaffir' labeled as unnatural the relationship between indigenous people and their rightful claim to the land. Instead, this was portrayed as a distorted, corrupt, and unfitting connection. Such a vision enabled the settlers to proclaim their own more fitting relationship with the land. Paul Carter theorizes this use of naming to erase prior meanings and create the space for new, imperial ones as "the theatricalization of the ground – its transformation into the *tabula rasa* of space which, by virtue of its emptiness, licenses the colonist's usurpation of it."[16] Blanketed by the adjective 'kaffir', the South African landscape was "saturated with

---

[13] Witz, "Beyond Van Riebeeck," 324.

[14] Graham Pechey, "Coetzee's Purgatorial Africa: The Case of *Disgrace*," *Interventions: International Journal of Postcolonial Studies* 4.3 (2002): 14.

[15] Edward W. Said, *Orientalism* (Harmondsworth: Penguin, 1991): 60.

[16] Paul Carter, "Turning the Tables – or, Grounding Post-Colonialism," in *Text, Theory, Space: Land, Literature and History in South Africa and Australia*, ed. Kate Darian–Smith, Liz Gunner & Sarah Nuttall (New York: Routledge, 1996): 24.

meaning" and turned into a stage for the events in which Europeans would be the centre and indigenous people would be acted upon.[17]

The third, and crucial, function of 'kaffir' was that it also signalled a boundary of *time*. The extraordinary fecundity of the word is tempered in the colonial setting into a formula for the creation of a *beginning*. If 'kaffir' marks corrupt indigenous meanings, then the settler relationship with the land institutes a new beginning. By marking the landscape, 'kaffir' actually marks a new beginning of history with settler arrival. At first the word looks mainly like a spatial gesture but, I argue, it is also a temporal one. Symbolically, 'kaffir' thus not only announces a claim to land but also marks a beginning.

This reading of 'kaffir' shows how racial identities became marked on bodies, the landscape, and even concepts of time, giving them an apparently ontological force; 'kaffir' was at the extreme end of the spectrum of words that distinguished 'European' from 'African" in the colonial period. Yet, as the analysis above shows, 'kaffir' also carries traces of the spatial, temporal, and racial entanglements created by colonialism.

III

It is to areas of entanglement that I turn next. Under apartheid, the terms 'African' and 'European' were freighted with racial meaning, where 'African' meant 'black' and 'European' meant 'white'. Yet the interstitial zone between them was the site of acute anxiety under apartheid. The place where the anxiety of difference was most intensively policed during apartheid was the racial category 'coloured'. In the racial hierarchy of apartheid, Islam gave added detail to the meaning of 'colouredness'.

'Colouredness' in South Africa exemplifies the way in which anxiety around linguistic slippage points to anxieties of 'race' and identity. In 1950, the Nationalist government passed the Population Registration Act, the legal basis of apartheid, creating three racial categories: white, coloured, and native, into which all South Africans would be placed.[18] Through this Act, the government attempted to give racial terms finite meanings, but it immediately faced the administrative and discursive problem of the elusive-

---

[17] Said, *Orientalism*, 84.

[18] Deborah Posel, "What's in a Name? Racial Categorisations under Apartheid and their Afterlife," *Transformations* 47 (2001): 56.

ness of naming and categorizing 'race'. After the passage of the Act in 1950, the task of assigning a legal racial category to every South African was at first given to census-takers, but the scale of the project eventually involved all public servants.[19] The apartheid State struggled particularly with the legal implications of the 'coloured' category because it created the possibility of 'reclassification', or movement from one racial identity to another. In effect, 'colouredness' was the *fluid middle* of the racial hierarchy in South Africa that revealed the permeability of whiteness and blackness. In 1959, the government tightened the meanings of the term 'Coloured', further dividing it into "Cape Coloured, Cape Malay, Griqua, Indian, Chinese, other Asiatic, and Other Coloured."[20] The proliferation of terms for naming 'race' indicated the fragility of the process of official classification.

In the essay "The Politics of Naming: the Constitution of Coloured Subjects in South Africa," Thiven Reddy argues that apartheid's hierarchical system of racial categorization, with white and black at its furthest extremes, was paradoxically both subverted and confirmed by the indeterminate category 'coloured'.[21] In contrast to the proclaimed stability of blackness and whiteness, this category represented the "'impure', mixed, the borderline, the unclassifiable [and] the doubtful."[22] To Reddy, colouredness was therefore both "the extreme Other of dominant racial discourse in South Africa, and also [...] its very ambivalent core."[23] In this formulation, colouredness stood for the stresses, contradictions, and evasions produced by the impossibility of racial purity, and its very indeterminacy provided a despised but necessary flexibility that absorbed the strains of the system.

Under apartheid, 'colouredness' thus played a crucial *holding* function. However, 'coloured' skin was also the focus of anxious vilification for marking racial impurity and embodying the instability of race. This intense surveillance of the elusive meaning of skin recalls Homi Bhabha's analysis of the colonial relation of visibility and interiority. Bhabha writes that even

---

[19] Posel, "What's in a Name?" 58.

[20] Thiven Reddy, "The Politics of Naming: The Constitution of Coloured Subjects in South Africa," in *Coloured by History, Shaped by Place: New Perspectives on Coloured identities in Cape Town*, ed. Zimitri Erasmus (Cape Town: Kwela, 2001): 75.

[21] Reddy, "The Politics of Naming," 65.

[22] "The Politics of Naming," 68.

[23] "The Politics of Naming," 68.

in the most visible sign of difference – the skin – meaning wavers.[24] The colonized subject seems always to be receding into an interior filled with secrets, and therefore the visibility and stability of their meaning has to be constantly re-produced.

The persistent fluidity of the category 'coloured' created an inherent instability in the whole apartheid system. Coloureds were coded as "residual, in-between or lesser [...] lacking, supplementary, excessive, inferior or simply non-existent."[25] Both because it was central to the system of racial classification and because it was always about to collapse this system, 'coloured' identity was among the most heavily policed concepts during apartheid and, significantly, also during the earlier colonial period.[26] In fact, Reddy argues that there was substantial continuity between the colonial and apartheid systems of 'race' classification.

Islam added a small but crucial detail to this picture. Muslims functioned as a part of the 'coloured' centre that was intended to stabilize the meanings of blackness and whiteness. While subject to the same intensity of surveillance as other 'coloureds', 'Malays' signalled in the official view a promise of purity. The focus in official discourses on the rituals of 'Malay' life, from clothing to festivities, were used to assert a sense of the cultural and *racial* distinctiveness of the 'Malays'.[27] In addition, compared with the supposed 'lack' of colouredness, Malays were associated with a *plenitude* of meaning. In the official discourse, Malays functioned as benevolent fillers between settler identity and the resistant African landscape. In a role established during the colonial period, Malays were portrayed as benevolent and reassuring, while lacking differentiation, change, and resistance. Under apartheid, Islam also provided a decisive indicator of race when people who were apparently white were also Muslim. Under apartheid, Muslims

---

[24] Homi K. Bhabha, *The Location of Culture* (London & New York: Routledge, 1994): xiii.

[25] Zimitri Erasmus, "Introduction: Re-Imagining Coloured Identities in Post-Apartheid South Africa," in *Coloured by History, Shaped by Place: New Perspectives on Coloured Identities in Cape Town*, ed. Zimitri Erasmus (Cape Town: Kwela, 2001): 15.

[26] Reddy, "The Politics of Naming," 65.

[27] Shamil Jeppie, "Reclassifications: Coloured, Malay, Muslim," in *Coloured by History, Shaped by Place: New Perspectives on Coloured Identities in Cape Town*, ed. Zimitri Erasmus (Cape Town: Kwela, 2001): 87.

could not be white, and therefore whites who converted to Islam also became another 'race'.[28]

Islam plays a signal role in the two South African texts analyzed in the rest of this essay: *Castaway* (1999) by Yvette Christiansë and *Mr Chameleon* (2005) by Tatamkhulu Afrika. The poetry collection *Castaway* constructs what I term a *biography* of St Helena, the island in the South Atlantic off the coast of South Africa, and a place known for its distance from Europe. It is most famous for being the place where Napoleon Bonaparte died in exile. *Castaway* recounts in fragments of imaginary documents the lives of the first inhabitant of the island, the disgraced Portuguese soldier Fernão Lopez, Napoleon, and the narrator's grandmother, who was born on the island. The reason for Lopez's fall from favour is that, after being left in command of a Portuguese outpost in India, he had converted to Islam.[29]

Mr Chameleon is the autobiography of the poet and political activist Tatamkhulu Afrika, who was born in Cairo in 1920 and died eighty-two years later in Cape Town, having converted to Islam in the 1960s during apartheid and having therefore chosen to decline the racial privilege of whiteness. Moreover, while his identity document named him 'Malay', Afrika chose to define himself as *African* when South Africa's inflexible racial terminology had named him 'European'. As an autobiography, *Mr Chameleon* is simultaneously a recounting of a politically engaged life and a meditation on the nature of identity, as Afrika writes of his conversion to Islam during the height of apartheid.

These two autobiographical texts trace in different ways the impossibility of a European identity untainted by Otherness, in the case of Fernão Lopez, the Otherness of Islam, and in the case of Tatamkhulu Afrika, Islam combined with the Otherness of an African identity. With neither Lopez nor Afrika does 'whiteness' prevent the possibility of becoming the Other or, more radically, being simultaneously Self and Other. Fernão Lopez, linked thematically with the other exiled or abandoned figures in *Castaway*, as well as Tatamkhulu Afrika, another 'white' convert, illuminates the impossibility of distinguishing absolutely between 'Africanness' and 'Europeanness'. In addition to their themes, the stretching and doubling of form in *Castaway* and *Mr Chameleon* also refuse certainties and boundaries.

---

[28] Posel, "What's in a Name?" 50–74.

[29] Yvette Christiansë, *Castaway* (Durham NC & London: Duke UP, 1999): 13.

Castaway's interlocking figures, looking out to sea both from a ship and from St Helena, create in their voicings a vision of the island that is momentarily clear and then recedes behind other views. Afrika's testimony of the changes that mark his eighty years – alluded to in the metaphor of the title *Mr Chameleon* and marked by his five names – is told from unexpected angles. Rather than recounting a gathering narrative that leads to his conversion to Islam, *Mr Chameleon* lingers in moments of fragile but luminous connectedness. Such experiments in form and content result, in these works, in fertile engagements with the terms 'African' and 'European' that allude to the partial, fissured, and unresolved aspects of the encounters between Africa and Europe.

IV

"The white man had the anguished feeling that I was escaping from him and that I was taking something with me. He went through my pockets. He thrust probes into the least circumvolution of my brain. Everywhere he found only the obvious. So it was obvious that I had a secret."[30]

Frantz Fanon theorized in "The Fact of Blackness" that the colonized subject seems to withdraw and withhold something from the colonizing gaze. In this section I consider the salience of a *private* realm – the insistently interior histories of the colonized, often hidden and secret, seen only in oblique ways, which trace a journey into the human. I argue that the realm of the 'private' is revealed through the silent and secret languages of the body. I explore such 'private realms' in *Castaway* through the figure of Fernão Lopez, the first inhabitant of St Helena, and in the story of Fin, the child of slaves who leaves St Helena for South Africa and longs for the island until her death-bed. Lastly, the autobiography of Tatamkhulu Afrika recounts an unsparingly honest, profoundly intimate journey of a public figure. By exploring the 'private' archive, I argue that Europe is also important to the identities of black South Africans – in other words, Europe seen through the eyes of the colonized. Among blacks in South Africa, an ambiguous relation to Europe is evident in claims of mixed heritage and

---

[30] Frantz Fanon, *Black Skin, White Masks*, tr. Charles Lam Markmann (*Peau noire, masques blancs*, 1952; tr. New York: Grove, 1967): 128.

European parentage.[31] Zoë Wicomb argues that there is a charged silence in the historical record as well as the consciousness of the descendants of slaves about the relation of slavery to the history of sexuality in South Africa. To uncover this relation engages with the trauma of memories of slavery. I discuss this matter further through the figure of Saartjie Baartman.

In reading the 'private' archives that explore the relation of Africans to Europeanness, my model is Saartjie Baartman, the woman taken from South Africa to Europe in 1810 and displayed publicly in London and Paris as the "Hottentot Venus." Baartman died in Paris in 1815 and her remains were exhibited for 157 years in the Musée de l'Homme. In her well-known essay "Shame and Identity," Zoë Wicomb reads Baartman as the locus of all the indictments of the colonial gaze for black women's bodies: their association with the shame of sexual lasciviousness and responsibility for miscegenation. Wicomb argues that this of "shame of having had our bodies stared at, but also the shame invested in those (females) who mated with the colonizer" resulted in the suppressed knowledge or "amnesia among blacks about slavery."[32] This intense, internalized shame is a sign of the ontological, physical, and social indictment which miscegenation brings, both the result of slavery for black people and that of which they are accused, generated a powerful form of forgetting: "the total erasure of slavery from folk memory"[33]

What does the recovery of Baartman's body from the history of her public display promise to restore? After her subjection to a notorious level of visibility during her lifetime and for 157 years after her death, the journey of Baartman's remains from France to burial in South Africa in 2002 was a stubbornly *private* one, as I argue below.

In death, whose bodies are buried, whose are studied and displayed, and whose unaccounted for? Judith Butler contends that the possibility of burial and mourning marks a crucial boundary of the human.[34] The deaths of those who are not regarded as human also lack in meaning. We can measure those who are counted as human by how their bodies are treated

---

[31] Zoë Wicomb, "Shame and Identity: The Case of the Coloured in South Africa," in *Writing South Africa: Literature, Apartheid and Democracy, 1970–1995*, ed. Derek Attridge & Rosemary Jolly (Cambridge: Cambridge UP, 1998): 100.

[32] Wicomb, "Shame and Identity," 92.

[33] "Shame and Identity," 100.

[34] Judith Butler, *Precarious Life: The Power of Mourning and Violence* (London: Verso, 2004).

after death – whether they are buried, displayed, or left unmarked. The return of Baartman's remains to be buried in South Africa in 2002 was, I believe, a return from the public to the private. The withdrawal of her body from public and scientific access was a return from "the shame of having had our bodies stared at"[35] to become once again a subject with an interior – and was thus also a return to the human.

The body plays a paradoxical role in the mediation of the public and private. Baartman's return to the private, I argue, occurred through the withdrawal of her body from access by the public gaze. Yet the body can also carry its privacy in other ways, through where it walks, is seen, and hides. In Cape Town, the visibility of bodies marked as slave was governed by a system of surveillance and extreme violence. In this context, the 'secret' codes of the body – often secondary meanings behind public visibility – become a way of reading the 'private' lives of slaves. Reading patterns of visiting and observance of ritual allows one to recover ways in which slave bodies retained a measure of interiority. For instance, the celebration of New Year by the descendants of slaves on 2 January, when slaves were given the day off, was a public holiday observed in Cape Town until the late twentieth century. More dangerously and privately, since public observance of Islam by slaves under the Dutch was punishable by death, the observance of ablutions, communal gatherings, and Friday prayers by Muslim slaves was transmuted into patterns of visiting on Thursday night. Subsequently, the tradition of Thursday-night prayer meetings has been retained among Muslims in South Africa into the twenty-first century.

The private realm can also be seen in the relation to the body in stories of food. In the past, popular South African cookbooks described similar dishes cooked by the descendants both of slaves and slave-owners, while underplaying the reality of slavery indicated by these continuities. In the 1970s, for example, a number of books extolling "Malay" cooking were published in South Africa, among them Betsie Rood's *Maleier Kookkuns* (Malay Cooking), Laurens van der Post's essay "East Meets West" in his book *African Food*, and Renata Coetzee's *The South African Culinary Tradition*, often referred to slavery as a picturesque historical detail.[36] By

---

[35] Wicomb, "Shame and identity," 92.

[36] Betsie Rood, *Maleier-Kookkuns* (Cape Town: Tafelberg, 1977). Laurens van der Post, *African Food* (New York: TIME–Life, 1970). Renata Coetzee, *The South African Culinary Tradition: The Origin of South Africa's Culinary Arts During the 17th and 18th Centuries, and 167 Authentic Recipes of this Period* (Cape Town: C. Struik, 1977).

contrast, the Muslim food historian Cass Abrahams noted that during the colonial period one could tell what cargo ships carried when they entered Cape Town harbour by smell – whether they carried spices or slaves.[37]

Coetzee's *The South African Culinary Tradition* defines the national culinary tradition by placing 'Malays' just after European influences on South African cooking, which are listed in turn as *The Dutch element, The German contribution, A French flair, An Eastern aroma, Edible wild plants and their influence,* and *Cape edible wild plants.* In the course of the book, it becomes clear that it is Afrikaans-speaking white South Africans who have absorbed various influences to become 'South African'. The book places the Malays in a serene past and slavery is described benignly in terms of the "skill" of the men as artisans and the "exotic oriental dishes" cooked by the women.[38] In this way, the slaves were characterized as a piquant *flavour,* as though they, like their food, gave a unique tincture to a broader South African history. The colourful visibility of Malays in these books functioned to give white, especially Afrikaans-speaking, South Africans a way to lay claim to a past with a substantial and elaborated history.

In fiction, as in the historical record, the body was the site where slavery exercised its authority over both slave and master. In Rayda Jacobs' novel about slavery in South Africa, *The Slave Book,* the protagonist Somiela is accused by the slave-owner's wife Marieta: "'We can see alright what she is. A naai-mandje'." As the slave owner Andries explains, "to naai was to sew or to have sexual intercourse; mandje was a basket."[39] The visible result of interracial sex, Somiela is accused here of what all slave women are fundamentally assumed to be guilty of. The virtuous Somiela's hair is cut off, she is beaten, and her jewellery and dress are confiscated. Yet, in the intimate and dangerous space of the kitchen (where slaves were suspected of plotting to poison slave owners), she takes subtle revenge. She does not poison the master. Instead, the food she flavours with chilies and spices is what the master desires to eat, rather than that made by the mistress.

Therefore, while a European identity in the South African colonies gained coherence by insistently defining itself against the African landscape, Africa also wrote itself onto Europeanness in desires that white

---

[37] Cass Abrahams, cook-book author; interview on food with Gabeba Baderoon (20 July 2002, Cape Town).

[38] Renata Coetzee, *The South African Culinary Tradition*, 45.

[39] Rayda Jacobs, *The Slave Book* (Cape Town: Kwela, 1997): 25.

bodies named as their own. In addition, whiteness in South Africa was complicated by the different and competing colonialisms of the Dutch and British Empires in South Africa. Interceding layers of Dutch, later Afrikaans, and English identities inflected distinct types of 'Europeans' in Africa. Through their name, Afrikaners proclaimed an intimate relationship with the continent, yet, contradictorily, under apartheid whiteness was named 'European'. English-speaking whites and visiting Europeans re-marked contemptuously on the entwined reality of Afrikaner (or "Boer") life and that of indigenous people. The ethnographer Gustav Fritsch, after travelling in the South African territories in the 1860s, observed that "it would not be possible to use Boer life as material for stories because in Boer life nothing ever happen."[40] This was contiguous, as Coetzee points out, with the 'idleness' perceived among indigenous Africans.

V

The body and its private meanings feature prominently in the linked poems of *Castaway* which tell the story of St Helena, the island so far from Europe it seems to be at end of the world, so far away that it is lost, and "married to the losses" (2). St Helena was a place of punishment, exile, and escape for its first inhabitant, the disgraced Portuguese soldier Fernão Lopez, who may have been the inspiration for Robinson Crusoe (13). Most famously, Napoleon was sent to the island to spend his last years in exile. In *Castaway*, Napoleon spends every day feeling his distance from the centre of power. To a man who was once "the measure of all things," simply to be on the island is a punishment. Lopez, who is one of the speakers in *Castaway*, names St Helena "the worst place" (1).

There are no innocent approaches to St Helena. The island was a source of slaves, and in *Castaway* ships leave with loaded holds. The book itself approaches St Helena in poems that are fragments of 'lost' texts by speakers in different eras – Lopez, Napoleon, and a woman embarked on a contemporary search for origins. Revealed only in fragments of intersecting narratives, the island itself can never be fully known. Frequently, the poems end with questions; "Is this real?" a speaker asks.

The island is a place of wind, mist, and constant change. Approaching the island, the ship dips beneath the waves, the horizon enfolded in fog and

---

[40] Coetzee, *White Writing*, 24.

endless sea. History layers St Helena like its perpetual mists and wind, and nature aids the island's resistance to being known; "There are things I know nothing of / things that go on in the island's sharp dark" (14). In *Castaway*'s telling, we are privy to an intimate, vertiginous vision of the island, different from the one seen from Europe. On the approach, the island appears and then recedes behind a wave, seen only in a shifting form.

Once on the island, we find the speakers in *Castaway* in transit or wanting to be elsewhere, like Napoleon and Lopez. The latter writes bitterly that by being left here he has been "taught about distance and desire" (16). But St Helena is also the island where Christiansë's family originates, and where Fin, her grandmother, was born, so *Castaway* also speaks differently of the island, intimately and with longing, as the locus of origin rather than of exile. Fin feels an intense and impossible desire for return to the island. "She longed / for the sea. Not any sea, / but that green sea / she knew" (7). Yet *Castaway* does not attempt to redeem the losses of slavery by returning Fin to the island and the poems do not claim to trace the truth that has eluded family memory. When the speaker asks about her grandmother's date of birth, the answer is 1898, with the caveat: "we think."

The poems revisit the cruel breadth of the Atlantic between Africa, Europe, and the Americas from this island off the west of Africa. The extent of the sea around St Helena cannot be tracked with the eye. In the poems the sea is loud and insistently present. The tide lines, birds, and ships that cross the vast stretch of ocean are *Castaway*'s central metaphor of change. In some poems, the sea is certitude, when "the fin of a sleek dark fish […] finds a current and slips clean into its long sweep all the way around the world without moving a muscle" (8).

But, because Fin was the child of slaves, and because of St Helena's long history of slavery, the sea also signals theft and loss. The poems take readers into the airless space of the ship's hold where slaves are packed in the dark without water. We are shown that the island's own darkness resembles the dark of a ship's hold, where slaves' cries reveal what Enlightenment Europe keeps hidden, that the trade in human beings was central to European notions of progress and expansion. In the poem "*The Enlightenment sees its face in a different light*," the slaves hidden beneath the surface in the hold become a "rigid silence / that threatens the deck" (66). Yet, unacknowledged and invisible, the presence of the slaves also sustains the ship. In its colonial territories, Europe defined itself by proclaiming itself separate from what it found, but in the poem the presence of the slaves is a "howl, those / sounds [...] grow into the hull's own song" (67).

To Europeans in the colonies, the separateness they saw between themselves and the 'Otherness' of colonized subjects was a compulsively policed difference. As a result, the mutability of the colonized body was a source of terror. Colonized subjects refused to be stable, to remain the same each time the colonist looked at them. Homi Bhabha writes that in the colonial setting the meaning of the most obvious sign of difference – the skin – is never definite; "skin, as a signifier of discrimination, must be produced [...] as visible."[41] Tatamkhulu Afrika named his autobiography after the chameleon, the animal that is always changing its skin and becoming like the landscape that surrounds it. This inherent ability of the skin to disappear against its background, to elude sight by its changeability, exactly fits the discursive elusiveness of the colonized body. Only one figure superseded the threat inherent in the changeable colonized body: a European in the colonies who rejected the role of the colonizer and became like the colonized. The story of such a figure is found in both *Castaway* and *Mr Chameleon*.

The exemplary story of mutability in *Castaway* is that of Fernão Lopez. It is, I suggest, a story of a journey into the private.

> Fernao Lopez travelled to Goa in the early 1500s with Afonso D'Albuguerque, Portuguese general and coloniser of the region, who left him in charge of a group of Portuguese to settle and 'rule' the local population. On his return, D'Albuguerque found that Lopez and others had converted to Islam and sided with Moslem resistance to the Portuguese. Upon capture, Lopez and other 'renegades' were punished by having their right hands and the thumb of their left hands severed. Their tongues, ears, and noses were also cut off as a reminder of their treachery. Lopez's hair and beard were scraped off with clam shells in a process known as 'scaling the fish'. He remained in India for some years until he was to be returned to Portugal. He left his ship at the then uninhabited island of St Helena, becoming its first exile and a figure of curiosity and myth. He planted lemon groves and tended a flock of goats. There are claims that Defoe based Robinson Crusoe on Lopez."(13)

---

[41] Homi K. Bhabha, *The Location of Culture* (London & New York: Routledge, 1994): 78–79.

Why was such remarkable violence shown toward Lopez's body? In *Castaway*, the character Lopez "says his name over and / over as if it is a limb he must massage or / lose to the butcher's field knife" (2). In this image, the body and the name are shown are both shown to be vulnerable to excision. For his conversion to Islam and becoming part of the resistance to the Portuguese in India, Lopez was punished by the returning Portuguese General D'Albuguerque in acts that were intensely intimate, against the skin. This was, I argue, a reaction to the inaccessible interiority represented by conversion to Islam. In the Cape Colony, Islam offered to slaves "a degree of independent slave culture" that did not fall under the control of slave-owners.[42]

Lopez personified the terror that usually resided in the insidious figure of the colonized – that the body and its meanings can change. For showing it was possible to shed the meaning of the skin, Lopez's skin, tellingly, was scraped in an enactment of the nature of his transgression – meaning was scraped from his body. Christiansë observes that Lopez may be the inspiration for Robinson Crusoe. Lopez, who had transformed himself through conversion, is transformed again through punishment for his conversion In remaking the island by planting lemon trees, and in his lost tongue, Lopez is at once Crusoe and Friday. Both because of the interiority of spiritual conviction and because such change betrayed the meaning of his European skin, Lopez's conversion to Islam can be seen as a journey into the private. In the figure of Lopez, Christiansë shows the possibility of discarding and creating a configuration of the self. Both Lopez and, as I will show below, Afrika illustrate that someone could move from one to the other: European to African.

VI

By the time of his death in 2002, the poet Tatamkhulu Afrika's extraordinary biography had become well-known in literary circles in South Africa. In often beautiful prose, *Mr Chameleon* tells a story ranging from Egypt to the Bo-kaap, reversing the colonial Cape-to-Cairo sweep up the continent. Within its continental range of reference, as an autobiography *Mr Chameleon* spirals inward toward intense self-reflection and unsparing honesty. In it, Tatamkhulu Afrika tells of the hard-earned selfhood of a

---

[42] Nigel Worden, *Slavery in Dutch South Africa* (Cambridge: Cambridge UP, 1985).

writer whose five successive name-changes and racial reclassification
confounded the certainties of apartheid. Tatakhulu Afrika was raised as a
white man in South Africa, and gave up this identity when he became Muslim. However, his biography confounds even this startling choice. Afrika
was born in Egypt in 1920 to a Turkish father and Egyptian mother, who
moved to South Africa when Afrika was two. After the death of his parents
shortly after their arrival in South Africa, he was raised by family friends as
a white child. Afrika fought on the Allied side in the Second World War
and later as part of *Umkhonto we Sizwe* (the armed wing of the African
National Congress) in the anti-apartheid struggle. In 1964, he legally
reclassified himself as a Muslim, ceding the privileges of a white identity.
The last of Afrika's five names, Tatamkhulu Afrika, which means 'Grandfather of Africa', was an honorific title given to him by fellow soldiers in
Umkhonto we Sizwe, and was one he adopted officially by deed poll.

Mr Chameleon is unsparingly honest about the slow, interior changes of
Afrika's life. In recounting a particularly hard part of his life, the painful
period in the 1960s when he was unemployed and, for five months, survived on one pint of milk and half a loaf of bread every day, Afrika lingers
on the slow processes of time changing. *Mr Chameleon* conveys the
vertiginous moral shift that comes from a continual failure to find work,
and how Afrika withstands the hardship of self-doubt and hunger during
this ungiving period. During this testing period comes the beginning of a
profound return to Islam when Afrika reads a second-hand copy of the
Qur'an. In its rendition of the unhurried growth of conviction, *Mr. Chameleon* conveys the movement inward into the private realm of identity.

For Afrika, the private is not, however, the solipsistic. The book also
conveys how he kept from distancing himself from others. Even in childhood, he notes in himself a capacity for absolute imperviousness to other
people. He also acknowledges the temptation to redeem himself for his
frequent failures, such as lies about his sexuality or his unforgiving attitude
to those who have hurt him, through the narrative tendencies of autobiography. At one point Afrika contemplates whether he is "bragging"
about his activities as a resistance fighter. The most moving moments in the
book emerge when he perceives the vulnerability of others and reciprocates
with openness. During the 1960s, he treats gays in Cape Town warmly,
though they were on the receiving end of violence and contempt at the
time. On the other hand, Afrika maintains an obdurate anger toward those
with whom he differs politically – for example, the coloured woman living

in Observatory who passes for white. After visiting her home and witnessing her rigid self-policing, he contemptuously rejects her, resolving never to see her again.

In contrast to Afrika's careful reflections about his internal shifts, the viciousness and absurdity of apartheid's racial categories are brutally displayed in *Mr Chameleon*. "[On] that night when they arrested us [they] at once separated me from my men because they thought that I was white- no, *insisted* that I was white" (406). Later on, offered the chance to have charges dropped against him by the Security Police if he betrays the rest of the group, Afrika realizes he has been made the offer because "after all, I was a white man, wasn't I?" (407). Under apartheid, the meanings of race stretch into every area of life. In jail, the food reflects racial division: "pork for blacks, mutton and beef for the other races" (417). When Afrika is taken for interrogation to the Security Branch's office in Loop Street in Cape Town,

> [the policeman] handed a file with my name on it, saying I was an Egyptian, and the clerk, fluttering anxious hands, protest that there was no such racial classification, so where must he put the file, and the squat one said not to ask him but why not try 'Indians' because they were both pretty much the same thing, weren't they? (411)

However, Afrika refuses these given categories, even declining, during Ramadan, to break fast at the same time as Sunni Muslims at sunset, but does so twelve minutes later, following the Shia requirement. Through his resistance, he embodies apartheid's anxiety about difference and change. In Afrika's refusals lies the threat that "the known [is] no longer known" (401).

Rejecting the 'Europeaness' which his upbringing and his light skin have given him, Afrika seeks Africanness through Islam, activism, and empathy with blacks. For Afrika, an African identity does not reside in the skin but is earned and recognized by others:

> When [Chris Hani] was assassinated a short while later, I mourned over him as a black should – as the Africanness that he had accepted in me and to which after such a long journeying I had returned. (406)

For Afrika, these moments of recognition are the basis for a humanity that is not based on the privileges of 'race'. Such moments mark crucial points throughout the book. When he first arrives at Victor Verster prison, although he cannot see him, Afrika recognizes the voice of the poet Sandile Dikeni shouting a greeting through a barred window.

What is most striking in the autobiography is where Afrika chooses to start and end his account. Near the beginning of the book, Afrika recalls a view seen through a window by his young self of a chameleon changing color to match its surroundings. Why does this happen, he asks the woman he knows as "Gran"? "'It's the way he gets what he wants, dear, and how he hides from those who want *him*'" (13). This is a manifesto that defines Afrika's life. By the end of the book, "Mr Chameleon" has changed his name five times, and owns nothing except his actions.

Yet the autobiography conveys something that goes beyond this hard-earned self-definition. What most distinguishes Afrika in a life of hardship and resistance are moments of deep recognition, of a tender meeting of the otherwise inaccessible interiors of two human beings. The book ends not chronologically with the period of writing in 2002, but with an event that occurred during the anti-apartheid struggle in the 1980s at the end of Afrika's imprisonment for acts of "terrorism."

The last sight Afrika recounts seeing from Victor Verster prison, and the event that closes the book, is not his fellow activists, but a non-political prisoner, a rent-boy on the verge of madness, whose resonant image ends the book. During the months of his imprisonment, Afrika had watched the young man polishing a pair of red boots every day, "an inwardness about him precluding any approach" (419). Eventually, through a series of encounters during which Afrika refuses either to abuse him or to ignore him, the man "unlocked the door to himself" (419). Afrika learns about that the boots that "I was the only one who had ever asked about them" and that they "were for him to put on the day he made his break across the wall" (419–20).

When the young man discovers that Afrika will be released, he flings the boots across the prison yard. On the day he leaves prison, just before stepping through the gates, Afrika walks across the yard to retrieve the red boots and places them again next to the young man. As he leaves, Afrika hears a shout and glances back in the autobiography across the incalculable distance of madness, and now time, separating him from the man, and remembers: "slowly he raised his hand" (420).

In a long life in which political activism and Islam play central roles, it is the "unlocking" of the door to the privacy of the self, and the mutual recognition of another person's humanity despite hopeless self-delusion and difference, that conclude *Mr Chameleon*.

VII

Islam is the means through which Tatamkhulu Afrika rewrites an African identity on an apparently European skin. Similarly, Fernão Lopez overwrote the meaning of his Portuguese identity by converting to Islam. In these figures, *Castaway* and *Mr Chameleon* contradict the notion that the meanings of Europeannness and Africanness are self-evident by showing that even the meaning of the skin can be remade. *Mr Chameleon* explores the anxiety behind the certainties of apartheid. Tatamkhulu Afrika's life belies the fantasy of a self-evident difference between Africans and Europeans at the heart of apartheid, and shows that whiteness can be indistinguishable from blackness. The recognition that grants humanity and an African identity in *Mr Chameleon* is not based on the skin, but on what is revealed by the "unlocked" self.

The two texts tell of inward transformations and a delicate and often uncertain reciprocity between people. In this view, shifts of identity are seen not as a betrayal but as part of a "long journeying" that manifests itself in tentative yet honest gestures of human connectedness. Approaching the subject through the stories of those who have been silenced, neither book proclaims any finality of the Self: in neither book is Africanness a point of arrival, nor is Europeanness a point of origin. By telling the stories of European identities that become African identities, *Castaway* and *Mr. Chameleon* suggestively point to intersections of identity which discourses of 'race' appear to keep apart. Through figures who begin their narratives as 'European' and end them as 'African', the two texts trace the role of these terms in crafting notions of belonging in South Africa. In South Africa, as in other African territories colonized by Europe, the meanings of the words 'European' and 'African' were shaped by the processes of colonialism. Literary works map areas of overlap and entanglement that stretch and contradict the certainties asserted by such labels. The two books discussed here expose the linguistic impossibility at the heart of apartheid and the colonial project to distinguish absolutely between black and white, and between 'Africanness' and 'Europeanness'.

WORKS CITED

Abrahams, Cass. Cookbook author. Interview on food with Gabeba Baderoon (20 July 2002, Cape Town).

Afrika, Tatamkhulu. *Mr Chameleon* (Johannesburg: Jacana Media, 2005).

Bhabha, Homi K. *The Location of Culture* (London & New York: Routledge, 1994).

——. "Remembering Fanon: Self, Psyche, and the Colonial Condition" (1986), foreword to Fanon, *Black Skin, White Masks* (London: Pluto Press, 1986).

Butler, Judith. *Precarious Life: The Power of Mourning and Violence* (London: Verso, 2004).

Christiansë, Yvette. *Castaway* (Durham NC & London: Duke UP, 1999).

Carter, Paul. "Turning the Tables – or, Grounding Post-Colonialism," in *Text, Theory, Space: Land, Literature and History in South Africa and Australia*, ed. Kate Darian–Smith, Liz Gunner & Sarah Nuttall (New York: Routledge, 1996): 23–36.

Coetzee, Renata. *The South African Culinary Tradition: The Origin of South Africa's Culinary Arts During the 17th and 18th Centuries, and 167 Authentic Recipes of this Period* (Cape Town: C. Struik, 1977).

Coetzee, J.M. *White Writing: On the Culture of Letters in South Africa* (New Haven CT & London: Yale UP, 1988).

Du Plessis, Izak David, & C.A. Lückhoff. *The Malay Quarter and Its People* (1953; Cape Town: A.A. Balkem, 1953).

Erasmus, Zimitri. "Introduction: Re-imagining Coloured Identities in Post-Apartheid South Africa," in *Coloured by History, Shaped by Place: New Perspectives on Coloured Identities in Cape Town*, ed. Zimitri Erasmus (Cape Town: Kwela, 2001): 13–23.

Fanon, Frantz. *Black Skin, White Masks*, tr. Charles Lam Markmann (*Peau noire, masques blancs*, 1952; tr. New York: Grove, 1967).

Henricks, Cheryl. "Ominous Liaisons: Tracing the Interface between 'Race' and Sex at the Cape," in *Coloured by History, Shaped by Place* (2001), ed. Erasmus, 29–44.

Jacobs, Rayda. *The Slave Book* (Cape Town: Kwela, 1998)

Jeppie, Shamil. "Reclassifications: Coloured, Malay, Muslim," in *Coloured by History, Shaped by Place* (2001), ed. Erasmus, 29–44.

Keegan, Timothy. *Colonial South Africa and the Origins of the Racial Order* (Charlottesville: UP of Virginia, 1996).

Lichtenstein, Henry. *Travels in Southern Africa in the Years 1803, 1804, 1805, and 1806*, tr. Anne Plumtre (1812; Cape Town: Van Riebeeck Society, 1928).

Pechey, Graham. "Coetzee's Purgatorial Africa: The Case of *Disgrace*," *Interventions: International Journal of Postcolonial Studies* 4.3 (2002): 374–83.

Pillay, Suren. "Experts, Terrorists, Gangsters: Problematising Public Discourse on a Post-Apartheid Showdown," in *Shifting Selves: Post-Apartheid Essays on Media,*

Culture and Identity, ed. Herman Wasserman & Sean Jacobs (Cape Town: Kwela, 2003): 283–14.

Posel, Deborah. "What's in a Name? Racial Categorisations under Apartheid and their Afterlife," *Transformations* 47 (2001): 50–74.

Reddy, Thiven. "The Politics of Naming: The Constitution of Coloured Subjects in South Africa," in *Coloured by History, Shaped by Place* (2001), ed. Erasmus, 64–79.

Rood, Betsie. *Maleier-Kookkuns* (Cape Town: Tafelberg, 1977).

Said, Edward W. *Orientalism* (Harmondsworth: Penguin, 1991).

Silva, Penny, Wendy Dore, Dorothea Mantzel, Colin Muller & Madeleine Wright, ed. *A Dictionary of South African English on Historical Principles* (Oxford: Oxford U P, 1996).

Van der Post, Laurens. *African Food* (New York: T I M E–Life Books, 1970).

Wicomb, Zoë. "Shame and Identity: The Case of the Coloured in South Africa," in *Writing South Africa: Literature, Apartheid and Democracy 1970–1995*, ed. Derek Attridge & Rosemary Jolly (Cambridge: Cambridge U P, 1998): 91–107.

Witz, Leslie. "Beyond Van Riebeeck," in *Senses of Culture: South African Culture Studies*, ed. Sarah Nuttall & Cheryl Ann Michael (Oxford & New York: Oxford U P, 2000): 318–39.

Worden, Nigel. *Slavery in Dutch South Africa* (Cambridge: Cambridge U P, 1985).

——, Elizabeth van Heyningen & Vivian Bickford–Smith. *Cape Town: The Making of a City* (Claremont: Verloren, 1998).

❖

Morountodun by Femi Osofisan

– ◇ – Marxism, Feminism, and an African Dramatist's Engagement with an Indigenous Heroic Narrative

WUMI RAJI

I

> The song cuts off in a general freeze. Lights come on in the auditorium. On stage, on opposing platforms, MOREMI and TITUBI are caught in harsh spotlight, looking at each other. BLACKOUT[1]

T HE SEQUENCE ABOVE closes *Morountodun*, Femi Osofisan's arguably most ambitious and most accomplished play to date.[2] "Morountodun" of the title is the name Marshall, the leader of the peasant fighters, gives to Titubi, the heroine of the play, the two having fallen in love with each other. As translated by the playwright himself, the word means "I have found a sweet thing" (ii). In giving her the name, Marshall seems to have openly articulated what Titubi represents to him.

The legend of Moremi is one of the two primary archives transformed in *Morountodun*. While the one is a mythico-legendary event, the other, the peasants' uprising that occurred in the Western region of Nigeria in the late 1960s, represents a concrete historical experience. At the precise point

---

[1] Femi Osofisan, *Morountodun and Other Plays* (Lagos: Longman, 1982): 79. Unless otherwise indicated, further page references are in the main text.

[2] The original version of *Morountodun* was first produced in 1979 at the Arts Theatre, University of Ibadan, in 1979. The published version was produced later the same year at the same venue by the Kakaun Sela Kompany. Both productions were directed by the playwright himself.

where the two narratives intersect, Osofisan erects a pole of opposition. Of course, Moremi, the legend, is the character who must yield ground in the ensuing confrontation. She is displaced from her acclaimed role as the saviour of the Yorùbá race and re-interpreted as a champion of hegemonic interests. This is to the extent that Titubi, the heroine for whom Moremi had hitherto stood as a great insipration, "had to kill the ghost of Moremi in (her) belly," declaring that she is not Moremi: "Moremi served the state, *was* the state, was the spirit of the ruling class. *But it is not true that the state is always right*" (70; my emphasis).

II

In the last chapter of his seminal book *African Philosophy: Myth and Reality* (1983), Paulin Hountondji articulates the processes of cultural mutation. He starts off by underlining the inherent plurality of all cultures, defining 'plurality' in three ways: the "coexistence" of different cultures; the acknowledgement and conscious promotion of the situation; and the "will" to utilize it, "either by preserving these cultures from mutual con-tamination or by organizing a peaceful dialogue among them for their mutual enrichment."[3] Hountondji proceeds further by stating that cultural pluralism itself constitutes a logical reaction against the cultural ethno-centrism of the West, and he considers it as important to note that the development itself first emanates from the West. As he argues, the "Europe that produced Lévi–Bruhl also produced Lévi–Strauss. The Europe that produced Gobineau also produced Jean–Paul Sartre. The Europe that pro-duced Hitler had previously produced Marx." This, then, is a sign that Western civilization is itself not unitary, that it is a "criss-cross of the most diverse tendencies." When, therefore, we speak of Western culture, there often exists "a danger that we will confuse currents that are opposed and irreconcilable" (156).

Is Hountondji, then, suggesting that it is impossible to conceive of cultural traditions in the singular? He answers in the negative. To him, however, the notion of the singularity of any civilization can be true only if applied to capture the "empirical unity of a specific geographical area" (160). In this sense, European culture will refer to the set of clashing values

---

[3] Paulin Hountondji, *African Philosophy, Myth and Reality* (London: Hutchinson, 1983): 156. Further page references are in the main text.

which have played themselves out on that particular continent over time, and which will continue to play themselves out in times to come. In the same vein, the term 'African civilization' may be applied to capture the agglomeration of an open, contradictory set of constructs which have been fielded, and which will continue to be fielded, on the continent of Africa. According to Hountondji, any attempt to take the concept of cultural unity beyond this point will simply result in untruth. It will be to deny culture, any culture, of its only important characteristic as an endless process of transition, forever incomplete, and eternally engaged in a dialogue both with itself and with other civilizations. Hountondji sees nothing unusual in the confrontation between precolonial African order and Western colonial traditions. Actually, as he says, the "decisive encounter is not between Africa as a whole and Europe as a whole":

> It is the continuing encounter between Africa and itself. Pluralism in the true sense did not stem from the intrusion of Western civilisation into our continent, it did not come from outside to a previously unanimous civilisation. It is an internal pluralism, born of perpetual confrontations and occasional conflicts between Africans themselves. (161)

Hountondji argues fiercely against any attempt at creating neat boundaries between cultures. He dismisses, for that matter, the notion of homogeneity or unanimity of African or any other civilization, and proceeds to launch a withering attack on what he describes as culturalism, defined as "the exclusive valorization of simplified, superficial and imaginary blueprint of cultural tradition" (162). He articulates a perspective of "cultural interpenetration," which, as stated earlier, he believes to be a characteristic of all civilizations, those of Africa included. To him, every culture is ceaselessly active, engaged in dialogue with itself and other traditions, enriching in the process both itself and the other traditions with which it continues to interact. For Hountondji, a culture is best conceived of as "a contradictory debate between people chained to the same destiny and anxious to make the best of it." He writes further:

> What we must recognize today is that pluralism does not come to any society from outside but is inherent in every society. The alleged acculturation, the alleged 'encounter' of African civilization with European civilization, is really just another mutation produced from within African civilizations, the successor to many

earlier ones about which our knowledge is incomplete, and, no doubt, the precursor of many future mutations, which may be more radical still. (165)

In other words, African traditions have never been closed; on the contrary, they have always been open. To investigate the precolonial African past is to be exposed to the innumerable upheavals and revolutions that these traditions have undergone in the course of history. It is to travel through the tortuous paths of negations and renewals that these cultures have passed through, to experience the conflicts and crisis they have triumphed over. Precolonial and postcolonial African cultures continue to interact and to influence one other. To try and establish an opposition between the two phases, then, is to miss the point. A culture grows when it is "exploited anew," when its meaning is stretched, countered, or re-articulated. Says Hountondji:

> What we must now realize is that this polarization (between pre-colonial and post-colonial traditions) has been disastrous and that its destruction is one of the first and most important conditions of our cultural renaissance. African culture must return to itself, to its internal pluralism and to its essential openness. We must therefore, as individuals, liberate ourselves psychologically and develop a free relationship both with African cultural tradition and with the cultural traditions of other continents. This will not be a process either of Westernization or of acculturation: it will simply be creative freedom, enriching the African tradition itself as an open system of options. (166)

III

If, as is the case, and especially because of the attitude of creative freedom displayed by its author, I have always regarded Femi Osofisan's *Morountodun* as a fascinating play, it is also true that my principal spur for selecting it up for detailed investigations in this essay is Paulin Hountondji's position, summarized above, on the mutual intermeshings of ideas and cultures. Indeed, on one level of reading, *Morountodun* could simply be seen to have set two local but opposing traditions against each other, with the sole purpose, perhaps, of achieving a mutation. On another level, however, and as the part of the quotation from the play which I highlighted above should demonstrate, it will be revealed that the weapons employed by the playwright in his attempt at threshing and re-moulding his materials can be seen, guardedly, to have been procured from another continent. At this point, it is probably important to state that Osofisan stands as perhaps the most prominent African playwright of English expression in the generation following Soyinka, and that he writes in a dialogic, even provocative style. In several of his dramas, essays, and interviews, he is often found engaging openly with the works of many of his predecessors and, in some cases, his contemporaries. Quite frequently also, he is discovered travelling around, exhuming different aspects of ancient identities and imbuing them with fresh interpretations. At other times, he may be caught ransacking the vast repertoire of Western drama, re-working such plays as he considers relevant for a particular, immediate context in his society.[4] The dramatist projects Wole Soyinka as his immediate point of departure, stating that he has worked at a "critical angle"[5] to him. The younger dramatist never tires of explaining what he means by this in his essays, speeches, and interviews. But while this may be true, it is also the case that the fire which burns in him has its origins in all kinds of sources. For one thing, and as has been stated, the playwright has a very close relationship with the abundant and various archives of his indigenous heritage and he explores them extensively in several of his works. However, and as he himself admits, while pursuing his postgraduate education in France in the period immediately following his country's independence, Osofisan came across the marxian-derived tenets of dialectical materialism. Once he had internalized these thoroughly, the tenets then became the major principles underlying his approach to transformatively representing the world in his works. Osofisan, as if in agreement with Hountondji, often establishes in his works a continuity between the precolonial and postcolonial traditions of Africa. To him, no cultural identity is ever univocal. When, therefore, he inserts himself into this contradictory discursive practice, it is with the aim of intensifying the debate or productively deepening disagreement. Beside Marxism, which represents the major point of departure for Osofisan, the principles

---

[4] In this regard, some of the relevant titles by Osofisan include *The Chattering and the Song* (Ibadan: Ibadan UP, 1977); *Another Raft* (Lagos: Malthouse, 1988); *Esu and the Vagabond Minstrels* (Ibadan: New Horn, 1991); *Yungba-Yungba and the Dance Contests* (Ibadan: Heinemann, 1993); and *Tegonni, an African Antigone* (Ibadan: Opon Ifa, 1999).

[5] Femi Osofisan, *The Nostalgic Drum: Essays on Literature, Drama and Culture* (Trenton NJ: Africa World Press, 2001): 248.

of feminist interpretation would also seem to be important in any honest attempt at understanding *Morountodun*. It is my intention in this essay to analyze the methods by which he presses the two Western-derived ideologies into service in his endeavour to interpret a local but dominant narrative in *Morountodun*.

As pointed out earlier, Osofisan's style of writing is often very discursive and extremely provocative. Any time he steps out, be it in his dramatic works or in his essays, it is always to invite the other party out for an open discussion. It is to engage, to initiate debate. "Ritual and Revolutionary Ethos" was originally written in 1976, but it has now been included in *The Nostalgic Drum*, Osofisan's collection of critical works published in 2001. In this highly reflective piece, Osofisan classifies Soyinka's dramatic works into two broad categories. In the first category, he puts together those works in which, he argues, the Nobel laureate presents the ancient African order literally, and untreated. To him – Osofisan, that is – these kinds of writing project a "reactionary" perspective on art and society, as he insists that any art "that stubbornly weaves around old mythologies, unmediated, prolongs the enfeebled past and is anti-progress."[6] On the other side, according to Osofisan, is a body of works produced by the same Soyinka but which puts the ritual form through the mill of transformation, thus presenting a dialectical view of history. Osofisan exemplifies the latter with *The Road*, a 1965 play, and the former with *Death and the King's Horseman*, a work he describes as having succeeded greatly in "recreating the complete, credible world of African ritual," but which in terms of vision reflects "a narcissism which seems to reinforce a decadent order."[7]

Osofisan is more detailed and painstaking in "And After the Wasted Breed?," another essay published in the same critical collection but first presented as a Janheinz Jahn memorial lecture in Mainz, Germany. In this latter essay, Osofisan seems to have taken further the argument of *No More the Wasted Breed*,[8] his play written specifically in response to Soyinka's *The Strong Breed*.[9] To him, indeed, Soyinka's "tragic perspective" has

---

[6] Osofisan, *Nostalgic Drum*, 95.

[7] *Nostalgic Drum*, 97.

[8] Femi Osofisan, "No More the Wasted Breed," in *Morountodun and Other Plays* (Lagos: Longman, 1982): 81–119.

[9] Wole Soyinka, "The Strong Breed," in *Wole Soyinka: Collected Plays I* (Oxford: Oxford UP, 1973): 113–46.

arisen out of the experience of the members of his (Soyinka's) generation. This generation, as the younger dramatist puts it, had grown up at the time of the struggle for liberation from colonialism, and had actively participated in it. Hopes had been very high when eventually independence was won by several of these countries in the late 1950s through the early 1970s. Unfortunately, these people were soon to find themselves as unwilling witnesses to the machinations of those who, on assuming the reins of power in the immediate post-independence years, began to pour water on the embers of people's optimism, and who embarked on the mass destruction of the talented children of the continent. The "grim and sombre epistemology" which Soyinka often offers in his works is, according to Osofisan, a "mirror of history, as he and his contemporaries have lived and experienced it."[10]

Osofisan argues that the body of works produced by the dramatists of his generation represents, essentially, a "refutation"[11] of Soyinka's position. To be sure, he himself admits that the older dramatist is indisputably the 'master', and acknowledges the debt of gratitude they all owe him. But Osofisan is unrepentant about the decision the younger writers have taken to open up a new perspective and work in different directions. He locates their motives in the kind of background they had and the nature of the education they received: "We were, do not forget, the generation born into independence":

> [We grew up] without the complexes of colonialism, and were beneficiaries of a better education that was more oriented towards our environment. In addition, we had gone on to study in the Europe of the post – World War Two, in which the ideas of socialism and dialectical materialism were fecund. We could see history therefore in a different light from our predecessors, as an arena of perpetual struggle and impermanent victories.[12]

Going further, Osofisan argues that another major area of weakness in Soyinka's reading of history is his perspective on heroism. Owing to his fixation with examples of individuals of outstanding endowment who volunteer in order that their society may be salvaged, Soyinka, inadvertently perhaps, has, in Osofisan's view, continuously failed to pay attention

---

[10] Osofisan, *Nostalgic Drum*, 253.
[11] *Nostalgic Drum*, 250.
[12] *Nostalgic Drum*, 256–57.

to the possible contributions that ordinary members of society can make to history. To be sure, Osofisan himself admits that it would be wrong to accuse an exceptionally sophisticated writer like Soyinka of ignoring the complex reality of his own society. While admitting that the universe of Soyinka's works is never entirely dominated by the highly placed of a given community, that his characters quite often include "a healthy number of the members of the lower classes and, even, of the dregs of society,"[13] Osofisan maintains that what Soyinka often fails to do is to lend these characters individual traits – to project them as people capable of separate initiatives instead of just making them dance around the main characters. Herein lies the point of departure of the dramatists of Osofisan's generation:

> We playwrights who come after the Soyinka generation aim, gradually to change all that. We aim to give voice to the active forces of our community, to democratize history, and demonstrate how participation is not only possible, but vital, for every level of society. I do not of course, on a personal level, mean by this that we shall idolize the farmers and peasants and the common working people of our cities. This will only be another form of exoticism […]. [On the other hand], I am not persuaded that the visionaries who will eventually lead us out of chaos will be discovered only among the elite, or the so-called 'elders,' or that they will necessarily all be male...."[14]

IV

The marxian concepts of *hegemony* and *tradition* are very important in any serious attempt at comprehending the relationship between Femi Osofisan and fellow dramatists of his generation, on the one hand, and Wole Soyinka and the other playwrights of the first generation, on the other; just as it is in grappling with the play *Morountodun*.

In *Marxism and Literature* (1977), Raymond Williams opposes the view of hegemony as a passive, totalizing system or structure, defining it instead as a complex, active social process which, when in practice, is constantly being re-worked, fine-tuned, defended, re-articulated and re-invented. As

---

[13] Osofisan, *Nostalgic Drum*, 260.
[14] *Nostalgic Drum*, 261.

Williams argues further, at no time is hegemony ever total or complete. On the contrary, what the marxist theorist has described as "forms of alternative or directly oppositional politics and culture"[15] often exists side by side with the dominant, and their effects on the hegemonic are often of great importance. This is to the extent that, as alternative practices, they often challenge or even threaten hegemony, while the latter, in turn, constantly struggles either to neutralize, to eliminate or to incorporate the former. Again, to the extent that alternative forms of struggles and cultural practices stand as "significant breaks" (114) beyond the hegemonic, they are evidence of what the dominant has had to struggle against and fight to control and/or transcend. "In this active process," Williams writes,

> The hegemonic has to be seen as more than the simple transmission of an (unchanging) dominance. On the contrary, any hegemonic process must be especially alert and responsive to the alternatives and opposition which question or threaten its dominance. The reality of cultural process must then always include the efforts and contributions of those who are in one way or another outside or at the edge of the terms of the specific hegemony. (113)

Going further, Williams establishes a connection between hegemony and tradition. He commences by rejecting the perspective of tradition as a fixed segment of the past, viewing it instead as a determining force – indeed, as a highly active shaping force, and consequently as the "most powerful practical means of incorporation" (115). In a given hegemony, Williams further suggests, what often is operative is never tradition unedited but, rather, a "*selective tradition*" (author's emphasis), a carefully packaged version of a "shaping past and a pre-shaped present" (113). This is not always difficult to prove, as Williams insists. From a broad spectrum of both the past and present of a given society, specific elements are deliberately chosen and foregrounded while others are deliberately ignored, repressed, and/or avoided. The foregrounded aspects are then presented as 'the tradition' – indeed, as that which is crucially required to guide the people as they continue to struggle with history. Driving his point home, Williams then defines tradition as an "aspect of contemporary social and cultural organization, in the interest of the dominance of a specific class," adding that, by virtue of

---

[15] Raymond Williams, *Marxism and Literature* (Oxford: Oxford U P, 1977): 113. Further page references are in the main text.

its being an aspect of the past which intersects with, and ratifies, the present, "what tradition offers in practice represents then a sense of *predisposed continuity*" (116; Williams's emphasis).

Williams believes that the above strong perspective on tradition –as opposed to its weak form, which proposes it to be fixed in the past, in contrast to "innovation" and the "contemporary" (116) – is simultaneously powerful and vulnerable. It is powerful because it links concretely with the present and continues in the future. But it is also vulnerable, because the aspects that it tries to distort, discard or destroy as part of an effort to preserve hegemony can in actuality be exhumed and revived. For those working in the opposition, then, the real responsibility lies in the subsequent struggle to recover the "discarded areas" and "redress [...] selective and reductive interpretations" (116). It is important to allow Williams to speak further for himself:

> It is at the vital points of *connection*, where a version of the past is used to ratify the present and to indicate directions for the future, that a selective tradition is at once powerful and vulnerable. Powerful because it is so skilled in making active selective connections, dismissing those it does not want as 'out of date' or nostalgic [...]. Vulnerable because the real record is effectively recoverable, and many of the alternative or opposing practical continuities are still available. Vulnerable also because the selective version of a 'living tradition' is always tied, though often in complex and hidden ways, to explicit contemporary pressures and limits [...]. This struggle for and against selective traditions is understandably a major part of all contemporary cultural activity. (116–17; author's emphasis)

Femi Osofisan's point of departure should be clear from the foregoing. Indeed, by the late 1970s, when, as a young man, he took the decision to embark on a writing career, Soyinka had become the greatest African dramatist of English expression, and his vision of heroism, drawing on his indigenous Yorùbá world-view but influenced also by the religious vision of the ancient Greeks, has become well-known.[16] The paradigm of Ogun, the Yorùbá god of iron and of creativity who, going by the tradition, plunged into the abyss, leading all the other gods on the day they decided to pay humanity a visit, stands at the centre of Soyinka's drama. The god

---

[16] See Wole Soyinka, *Myth, Literature and the African World* (Cambridge: Cambridge UP, 1976).

exemplifies Soyinka's idea of the much-needed individuals of talent in a society struggling to salvage itself from history. Osofisan, who, while studying abroad for a doctorate, had had to read and internalize the Marxist principles of collective struggle, considers Soyinka's approach to be both selective and reductive, and he therefore decides to kick against it, even if, as he seems well aware, he stands only on the fringes of hegemony. Thus, in appropriating the Môrèmi script in *Morountodun*, what seems paramount in the playwright's mind is this attempt, very much as stipulated by Marxism, to give voice to the otherwise repressed majority of his society. To do this, he knows he has to dispel the dominant interpretation of the well-circulated archive and instil a fresh meaning, as well as to recover an aspect of its implication that has long been sidelined. To achieve success in this, Osofisan considers it important to introduce another aspect of tradition which, though more recent and more concretely historical, the dominant order seems determined to set aside. In doing so, the playwright himself claims to be aware that he cannot always bring everybody to agree with his point of view. To him, however, it will be enough achievement if, to use his own words, he is able "to demonstrate that the world is just as our stage is, a platform of constant revision and of innumerable possibilities."[17]

V

As can be seen, the approach adopted by Osofisan as he presses a Western ideology into the service of cultural analysis in *Morountodun* is quite complex. To restate the point, his chief goal is to interrogate a dominant, mytho-legendary archive in the oral library of Yorùbá received tradition by knocking it against a rather marginal aspect of the same heritage, the consequence being a destabilization of the received perspective on the hegemonic narrative. But the process entails more: it involves subversion of an earlier dramatic transformation of the widely acknowledged archive, which transformation simply re-produces the long-accepted perspective on the tradition.[18] It also involves a similarly covert engagement with the works of some of Osofisan's predecessors which, either directly or indirectly, can be

---

[17] Osofisan, *Nostalgic Drum*, 262.

[18] I refer here to Duro Ladipo's dramatization of the same story in a play that derives its title from the name of the heroine. See Ladipo, "Moremi," in *Three Nigerian Plays* (London: Longman, 1967).

interpreted as betraying some measure of sympathy for the expressed position of the entrenched story.[19] Osofisan is certainly unperturbed about the source of the fire that he carries in his belly. To him, what matters is that it burns well; that, indeed, it is applicable, as he once told Ossie Enekwe in an interview, to the "immediate, relevant problems of our society."[20]

Now, to proceed with the story: Môrèmi, the personage in the dominant discourse engaged in the play under discussion, is actually the subject of two important festivals in the towns of Ilé-Ifê and Offa respectively. There is some slight disagreement about the exact temporal location of the story. While some scholars, including Samuel Johnson in his *History of the Yorubas*, speculate that the incident took place during the reign of Oranmiyan, the legendary grandson of Oduduwa and acknowledged husband of Môrèmi, others contend that it happened after Oranmiyan died and Alaiyemore took over as Ooni of Ife. At any rate, the root of the crisis dated much further back. By all accounts, it can be traced to the day on which Oduduwa first invaded Ilé-Ifê in order to forcibly displace the Igbos, who were said to be the original inhabitants of the land. Following his victory, Oduduwa was said to have simply settled his people on the land without making necessary propitiations to the goddess of Esinmirin river under whose aegis Ilé-Ifê fell. So the Igbos continued to make visitations on the Yorùbá, capturing them as slaves and carting away their property. And all efforts – spiritual and practical – by the people to stop their tormentors failed, until Môrèmi stepped in. Samuel Johnson writes:

> Now, this Moremi, fired with zeal and patriotism, was determined to do what she could to free her country from this calamity. She was resolved to find out what these Igbos really were, and how to fight them. To this end she repaired to a stream called Esinmirin, and there made a vow to the deity thereof, that if she was enabled to carry out her plans, and they proved successful, she would offer to the god the most costly sacrifice she could afford.[21]

---

[19] My reference here, specifically, is to Wole Soyinka's *Death and the King's Horseman*, which will also be touched on in this essay.

[20] Muyiwa Awodiya, *Excursions in Drama and Literature: Interviews with Femi Osofisan* (Lagos: Kraft, 1993): 19.

[21] Samuel Johnson, *History of the Yorubas* (London: George Routledge & Sons, 1921): 147.

Assured of the goddess' support, Môrèmi then allowed herself to be captured by the Igbo invaders when next they raided the village. On her arrival
in Igbo territory, and being a woman of charm and beauty, she naturally
became part of the harem of the ruling Igbo king. Môrèmi settled in quickly
and soon dispelled all suspicions surrounding her. Again, as a woman of
great charisma, she was soon to attain the position of the foremost wife of
the king. After some years, and having used her privileged position to
obtain the information she needed, Môrèmi made her escape back to Ilé-Ifê.
With the secrets of the Igbos now revealed, all attempted raids by them
were thenceforth to end in great disasters for the invaders. In fulfilment of
her pledge, Môrèmi returned to Esinmirin to offer the stream a sacrifice of
choice animals. This the goddess spurned, and, as eventually divined by
priests, it was to be discovered that what she actually wanted as sacrifice
was Oluorogbo, Môrèmi's only son. Painful though it was, Môrèmi offered
up the boy, and the Ife nation "bewailed her loss and promised to be sons
and daughters to her, for the loss she had sustained for the salvation of her
country."[22] This was how Môrèmi became transformed into a goddess
whose memory is commemorated yearly in the Edi festival. Here is what
Benjamin C. Ray has to say about it:

> This legend is re-enacted each year at Moremi's festival at Ife. It is
> part of a larger agricultural festival and includes a mock combat
> between two men representing the Yoruba and Igbo forces. In the
> course of the "battle," the marked Igbo leader finally flees before a
> flaming torch carried by the Yoruba warrior, for this was Moremi's
> successful strategem against the Igbo troops. Later, the Igbo warrior
> again appears before the Oni and expresses his loyalty to the king.[23]

Duro Ladipo's appropriation of the story, titled after the heroine herself,
stands as a prior dramatic transformation of this particular myth. Ladipo is
the author, producer, and director of *Oba Ko so*,[24] arguably the best known
work in the repertory of Yorùbá operatic tradition. The play dramatizes the
story of Şango, an ancient tyrannical ruler of the old Oyo Empire who had

---

[22] Johnson, *History of the Yorubas*, 148.

[23] Benjamin C. Ray, *African Religions: Symbols, Ritual and Community* (Englewood
Cliffs NJ: Prentice–Hall, 1976): 45.

[24] Duro Ladipo, "Oba Ko so," in *Three Yoruba Plays: Oba Ko so, Oba Moro, Oba
Waja* (Ibadan: Mbari, 1964): 1–28.

to commit suicide after being forced to abdicate the throne by one of his war generals. However, in a desperate bid to protect his memory, the leading chiefs of Oyo decided to put out word that Ṣango did not die and had instead ascended to heaven to become the god of thunder and lightning. With the people accepting this to be true, Ṣango consequently became a deity, and his festival is still celebrated today in various parts of Yoruba-land. Duro Ladipo's dramatic transformation of the story in *Oba Ko so* is a powerful reinforcement of the hegemonic thrust of the saga of Ṣango. His is an example of what Hountondji has referred to as culturalism, an attempt at presenting the past in an originary, uncontaminated form.

Ladipo carries this attitude further in his creative intervention in the Môrèmi narrative. The play is an unequivocal acceptance of the orthodox perspective promoted by the original rendition of the story.[25] The heroine dominates the play throughout. The women grovel before her at the market. Her views sway discussion at Ooni Alaiyemore's palace. And, on arrival in Igboland, her presence becomes so overwhelming that the Igbo king cannot resist taking her on as a queen despite a strong warning to the contrary by the palace prophet. On her return, the entire city of Ife bursts into celebration. And having offered her son, Oluorogbo, in sacrifice to Esinmirin at the close of the play, Môrèmi is celebrated as the woman "who fights when others are feasting. / One with a strong cloth to carry a child, / One who

---

[25] In his introduction to the English translation of Duro Ladipo's *Moremi*, Ulli Beier points out two important aspects in which the dramatist departs from *History of the Yorubas*. "In Johnson," Beier says, "Moremi does not realise the gravity of her promise to the river goddess Esinmerin. Rather, she is being tricked into the situation where she has to sacrifice her child. Ladipo on the other hand gains tragic and dramatic intensity by making the sacrifice a voluntary decision. Moremi then becomes the real heroine who places the welfare of the town above her personal happiness." Beier goes on to underline a second important aspect: "Johnson, rather naively, is trying to tell us that the Ifes mistook the Igbo masks for divine beings dressed up as spirits and that firebrands would burn the dry leaf masks. Ladipo rightly thinks that it is difficult to imagine that the ancient Ifes did not realise that the masqueraders were human. What they did believe, however, was that the masks gained supernatural powers from the ancestors whom they represented. It is Moremi's task, therefore, to find the right magic formula that will successfully counteract this supernatural power." Ulli Beier, "Introduction" to *Three Nigerian Plays* (London: Longman, 1967). Beier is doubtless correct in his claim about Ladipo's departure from his primary material, but the deliberate aim of his (Ladipo's) intervention, as can be inferred even in Beier's statement above, is to further promote the entrenched perspective on the story.

gave her child / to buy peace."[26] In the play, clearly, the acceptance of Môrèmi is total by virtue of this feat, as the saviour and redeemer of the race, while Oluorogbo is projected as the "messenger between heaven and earth," one whose "blood / protect(s) this town forever."[27]

As can be seen, Duro Ladipo's attitude to the story is direct and straightforward, being, as it were, an uncomplicated projection of the Yorùbá metaphysical world-view. There is a crisis in the land which has hitherto defied solution. A prominent woman steps forward, with a determination to get to the root of the problem. She goes before a goddess to seek protection, promising to perform the necessary propitiatory rites should she succeed in her mission. She embarks on the adventure, returns safely, and with a secret solution the problem besetting the land. She offers up her son as sacrifice in fulfilment of the pact with the goddess. Order is restored. The community celebrates.[28]

For Femi Osofisan, who stands at the threshold of two great traditions, the matter cannot be so clear-cut. There is no doubt that, even in the contemporary context, the Môrèmi story continues to offer great potential, and that it is treated with considerable reverence by the people. The legend remains an icon even in the age of postcolonialism. As mentioned earlier, annual festivals continue to be celebrated in her honour. Edifices continue to be dedicated to her, while children are named after her.[29] Osofisan himself seems to be aware of the details, and perhaps a little more. In *Morountodun*, the necklace which Titubi wears is called Môrèmi. "You taught me her story, [...w]hen I was still too young to understand," the play's protagonist tells her mother, as the latter struggles to discourage the young

---

[26] Duro Ladipo, *Moremi*, 32.

[27] *Moremi*, 32.

[28] The myth actually has it that Oluorogbo, very much like Jesus Christ, rose from the dead, and with the aid of a rope "climbed up into heaven; and all Ifes to this day have a full hope that he will come again to this world, and reap the full reward of his good deeds"; Johnson, *History of the Yorubas*, 148.

[29] An important women's hostel in Obafemi Awolowo University, Ilé-Ifè, Nigeria and another at the University of Lagos are officially designated as Moremi Hall. Also in Ilé-Ifè, a secondary school attended by wards and children of the Obafemi Awolowo University's staff is also known as Moremi High School. In the town of Ilé-Ifè itself, a residential estate of middle-class standard is known as Moremi estate. Finally, a major Nigerian writer, of a generation before Osofisan's, was also said to have given one of his daughters the name Moremi; she is now an adult and has retained Moremi as her first name.

lady who has just volunteered to infiltrate the camp of the peasants who have taken up arms in protest against the state. She would never forget her, Titubi says, "Moremi, the brave woman of Ile-Ife, who saved the race" (31).

As he travels, to Ilé-Ifê to meet Môrèmi, Osofisan carries with him this other box in which are kept the materials he procured while studying in Europe. Among other objects, the contents of the box include the tools of dialectical materialism and feminism, as Osofisan himself has earlier confessed. It also contains a text offering another interpretation of the concepts of hegemony and tradition. It is with the aid of these tools that the dramatist decides to explore the story a little further, to probe more closely into its depths and bring a few things up to the surface. With them, Osofisan is able to raise some hitherto unasked questions regarding the story. Not least of these are the interests which the heroine herself represents, the implication of her sexual identity, and the factors impelling her to action. Not for this playwright an unmediated acceptance of the story as it has been handed down over the ages, the hegemonic perspective that it promotes, the feudalistic world-view it propagates, the patriarchal vision it entrenches. In resurrecting the ghost of Môrèmi, therefore, Osofisan considers it important to make her address some of the questions that have been awaiting her for hundreds of years.

Osofisan's supreme strategy in the play is to initiate a dialogue between the Môrèmi tradition and a concrete, more recent, but, in relative terms, grossly marginal historical incident. In the late 1960s, precisely at the same time as the civil war was raging in the eastern part of Nigeria, the farmers and peasants in the western region had also taken up arms in revolt against the government of that part of the country, the immediate grounds for protest being heavy taxation and levies.

Briefly, and as can be deduced from Gavin Williams's *State and Society in Nigeria*[30] (1980) and E.E.C. Beer's *The Politics of Peasant Groups in Western Nigeria* (1976), the rebellion of the 1960s was evidently a consequence of the development of peasant consciousness. Over the years, according to these two authors, successive governments had sought to maximize surpluses from sales of cocoa crops for infrastructural development. The consequence of this was an ever-increasing reduction in the price of the crop relative to its value on the world market. In addition to this, the administration had also sought added revenue by increasing direct taxation

---

[30] Gavin Williams, *State and Society in Nigeria* (Idanre: Afrographica, 1980).

and levies on the populace. What it did was to introduce flat-rate taxation without making allowance for people of extremely low income, or of no income at all, and without considering the fact that the people enjoyed very little compensation for the huge fiscal contribution they were being forced to make to the State. Beer, who makes extensive use of the report of the Ayoola Commission set up to investigate the cause of the disturbances, writes of how "Akodas, or council tax collectors, often demand bribes from those who do not wish to, or cannot, pay the full amount," and how many of the tax collectors consequently grew "wealthy from the exercise of their office." He also writes of how tax-raid exercises conducted to round up defaulters "were both provocative and inhuman, a common tactic being to force those not in possession of tax receipts to suffer prolonged exposure to the sun on the burning iron roofs of council offices."[31] The farmers initially reacted to this with a series of constitutional actions which included marches to the palace of Olubadan, the traditional ruler of Ibadan, and written petitions sent to the office of the governor. This achieved absolutely no result and the farmers started fighting back the tax collectors, beating them up and even detaining them. Policemen sent to the villages were ambushed and beaten back. Gradually, the hostilities escalated into a full-blown war which went on from November 1968 to July 1969, when hostilities finally ceased following the dramatic intervention of Chief Obafemi Awolowo, then Federal Commissioner for Finance and Vice-Chairman of the Federal Executive Council.

From his obviously Marxist perspective, the incident in the western region stands for Osofisan as a prime instance of class conflict, of a situation in which the socially marginalized resolve to take their fate in their own hands. This, at least, represents the way Osofisan projects the matter in *Morountodun*. To illustrate this, it is perhaps best to go to scene four where Superintendent Salami, the officer charged with the responsibility of crushing the rebellion, comes face to face with Alhaja Kabira, Titubi's mother and head of the market women. Alhaja Kabira has come to the prison determined to prevent Titubi from embarking on her course of action; Salami enters, and the following exchange ensues between the two of them:

---

[31] E.E.C. Beer, *The Politics of Peasant Groups in Western Nigeria* (Ibadan: Ibadan UP, 1976): 164–65.

SUPERINTENDENT: Listen to me. The peasants out there are
not more than a thousand strong. Let's say, even two thousand. Two
thousand men, armed mostly with crude dane guns, matchets, bows
and arrows. What's all that before the awesome apparatus of the
State? Before our well-trained and well-equipped fighting squads? A
wall of vegetables! So why have we not been able to crush them?

ALHAJA: Are you asking me?

SUPERINTENDENT: You should know, Alhaja. After all, these
rebels are of your own creation, you who are used to feeding on
others.

ALHAJA: Look here –

SUPERINTENDENT: I'll tell you. The peasants are strong, and
seemingly invincible, because they are solidly united by the greatest
force in the world: hunger. They are hungry, their children die of
kwashiorkor, and they have risen to say no, no more!

ALHAJA: It's a lie! No one has ever died of hunger in this country! I am surprised at you, a police officer, carrying this kind of
baseless propaganda...

SUPERINTENDENT: They claim that you and your politicians
have been taking off the profits of their farms to feed your cities, to
feed your own throats and buy more jewels and frippery. And so, at
last, they are coming for the reckoning. (24)

Morountodun, then, is at the opposite end of the Môrèmi story where
ordinary people are completely marginalized, where they are hardly seen
and their voices hardly heard. Confronted with a crisis of calamitous proportions, the original Môrèmi narrative projects the people as totally help-
less, wholly incapable of any thinking or initiative until a woman member
of the class of the ruling aristocracy steps forward. In Osofisan's own play,
as in the Agbekoya story on which it is based, it is the farmers themselves
who decide to put an end to oppression and exploitation. On their own, they
resolve to constitute themselves into a resistance movement and, when
push comes to shove, to wage war in defence of their position. We see them
launch an attack against the prison in scene five of the play, freeing their
captured colleagues as well as a number of other detainees. And in scene
nine, the spectators are taken down to the village, to the abode of the
farmers. They are presented on stage as they plan their strategies, as they
take care of the wounded, as they mourn their losses, as they try the people
they capture, as they, in short, work together, men and women, young and

old, strong and weak. It is a very long scene, coming right in the middle of the play, with the action covering the entire stage area and with the people portrayed (if I may adopt the parlance of dialectical materialism) as actualizing themselves in history, showing themselves as the true heroes of any and all struggles.

It is perhaps necessary at this point to mention the fact that Osofisan is not the only playwright who has appropriated the Agbekoya uprising in a stage-play. Bode Sowande, another member of the second generation of Nigerian dramatists of English expression, actually dealt with the story one or two years before Osofisan. Sowande's approach is also socialist, but the ideology this time is tempered with what the playwright himself has described as spiritualism. To Sowande, as he tells Olu Obafemi in an interview, the ideal postcolonial state is both a "socialist utopia and a spiritual state." There is no difference, he goes on, "when we say there should be dignity of labour, that the man who has more should give to the man who has less, it is both spiritual as well as ideological."[32] Indeed, when the audience first encounters the farmers in *Farewell to Babylon*,[33] the play by Sowande in question, they are seen engaged in an intense ritualist ceremony. The men are presented as forming "a circle round a symbolic mortar [as] Oduloju and another young farmer pound to the rhythm as the song proceeds." Guarding this circle, in turn, are Dansaki and two other farmers as they stand, "strategically, holding their guns."[34] The stage is overwhelmed by heavy drumming, heavy pounding of mortars and pestles, and sustained chanting. The circle is the central organ of the farmers' state, and only the initiates are allowed into it. Not even Onita, the ivory-tower intellectual who believes that the farmers represent the alternative to the injustice of Nigerian life, would be accorded the privilege.

But the important point to make is perhaps that, as in *Morountodun*, Sowande's play also projects the farmers and the peasants as the main focus, their struggle the primary concern of the action. Moved by their example, Onita abandons his job at the university, resolving to join them. He is to discover, however, that the processes involved are not so simple.

---

[32] See Awodiya, *Excursions in Drama and Literature*, 377.
[33] Bode Sowande, *Farewell to Babylon and Other Plays* (London: Longman, 1979).
[34] Sowande, *Farewell to Babylon*, 70.

VI

To return to *Morountodun*: the play opens with an itinerant amateur theatre company taking the stage and trying to mount a performance, as the group's own way of intervening in the raging storm. The stage is soon invaded by another group bent on stopping the performance. In contrast to the theatre group, whose members are obviously ordinary citizens, this new band is said to be "superbly dressed, with lots of jewellery and make-up, and wearing conspicuously the 'Moremi necklace' then in vogue" (37). The latter group is led by the head of the market women and daughter of Alhaja Kabirat, Titubi, who is described as a "pretty, sensual, and obviously self-conscious woman." To Titubi, the play being mounted by the original group and its purpose represent an insult to her and her class, and she and her followers have come to disrupt it. What if there is a peasant rebellion?, she asks rhetorically. After all, as she states further, it is not a crime to be rich. For too long, she goes on, the insults and the lies have continued. But she is determined to put a stop to it: "This is our country too, and we shall not run away! I, Titubi, daughter of Alhaja Kabirat, I am stopping this play tonight" (7).

The police presently arrive, and Titubi soon finds herself in confrontation with Salami, the Deputy Superintendent of Police. The man is an intelligent police officer, if ever there was one, and he understands Titubi's psychology. This he plays upon as he tries to enlist her support in his efforts to quell the rebellion. "I'd like to say how terribly impressed I am by this show you've put up here." He tells the young lady at long last:

> So you are Titubi, the Amazon going to war! You're wealthy, your
> mother owns the town, and you're going to defend with your very
> life all that possession. But tell me, if you're really serious, if you
> really want to save your fat-arsed class, why haven't you offered
> your services to crush this peasant revolt? You know there is a battle
> going on now, don't you? That the farmers and villagers around us
> have risen in open rebellion, and are marching down upon the city?
> When they arrive, who do you think will be the first target? But you
> don't volunteer to help in fighting them. No. This mere wooden
> platform is your battlefield... this is where you come to put up a
> gallant fight, wasting my time! Go on. Titu-Titu, the magnificient
> Moremi of the sixties! Make your show, let them clap for you!
> Destroy the theatre! Burn it down! They'll put your name in the
> national archives! (14)

It is a well-delivered speech, a well-calculated strategy. Salami is certain that it will at least deflate Titubi's ego and discourage her from her plan to disrupt the show. But the move achieves more than this. Titubi calls back the Superintendent of Police as the latter turns to go. In a move reminiscent of Môrèmi, she volunteers to help capture the leader of the farmers' rebellion by infiltrating their camp. But as she waits in her cell at the maximum security prison, in the expectation that it will soon be invaded by the farmers, fear creeps in. "No! Moremi was not afraid!," she shouts, as she tries to overcome her feeling of trepidation. The stage direction specifies how she picks up the Môrèmi necklace from the floor and looks at it as she talks to herself, struggling desperately to reassure herself: "She was a woman, like me. And she waited all alone, for the Igbo warriors. All her people went into hiding, but she alone stood and waited" (30).

Presently, we are taken back in time to the historical context of the Môrèmi story. It is the beginning of scene five and the legend herself is presented, sitting in the market square, waiting for the Igbos. In this scene, as well as the next, Osofisan presents what he imagines must have transpired at the time, as opposed to what has been passed on through the ages. Underlined first is Môrèmi's courage and determination, as she goes before Esinmirin to make her pledge, as she bids her son goodbye, and as she takes a last walk round the streets. Then there is her sense of fear as she finds herself alone in the market square, waiting to be captured. There is also a complex exploration of her motivation as her friend Niniola comes in to try and dissuade her for the last time. Môrèmi herself admits that she might indeed have been prompted by a quest for fame. "When I see the stars," she says, "I long desperately to touch them... I am jealous of the gods" (33). And just as Niniola yells in fright, thinking that her friend is going too far, Môrèmi begins to question the supernatural, launching into direct blasphemy: "We fall on our knees, we multiply our supplications, we pile up the sacrifices," she says, "but suppose, Niniola, just suppose the gods are indifferent to us" (33). And when Niniola prays, Môrèmi counters by describing the effort as futile. "What more shall we do to learn that the gods will not help us?," she asks rhetorically, adding: "I have decided. Moremi shall be the clay which the race requires to remould itself" (34). Seeing that there is no use trying to dissuade her friend from what she has resolved to do, Niniola gives up, and the Yeye Oba group comes in to dance with the legend, trying to accord her moral support and bolster up her courage.

The sixth scene is entirely between Môrèmi and Oronmiyon, her husband. But more on this later. Suffice it to state for now that at the end of this latter scene Môrèmi freezes to become a statue, just as the playwright takes the spectators to the next one, where the farmers descend on the maximum security jail, freeing all of the detainees, including Titubi, who follows them.

In spite of herself, Titubi arrives at the farmers' camp to commence a process of (un)learning. Living with the peasants, interacting with them on a day-to-day basis, she cannot help but listen to their stories, to the tales of woe, of poverty and deprivation, and of humiliation and exploitation. Among the women of the camp, Titubi learns of the exorbitant taxes the men are forced to pay, the high-handedness of council officials, and the total indifference of the government with which the farmers have filed petition upon petition. Once, as the women dramatize snippets of their experiences at the hands of people of power, Titubi cannot help but confess: "You know[…]," she says, "before this […] I could never have believed that life was so unkind to anybody" (65). Moved, finally, by the justness of the farmers' cause, Titubi decides to re-think some of her positions. The process of her ideological conversion is complete. Listen to her:

> I saw myself growing up, knowing no such sufferings as these. With always so much to eat, even servants feed their dogs. Yet, here, farmers cannot eat their own products. For they need the money from the market. They tend yams but dare not taste. They raise chickens, but must be content with wind in their stomachs. And then, when they return weary from the market, the tax man is waiting with his bill. It could not be just. In our house, mama, we wake to the chorus of jingling coins. And when we sleep, coiled springs, soft foam and felt receive our bodies gently. But I have lived in the forest among simple folks, sharing their pain and anguish … and I chose …. (66)

And she decides to kill the Môrèmi in her; for the original Môrèmi in the context of the current struggle will be a villain and not a heroine – a reactionary, not a revolutionary. For Titubi to stick to the old Môrèmi would be for her to fight on the side of the ruling power, which, as she now sees it, is wholly in the wrong. Her new learning having taught her to fight only in defence of what is just, she resolves to hand the gun over to Marshall, the leader of the farmers' struggles, urging him to "let a new life begin" (66).

VII

While, as I hope to have demonstrated, the two archives which Osofisan engages in *Morountodun* are decidedly local, the idea that powers his investigation derives in part from Marxism, an ideology which, as has again been pointed out, Osofisan encountered during his sojourn in the West. Part of the cardinal assumptions of this ideology has to do with its conception of ordinary people as the true makers of history. Early in this essay, I pointed out what Osofisan indicates as part of his disagreement with Soyinka, including what he sees as the Nobel Prize winner's consistent failure to demonstrate the "dynamic participation of the other classes of society in the making of history."[35] He admits, to be sure, and if only to reiterate the point, that Soyinka's cast often includes a representation of the lowly in society, adding nonetheless that "these characters are almost always presented as a mass of items, without individuation, and in supportive, subsidiary roles, playing chorus to the characters that matter, the grand, visionary heroes."[36]

There is no doubt a grain of truth in this assertion, and Soyinka's play that probably illustrates this best is *Death and the King's Horseman*. Again, like *Morountodun*, the play dramatizes an actual incident in the history of the Yorùbá. In 1946, in the ancient city of Oyo, Elesin Oba, the human carrier, failed to commit ritual suicide as demanded of him by tradition following the intervention of the white district officer. Soyinka projects this incident in his play as one of profoundly tragic proportions for the Yorùbá people. Described literally in the play as his "tail,"[37] Elesin is followed by a retinue of praise singers, drummers, dancers, women, and children, as he takes a last dance round the community, the entirety of which looks up to him as saviour and redeemer. In addition to this support for the old feudalist order is Soyinka's promotion in the play of the people's patriarchal worldview, one of Soyinka's choices in the drama being the decision by Elesin Oba to take a new wife in his last few hours on earth. Having set his eyes on a young virgin who is already betrothed to the son of Iyaloja, the hero decides to shed some weight before embarking on the final journey. The

---

[35] Osofisan, *Nostalgic Drum*, 260.
[36] *Nostalgic Drum*, 260.
[37] Soyinka, "Death and the King's Horseman," in Soyinka, *Six Plays* (London: Methuen, 1984): 170.

affected lady herself is allowed no say in the matter. Having insisted, the people have no choice but to grant Elesin his last wish on earth.

Femi Osofisan's *Morountodun* presents us with an entirely different order when it comes to the role of women. In the farmers' camp, women are portrayed as full participants in the overall decision-making process. They are part of the resolution to go to war, part of strategic planning, and, indeed, part of the process of putting traitors on trial. And while men go to the battle-field, the women stay behind to nurse the wounded and the children. The substantial part of Titubi's process of (re-)education comes through the women.

In her seminal introduction to *Ngambika: Studies of Women in African Literature*,[38] Carole Boyce Davies concedes that there is a connection between African and Western feminism, adding that what they share lies in the recognition of the "woman's position internationally as one of second class status and 'otherness'"[39] and the agreement on the need to change the situation. Beyond this, she condemns the "failure" of Western feminists "to deal with issues that directly affect Black women and their tendency to sensationalize others."[40] She contends further that white women have often been complicit in the oppression and exploitation of the different peoples of the African continent, both men and women, and she cites the example of South Africa under apartheid. On the specificities of African feminism, Boyce Davies argues that, theoretically, the movement emphasizes the connections between and among sexism, racism, and class oppression, a fact which, she contends, makes it "socialist"[41] in orientation. Among others, one very important point that Boyce Davies makes is that African feminism recognizes that certain aspects of precolonial African traditions contain elements which accord women substantial dignity and even equality. "Revised historical records," she says, "are indicating that African women in the pre-colonial period and in antiquity were competent rulers, warriors and participants in their societies."[42] Boyce Davies exemplifies this with the

---

[38] Carole Boyce Davies & Anne Grave Adams, *Ngambika: Studies of Women in African Literature* (Trenton NJ: Africa World Press, 1986).

[39] Boyce Davies, *Ngambika*, 10.

[40] *Ngambika*, 10.

[41] Boyce Davies, *Ngambika*, 11.

[42] *Ngambika*, 9.

Gikuyu story of Mumbi but, in my view, she could also have included that of Môrèmi.

But, at this point, and to link up with Carole Boyce Davies in her statement about the general assumptions of feminism, it is probably necessary to state that the Yorùbá traditional order, like those of several other African societies, subscribes to what Molara Ogundipe–Leslie once termed "sex asymmetry,"[43] holding males to be superior to their female counterparts and attributing to them positive qualities of strength, chivalry, courage, valiance, reliability, intelligence, and trustworthiness. The female sex, on the other hand, is, broadly speaking, projected negatively as weak, fickle, indiscreet, and shallow in thought. Because of her inherent weaknesses then, a woman is not considered capable of such great feats as winning wars or running empires or kingdoms. Rather, her roles are seen to be marginal, consisting in keeping house and in bearing and bringing up children. The Hausa saying quoted in Trinh T. Min-ha's "Mother's Talk" which precisely states that 'He who follows a woman's plan is bound to drown'[44] will find the approval of any typical Yorùbá male. The legend of Môrèmi, in my view, is a metaphor cast up within this same Yorùbá ethos negating female stereotypes. Yet, to the best of my knowledge, this story does not seem to have captured the attention of many African feminist writers, researchers, scholars, intellectuals, and even activists. Indeed, Môrèmi is Medea's counterpart in the political arena. The latter is the heroine in Euripedes' play of the same title who makes enormous sacrifices – which include killing her own blood brother – in the process of demonstrating her love for and devotion to Jason, whom she later marries.[45] As I suggested earlier, she serves to bear out Carole Boyce Davies' assertion regarding the existence of women in precolonial Africa who participated actively in the affairs of their societies and who proved themselves to be competent planners and leaders. At a time when the male hegemonists of her society

---

[43] Molara Ogundipe–Leslie, *Re-creating Ourselves: African Women and Critical Transformations* (Trenton NJ: Africa World Press, 1989): 34.

[44] Trinh T. Min-ha, "Mother's Talk," in *The Politics of Mothering: Womanhood, Identity, and Resistance in African Literature*, ed. Obioma Nnaemeka (London & New York: Routledge): 29.

[45] Ato Quayson uses the story of Medea to preface his discussion of what he describes as the "affective foundation of the companionate nuclear family set-up" and the problem which African women who find themselves in such situation often have to tackle. See Quayson, *Postcolonialism: Theory, Practice or Process* (Cambridge: Polity, 2000): 121.

seemed to be totally lacking in strength, when courage seemed to have failed all of them, and when they seemed to be quite bereft of ideas, this woman stepped forward, came up with a brilliant idea, and proceeded to execute it at great personal risk. This member of the sex that is considered untrustworthy did not jettison her cause at any time. She kept to it and kept it to herself even in the land of her captors, staying with it till the very end. She was to further demonstrate her strength of character and commitment to her land by agreeing to sacrifice her son to the goddess of Esinmirin river.

To emphasize the point, the story of Môrèmi is one that deserves to be interpreted and re-interpreted, appropriated again and again and re-visioned and re-articulated by people committed to feminist transformation and the question of female agency in social, political, and discursive arenas of Africa; and it is somewhat surprising that this has not been the case. On the contrary, what seems to have happened over time is the abandonment of the story to preservers of male hegemony who clearly have taken it as their own and have continued to project it *selectively*.

It is intriguing that, over several centuries of the re-enactment of Môrèmi story, in the annual traditional festival dramas in Ife and Ofa, and in Duro Ladipo's own transformation in *Moremi*, the chief concern seems to be the entrenchment of the traditional order. Always, the simple message is that at a moment of turmoil in the land, an individual steps forward from the palace, taking great risks in an attempt to rescue the race. The fact that this particular saviour belongs to a greatly disrespected and marginalized sex is often conveniently ignored by the authors and sponsors of the performances. Osofisan scores another positive here, then, being the first to draw attention to the implications of the sexual identity of the heroine of the narrative in the course of several centuries of its re-enactment.

Of course, in *Morountodun* Osofisan underlines Môrèmi's complex motivation in undertaking her action, and he also takes care to point out that ultimately, the woman's action was on behalf of the ruling hegemony. In addition to this, however, the dramatist draws the attention of his audience to the possibility that Môrèmi's original decision would have at least created some confusion in the hearts and minds of the male hegemonists of the time. This comes out clearly in scene six, which takes place in the market square, between Oronmiyon and his intrepid wife. As revealed, the overall aim of Oronmiyon in the scene is to dissuade Môrèmi from her course of action. "It is not too late to change your mind," he tells Môrèmi as soon as recognition dawns on the latter regarding the identity of the person standing before her. To the question of what the people will say afterwards of Môrèmi, whether they would not laugh at "the brave, brave hero [sic] who lost her nerve at the crucial moment and fled with her tail between her spindly feet" (36), Oronmiyon simply asks her not to worry, as he alone stands as the will of the people. In any case, "subjects only echo the ruler's caprices" (37). But Môrèmi continues to prove stubborn until Oronmiyon can no longer hold back, making the ultimate slip: "*And which husband, be he king and all, will dare walk proud again, who has openly sacrificed his wife to ward off his own death?*" (38; my emphasis). Precisely for reasons bordering on egoism, therefore, Oronmiyon is ready to do anything to thwart Môrèmi's plans. But the latter also proves to be a very smart individual. She knows she has to think fast, having realized the extent to which her husband is ready to go in an attempt to make sure she changes her mind. Môrèmi cooks up a story and it works, just like magic.

To be sure, Titubi does not possess the maturity and consciousness of her mythical predecessor when she resolves to embark on the adventure. In a real sense, then, she has simply yielded to the subtle manipulation of the wily police officer, Superintendent Salami. It is after her arrival at the farmers' camp that she begins to comprehend issues in all their complexity. By the time she re-appears in the city a few weeks later, she is completely transformed. She is clear now in her mind about what she has stepped into, and understands the kind of bargain she wishes to negotiate for herself. As she sees it, in the context of the fight for justice which the farmers' struggle of the time represents, it would be wrong of her to remain Môrèmi. As a mature woman with a clear understanding of events and history, she has resolved to travel in a different direction.

VIII

Which returns us to Paulin Hountondji's position on the inherent plurality of all cultures, and on the need to transcend the artificial polarization between precolonial and postcolonial traditions in Africa. Because what Osofisan has done in *Morountodun* is to ransack the huge storehouse of his inherited traditions, settling on a revered discourse, a hegemonic construct, which nonetheless projects contradictory implications but which, over the ages, has been selectively interpreted. The playwright does not just draw attention to the discarded aspect of this heritage, he also juxtaposes the latter with a less familiar aspect of postcolonial history, a marginal one with an unequivocal element of oppositional politics. As the two archives engage each other in a heated debate, the limitations and contradictions of the older material is thrown into bold relief. As he himself admits openly, Osofisan's major sources of inspiration as he sets the dialogue in motion are feminism and Marxism, two ideologies that are unquestionably of Western origin. To the playwright, the source of the ideas that he has appropriated is not so important. What is important, in his view, is their effectiveness or otherwise in a given pragmatic context. A traditional story like that of Môrèmi needs to be updated; and considering dialectical materialist and feminist thought to be suitable for the kind of project he has in mind, the dramatist simply reaches out for them without hesitation. Indeed, what Osofisan conveys as he sets the legend of Môrèmi against the story of the Agbekoyas in *Morountodun* is a palpable sense of confidence. Of course, the implication of his conclusions is not that the Môrèmi myth be set aside altogether. He actually articulates the profound possibilities of the tradition; not least of which is the heroic daring of the original protagonist, which itself serves as the primary impulse behind Titubi's action in the drama. And this alongside the feminist thrust of the story, which, up to this particular point and to the best of my knowledge, had been de-emphasized, if not consciously repressed. If, therefore, the dramatist ends up doing violence to the linear logic of the narrative, this is simply because (as can be deduced from Paulin Hountondji's position) no cultural text can emerge unmediated when applied in a different – spatial as well as temporal – context. Once, as is the case in the present situation, autochthonous material confronts postcolonial realities, it inevitably undergoes transformation.

WORKS CITED

Awodiya, Muyiwa, ed. *Excursions in Drama and Literature: Interviews with Femi Osofisan* (Lagos: Kraft, 1993)

Beer, E.E.C. *The Politics of Peasant Groups in Western Nigeria* (Ibadan: Ibadan UP, 1976).

Beier, Ulli. "Introduction" to *Three Nigerian Plays* (London: Longman, 1967): vii–xviii.

Davies, Carole Boyce. "Introduction: Feminist Consciousness and African Literary Criticism," in *Ngambika: Studies of Women in African Literature*, ed. Davies & Graves, 1–23.

——, & Anne Adam Graves. *Ngambika: Studies of Women in African Literature* (Trenton NJ: Africa World Press, 1986).

Hountondji, Paulin. *African Philosophy: Myths and Reality* (London: Hutchinson, 1983).

Johnson, Samuel. *History of the Yorubas* (London: George Routledge & Sons, 1921).

Ladipo, Duro. "Moremi," in *Three Nigerian Plays* (London: Longman, 1967).

——. "Oba Ko so," in *Three Yoruba Plays: Oba Ko so, Oba Moro, Oba Waja* (Ibadan: Mbari, 1964): 1–28.

Minh-ha, Trinh T. "Mother's Talk," in *The Politics of (M)Othering* (1997), ed. Nnaemeka, 26–32.

Nnaemeka, Obioma. *The Politics of (M)Othering: Womanhood, Identity, and Resistance in African Literature* (London & New York: Routledge, 1997.

Ogundipe–Leslie, Molara. *Re-Creating Ourselves: African Women and Critical Transformations* (Trenton NJ: Africa World Press, 1989).

Osofisan, Femi. *Another Raft* (Lagos: Malthouse, 1988).

——. *Esu and the Vagabond Minstrels* (Ibadan: New Horn, 1991).

——. *Morountodun and other Plays* (Lagos: Longman, 1982).

——. *Tegonni, an African Antigone* (Ibadan. Opon Ifa, 1999).

——. *The Chattering and the Song* (Ibadan: Ibadan UP, 1977).

——. *The Nostalgic Drum: Essays on Literature, Drama and Culture* (Trenton NJ: Africa World Press, 2001).

——. *Yungba–Yungba and the Dance Contests* (Ibadan: Heinemanns, 1993).

Quayson, Ato. *Postcolonialism: Theory, Practice or Process* (Cambridge: Polity, 2000).

Ray, Benjamin C. *African Religions: Symbols, Ritual and Community* (Englewood Cliffs NJ: Prentice–Hall, 1976).

Sowande, Bode. *Farewell to Babylon and Other Plays* (London: Longman, 1979).

Soyinka, Wole. "The Strong Breed," in Soyinka, *Collected Plays I* (Oxford: Oxford UP, 1973): 113–46.

——. *Myth, Literature and the African World* (Cambridge: Cambridge UP, 1976).

——. "Death and the King's Horseman," in Soyinka, *Six Plays* (London: Methuen, 1984): 143–220.

Williams, Gavin. *State and Society in Nigeria* (Idanre: Afrographica, 1980).

Williams, Raymond. *Marxism and Literature* (Oxford & New York: Oxford UP, 1977).

◁▷

Europe Discarded
– ‹›› – Ken Bugul and the Twenty-Eighth Wife of a Marabout

JARMO PIKKUJÄMSÄ

I

"IT TAKES A VILLAGE TO RAISE A CHILD" – this oft-quoted proverb from an unknown source seems to materialize in Mbaye Biléoma's[1] sequence of three autobiographical novels from *The Abandoned Baobab* (1991) via *Cendres et braises* to *Riwan ou le chemin de sable*.[2] Her own itinerary from Senegal to Belgium and France, and back again to the village in the heartland of one of the Senegalese Sufi orders – the Mourides – allows her to use writing not only as an empowering tool, but also to break barriers between European languages and religious brotherhood traditions in Senegal, challenge gender roles, and build critically upon North–South dichotomies and also, *en passant*, on the social structures of Senegal, her home country. Each of these three novels stands alone as an artistic entity, yet this article hopes to establish a link between them by interpreting these narratives as a series of stories that build upon each other. The exilic experiences that the main character, Ken, goes through in the West eventually lead to her return to Africa.

---

[1] Ken Bugul's real name is Mariètou Mbaye Biléoma. In order to avoid any confusion, "Ken" in this article makes allusion to the main character of the stories, while Mariètou Mbaye Biléoma alone is used in connection with the author.

[2] *The Abandoned Baobab: The Autobiography Of A Senegalese Woman*, tr. Marjolijn de Jager (*Le Baobab fou*, Dakar: NEA, 1984; tr. New York: Lawrence Hill, 1991).

In *The Abandoned Baobab*, the home village symbolizes much more than a place; it is a "symbol of warmth and light, [where the] baobab tree represents the positive forces of life: tradition, fertility, continuity, and survival."[3] In *The Abandoned Baobab*, upon Ken's return, she discovers that the tree has "gone mad" and died; she is referring perhaps to herself and her own alienating experiences in Europe, whereas now, her return to Africa at the end of the story marks a new chapter that is about to begin in her life. This symbolism functions as closure in the novel, and the reader will have the opportunity to discover this new chapter in detail only much later in her third novel, *Riwan ou le chemin de sable*. In between these two novels, Mbaye Biléoma published *Cendres et braises*, which is yet another account of alienating experiences in a devastating relationship, this time in France. During this relationship, Ken experiences such a sense of alienation that whenever she follows her companion on his business trips to Senegal, she consciously denies her Senegalese background and avoids any contact with the Dakarois surroundings and the locals, staying in the hotel for fear that she might be recognized by someone if she went out. Her motives for such behaviour can be explained partly by her painful memories of her mother abandoning her when she was a small girl, an event which she vividly describes in *The Abandoned Baobab*, and also by a strong sense of guilt for having left behind her nearest and dearest in the village and losing touch with them and her origins over a long period of time. *Cendres et braises* articulates Ken's painful failure to hold on to a tragic love story with a married man, and to fit properly into the Parisian bourgeois setting. She admits to herself that she is trying to live a false and exteriorized dream in the beautiful City of Light, the embrace of which turns out to be anything but warm. Her inward battle to make sense of these experiences almost numbs her, but at the same time it only intensifies the vividness of her memories of village life back in Senegal. Memories construct a welcome opposition to and relief from Ken's extreme solitude, and she is eventually able to change the course of her life with the aid of the village marabout, who helps her to accept herself again and "to find belief in God, belief in life."[4] The importance of the role of the marabout in Ken's life from here

---

[3] Susan Stringer, *The Senegalese Novel by Women: Through Their Own Eyes* (New York: Peter Lang, 1996): 133.

[4] Ken Bugul, *Cendres et braises* (Paris: L'Harmattan, 1994): 164. [...] découvri[r] la foi en Dieu, la foi en la vie. Apart from *The Abandoned Baobab*, all quotations from the novels of Ken Bugul are my translations from the French.

on is to be demonstrated on many occasions, not so much in religious terms as in terms of sharing with or submitting one's life as a woman to a venerated holy man, better known in Wolof as *Sërîñ*. In an interview, Mbaye Biléoma herself calls the life experiences that she describes in *Cendres et braises* her "descent to hell,"[5] from which she recovers only by returning to the village and, eventually, by getting married. The textual representations of Ken's long itinerary thus culminate in *Riwan ou le chemin de sable*, in which the memories of village life again take the form of both autobiography and fiction, and in which the village is presented as a space that provides a protective shelter, a place for 'healing from the West'. The village and tradition are employed in the narrative as a tool for Ken to finally complete a more coherent subjectivity. To some extent, the village also articulates a topos of patriarchy, and Mbaye Biléoma puts the solidity and the unchanging nature of this topos to the test in her writing.

Susan Stringer asks whether Senegalese women writers "pass through a primary autobiographical stage and then turn to more universal themes"[6] – the example of Mbaye Biléoma confirms this view – and concludes that as far as the literary categories are concerned, they can be encompassed in multiple ways, including, for instance, Kenneth Harrow's categories of "autobiographical, social or historical *littérature de témoignage.*"[7] Julia Watson has given evidence of how Mbaye Biléoma uses European confessional autobiography to "decolonize herself from European values and belief" and how at the same time "she is also and necessarily complicit in its writing practices."[8] Mbaye Biléoma completely lacks interest in labelling *The Abandoned Baobab* a novel or an autobiography. Rather than giving importance to genre, the author advocates self-expression, which entails a social dimension with a very personal inventory of the traces that her experiences in Europe inflicted upon her. This inventory clearly func-

---

[5] Gnimdéwa Atakpama, "Rue Félix-Faure de Ken Bugul," *Amina* 422 (June 2005): 86–87.

[6] Stringer, *The Senegalese Novel By Women: Through Their Own Eyes*, 18.

[7] Kenneth W. Harrow, "The Poetics of African Littérature de Témoignage," *African Literature Studies: The Present State*, ed. Stephen Arnold (Washington DC: Three Continents, 1985): 143–44.

[8] Julia Watson, "Self-Decolonization And Bodily Re-Membering In Ken Bugul's *The Abandoned Baobab*," *Writing New Identities: Gender, Nation and Immigration in Contemporary Europe*, ed. Gisela Brinker–Gabler & Sidonie Smith (Minneapolis & London: U of Minnesota P, 1997): 150.

tions as her personal 'counter-history', which seeks to define who Ken really is and how her persona develops within the conflicts of values that emerge along the axis of 'modern' and 'traditional'. This theme is often present in the wonderfully prolific Senegalese literature and film, and it is particularly the case among women writers such as Mariama Bâ, Aminata Sow Fall, and Aminata Maïga Ka, to name but a few. How is the notion of return inscribed in fiction? Generally speaking, from the first slave narratives and the different ideological expressions of movements such as pan-Africanism and *négritude* onwards, examples of fictive characters' experience of the West and return to Africa are numerous. Male writers have often written about the experiences of exile and the return of male characters. In this respect, the gender balance has been counterweighted by a multitude of female writers – from Ama Ata Aidoo and her "imperative of return"[9] to the most recently published African writers and those who form newer literary categories such as immigrant literature or refugee literature, to Mbaye Biléoma's fellow countrywoman Fatou Diome and the themes of her novel, which suggest one should never even consider leaving the African continent in the first place.[10] I would argue that in her first three novels Mbaye Biléoma looks with an increasingly critical eye at Europe and the Western woman as role model, and her narratives exemplify a refusal to accept them as key elements for defining an identity.

Ken is a woman returnee who has now turned her back on a Europe that for so many still represents the ultimate Promised Land, a dream worth fighting for at almost any cost. Her return to the village takes us behind the walls of the compound of her village's *Sëriñ*, the highly respected local spiritual leader. The village scenario includes contradictory views: At the same time as she describes how young girls are destined to marry the *Sëriñ*, either by communal agreement between him and the girls' parents, or by the one-sided decision of the latter, Ken herself chooses to become his "twenty-eighth wife" and by doing so obtains the title of a *Soxna*.[11] Against

---

[9] Ama Ata Aidoo, *Our Sister Killjoy* (New York: Longman, 2004). Aidoo's work is assessed in detail in Carmen Nge, "The Return of the 'Native': Visualizing Place and Narrative Homecoming" (doctoral dissertation, Brandeis University, 2004).

[10] Fatou Diome, *Le Ventre de l'Atlantique* (Paris: Anne Carrière, 2003).

[11] *Soxna* (Wolof): Lady; wife (especially wife of a spiritual leader). Wolof terminology is rendered according to the transliteration system introduced in *Dictionnaire wolof-français*, ed. Arame Fal & Rosine Santos & Jean Léonce Doneux (Paris: Karthala, 1990), except for direct quotations from the novels.

this background Mbaye Biléoma juxtaposes polygamy, a practice common in Senegal, with that of the Western women's so-called 'choices', arguing, through her text, that the available role models for women, who want to be 'modern', sometimes reveal themselves to be nothing but ostentation. Polygamy is a common topic in the artistic expressions of Senegal, and Mbaye Biléoma's representation of polygamy is to be seen within the context of Western assumptions. She considers it necessary on several occasions to underline the fact that polygamy is not an institution. In the autobiographical work under examination here, this can be interpreted as the defence of her own very personal quest. We will return to this question later. Through the substantial amount of terminology and references in Wolof and through the re-lexification of the phenomena that describe traditional Senegalese culture or Islamic practices, Mbaye Biléoma creates a larger context for the concept of polygamy. This concept, like other customary practices within Senegalese village life, can all too easily be misinterpreted unless the entire context is explained to the reader.[12] This is indeed what Mbaye Biléoma does quite successfully, particularly in *Riwan ou le chemin de sable*, which focuses on the social roles of the village protagonists and on the ways in which a Mouride community is able to set its members back on "more solid ground." This is Ken's *chemin de sable*, at the same time – albeit more latently – her very own spiritual path and more visibly that "sandy road" which leads her to her beloved *Sëriñ* and to an ongoing process of self-empowerment. Her critique of some of the customs of traditional village life is at once subversive and gentle. Moreover, her questioning of the gender roles and some of the hierarchies that condition polygamous life is mixed with admiration and wonder with regard to the beloved *Sëriñ*.

II

An almost unavoidable phenomenon in the study of the Senegalese novelists is the Mouride brotherhood, a Senegalese Sufi movement and its founder Amadou Bamba (1850–1927), his descendants, religious notables,

---

[12] Ahmed S. Bangura has studied the frequent presence of Wolof terminology in Aminata Sow Fall's novels and argues, that such strategies can be expected in narratives whose central theme is the encroachment of Western values and the threat they pose to the survival of traditional Senegalese culture. Ahmed S. Bangura, *Islam and the West African Novel: The Politics of Representation* (Boulder CO & London: Lynne Rienner, 2000): 85.

and leaders (*marabout, sheikh*), or their disciples. Historically, the brotherhood originated in the late nineteenth century as a response of the Wolof
people of north-western Senegal to changes brought about by the French. In
1971 it was estimated that the movement attracted over half a million members, while today's estimates vary between three and five million suppor-
ters, about one-third of the total population of the Republic of Senegal.[13]
The movement has achieved strong political and economic success, based
on hereditary leadership and encouraged by a religious ideology according
to which manual labour performed in the service of God provides the loyal
disciple not only with economic security through material aid but also with
the prospect of paradise in the afterlife. As a result of the immense popularity of the movement, Cheikh Amadou Bamba, who, among the members of
the brotherhood, is considered a saint, "is never criticised in the Senegalese
novel."[14]

However, as Debra Boyd–Buggs points out, when one turns to examine
novelists' perceptions of the basic concepts of Mouride doctrine, one finds
Mouridism viewed as "having established a system of domination and
exploitation in which a religious elite distorts Bamba's teaching, abusing
their privileges vis-à-vis their *talibés* or disciples for their own personal
gain."[15] Mbaye Biléoma never establishes a direct link to this more abusive
side of Mouridism. Instead, Ken's account essentially builds on roles and
practices connected to the movement through the relationship of the female
disciple and her spiritual guide. The latter remains at a respectful distance
throughout these three novels, and is criticized much less severely when
brought together for comparison with other Senegalese novelists. Ken's
return from her exilic years in Brussels and Paris is characterized by her
return not only to her home village but also to a framework of ideas within
which individuals are evaluated.

A substantial part of life in the Senegalese Mouride brotherhood is
organized around work – almost as a form of prayer – for the benefit of
one's very personal *Sëriñ*, who, by his (or, in rare cases, her) consequently

---

[13] Donal B. Cruise O'Brien, *The Mourides of Senegal: The Political and Economic
Organization of an Islamic Brotherhood* (Oxford: Clarendon, 1971): 1. There are two
dominant brotherhoods in Senegal, the Tidjaniyya and the Mouridiyya (or Mourides).

[14] Debra Boyd–Buggs, "Mouridism in Senegalese Fiction," in *Faces of Islam in African Literature*, ed. Kenneth W. Harrow (Porsmouth NH: Heinemann & London: James
Currey, 1991): 201.

[15] Boyd–Buggs, "Mouridism In Senegalese Fiction," 20–25.

increased *baraka* (blessing, divine power), is able to provide the disciple with a comprehensive well-being in both spiritual and economic terms. Interestingly, the idea of leaving is rooted in the Mouride agenda as one form of following one's submission to the Sufi path. Scott L. Malcolmson points out in his survey that today's Mouride immigrants find that "because knowledge comes from God, it would be an insult to Him not to seek it. Because God commands us to work, not seeking work would also be an insult to God."[16] An inseparable part of this agenda is – one day – to return. In the minds of the Mouride immigrants, the Promised Land is not in the West but in Africa, in Touba, which is the holy city of the Mouride order. Even though this example is drawn from the reality of migratory movements in today's world, it is exemplary of the imaginative geography largely present in Senegal and particularly among its Mouride disciples.

In this regard, the magnitude of the trauma that Ken experiences upon her return from Europe can be better understood – her return does not provide any evidence of success; quite the contrary. Let us first look at one very inspirational example of how the return from exile in the West can be articulated. The novels of Mbaye Biléoma and Tayeb Salih contain surprising similarities in their internal quest for meaning in life. The gender dynamics constitute the most obvious and, in my view, most interesting parallel to the comparison of Ken's itinerary with that of the exiled character Mustafa Sa'eed, or his alter ego – the narrator – in *Season of Migration to the North*. Listen to what he says upon his return to Sudan:

> I want to give lavishly, I want love to flow from my heart, to ripen and bear fruit. There are many horizons to be visited, fruit that must be plucked, books read, and white pages in the scrolls of life to be inscribed with vivid sentences in a bold hand [...] *I feel a sense of stability, I feel that I am important, that I am continuous and integral.*[17]

In contrast to this, having returned to the village Ken sees herself in *Riwan ou le chemin de sable* as "a broken doll, abandoned one night in a

---

[16] Scott L. Malcolmson, "West Of Eden," *Transition* 71 (1996): 44.

[17] Tayeb Salih, *Season of Migration to the North* (Harmondsworth: Penguin, 2003): 5; my emphasis.

garbage container in a deserted street."[18] Already in *Cendres et braises* her final return home is filled with negative sentiments and she is completely shattered and unable to engage in daily life. Ken's self-esteem has long been disrupted and, with no social status acquired, she remains marginalized, first, even among the members of her home village. She feels that by having left home and been absent so long she has caused embarrassment to her mother, and her current situation as a single woman is not helping the matter. Ken is absorbed by her vivid memories of a friend called Mbène Sarr, a 'stayee', who for Ken seems to symbolize continuity and stability and who "put in the world only twins," and whose family, following the Mouride brotherhood's mission, was "dynamic and harmonious in work."[19] In contrast to Mbène Sarr, she sees herself as an object of gossip:

> Elle n'est pas mariée?
> Non.
> Elle a des enfants?
> Non?
> Elle travaille?
> Non.
> Elle est saine d'esprit?
> Non[20]

The difficulty of Ken's return is expressed by her memories of being among the village women and taking part in the hard everyday tasks as a little girl; upon her arrival after years abroad she now feels that she owes something to these women and that she has let them down. Beneath the surface of what Mbaye Biléoma describes here lies what in Wolof society is called *ligéey u ndey*, a belief according to which a child is the reflection of the behaviour of its mother:

> Revenir à la Mère, revenir aux origines, revenir aux sources des choses, revenir dans l'environnement, revenir dans l'atmosphère, revenir au familier, revenir *pour la confrontation.*[21]

---

[18] Bugul, *Riwan ou le chemin de sable*, 154. [...] une poupée brisée, abandonnée dans une poubelle, un soir, dans une rue déserte.

[19] Bugul, *Cendres et braises*, 23. [...] ne mettait au monde que des jumeaux [...] une famille dynamique, harmonieuse dans le travail.

[20] *Cendres et braises*, 22. Is she not married? No. Has she got children? No. Is she working? No. Is she mentally well? No.

Ken's return to the village is soon followed by her becoming the twenty-eighth wife of a *Sëriñ*, which the reader is to perceive as a soothing experience that helps her restore her identity. In a very thorough analysis of *The Abandoned Baobab* and of Mbaye Biléoma's attempts to remember herself as an African female subject, Julia Watson demonstrates how "caught in a representational dilemma between the sexual licentiousness of the West, where she is acclaimed as the perfected exotic other, and the moral strictures of Islam in the village that exclude and 'abandon' her, Ken finds no tenable space of subjectivity."[22] That certainly is the case in *The Abandoned Baobab,* but as *Riwan ou le chemin de sable* then shows, Ken's return articulates interesting ambiguities in that "tenable space of subjectivity" and these ambiguities centre on the persona of the *Sëriñ* more than anything else, as we will later see. The author herself points out:

> Looking back at my novels you can see how I absolutely needed to return to my origins. As I have sometimes said, I wanted to return to my mother's belly. For me it was a necessity. When I left my origins I may not have believed that my origins were absolute. But upon return, the country made no sense, the deception was even worse.[23]

In order to get a better understanding of Ken's stance *vis-à-vis* the expectations determined by external signs of success for anyone returning from the West, it suffices to look at the symbolism of the titles of these novels. This symbolism expresses what she considered essential in her itinerary: personal choices and their consequences. The title of *The Abandoned Baobab* has already been discussed above. *Cendres et braises* ('ashes and embers') characterizes the state of mind of Ken and also her continuous memories of the home village, memories not quite dead yet but burning in embers. As already suggested, the full scale of these memories is then exposed in *Riwan ou le chemin de sable*. Again the choice of title carries a message; *chemin de sable*, or the sandy road, is partly her childhood memory of walking on errands, barefoot, in the village with the relative

---

[21] Bugul, *Cendres et braises*, 33, my emphasis. Return to the Mother, return to origins return to the source of things, return to the environment, return to the atmosphere, return to the familiar, return *for the confrontation.*

[22] Watson, "Self-Decolonization and Bodily Re-Membering in Ken Bugul's *The Abandoned Baobab*," 158.

[23] Personal interview with Mariétou Mbaye Biléoma (Dakar, Senegal, 20 December 2006).

ease of a child; this soft sand can also be read allegorically to mean having no more obstacles in your way as compared to what used to be. Riwan, one of the male characters of the novel, represents an example of the more spiritual side of what may be needed on that sandy road. Riwan gives his oath of submission to the *Sërin* by pronouncing *jëbellu*,[24] and from this day on his itinerary is trouble-free, because so clearly defined by the guidelines that show how to follow the Sufi path; complete servitude to *Sërin* is all that is needed.

The female characters outnumber their male counterparts in these three novels. Ken is in a privileged position to survey the lives of women from all sides of life and her accounts embody a variety of female figures who are intermittently in relation with each other, individually and collectively. The embodiments of these figures under investigation in this article include Ken as an *évoluée* and a returnee and her relation to the 'stayees', and the female images articulated by the collective of the *Sërin*'s wives. Ken often expresses regret and nostalgia for having left her village, especially when she sees how her childhood friends, those who stayed and never left, have become wives and mothers and have obtained a notable status in the village. She says:

> J'étais de toutes celles avec qui j'avais grandi ici, la seule qui était partie au loin et qui n'avait rien ramené. Ni malles remplies de trésors, d'étoffes rares à distribuer, ni assez d'argent pour faire taire les langues les plus venimeuses, ni de riches parures, ni d'habits chatoyants pour faire pâlir d'envie celles qui étaient restées au village. Je n'avais ramené ni mari, ni enfant. Rien.[25]

---

[24] *Jëbellu* (Wolof): Personal and physical surrender; initiation ritual in which the Mouride disciple declares to his master: "I submit myself to you, in this life and in the next. I will do everything that you order me. I will abstain from anything you forbid me." Cruise O'Brien, *The Mourides of Senegal: The Political and Economic Organization of an Islamic Brotherhood*, 143.

[25] Bugul, *Riwan ou le chemin de sable*, 162. Among all those with whom I grew up here, I was the only one who left and went far away and who brought nothing back. No suitcases full of treasures, no rare fabrics to give away, not enough money to shut up the most poisonous tongues, neither rich decorations, nor glittering dresses to make those who had stayed in the village go pale with envy. I had brought neither husband nor a child. Nothing.

Ken's return empty-handed is evoked especially in regard to her female friends and village inhabitants. Her regrets only confirm what has been at the core of the social acceptance granted to the returnees: material signs of success, inverted to symbolize not only the respectability of the person who travelled but also to mark the esteem of the returnee's family members and even neighbours. Ken is, first of all, an ambiguous character and the almost disturbing signs of her alienation can be read, for instance, in the fact that the internal structure of *The Abandoned Baobab* is divided into two parts: "Ken's Prehistory" and "Ken's History." What adds to the confusion is her use of a pseudonym and the fact that the narrator sometimes, but not systematically, addresses herself in the third person:

> Ken Bugul se souvient [...] Je partais. Les autres restaient. Je partais très loin. Je m'arrachais pour tendre vers le Nord. Le Nord des rêves, le Nord des illusions, le Nord des allusions, le Nord référentiel, Le Nord Terre Promise.[26]

Here Ken is already looking back at the moment of her departure for Europe; she describes this moment in somewhat cynical terms and underlines the disruptiveness of leaving when she is "tearing herself away" to the illusory Promised Land that will only disappoint her expectations. Europe as a "frame of reference" in the Senegalese mind reflects the images of Europe first provided by the French colonizers, which the author occasionally addresses in her writing. These images are then reinforced or re-shaped by the African returnees who had been to Europe, most often France, to get an education and who cultivated the image of the often admired *évolué(e)s*, the 'been-there' men and women and the *'venu(e)s de France'*, who were to be looked up to by the 'stayees'. Ken looks back at this from a distance and remembers how, after her very first visits back to Senegal, she spent time only with those who had also stayed in Europe, or with those who imitated the lifestyle of the Europeans. The *évoluées* wanted to exhibit their knowledge of elsewhere and even shared a common language that they deformed: "We spoke the language of elsewhere among

---

[26] Bugul, *Le Baobab fou*, 33. "Ken Bugul remembers [...] I was leaving. The others were staying. I was leaving to go very far away. Tearing myself away to head North. The North of dreams, the North of illusions, the North of allusions. The frame of reference North, the Promised Land North." Ken Bugul, *The Abandoned Baobab: The Autobiography of a Senegalese Woman*, tr. Marjolijn de Jager (New York: Lawrence Hill, 1991): 23.

us, especially in public."[27] The "elsewhere" had become a myth. On the one hand, Ken had rebelled against the previous generation, and this is manifested through the new lifestyle of her own generation: Young single women go out as they please and come back home late at night. Her excuse for this kind of behaviour, unacceptable in the Muslim community, was that she was already alienated, since she had lived elsewhere. These liberated young women, Ken explains, were just as keen as everyone else to get married, but the young men of their own generation favoured the supposedly more innocent younger girls who had not known exile, so that the *évoluées* became a kind of merchandise. In *Riwan ou le chemin de sable*, Ken explains that marriage only came second on her list of priorities:

> En ces premières années d'indépendance, je ne songeais qu'à mon émancipation. Je voulais être une femme bardée de diplômes qui épouserait un homme bardé de diplômes de l'école occidentale. [28]

In contrast to the above, Ken is not completely at ease among the *évoluées* and feels excluded from their camp as well. Ken's life in Europe and her being away from her closest family and friends has marked her profoundly, and she regards the new generation as condemned, without hope, realizing that she has nothing in common with them; her life story has given her the role of an outsider. Whatever the case, her experiences of different lifestyles translate the presence of Europe in the imaginary of Ken into a certain cosmopolitan voice; it is often accompanied with a particular attachment to labels, partly reflecting the attachment to beautiful things designed for women, but more importantly also carrying a political message requiring a social change in consumer habits:

> [...] les épouses de nos Chefs portent des robes étranges qui coûtent des fortunes, des habits qui ne sont pas confectionnés chez nous, des bijoux qui ne sont pas fabriqués chez nous. Donnons du travail à nos artisans et promouvons leur travail en dehors des circuits folk-

---

[27] Bugul, *Cendres et braises*, 44. Nous parlions la langue de l'ailleurs entre nous, surtout en public.

[28] Bugul, *Riwan ou le chemin de sable*, 39. In those first years of independence, I opted only for my emancipation. I wanted to be a woman loaded with diplomas, who would marry a man loaded with diplomas from his Western education.

loriques qui ne débouchent sur rien du tout et permettent seulement
aux autres de recopier et d'imiter sans vergogne nos créations.[29]

Ken's observation can also be explained by the fact that beauty and
femininity are highly important values in Senegal; Ken's response in the
above passage is clear: it is time to take local Senegalese work seriously
and value not only the artisanship directed at visitors to the country and
thus in some ways also dictated by the demands of the tourist industry, but
to respect the fact that the Senegalese production in itself is responding to
the demands of local fashion. Ken ends her plea by listing an impressive
number of local Senegalese designers whose work should be valued more,
in the name of God, "*Bilahi!*"[30] Ken's earlier experiences in Europe went
deeper than following the latest trends: In *The Abandoned Baobab*, she
bitterly accepts the orientalized role ascribed to her in Brussels, and the
narrative shows her reduced to the classic stereotype of the African woman
as a mere object of the Western/male gaze. The same externalization of
one's self can be read also in her life in Paris, where she and her Fulani
friend Jimmy Moussa Sarr created a sensation by dressing up in order to
accentuate their African origins: "We had the courage to dress the way we
felt. Black skin was no longer hidden, it was an advantage."[31] For a while,
Ken plays around with the novelty of using her black femininity and
sensuality as means of seduction, but with time it leads her to an enclosed
world of solitude and objectification with no easy way out.

Susan Stringer has looked at the images of women in works written by
African men, on the one hand, and more particularly at the images of men
in Senegalese novels by women, on the other, and provides a summary set
of categories of female and male roles as seen by both sexes.[32] With some
rare exceptions, both seem to portray the protagonists of the opposite sex as
stereotypes and flat characters. Mbaye Biléoma's depictions of the sister-

---

[29] Bugul, *Riwan ou le chemin de sable*, 150–51. [...] the wives of our chiefs dress in
foreign clothing that costs a fortune, clothes that are not made by us, jewellery that was
not made by us. Let us give our craftsmen work and promote their work beyond the
folkloric circles, which are of no use and only allow others to copy and shamelessly imi-
tate our creations.

[30] Bugul, *Riwan ou le chemin de sable*, 151.

[31] Bugul, *Cendres et braises*, 64. Nous osions nous habiller comme nous le sentions.
La peau noire ne se cachait plus, elle était un atout.

[32] Stringer, *The Senegalese Novel by Women: Through Their Own Eyes*, 148–51.

hood of the village women, on the one hand, and the *Sërin* and his exuberant charisma, on the other, are much more profound than her characters –
both male and female – in Belgium or France, and form an important contribution to Ken's affirmation of self. With gender as a defining element,
she makes a sweet memory out of her childhood, during which she is
constantly in the presence of women, surrounded by their beauty and their
sensual, perfumed bodies; or she remembers how she enjoyed sharing the
hardship of work with the women of the village, tasks that are summarized
by one word: endurance. These memories are then extended into a celebration of African womanhood, which is characterized by the "healing
African village," whose women provide protection through warm sisterhood. Sensuality is the key word in this context: as one of the wives of the
Sërin, Ken witnesses various forms of expressions of female sensuality,
though it can be debated whether, at times, it may also be regarded as a
translation of sexual frustration among the multiple co-wives who share
one husband. *Riwan ou le chemin de sable* describes how women channel
their sexuality among themselves; the behaviour of one character, Bousso
Niang, in particular, shows exemplary transgressiveness in her freedom – in
more than one sense – because she belongs to the caste of blacksmiths and
is not tied to the *Sërin* by marriage or by familial bonds. She excites the
Sërin's co-wives by her sensual and even vulgar dances. Ken describes her
as someone who dared to say and do everything, and because she is the
only woman who is allowed to leave the compound, Bousso Niang also
serves as an important link to the outside world. Her sensuality and eroti-
cism excite the wives, who are "dressed up like Senegalese dolls" and who,
in the secrecy of the night, "engage in even more vicious dances"[33] among
themselves, which lead to pleasures that help them channel their sexual
needs. The whole compound vibrates with the presence of women, which
also embodies a latently homosexual subtext in the narrative. The beauty
and sensuality of the Western women that Ken encounters never receive
similar applause. It can also be suggested that a male writer would not
easily have access to the aspirations of the group of co-wives or even the
imagination to describe them in such detail, even though the attitude to
sexuality and gender in traditional Senegalese society has been explored in
depth, for instance, by Senegalese film directors. One of the latest examples

---

[33] Bugul, *Riwan ou le chemin de sable,* 88–89. […] parées comme des poupées séné-
galaises […] qui s'adonnassent à des danses plus vicieuses […].

that could be compared to Bousso Niang's self-inflicted autonomy and agency is Joseph Kaï Ramaka's film *Karmen Geï*, an adaptation *à la séné-galaise* of Prosper Mérimée's text, perhaps most famously known from Bizet's opera.[34] Ramaka's film is a complex and complete re-interpretation of the main character, Karmen, whose Amazonian presence and almost mythic heroism is expressed through her sexuality and through ways in which she "transgresses gender constructions and expresses sexual libera-tion in its full potential."[35] Similarly, Mbaye Biléoma's novels are linked to the Senegalese tradition of depicting strong women, who take matters into their own hands and transmit traditional values that demonstrate sometimes surprising forms of freedom and, more importantly, expressions of femin-ine agency. The importance of this agency is summarized by the author:

> Other women's role in the village and in the polygamous marriage was to help me become aware of my individuality and rely on it and they taught me also how to get rid of jealousy. Even without poly-gamy my rehabilitation would have been total but without the pres-ence of other women the problem of the individual would have remained.[36]

The memories of the warm presence of women reinforce Ken's own sense of belonging; the role of these memories can be regarded as a counter-image to the overwhelming solitude that she goes through in Europe, where her female friends remain somewhat two-dimensional char-acters. This sisterhood encompassed in the lives of the women of the com-pound also includes the other side of the medal – a sense of competition between the co-wives. From an early age, girls learn methods of seduction taught to them by their elders, and when the time comes, they go through the traditional test of *xaxar*;[37] it is a ritual imposed on the latest arrived wife to test whether the polygamous ménage in her case is to last or not:

> *Xaxar* is a procedure that no longer exists, the new generation does not know what it is. It's an extraordinary tradition that requires

---

[34] Joseph Gaï Ramaka, *Karmen Geï* (Senegal: 2001; D V D: Kine Video, 2005).

[35] Ramaka, *Karmen Geï*, interview with Dr Joanna Grabski (23 November 2004).

[36] Personal interview with Mariétou Mbaye Biléoma (Dakar, Senegal, 20 December 2006).

[37] *Xaxar* (Wolof): the welcoming ritual of the newly wed by making her the target of insulting gossip.

creative genius. You would ask for a specialist in *xaxar* to come to
the proceedings: they are the kind of *griots* and *griottes* who do
research on the family, they look for the weak spot in the family,
they can even physically tie the bride to embarrass her and to break
her pride and vanity. And the next day you exchange your good
mornings and how are yous again. With this procedure you remove
the potential ideas of rivalry, and it leaves no room for discordance.
Everything is fine. And if you ask me, that's the best polygamous
ménage, that's how our parents lived![38]

Rama, a character whose detachment from the family and marriage to
the *Sërin̄* are described in great detail, brings a critical perspective to the
polygamous tradition in *Riwan ou le chemin de sable*. The example of
Rama shows the disappointment of a young girl who is given to the *Sërin̄*
and who, as a freshly wedded wife, obtains frequent attention from him, but
who eventually has to make way for potential and even likely newcomers,
and adapt to the codes of polygamy. At the end of the novel, Rama is
revealed to be a merely symbolic character – to some extent we may say
she is another alter ego of Ken – who has been introduced in the story to
represent all those young girls whose lives are bound to the *Sërin̄*. A rather
mystical curtain falls over the life of Rama, who later escapes from the
compound. Ken wonders: "Escape from the *Sërin̄*? The *Sërin̄*, who opened
the gates of Paradise?"[39] No answers are given to these questions, because
Rama's return to her home village late at night ends in a cathartic fire,
leaving no trace of her, her parents, or their house. A complete silence follows, insinuating that Rama symbolizes more generally that strong sense of
shame that befalls a failed marriage, a failed commitment to a *Sërin̄*, and
fear of dishonour falling upon the family. As a character in a story, Rama is
perhaps the most harmonious among the numerous female figures, who are
all only briefly introduced in the novel. Her story serves as a critical device
to illustrate, on the one hand, how difficult it may be to accept a polygamous ménage, and, on the other, how hard it can be to walk out of it and
break the disciple–wife dependency.

---

[38] Personal interview with Mariétou Mbaye Biléoma (Dakar, Senegal, 20 December
2006).

[39] Bugul, *Riwan ou le chemin de sable*, 221. S'enfuir de chez le Serigne? Le Serigne
qui ouvrait les portes du Paradis?

III

Mbye B. Cham's general overview of the Senegalese artists' creative response to Islam suggests that they are more prominent and influential in Senegal than perhaps anywhere else in sub-Saharan Africa.[40] While Mbye B. Cham's survey concentrates primarily on the works of Cheik Hamidou Kane, Aminata Sow Fall, and Amar Samb, and on the filmmakers Mahama Traoré and the iconic Ousmane Sembène, his categorizations help locate each artist in the creative spectrum between advocacy of religious ideals and denunciation of the abuse of Islamic institutions and principles. Whatever the stance of the individual artist, one key character in their work is unavoidably always present: the *Sëriñ*. He is, as Cham puts it, "the most pious earthly symbol of Islam."[41] His devoutness is, of course, not only venerated but also ridiculed – for instance, in Wolof satirical narratives, which "temporarily rob this sacred figure of certain trappings of sanctity, reduc[ing] him to the level of an ordinary mortal person."[42] Abdoulaye Berte divides the marabouts into two categories, the regular and the secular, the former enforcing strict observation of Qur'anic law, the latter designating leaders who choose to "live in their time, in the world, outside of major religious constraints."[43] It is a little surprising that, given the title of his essay, it looks only at male novelists, but let us not be disturbed by the somewhat overlapping nature of his categories; clearly, the *Sëriñ* portrayed in *Cendres et braises* and *Riwan ou le chemin de sable* has features from both of them. Mbaye Biléoma's talent is articulated in a most subtle way when she describes the *Sëriñ* as a person exercising his powers on both Ken and on the other members of his religious associations – here the marabout is not a healer or a man who solves no matter what problem with or without the help of a *gris-gris* (amulet), nor is he a manifestly fanatical exploiter of the people. The development of their relationship into love, not only in the spiritual but also in the more carnal form, is depicted with tact:

---

[40] Mbye B. Cham, "Islam in Senegalese Literature and Film," *Journal of the International African Institute* 55.4 (1985): 1.

[41] Cham, "Islam In Senegalese Literature And Film," 3.

[42] "Islam In Senegalese Literature And Film," 19.

[43] Abdoulaye Berte, "L'Image du marabout dans le roman négro-africain francophone," *Éthiopiques* 66–67 (2001): np.

Elle avait usé des meilleures techniques de massage de son
répertoire acquis depuis mais, dès qu'elle commençait, le Serigne
s'endormait en ronflant légèrement. Elle interrogeait alors ses yeux
fermés, sa bouche légèrement entrouverte, ses grandes et belles
mains, sans réponse hélas. Elle continuait à remplir son devoir
d'épouse à un Serigne, en espérant un autre paradis, s'il en existait.[44]

In the above passage, the privacy of the *Sërin*'s more intimate life is
exposed in its more unpleasant form; Rama, who is giving a massage here
to the snoring *Sërin*, displays the wiles of a young girl who has to make her
expectations of the marriage adapt to the realities of being a co-wife and
sharing her husband with many. The above example demonstrates that even
in the presence of the *Sërin* you can be rejected and feel abandoned, if or
when the *Sërin* loses interest in you. Rama, whose exuberant beauty is
depicted in great detail in the novel, exemplifies the tragedy that lies in the
fact that suddenly, at the time when she is blossoming, the *Sërin* has
forgotten her, for whatever reason. This is as far as Mbaye Biléoma's critique on the *Sërin* really goes. As we saw above, the Senegalese novel practically never criticizes the Mouride founder Amadou Bamba, and in the
same way Ken's *Sërin*, one of the critical figures in her itinerary, remains
after all a rather distant and almost sacred personage. Already in *Cendres et
braises*, where the only direct reference to the venerated founder of the
brotherhood appears, the *Sërin* is described as "this man who was the hope
of thousands of people, reaching across the oceans, a descendant of Cheikh
Amadou Bamba."[45] Ken further describes how the charisma of the *Sërin*
reaches everybody in the village: little girls follow the example of their
mothers very early on by almost auto-suggestively putting their sensuality
on display for him; mothers – including Ken's own mother – have no other
option than to consent to his marriage proposals, because "you don't refuse
the *Sërin* anything" and "no, you don't count the *Sërin*'s wives."[46] Among

---

[44] Bugul, *Riwan ou le chemin de sable*, 139–40. She had used the best massage techniques in her repertoire that she had ever since acquired, but as soon as she started, the
Sërin fell asleep, snoring lightly. She then studied his closed eyes, his mouth slightly
open, his beautiful big hands, but without any response. She continued to fulfil her duty
as a wife submitting to a Serigne, hoping for another paradise, if such a thing existed.
[45] Bugul, *Cendres et braises*, 54. […] cet homme qui était espoir de milliers de per-
sonnes jusqu'au-delà des océans, descendant de Cheikh Ahmadou Bamba.
[46] Bugul, *Riwan ou le chemin de sable*, 152–53. On ne refusait rien au Serigne […].
Non, on ne comptait pas les épouses du Serigne.

the wives, there are also those who never have the honour or pleasure of spending the night with the *Sëriñ*. This, according to Ken, is an unarguable part of *ndigal*, the central concept of Mouridism, according to which only submission to the *Sëriñ* counts, and "once a woman was submitted to the *Sëriñ*, a choice of life had been carried out for her and this choice also implied the silence of the senses."[47]

In addition to the *Sëriñ*, *Riwan ou le chemin de sable* portrays another male character: the novel opens with a passage in which Ken witnesses how some of the powers of the *Sëriñ* are put to use when Riwan, a somehow disturbed person, is brought before the *Sëriñ*; the latter, by his simple presence, calms Riwan down, who then takes an oath and submits himself to the will of the *Sëriñ*. Riwan is mysterious, living entirely under *ndigal*, and his presence and actions show examples of the gender divide in the village life and demonstrate how submission to the *Sëriñ* is not only a practice for women who are to become the *Sëriñ*'s wives. Ken is puzzled by the nature of Riwan's absolute submission, illustrated by the fact that he never looks up at the wives of the *Sëriñ*: he recognizes individual wives only by the timbre of their voice. The extent of his spirituality is expressed through his apparent lack of sexual desire. Riwan is a *bëgg-néeg*,[48] the most loyal disciple of the *Sëriñ*, and expresses *ndigal* through all his actions. Indeed, *ndigal* is a very personal choice, and Ken seems to suggest that such degrees of loyalty and spirituality can be reached not only by male *taalibés* (disciples) but also by women like her. As much as Riwan's acts exemplify the embodiment of respect for the practices that organize the Mouride way of life, and fear of failing it, Ken also speculates about Riwan's total submission to the *Sëriñ* by asking what would happen if Riwan were a woman. In other words: Ken *is* Riwan, and Ken's question motivates us to consider further how gender may affect the relationship between the *Sëriñ* and his closest disciple. Although Ken is not considered the *Sëriñ*'s closest disciple in the novel, neither is she the conventional wife among the co-wives; the reconciliatory nature of her marriage to the *Sëriñ* suggests that, for Ken, in terms of spirituality, it reaches a degree as high as that of a *bëgg-néeg*. At the same

---

[47] Bugul, *Riwan ou le chemin de sable*, 135. Quand une femme était remise à un Serigne on lui avait fait un choix de vie. Et ce choix impliquait aussi le silence des sens. — *Ndigal* (Wolof) literally means 'order, directive, instruction, recommendation, piece of advice'.

[48] *Bëgg-néeg* (Wolof) = confident of ruling or religious authority.

time, Ken shows that the hierarchical structures of the Sufi brotherhoods can be examined and questioned. Generally, women in the Sufi brotherhoods in Senegal form groups of disciples – most often, though not exclusively, all-female groups – that express their spirituality and their allegiance to their leader in religious associations, *daa'iras*. There are also examples that demonstrate how spiritual leadership within the Sufi brotherhoods is not entirely a monopoly of men, yet these examples of female leaders remain in the margin both in Senegal and in the Senegalese diaspora.[49]

Marriage remains uncompromisingly one of the most important events in the lives of the village members, despite the fact that today, especially in urban Senegal, its importance is becoming more and more questioned. Ken reveals that her plan in life initially was not to marry, and one of the reasons for this, she explains, is the image of the African male, which can hardly be called flattering. Again with echoes from the colonial past, Ken explains how she was taught at school that the men of her own village were:

> De véritables brutes qui passaient leur temps à s'entre-tuer [...] je n'avais pas envie de faire des projets de mariage avec quelqu'un de mon village, ni d'ailleurs, sur mon Continent, surtout pas avec un de ces Dahoméens fétichistes et sanguinaires.[50]

Despite such warnings, Ken does marry a man from her continent. She points out what is involved in the bargain: not only does a woman marry a man but, more importantly, she engages with a mental and moral responsibility, following the example of her mother and all mothers, and from that moment on "life [...] would be what she was going to make of it herself, against all beliefs."[51] Ken's description of the physical side of the relation-

---

[49] Codou Bop, "Roles and the Position of Women in Sufi Brotherhoods in Senegal," *Journal of the American Academy of Religion* 73.4 (December 2005): 1102. Codou Bop points out that gender and class relations in Senegal will change faster through secularism and the promotion of women's political, economic, social, and cultural rights than through the *tariqas*, which do not provide women with the knowledge of Islamic texts that is central to being respected as learned persons.

[50] Bugul, *Riwan ou le chemin de sable*, 39–40. Real brutes, who spent their time killing each other [...]. I didn't feel like planning a marriage with someone from my own village, neither, by the way, from my continent, and certainly not with one of these blood-thirsty fetishistic Dahomeans.

[51] Bugul, *Riwan ou le chemin de sable,* 108. La vie [...] serait ce qu'elle en ferait elle-même, contrairement à ce que l'on croyait.

ship and her marriage consumed with the *Sëriñ* is very graphic, and as such
again demonstrates how much more significance she gives to this relationship than to her promiscuous years in Europe. Her very direct voice and the
ease with which she talks about her sensuality and the female body may
initially have been behind the suggestion of the editor to use a pseudonym
upon the publication of *The Abandoned Baobab*. In *Riwan ou le chemin de
sable*, this explicit style is still present, but now, with the marriage to the
Sëriñ, the tone is different: her experiences are uplifting and we are invited
to follow the process by which she becomes a new person. Ken's 'morning
after' with the *Sëriñ* is filled with an ecstatic poem that immortalizes this
moment in her life:

> Adja, tu étais là.
> Adja, tu allas.
> Adja, hélas, tu allas.
> Adja, tu allas, hélas.
> Hélas, Adja, allas.[52]

Adja, who is Ken's nephew, happens to witness Ken's joy that particular
morning, and the poem's highly connotative style here stresses the importance of the moment. In my reading, it advocates a sense of freedom that is
almost transgressive; Ken is using one of the Sufi elements to her purposes
and demonstrates flexibility and informality in expression by complement-
ing in this way the common prayer practices of the Sufi way of life. She
recites her very own *wird*, an arrangement of standard litanies or repeated
formulae that is usually given to the disciple by his or her sheikh, to be
regularly recited in specific circumstances.[53] Ken's prayer-like poem invites the reader to comprehend the extent to which this moment of great
intensity – measured against her years in Europe – is something that had
long been lacking in her life. Moreover, she contrasts this ecstatic feeling
with her earlier experiences of intimate encounters with men, which she

---

[52] Bugul, *Riwan ou le chemin de sable*, 165. Note: It is pointless to translate this poem
because its significance resides not in its literal content in French but in the phonetic
content produced when recited aloud. The verb form *allas* phonetically evokes God
(*Allah* in Arabic).

[53] *Wird* (Arabic) is a composition of pious recitations specific to each brotherhood.
See Lamin O. Sanneh, *The Crown and the Turban: Muslims and West African Pluralism*
(Boulder CO: Westview, 1997).

sees, on the one hand, as too rational and exteriorized and, on the other, as
wholly pretentious and banal:

> Tout ce que j'avais connu, c'était l'amour discuté, expliqué, analysé,
> planifié [...] Et combien de fois j'avais joué au jeu de la jouissance,
> comme des milliers de femmes, qui, comme moi, jouaient aux
> femmes émancipées, aux femmes modernes.[54]

Mbaye Biléoma does not explicitly refer here to Western women, yet the
target of her 'modern woman' sarcasms is clear. Now, as a returnee and a
soxhna, with the reconciliatory blessing provided by the *Sëriñ,* her life is
reconnected with the past, for so long lost during the disorderly and drifting
years spent in Europe:

> Je guérissais comme d'une longue et douloureuse plaie intérieure
> [...]. Ainsi le Serigne m'avait offert et donné la possibilité de me
> réconcilier avec moi-même, avec mon milieu, avec mes origines [...]
> avec mon monde sans lesquels je ne pourrais jamais survivre.
> J'avais échappé à la mort de mon moi, de ce moi qui n'était pas à
> moi toute seule. De ce moi qui appartenait aussi aux miens, à ma
> race, à mon peuple, à mon village et à mon continent.[55]

Ken is weighing her choice of marriage against her earlier desperate
hopes of resembling her contemporaries and becoming a 'modern woman'
living a monogamous life. These hopes were never met when she lived as a
mistress to a married man in Paris, where "the men married a woman, had
mistresses and lived in continuous infidelity" whereas in Senegal "the
[polygamous] marriage sorted out such situations."[56] She is not even sure if

---

[54] Bugul, *Riwan ou le chemin de sable,* 165. All I had known was love discussed, explained, analyzed, planned [...]. And how many times had I played the game of orgasm,
like thousands of other women who, like me, pretended to be emancipated women, modern women.

[55] Bugul, *Riwan ou le chemin de sable,* 167–68. It was as if I were healing from a long
and painful interior wound [...]. This is how the *Sëriñ* had offered and given me the
possibility to be reconciled to myself, to my surroundings, to my origins [...] to my
world, without which I would never survive. I had escaped the death of my self, this self
that did not belong to me only. This part of me that belonged also to my own people, my
race, my village, and my continent.

[56] Bugul, *Cendres et braises,* 79. [...] les hommes ici épousaient une femme, avaient
des maîtresses et vivaient dans l'infidélité permanente [...] dans mon pays le mariage
arrangeait ces situations.

she had been true to herself in the first place with her hopes of a monogamous relationship, and her hesitation only adds to the frankness of her
voice throughout her memories. Her critique goes on to undermine the life-
style of a 'Français moyen' that she had observed in the Parisian suburbs.
She sees the average Frenchmen's attempts at being bourgeois as ridi-
culous; the ever-present compulsive urge to be individual is watered down
in mass behaviour, everything comes in series. Women make housekeeping
their life's objective and, year in year out, everybody eats "the same old
tasteless, shapeless steak."[57]

In my view, these first three novels – if we are to look at their narratives
as a whole – also articulate a response, particularly so in *Riwan ou le
chemin de sable*, to potential arguments against polygamy and against the
choices Ken made. In Mbaye Biléoma's own words, after having written
Riwan ou le chemin de sable, she was accused of "putting African women
fifty years back in time."[58] In this light, I consider Obioma Nnaemeka's
study of some of the misinterpretations of Mariama Bâ's novel to be useful
for the focus of this article.[59] Obioma Nnaemeka considers polygamy in
Bâ's work to be a "cultural hemorrhage," a phenomenon in which the existing feminist criticism has failed to capture the different voices that Bâ's
novel develops on polygamy. She argues:

> It is troubling, but understandable that feminism which has made the
> issue of 'choice' the centrepiece of its theorizing and activism is
> reluctant to factor the same issue in its analysis of African women's
> lives.[60]

Ken looks at village life from her own female perspective – and her gaze
may be even sharper, given the fact that she has been away for a long time
– and presents different female voices that show distinct facets of poly-

---

[57] Bugul, *Cendres et braises*, 84. […] l'éternel steak sans goût, sans forme.

[58] Personal interview with Mariétou Mbaye Biléoma (Dakar, Senegal, 20 December
2006).

[59] Obioma Nnaemeka, "Urban Spaces, Women's Places: Polygamy as Sign in Mariama Bâ's Novels," in *The Politics of (M)Othering: Womanhood, Identity, and Resistance in African Literature*, ed. Obioma Nnaemeka (London & New York: Routledge,
1997); Mariama Bâ, *So Long A Letter*, tr. Modupé Bodé–Thomas (*Une si longue lettre*;
Dakar & Abidjan & Lomé: NEA, 1979; tr. London: Virago, 1982).

[60] Nnaemeka, "Urban Spaces, Women's Places: Polygamy As Sign In Mariama Bâ's
Novels," 167.

gamy, not simply as something that dehumanizes all these women who share one man but also as something valuable. Ken realizes that her marriage to the *Sëriñ* has given her a new opportunity to live her life differently, to concentrate more on herself and others and to create new passions in her life – writing included – instead of waiting for "a man to take hold of [her] existence."[61] Undoubtedly, her novels indicate how post-independent Senegal is booming with a generation of young people who are willing, and many of whom are also able, to become *évolués*. When Ken narrates her experiences of Europe, this is shown in the light of a *lack* of true choices for women, who compress themselves into the same mould of a 'modern woman'. To summarize, Mbaye Biléoma asks: How is this 'modern woman' a choice?

IV

After her first three novels, Mbaye Biléoma moves on to other themes, in which she distances the key characters from herself, yet she does not seem to move too far from what is familiar to her from her own life experiences. Her later narratives, in general, are less concerned with Europe, and she not only lends more importance to the memory of Senegal and her home village but allows herself an even more imaginative pen; for instance, *La Folie et la mort* is almost an epic description of the decay of the independent African countries, and further on, in *Rue Félix Faure*, she concentrates on more specific difficulties that women face in the urban setting of today's Dakar.[62] Likewise, in her most recent novel, *La Pièce d'or*, the narrative focuses on contemporary Senegalese society, which mirrors the status quo of the whole continent and in which the presence of Europe and the legacy of colonialism are obliquely echoed through her critique of corruption and the broken promises made by the post-independence elite.[63] What is crucial to the work of Mbaye Biléoma is the fact that, whatever narrative setting she uses, she gives a voice to women. It is first and foremost through her very own alter ego – Ken – and later also through the insights of other

---

[61] Bugul, *Riwan ou le chemin de sable*, 200–201. ([…] qu'un homme vînt s'emparer de mon existence.

[62] Ken Bugul, *La Folie et la mort* (Paris & Dakar: Présence Africaine, 2000). *Rue Félix-Faure* (Paris: Hoëbeke, 2005).

[63] Ken Bugul, *La Pièce d'or* (Paris: UBU, 2006).

female characters, that she deploys the agency of the African woman, or, as some of her examples show, the lack of it. For Ken, the 'healing elements' of the African village in her long itinerary from Senegal to European metropoles and back embody a rich gallery of village personages, who assume key roles in the juxtaposition of traditional society and the 'stayees' with Ken as a 'returnee'. On the other hand, the Western characters in these three novels, when compared to their African counterparts, lack dimension and their roles are diminished against the charisma of the *Sërin* and the vibrant sisterhood provided by the presence of the African women in Ken's memories. The significance of marriage to Ken and to her fellow country-women is at the centre of all these stories, and the social roles connected to marriage in a Senegalese Mouride community reveal how a traditional soci-ety is able to demonstrate some of its practices in flexible terms. These practices organize the world, and the fact that Ken felt she had abandoned that world and was excluded from it for many years of exile in Europe only intensifies her attachment to it when she returns. What did eventually make sense to Ken was that, even if first rejected by her own, she was re-inserted into the community by the *Sërin*:

> The role of the *Sërin* was to recuperate the widows; you could attach
> yourself to the *Sërin and then move on*; so some of the women were
> only temporarily in the concession; it was often very young widows
> or sterile women.[64]

What is noteworthy here is the fact that the submission to the *Sërin* is not viewed in the narrowest possible way only as an abusive practice – the tradition apparently does resolve Ken's dilemma. *Riwan ou le chemin de sable* demonstrates that, in her case, finding a sense of belonging in the village was a process eased not only by the *Sërin* but also by other women, who have an active and even crucial role in Ken's affirmation of coherent subjectivity. If Julia Watson, in her analysis of *The Abandoned Baobab*, can point out that Ken was "exiled from both the traditional African and the modern European worlds, without a habitable social place,"[65] *Riwan ou le*

---

[64] Personal interview with Mariétou Mbaye Biléoma (Dakar, Senegal, 20 December 2006), my emphasis.
[65] Watson, "Self-Decolonization and Bodily Re-Membering in Ken Bugul's *The Abandoned Baobab*," 144.

chemin de sable seems to prove otherwise and this, in my view, is what gives a unique voice and perspective to the novel.

The assertiveness in the construction of Ken's identity is briefly revisited when Mbaye Biléoma returns to the topic in her story "La Femme du gouverneur."[66] The heart-warming reminiscences of her childhood reveal her very first encounter with a white woman in her village, and here again it is tradition that defines the nature of the event: in the skull-boiling heat of the day she finds a white woman standing under a tamarind tree, smiling at her. Under no circumstances would a local stay under this tree, because it is considered one of the devil's predilections. Frightened by this sight, Mbaye Biléoma runs away, convinced that she has seen a glimpse of the devil's wife, and she now reminds us: *"Where I come from, the devil was white."*[67] The gravity of the moment is then articulated in her later profound desire to resemble that white woman, and the short story takes us back to all the decades from the 1960s onwards to show the evolution of Western (French) femininity and all those laborious measures that her female compatriots – *évoluées* and 'stayees' alike – would take to achieve the most recent ideals of beauty. Ken walked out of these clichés by returning to her home village, where she was able to open alternative possibilities for life as a *soxhna*. In this story, the author walks out of the same clichés again by closing on an affirmative note: "I no longer wanted to be the wife of the white devil. I wanted to be the wife of the black devil. I wanted to be myself."[68]

One of the objectives of this essay has, I trust, been met by my demonstrating how Mbaye Biléoma engages the reader in actively understanding the complexities of gender dynamics attached to traditional Senegalese culture, and how they are constructed. Ken's return is presented in connection with a society which is organized by a set of traditions that is able to 'save' her. Even if the example of Ken seems an isolated case, her rejection of the alternatives available for women in Europe undermines the admiration for the behaviour and attitudes of the *évoluées*, on the one hand, and the *'métro-boulot-dodo'* life-style – a common reality for all lower-class

---

[66] Ken Bugul, "La Femme du gouverneur," in *L'Europe, vues d'Afrique* (Paris & Bamako: Le Cavalier Bleu / Le Figuier, 2004): 123–36.

[67] Bugul, "La Femme du gouverneur," 127. *Chez nous, le diable était blanc.*

[68] Bugul, "La Femme du gouverneur," 136. Je ne voulais plus être la femme du diable blanc. Je voulais être la femme du diable noir. Je voulais être moi-même.

members of society in the Western metropolis – on the other. Mbaye Biléoma is highly critical of the phenomena connected with the image of the
évoluées in Senegal, and she shows how tradition can provide a high social
status without the elements that she regards as a burden for the 'modern
woman'. As we saw above, Ken's identity-formation is strongly connected
with reflections on her Senegalese origins and memories triggered by her
exilic experiences. Although the binary dichotomy of African village/Euro-
pean metropolis is very much present, a certain balance can be observed in
Biléoma's critique: the often nostalgic views of the African village are disrupted by problematizing gender hierarchies and male dominance in the
everyday life of the *Sërin* and his disciples. It would also be interesting to
explore further whether and how her more recent novels *Rue Félix Faure*
and *La Pièce d'or* open up new configurations of Senegalese society, so
ordered by religion and *ndigal*. For instance, her views with regard to Islam
in Africa in *Rue Félix Faure* point to a clear distinction that she wants to
make between the faith of the people and questionable intermediaries who
promote Islam with hidden and abusive agendas. *Rue Félix-Faure* repeatedly reminds the reader that God is in people's minds and prayers all the time,
despite the attempts of what the author calls "false gurus and *moqaddems*"
to make everyone follow their way.

WORKS CITED

Aidoo, Ama Ata. *Our Sister Killjoy* (New York: Longman, 2004).
Atakpama, Gnimdéwa. "*Rue Félix-Faure* de Ken Bugul," *Amina* 422 (June 2005):
    86–87.
Bâ, Mariama. *So Long A Letter*, tr. Modupé Bodé–Thomas (*Une Si longue lettre*;
    Dakar & Abidjan & Lomé: NEA, 1979; tr. London: Virago, 1982).
Bangura, Ahmed S. *Islam and the West African Novel: the Politics of Represen-
    tation* (Boulder CO & London: Lynne Rienner, 2000).
Berte, Abdoulaye. "L'Image du marabout dans le roman négro-africain franco-
    phone," *Ethiopiques* 66–67 (2001), online: http://www.refer.sn/ethiopiques /article
    .php3?id_article=1283 (accessed 21 November 2006).
Bop, Codou. "Roles and the Position of Women in Sufi Brotherhoods in Senegal,"
    Journal of the American Academy of Religion 73.4 (December 2005): 1101–1109.
Boyd–Buggs, Debra. "Mouridism In Senegalese Fiction," in *Faces of Islam in
    African Literature*, ed. Kenneth W. Harrow (Portsmouth NH: Heinemann; Lon-
    don: James Currey, 1991): 201–14.
Bugul, Ken. *Cendres et braises* (Paris: L'Harmattan, 1994).

——. "La Femme du gouverneur," in *L'Europe, vues d'Afrique: Nouvelles* (Paris & Bamako: Le Cavalier Bleu/Le Figuier, 2004): 123–36.

——. *La Folie et la mort* (Paris & Dakar: Présence Africaine, 2000).

——. *La Pièce d'or* (Paris: UBU, 2006).

——. *Le Baobab fou* (Dakar: NEA, 1997).

——. *Riwan ou le chemin de sable* (Paris & Dakar: Présence Africaine, 1999).

——. *Rue Félix-Faure* (Paris: Hoëbeke, 2005).

——. *The Abandoned Baobab: The Autobiography of a Senegalese Woman*, tr. Marjolijn de Jager (*Le Baobab fou*, 1984; tr. New York: Lawrence Hill, 1991).

Cham, Mbye B. "Islam in Senegalese Literature and Film," *Journal of the International African Institute* 55.4 (1985): 447–64.

Cruise O'Brien, Donal B. *The Mourides of Senegal: The Political and Economic Organization of an Islamic Brotherhood* (Oxford: Clarendon, 1971).

Diome, Fatou. *Le Ventre de l'Atlantique* (Paris: Anne Carrière, 2003).

Fal, Arame, Rosine Santos & Jean Léonce Doneux, ed. *Dictionnaire wolof–français* (Paris: Karthala, 1990).

Harrow, Kenneth W. "The Poetics of African *Littérature de Témoignage*," in *African Literature Studies: The Present State*, ed. Stephen Arnold (Washington DC: Three Continents, 1985): 135–49.

Malcolmson, Scott L. "West Of Eden," *Transition* 71 (1996): 26–45.

Nge, Carmen. "The Return of the 'Native': Visualizing Place and Narrative Homecoming" (doctoral dissertation, Brandeis University, 2004).

Nnaemeka, Obioma. "Urban Spaces, Women's Places: Polygamy as Sign in Mariama Bâ's Novels," in *The Politics of (M)Othering: Womanhood, Identity, and Resistance in African Literature*, ed. Obioma Nnaemeka (London & New York: Routledge, 1997): 162–91.

Ramaka, Joseph Gaï. *Karmen Geï* (Senegal: 2001; DVD: Kine Video, 2005).

Salih, Tayeb. *Season of Migration to the North* (Harmondsworth: Penguin, 2003).

Sanneh, Lamin O. *The Crown and the Turban: Muslims and West African Pluralism* (Boulder CO: Westview, 1997).

Stringer, Susan. *The Senegalese Novel By Women: Through Their Own Eyes* (New York: Peter Lang, 1996).

Watson, Julia. "Self-Decolonization and Bodily Re-Membering in Ken Bugul's *The Abandoned Baobab*," in *Writing New Identities: Gender, Nation And Immigration In Contemporary Europe*, ed. Gisela Brinker–Gabler & Sidonie Smith (Minneapolis & London: U of Minnesota P, 1997): 143–67.

◁▷

"France, effaced but venerated"[1]

– ◇ – Marie Cardinal's *Au pays de mes racines*

ANN-SOFIE PERSSON

I

MARIE CARDINAL (1929–2001) was born into a wealthy family of French settlers in Algeria and raised both on the farm which had been in the family for generations and in the city of Algiers. She later lived in Europe (Greece, Portugal, Austria, and France) and North America (Quebec), but she always considered Algeria her place of origin, despite the distance imposed by the Algerian war of independence. After twenty-four years of absence, she decides to make a trip to Algeria, returning, in a sense, to her country. The thoughts and preparations preceding the trip, the stay in Algeria itself, and the period immediately following it are recorded in an autobiographical narrative in the form of a journal, kept between 29 April and 7 June 1978,[2] and published under the title *Au pays de mes racines* (1980).[3] In this journal, the colonization of Algeria by France starting in 1830, the Algerian war of independence (1954–62), and the departure of the descendants of the French settlers,

---

[1] Marie Cardinal, *Au pays de mes racines suivi de Au pays de Moussia par Bénédicte Ronfard* (Paris: Grasset & Fasquelle, 1980): 13. All English translations of this work are mine. The original is: "la France, effacée mais vénérée."

[2] The Cardinal family left Algeria in 1954, thus the year of Cardinal's return would be 1978, but no date is given inside the text.

[3] *Au pays de mes racines* could be translated either as 'In the country of my roots' or 'To the country of my roots', since the French original can express the fact of being in the country as well as the fact of going there.

known as *pieds-noirs*, are omnipresent events. Cardinal's narrative illustrates how the *pied-noir* identity is constructed as both French and Algerian, and at the same time as neither. Eventually, it becomes evident to the reader of *Au pays de mes racines* that Cardinal identifies with Algeria more than with France. Given the author's way of inscribing herself in the context of Algeria as the homeland, although she belongs to the settler community, it seems appropriate to say that through Cardinal, Africa is writing Europe. It is certainly a different Africa from that of a writer of Arab origin, but it is also an entirely different version of Europe from one written by a French writer born and raised in France. This study will focus on the images of France as representative of Europe, as opposed to Africa, offered by Cardinal in *Au pays de mes racines*. The techniques or the themes that will receive particular attention in the investigation of how Cardinal constructs an image of Europe are the use of contrasting images of Africa and Europe, the child's perspective as a pupil of the colonial school, hierarchical patterns, the idea of being French and Algerian, and that of being a woman and a feminist.

I

When Cardinal constructs an image of France, Algeria is often used as a contrast which in turn tells us what France is not. The representation of Africa, in itself very interesting, will here be studied only as a different manner of writing Europe. In the opening pages of *Au pays de mes racines*, we find an attempt to define the meaning of living in and outside of Algeria. Since Cardinal was living in France when writing the book and has mainly lived in different places in Europe, one can probably conclude that when she talks of what life is like outside Algeria, she is referring to European countries. The European way of life is described in the following manner:

> Vivre ailleurs que là a changé pour moi le sens du mot vivre. Vivre ailleurs est devenu synonyme de besogner ma vie, organiser ma vie, structurer ma vie, prévoir ma vie.
> (Living elsewhere has changed the meaning of the word to live for me. Living elsewhere has become synonymous with working with my life, organizing my life, structuring my life, planning my life).[4]

---

[4] Cardinal, *Au pays de mes racines*, 6.

The words used are all associated with activity, but in the sense of excessive control and incapacity to enjoy life unconditionally. Living in Algeria is described as a fundamental kind of being, of seizing the moment, of belonging and being a part of a cosmic whole. Her present life in France is governed by binary oppositions, by rules, by research, by Western values about knowledge:

> Désormais une vie conforme aux manuels de psychologie, de physiologie, de sociologie. Heureuse–malheureuse. Agréable– désagréable. Passionnée–ennuyeuse. Violente–douce. Comme une vie d'humaine homologue.
> (From now on a life in accordance with textbooks in psychology, physiology, sociology. Happy–unhappy. Pleasant–unpleasant. Passionate–boring. Violent–gentle. Like a homologated human life).[5]

The image of Europe is here constructed through elliptical comments on opposing feelings associated with the European way of life, but also through abundant references to the idea of intellectual rules and conformity. Human life must be approved by the authorities. According to Marie–Paule Ha, France is considered "a stifling space regulated by numerable moral, religious and social interdictions."[6]

What Cardinal misses outside Algeria is "la connivence avec un espace, la complicité avec un rythme naturel, la compréhension parfaite des signes colorés, odorants, bruyants" (the connivance with a space, the complicity with a natural rhythm, the perfect understanding of coloured, perfumed, noisy signs).[7] Being able to read signs involving different senses – sight, smell, sound – signifies cultural belonging in the Algerian context. In contrast, the European way of life is described as a total lack of contact with the surrounding world: "Ici je me perds, je m'effiloche, je me dilue, je suis une décalcomanie" (Here I lose myself, I get frayed, I get diluted, I am a decalcomania).[8] The sense of identity is troubled, the self displaying characteristics associated with objects rather than humans: it is frayed just like a

---

[5] *Au pays de mes racines*, 7.

[6] Marie–Paule Ha, "Outre-mer / autre mère: Cardinal and Algeria," *Romance Notes* 36.3 (1996): 317.

[7] Cardinal, *Au pays de mes racines*, 43. In the French original, one notices the alliteration in /co/ which is partly lost in the English translation, taking away some of the harmony of the life described expressed through form.

[8] Cardinal, *Au pays de mes racines*, 43.

piece of fabric or diluted like a liquid or a powder, hence losing strength, concentration, and structure. The self is lost, replaced by a pale copy.[9] Although the self affirms itself through the syntactical structure with the repetition of "I" at the beginning of each part of the sentence, this affirmation is only valid on the level of grammar and not on any deeper level. France, then, becomes a site of illusory selfhood, of fruitless and reductive imitation.

Just as European life is associated with a lack of unity, Cardinal's own identity is split. This division is presented through contrasting images of Africa and Europe, as an attempt to combine successfully these two different rhythms:

> Ce n'est pas rien de vivre avec, emmêlés au fond de soi, le rythme nonchalant de la sieste algérienne et l'activité besogneuse des début d'après-midi français ; les aubes ensoleillées et fraîches et les petits matins frileux percés du néon des bistrots aveuglés de buée ; les crépuscules qui deviennent rapidement la nuit, juste le temps de laisser les notes d'une flûte de roseau grimper jusqu'aux branches de l'olivier, et les soirées lumineuses de France qui s'étirent longuement, ni jour ni nuit, dans les bavardages avec les commerçants, sur les terrasses des cafés, comme si la vraie journée commençait là.[10]

Placed within the logic of the division of the day, these opposing images of Algeria and France are largely constructed as an imbalance, with France carrying more negative connotations. French afternoons are filled with uninteresting and tiresome work. French mornings are associated with coldness, raw artificial light, and café windows blinded by moisture. When it comes to French evenings, the words used are more positive than for the other parts of the day, but there is a discomforting feeling of not being able

---

[9] This could be linked to what Édouard Glissant calls the illusion of a successful mimesis in the case of the Antilleans and their assimilation to French society and cultural identity. Glissant, *Le Discours antillais* (Paris: Gallimard, 1981): 41.

[10] Cardinal, *Au pays de mes racines*, 17–18. Living with the careless rhythm of the Algerian siesta and the busy activity of the early French afternoons; the fresh, sunny dawns and the chilly morning hours with the neon lights of the bistros blinded by moisture breaking through; the dusk turning quickly into night, leaving time only for a few notes of a reed flute to climb up the branches of the olive tree, and the bright evenings of France that stretch out for so long, neither day nor night, while one is chatting with the shop keepers, outside the cafés, as if the real day started there; living with all this entangled deep down within, is far from nothing.

to distinguish afternoon from evening. This underlines the narrator's lack of knowledge when it comes to the French cultural codes. Even such an easy thing as knowing what time of day it is, based on the light and the activity performed, becomes difficult in the European context. Europe, which here seems synonymous with Paris or at least a large French city, is a place where time seems artificial, disconnected from nature. The Algerian olive tree is replaced by the neon lights of Parisian cafés. Ha underlines in her study that "the most recurring topos in Cardinal's evocation of her Algerian childhood memories is the Edenic garden which, in opposition to the drab, dreary and sordid Parisian streets, is depicted in highly sensuous and colourful tones."[11] Thanks to these positive descriptions of Algeria, France stands out as even more negative and dull, as a place where things are no longer linked to nature.

This idea of a displaced order of things is also associated with French landscapes, history, and geography. Cardinal explains that she does find France beautiful, but it is not her home. The description of the family trips to France displays this feeling of strangeness:

> Je me souviens, dans mon enfance, quand nous venions en France, les marronniers m'impressionnaient plus que les châteaux et les musées. Je les trouvais raffinés, royaux, civilisés. [...] Les marronniers [...] étaient faits pour des princesses endiamantées jouant aux bergères, pour des courbettes, pour du langage châtié, pour du satin, pour border des allées à carrosses. La campagne française me stupéfiait, tellement elle était verte, tellement elle était faite de petits bouts. Tout cela me frappait et m'ennuyait finalement. Cette mère Patrie, quelle barbe, tout y était bien, même la mauvaise herbe! Il me tardait de rentrer chez moi.[12]

---

[11] Ha, "Outre-mer / autre mère: Cardinal and Algeria," 319.

[12] Cardinal, *Au pays de mes racines*, 97–98. I remember when we went to France in my childhood, I was more impressed by the chestnut trees than by the castles and the museums. I found them refined, royal, civilised. [...] The chestnut trees [...] were made for princesses with their diamonds, playing shepherds, for bows, for polished language, for satin, for lining alleys where coaches passed by. The French countryside amazed me – it was so green, so made out of little pieces. All this struck me and finally annoyed me. This "motherland," what a bore, everything was in its place, even the bad weeds. I was eager to go home.

France is the country of chestnut trees, of fairytales with beautiful princesses. In fact, the sight of these trees throws the child into a pre-1789 France built on court life and royal power. One easily imagines the source of this image of France also to be literary, meaning that the child as a consumer of images of France also becomes a (re)producer of these images in her imagination. France is fascinating and boring at the same time. Perfection, which in France seems to apply even to weeds, is paralyzing. The perspective of the child is used to convey the alternative hierarchies where nature is placed before culture, chestnut trees before castles and museums. The juxtaposition of the terms *mère Patrie* (Motherland) and the familiar expression of *quelle barbe* (what a bore) is quite ironic, since the former implies a serious patriotic relationship between the colonies and France while the latter expresses the child's non-political point of view on France, a boring place that makes her homesick.

The image of French history is built on the personification of History, behaving as a human being, trying to attract everybody's attention: "Il y a son Histoire partout qui fait de l'œil, qui tape du pied, qui hèle, qui gémit, qui parade, qui brouille les reliefs" (Its History is everywhere, making eyes at you, stamping her foot, hailing, groaning, showing off, blurring the outlines).[13] History cannot be ignored in France. Each city, lake or landscape is associated with historical events. By comparison, Algerian history is said to be told or narrated rather than built.

The history of colonization and decolonization can be seen in the representation of the geographical setting of Algeria and its relation to France when Cardinal writes:

> Avant, l'Algérie faisait partie de l'Afrique du Nord, mais l'Afrique du Nord, ce n'était pas l'Afrique. L'Afrique du Nord était reliée à l'Europe par la Méditerranée; la France, c'était la plage d'en face, le drapeau bleu blanc rouge unissait les deux côtes. Aujourd'hui, l'Afrique du Nord est séparée de l'Europe par la Méditerranée!
>
> L'Afrique du Nord était séparée de l'Afrique par le Sahara. Aujourd'hui, l'Afrique du Nord est attachée à l'Afrique par le Sahara.[14]

---

[13] Cardinal, *Au pays de mes racines*, 24.

[14] Cardinal, *Au pays de mes racines*, 194. Before, Algeria was a part of North Africa, but North Africa wasn't Africa. North Africa was linked to Europe by the Mediterranean; France was just the opposite beach, the blue, white and red flag united the two

The limits between what is Africa, what is North Africa, and what is Europe here seem difficult to draw clearly. Water – the Mediterranean Sea – was previously a linking element whereas sand – the Sahara desert – was a dividing one. These two elements now have opposite functions: water creates distance, sand proximity. Interestingly enough, this means that the fluid element so often associated with the female/mother has shifted from that which signifies community, bonding, and safety to the element which signals dividedness, disruption, and insecurity. A particular significance can be assigned to this shift when one is familiar with the role of the mother in Cardinal's life and writings. In *The Words to Say It*, Cardinal explains how, at the age of ten, she heard her mother tell her that she was not wanted, that the mother tried to terminate her pregnancy. This experience is a starting-point for the mental problems Cardinal describes in *The Words to Say It* (1975). The telling of this particular event is also the most obvious link between *Au pays de mes racines* and *The Words to Say It*, since the above-mentioned passage from the earlier text is inserted in the latter.[15] Cardinal seems to be saying that just as her mother refused to offer her love and protection, in fact refusing the role of the mother bestowed upon her, the Algerian war mirrors this personal situation by shutting her out of the place she loves and considers her home. Marie–Paule Ha argues that the "love–hate rapport with the mother is reproduced in Cardinal's relation to the Me(re)tropole, for, in more than one way, the maternal space overlaps

---

coasts. Today, North Africa is separated from Europe by the Mediterranean! North Africa was separated from Africa by the Sahara. Today, North Africa is attached to Africa by the Sahara.

[15] Marie Cardinal, *The Words to Say It* (London: Women's Press, 1983). The order of the sequences has been slightly changed and certain elements are not exactly identical, but since Cardinal herself indicates in *Au pays de mes racines* that she is recycling an earlier text, the reader is invited to read the two texts as one unit. This is also the reason why I consider results presented in studies of *The Words to Say It* to be relevant for my study of *Au pays de mes racines*. Although Cardinal may have published *The Words to Say It* as a novel, several critics have studied it as autobiographical. Françoise Lionnet includes *The Words to Say It* in her book *Autobiographical Voices* and states that Cardinal "[draws] heavily on [her] personal colonial experience but [publishes her work] as [*roman*]." Lionnet, *Autobiographical Voices: Race, Gender, Self-Portraiture* (Ithaca NY: Cornell UP, 1989): 191.

with the me(re)tropolitan space."[16] This further complicates the picture, in that it places Algeria as the alternative mother. The biological mother is dead when Cardinal returns to the country of her roots, where she may instead get a second chance with Algeria, the true mother. France is thus associated with biological but negative motherhood, which in turn is associated with authority.

Following this line of argument, it is logical to find that French geography is shaped by authorities, but other than that of the mother:

> C'est une géographie de pays fertile où la terre est divisée en lopins et où, depuis des siècles, les voies sont indiquées avec autorité afin que les errances n'aillent pas fouler les trésors campagnards des familles qui logent autour de leurs clochers. Multitude de clochers hérissant les vallons, les vallées, les plaines, les montagnes et les côtes.[17]

Cardinal evokes the quilt-like landscape of agricultural Europe, where every piece of land has its rightful owner, where all possible directions are indicated, where all roads lead somewhere, and where church towers function as the thread that holds the quilt together, regardless of the character or the fabric of each individual piece. The positive effect of religion as a cohesive element in the community is undermined when Cardinal opposes this landscape filled with church towers to her country where the minarets are rare, but God is everywhere. Muslim traditions seem more natural, less controlled by human authorities than their Catholic counterparts. The child has already chosen the Muslim paradise, associated with pastries and sweets, instead of the Catholic one:

> Je crois que j'imaginais le paradis d'Allah plein de beignets encore grésillant de friture et de *zlabias* dégoulinant de miel. Tandis que dans l'autre il fallait jouer de la harpe, réciter son chapelet, se tenir

---

[16] Ha, "Outre-mer / autre mère: Cardinal and Algeria," 317. *Mère* means mother, thus the (re) in Me(re)tropole refers to the fact that the biological mother is linked to France as the motherland.

[17] Cardinal, *Au pays de mes racines*, 24. It is a geography of fertile soil where the land is divided into patches and where roads for centuries have been drawn up by the authorities so that wanderers do not trample on the country treasures of families living around their church towers. A multitude of church towers bristling in the small vales, the valleys, the plains, the mountains, and on the coasts.

assise sagement, les genoux serrés, sur des nuages, et ça ne me disait
rien.
(I think that I imagined the paradise of Allah filled with fried dough-
nuts still sizzling and of *zlabias* dripping with honey. Whereas in the
other you had to play the harp, tell your beads, sit quietly, knees
together, on clouds, and that didn't appeal to me)[18]

Pleasure is opposed to duty. Going to the paradise of little French girls is
associated with boring activities and good behaviour. The image of the
French version of paradise appears as an image within another image – that
of France – in turn constructed in opposition to the Algerian version of
paradise.

The text continuously sets up Algeria and France as opposites. Alongside
the images related to meteorological observations, people's activities, history and geography, communication and language as well as bodily perceptions are used to produce conflicting images of France and Algeria. Cardinal's description of the art of conversation dismantles the idea of the French
as masters of conversation:

> Pouvoir laisser s'embrouiller les conversations divaguantes où pas-
> sent les sensations, les émotions, les cris, la peur des esprits, la
> crainte amoureuse de Dieu, l'excitation de l'agora, et les raisonne-
> ments logiques où tout le mot doit couler d'une réflexion pondérée
> et froide, raisonnable, et pour laquelle les sensations sont des tares
> [...] Les mots qui poussent comme de la mauvaise herbe, ceux qui
> poussent comme des betteraves, en rang.[19]

Whereas Algerian conversational practices seem full of chaotic and inspir-
ing energy, French conversation stands out as boring and cold, controlled
by reason and deprived of all feelings. The only advantage of it is that it
pays off, it bears fruit in the image of beetroots growing, but only in strict
rows as opposed to the wild weeds of Algerian words exchanged.[20] This

---

[18] Cardinal, *Au pays de mes racines*, 46.

[19] *Au pays de mes racines*, 18. To be able to allow rambling conversations to become
entangled in feelings, emotions, cries, the fear of spirits, the loving fear of God, the
excitation of the agora, and the logical reasonings where the whole word should flow
from a ponderous and cold reflection, based on reason, and where feelings are a blemish
[...] The words that grow like weeds, those that grow like beetroots, in rows.

[20] Lionnet writes about how Cardinal, in *The Words to Say It*, expresses a fear of writing because of the repressive rules of grammar and the critical eye of the great masters

should of course be compared to the previously analyzed image of France where even weeds are in their place. One could, then, imagine that weeds represent something which grows freely and without complying with rules, and that when France tries to adopt some of the freedom Cardinal places in the Algerian *pied-noir* way of life, it is still submitted to strict lines. This contrasting image of French and Algerian ways of conversing tells us something about how Europe is perceived through an African gaze: human interaction is rigid and dry, especially when compared to African habits.

The same fundamental idea is found when it comes to differences in the perception of the body. Discussion with some Algerian women interested in her writing, during her stay in Algiers, prompts Cardinal to observe their non-European way of moving, which she in turn evokes in the following manner:

> J'ai souvent remarqué que les Occidentaux ont les membres raides, que leurs articulations des hanches et des épaules et surtout celles des coudes et des poignets, sont moins mobiles que celles des autres peuples.
> (I have often noticed that Westerners have stiff limbs, that the articulation of their hips and shoulders and most of all of their elbows and wrists, is less mobile than that of other peoples)[21]

It would seem, then, that stiffness of character goes hand in hand with limited capacity to move the body. People in Europe have bodies that are more restricted in their movements, more mechanical, like their minds. Once again, the image of Europe is conceived in contrast to Africa, which from the comparison acquires greater value. Cardinal again uses contrasting images when describing the body:

> Les pieds nus qui tâtent le visqueux, le poudré, le doux et le pointu, les hanches qui balancent, les poignets et les chevilles qui tournent, les fesses et les seins sous les libres cotonnades qui frôlent... et les

---

and how "she has to learn to let the words flow freely, without regard for grammatical rules or objective reality: the flow of words must mimic the anarchic flow of blood and eventually replace it." Lionnet, *Autobiographical Voices: Race, Gender, Self-Portraiture*, 197–98. When put side by side, I would argue that these two descriptions of Cardinal's attitude towards language reveal complex structures of correspondence between freedom, body and flow.

[21] Cardinal, *Au pays de mes racines*, 157.

chaussures, les bas, les gants, les gaines, les vêtements importants qui cachent le corps, le déforment, et désignent l'état, la condition.[22]

The Algerian body interacts with its surroundings, touching all kinds of surfaces. Different parts of the body move and play active roles in the syntactical segments where they occur: feet touch, hips sway, wrists and ankles turn, buttocks and breasts move freely. Unlike the Algerian body, the French body is never in contact with anything other than clothes. In fact, it never appears in the text. A list of different pieces of clothing is the only way the body is conveyed, through what imprisons it, deforms it, and indicates the social standing of the person wearing them. Even the syntax of the passage expresses the conformity of the French through the monotonous enumeration of pieces of clothing and the punctuation which adds to the impression of imprisonment. Given that the bodies in question are female – we are told that the Algerian bodies have breasts, the French wear stockings and girdles – Cardinal seems to challenge the idea of the North African female body's confinement, underlining the fact that it is French women who are not free when it comes to bodily control. The use of the technique of contrast also says something about Cardinal's France which is never thought of without its link to Algeria, the lens through which Cardinal sees France, the alphabet with which she writes Europe. All these images are the product of the adult narrator's comparison between France and Algeria, made possible by the experience of both. Other images of Europe are constructed from the child's perspective on France, still considered a quite foreign world, since Cardinal did not live there as a child.

II

France as seen through the eyes of the child is closely linked to her experience as a pupil at the colonial school in Algeria. She writes:

Les livres de classe de mon enfance étaient français, faits pour des petits Français vivant en France. Des saisons inconnus les rythmaient de feuilles de houx, de brins de muguet, de chaumières en-

---

[22] Cardinal, *Au pays de mes racines*, 18. The naked feet that touch what is sticky, powdered, soft and pointed, the hips that sway, the wrists and ankles that turn, the buttocks and the breasts brushed by the loose cotton fabrics... and the shoes, the stockings, the gloves, the girdles, the important clothes that hide the body, deform it, and indicate the state, the condition.

neigées, d'écoliers en sabots.... Visions incompréhensibles. Tout
m'était incompréhensible dans ces bouquins, sauf les croisades où
les Français rencontraient les Arabes. Quoique ces derniers, sur les
illustrations, eussent l'air de grands mamamouchis, mais après tout
pourquoi pas puisque les Français, eux, dans leurs armures, avaient
l'air d'obus articulés.[23]

The first sentence in this example defines Frenchness as something that can
only exist on European soil. Elements of botany, inscribed in a system of
seasons and weather foreign to the African context, exotic architecture, and
dress codes – all the classic examples of how the colonial school imposed
French reality upon schoolchildren in the colonies are present. In Lucille
Cairns' words, "French cultural imperialism created a preposterous disjunc-
tion between the nature and the seasons she experienced in real life and
those depicted in schoolbooks."[24] France becomes that which is Other, incomprehensible. The narrator speaks of incomprehensible visions, but how
can one see what is absent, except in the imagination? The characters encountered in this strange land of French textbooks are caricatures of cultural
identity, and in order to get closer to these strange figures, to give them
meaning in the child's universe, the narrator places the French crusaders next
to an uninteresting everyday item in the image of "un beau jeune homme
luisant comme une boîte de sardines" (a handsome young man shining like
a can of sardines).[25] The humour of the narrator is expressed through this
surprising parallel established between something as serious as a crusader
and something as trivial as a can of sardines. Cardinal shows the process of
making the foreign familiar, of using the already known to understand the
unknown, filtered through the child's eyes.

---

[23] Cardinal, *Au pays de mes racines*, 103. The textbooks of my childhood were
French, made for little Frenchmen living in France. Unknown seasons gave them
rhythms with holly leaves, blades from the lily of the valley, cottages with thatched
roofs covered with snow, schoolchildren in clogs.... Incomprehensible visions. Everything was incomprehensible to me in these books, except the Crusades where the French
encountered the Arabs. Although the latter, in the pictures, looked like big *mamamouchis*, but then again, why not, since the French, in their armour, looked like articulated shells.

[24] Lucille Cairns, "Roots and Alienation in Marie Cardinal's *Au pays de mes racines*,"
Forum for Modern Language Studies 29.4 (1993): 348.

[25] Cardinal, *Au pays de mes racines*, 104.

The narrator goes on to explain how fascinated she was by knights and the Crusades, and depicts herself as a small girl imagining herself as the fair lady of the knight bidding her beloved farewell as he goes off to protect her from the infidel. The narrator obviously seems quite ironic when describing the naive perspective of the child. Through these reductive representations themselves and by showing how they constitute sources of inspiration for the child's imagination, Cardinal manages to bring out how, as a member of the *pied-noir* community in Algeria, she falls between cultural identities and how Europe, through colonial education, offers an image of the Other (Arab) as well as of the Same (French). From her position within Africa but outside the Arab population, Cardinal writes both Europe and North Africa as Others.

Although this history lesson about the Crusades makes the reader aware of the dangers of cultural stereotypes, the narrator does underline that there is a possibility for the child to recognize a small part of her reality, even if it is twisted. Other parts of her history lessons do not even offer this slim possibility:

> Tout le reste de cette Histoire était beaucoup trop subtil pour moi. J'avoue que les combats au sujet du Piémont, des Flandres ou de l'Alsace–Lorraine me laissaient de marbre. C'était où tout ça? En tout cas, ni du côté d'Oran ni du côté de Constantine.[26]

Cardinal stresses the point that France / Europe is just a set of geographical names deprived of reality and with no interest for the pupil at the colonial school that she once was. The expression that compares her to marble underlines the complete lack of identification with this distant geography by dehumanizing her, turning her into stone.

The physical space where this knowledge was transmitted to her, the school she went to as a child, is one of the places she visits with her daughter during their trip to Algeria. This reunion is described in the following manner:

> Onze années passées là-dedans. Onze années à m'empiffrer des interdits et des grâces de ma religion avec, en prime, quelques con-naissances culturelles dans le genre 'nos ancêtres les Gaulois', 'rosa-

---

[26] *Au pays de mes racines*, 104. The rest of this History was all much too subtle for me. I confess that the battles of the Piedmont, Flanders or Alsace–Lorraine left me cold as marble. Where were they all? In any case, neither close to Oran, nor to Constantine.

rosae', 'les sous-préfectures des départements français', 'la dérivée d'X^2 c'est 2X', etc.[27]

Interestingly enough, the narrator describes all these forms of knowledge as cultural, although they belong to history, Latin grammar, geography, and mathematics. Should we understand this as a subtle way of saying that knowledge is always culturally determined, that what is knowledge depends on the cultural context? In this case, what we see here is an image of France through the knowledge transmitted in school. Both linguistic and ethnic origins, present-day geography with embedded power-structures, and mathematics are constituents of what France is.

In short, Cardinal's narrative offers several examples of what was taught in the Algerian colonial school of her childhood and of the image both of Europe and of North Africa transmitted through textbooks. The double alienation of the children in the *pied-noir* community is expressed as an impossibility to identify with either culture in its stereotypical representations. Instead of a degrading image of the self, so common in the colonizer's discourse on the colonized, the *pied-noir* finds either a void, no image at all, or the image of a hybrid, a neither–nor. Still, hierarchies govern the relations between these different groups, and Cardinal shows how the little girl is taught to reject the Arab community and associate herself with the French.

III

The obvious hierarchical patterns that Cardinal's narrative presents are connected to identity-building as a process in which the goal is to form a French identity as opposed to an Algerian one. Cardinal expresses this dissociation from everything Arab through the eyes of the little girl she once was when telling of a funeral for drowned kittens she organizes with her friends at the family farm. The ceremony is said to be half-Catholic, half-Muslim. The problems arise when the little girl uses the set of doll plates that used to belong to her great-grandmother, and they get stolen. When her mother tries to explain to her why she is so upset by the stolen plates, a

---

[27] Cardinal, *Au pays de mes racines*, 145–46. Eleven years spent in there. Eleven years stuffing myself with the interdictions and the graces of my religion with, as a bonus, some cultural knowledge like "the Gauls our ancestors," "rosa-rosae," "the subprefectures of the French districts," "the derivative of X^2 is 2X," etc.

clear line between 'them' and 'us' is established. The great-grandmother was born in Algeria, but her family came from Italy, which is compared to France:

> L'Italie c'est pas la France, mais c'est en face quand même, de l'autre côté de la mer, du bon côté.... Tout ce qui touche à ça, tout ce qui vient de là, est sacré. C'est plus sacré que tout ce qu'il y a de sacré ici.
>
> (Italy is not France, but it is still across from here, on the other side of the sea, on the good side.... Everything that has to do with that, everything that comes from over there, is sacred. It is more sacred than anything that is sacred here)[28]

The idea of Europe as the other side, the good side. is also linked here to the sacred. The fact that her playmates at the farm are incapable of recognizing the sacredness of these particular plates throws the little girl into a state of profound solitude. She feels as if she is forced to choose sides against her family or against her friends, knowing at the same time that even the thought of not choosing to side with the family is absurd:

> C'était ailleurs, dans le domaine de la morale, que se situait l'alternative: aimer le bien ou aimer le mal. Eux étaient le mal, nous étions le bien. Qui choisit délibérément le mal à l'âge de cinq ans, de huit ans, de dix ans...? Pas moi en tout cas, je n'avais pas cette force-là.
>
> (It was elsewhere, in the moral sphere, that the alternative was situated: to love Good or Evil. They were Evil, we were Good. Who would deliberately choose Evil at the age of five, eight, ten years...? Not me in any case, I didn't have that strength)[29]

Sympathizing with the Arab community, be it children and playmates, is morally wrong according to the set of values defended by Cardinal's family. In their view, this has nothing to do with politics, history or the worth of each individual, but it is a moral query. Good and Evil structure the Catholic upbringing Cardinal describes, and this structure is doubled by a split in the world between 'us' and 'them'.[30] France is what separates these two groups:

---

[28] Cardinal, *Au pays de mes racines*, 30.

[29] *Au pays de mes racines*, 31.

[30] In her study of *The Words to Say It*, Christina Angelfors points out that the opposition between classes mirrors the opposition between French and Arab, colonizer and

La France faisait qu'on supportait moins bien les mouches que les
'indigènes,' qu'on s'habillait autrement, qu'on apprenait les fables
de La Fontaine, qu'on avait des églises. La France créait la diffé-
rence en nous haussant puisque tout ce qui venait d'elle était
'meilleur.' Loin de nous l'idée que ce 'meilleur' était une culture.
Idée plutôt que la France nous mettait des galons, une casquette,
éventuellement un fusil entre les mains, elle nous conférait une force
indiscutable – et indiscutée d'ailleurs... [31]

The hierarchical patterns are easily spotted, but the details chosen to
express the superiority of everything French hint at the flaws in these same
patterns. There is an apparent irony in the fact that the ability to tolerate
flies less well seems positively connoted, through the simple fact that it is
associated with the French, when it is in fact a negative characteristic.
Cairns characterizes Cardinal's family as "profoundly chauvinistic, considering themselves superior to the autochthonous Algerians simply by
virtue of their French origins."[32] The superiority of France is associated
with military action, but also with clothing, traditional literary texts, and
churches, and the top position is never questioned. France is personified,
playing the role of a high-ranking officer. When speaking about the civil
war, however, this image changes. France is no longer what she used to be:

C'est la guerre civile pour que renaisse la France de Jeanne d'Arc, la
France des croisades, la France des conquêtes, la France sainte et
souveraine. La France belle, jouisseuse, gourmande, forte, pure. La
France dont sont amoureux ceux qui en sont tenus éloignés, amoureux fous. Ils la révèrent, ils l'idolâtrent et ils tâchent de la célébrer et

---

colonized, rich and poor, bourgeois and working class. To this series of oppositions
present also in *Au pays de mes racines,* could be added the opposition between Catholic
and Muslim, Good and Evil. See Christina Angelfors, *La Double Conscience: La prise
de conscience féminine chez Colette, Simone de Beauvoir et Marie Cardinal* (Lund:
Lund U P, 1989): 212.

[31] Cardinal, *Au pays de mes racines,* 14. France made us tolerate flies less well than
the 'natives', dress differently, learn the fables of La Fontaine, have churches. France
created the difference by uplifting us, since everything that came from her was 'better'.
Far from us the idea that this 'better' was a culture. Rather, the idea that France gave us
braids, a cap, possibly put a rifle in our hands, she gave us an indisputable strength –
which was in fact undisputed....

[32] Cairns, "Roots and Alienation in Marie Cardinal's *Au pays de mes racines,*" 350.

de la séduire dans ces morceaux de terre qu'elle leur a lancés à travers le monde: les colonies.[33]

The image of France produced here is based on the idea of lost ideals: war and conquest in the name of religious and ethnic purity need a revival. As the holder of the highest moral values, France is required to uphold the hierarchies established earlier and reclaim the superiority given by faith and warfare. The *pied-noir* community described here is clearly inferior to France, but of course superior to the Arabs. The relation between *pieds-noirs* and the French continues to build on the personification of France:

> Qu'a fait la belle et coquette France, dans sa sagesse et sa sainteté, depuis qu'elle a conquis l'Algérie? Dans un premier temps elle s'est laissé aduler par ces amants fougeux qui sentaient un peu trop l'aïl et le patchouli. Mais ils lui offraient leurs corps et leur fanatisme pour ses guerres et elle en a bien usé [...] Elle leur donnait des décorations, des rubans, des babioles, qu'ils vénéraient comme des reliques.[34]

France is a queen who takes advantage of the *pieds-noirs* lovers although she finds them unrefined, but useful in war because of their fidelity and their worship of whatever junk she offers in compensation for their efforts. The hierarchical patterns indicate that although the *pieds-noirs* are placed above the Arabs, they are only second-class citizens in the eyes of the metropolis. Once conqueror, always conqueror, Cardinal seems to say:

> L'Occident est un colon qui a perdu ses terres, ce qui ne l'empêche pas d'avoir une mentalité de colon. Un colon est un homme qui s'exile en terre étrangère afin de cultiver cette terre au profit de son

---

[33] Cardinal, *Au pays de mes racines*, 67. There is a civil war so that the France of Joan of Arc, the France of the Crusades, the France of the conquests, the holy and sovereign France can be born again. The France of beauty, pleasure, good eating, strength, purity. The France with which those who are kept far from her are in love, crazily in love. They revere her, idolize her, and they endeavour to celebrate and seduce her in those pieces of land that she has thrown to them across the world: the colonies.

[34] Cardinal, *Au pays de mes racines*, 67–68. What has the beautiful and coquettish France done, in her wisdom and holiness, since she has conquered Algeria? At first she let herself be flattered by these passionate lovers who smelled a little bit too much of garlic and patchouli. But they offered her their bodies and their fanaticism in her wars and she used them well [...] She gave them decorations, ribbons, knick-knacks, that they venerated like relics.

pays et à son propre profit [...] Il travaille dur et il se sert de son
idéal national comme d'une trique. Le colon veut s'enrichir au
meilleur prix et il fait cela sans vergogne car il est sûr de son bon
droit puisqu'il est supérieur. Sa morale est la meilleure, son rythme
est le meilleur, ses règles de vie sont les meilleures, ses régimes et
ses lois sont les meilleurs, sa religion est la meilleure. En imposant
cela il fait donc le bien.[35]

The French and the colonist are one and the same and their superiority
entails the duty to civilize the world in order to better it from a moral, political, and religious point of view. In the colonist's world structure, there are
those who give and those who receive, those who make the rules and those
who obey them. The colonist is depicted as crude; "the cudgel image con-
notes brutality and lack of subtlety," in Cairn's words.[36] Cardinal's childhood universe contains different layers of people, some considered better
than others, and there seems to be a conflict between the conscious respect
for this order of things and the child's unconscious desire for the Arab
Other. Evoking lullabies from her childhood, Cardinal describes how the
split between two cultures, two rhythms, provokes a bad conscience:

> La berceuse est douce mais elle l'est trop quand c'est ma mère qui la
> chante. Quand c'est Carmen, elle est plus proche de moi. Quand
> c'est Daïba, elle me plaît tout à fait, pourtant je me sens déjà cou-
> pable de me laisser endormir par elle. Je sais déjà que c'est le
> rythme de ma mère qui est le 'meilleur'. Il est raisonnable, char-
> mant, et entraîne des mots mignons qui vont bien au 'gazouillis' des
> enfants: dodo, poupée, papa, maman... Il n'est pas question de ça
> dans les berceuses de Carmen ou de Daïba, elles sont plus sauvages.
> Rythmes des saisons, rythmes des chansons, rythmes des mots.[37]

---

[35] Cardinal, *Au pays de mes racines*, 52–53. The West is a colonist who has lost his
land, but this doesn't stop him from having the mentality of a colonist. A colonist is a
man who goes into exile in a foreign land in order to cultivate this land for the profit of
his country and his own profit. [...]. He works hard and he uses his national ideal as a
cudgel. The colonist wants to get rich at the best price and he does this shamelessly
because he is sure of being right, since he is superior. His morals are the best, his rhythm
is the best, his norms are the best, his regimes and his laws are the best, his religion is
the best. When imposing this, he thus does what is good.

[36] Cairns, "Roots and Alienation in Marie Cardinal's *Au pays de mes racines*," 351.

[37] Cardinal, *Au pays de mes racines*, 27. The lullaby is pleasant but too much so when
it is my mother who sings it. When it is Carmen, it is closer to me. When it is Daïba, it

The feelings of guilt, Christina Angelfors claims in her analysis of *The Words to Say It*, come from the child's knowledge of the hierarchy between the French and the Arabs.[38] The classic division between reason and feeling, sense and sensibility, illustrates how the child is brought up to reject what seems to attract her naturally and embrace that which her conscience and upbringing tells her to prefer. This division is seen as an expression of Frenchness:

> Cette habitude française de mettre les sensations d'un côté et la raison de l'autre, je ne l'aime pas, car, personnellement, je ne parviens pas à les dissocier (This French habit of putting feelings on the one side and reason on the other, I don't like it, because personally I can't mangage to dissociate them).[39]

In a sense, early childhood is associated with Algeria, whereas France imposes itself as the child grows up. Angelfors remarks that, in *The Words to Say It*, childhood, authenticity, happiness, land, and nature are associated with Algeria. France, by contrast, represents the constraints and rules of a world considered 'civilized'.[40] The same oppositions are, not surprisingly, found in *Au pays de mes racines*. Given the hierarchy between what is French and what is Algerian, sympathizing with one side or the other has consequences. In *Au pays de mes racines,* Cardinal analyzes the process through which she is distanced in her rapport to Algeria and brought closer to France and encouraged to identify with her.

I V

Saying that Algeria represents childhood and France adulthood does not imply that Cardinal as a child was Algerian and as an adult French. Since Algeria was French when Cardinal was born, and she never lived there after independence, she of course never was of Algerian nationality. Con-

---

pleases me entirely, yet I feel guilty when she puts me to sleep. I already know that it is my mother's rhythm that is the 'best'. It is reasonable, charming, and carries with it cute words that fit well with the 'babbling' of children: bye-bye, doll, daddy, mummy... It is never about that in Carmen's or Daïba's lullabies, they are wilder. Rhythm of the seasons, rhythm of the songs, rhythm of the words.

[38] Angelfors, *La Double Conscience*, 173.

[39] Cardinal, *Au pays de mes racines*, 100.

[40] Angelfors, *La Double Conscience*, 172.

cluding that she is neither Algerian nor French but *pied-noir* is only a
partial truth, since being *pied-noir* in many ways bears with it the complexity of being both Algerian and French and at the same time neither. Being
French or Algerian, then, will be considered here not as an indication of
nationality, but as some kind of complicity established between the individual and each one of the physical spaces. When preparing for her trip to
Algeria, the narrator phones the embassy and learns that because she is of
French nationality, she does not need a visa. Her feelings are then described:

> Il y a un creux en moi, un manque, un trou, une plaie, au moment où
> je dis ça. Qu'est-ce qui me prend? Ordinairement ça ne me gêne pas
> de dire que je suis française.
> (There is a hollow in me, a lack, a hole, a wound, when I say that.
> What has come over me? Usually it doesn't bother me to say that I
> am French)[41]

Being French is synonymous with losing a part of one's self, of being hurt
and embarrassed. "The absence suggested by 'creux', 'manque' and 'trou'
is obviously that of Algeria: to deny that part of her identity is a spiritual
ablation," Cairns suggests.[42] In addition, the frustration comes from the fact
of feeling and behaving as a tourist in one's own country, so to speak. For
Cardinal, visiting Algeria as a tourist is metaphorically mutilating, revealing the distance between her present self and the childhood perception of
being a part of the natural environment on the family farm. The experience
of not belonging in Algeria is not, however, a wholly new experience. Even
when she used to live in Algiers she tells of excursions into the Casbah
with her playmates as a strange adventure:

> La Casbah autour de laquelle la ville européenne s'enroulait était le
> lieu de dépaysement, l'étranger, dans lequel nous nous enfoncions le
> cœur un peu battant avec, inconsciemment, l'impression de violer –
> touristes dans notre propre ville. Je crois qu'en grimpant ou en valant
> les ruelles de la Casbah, qui sentaient les épices et l'égout, nous
> savions que nous étions les héritiers des conquérants vainqueurs.[43]

---

[41] Cardinal, *Au pays de mes racines*, 27.

[42] Cairns, "Roots and Alienation in Marie Cardinal's *Au pays de mes racines*," 348.

[43] Cardinal, *Au pays de mes racines*, 56. The Casbah around which the European city
rolled itself was the place of disorientation, the unknown, into which we penetrated with

Being French, even as a child, equals being a tourist, an intruder, a conqueror, negatively connoted. Cairns asserts: "The use of the verb *violer* is politically pregnant, connoting rape, a concept common in diatribes against colonialism."[44] The common image of Europe is that of the rapist attacking the victim, Africa. Here, the image of the tourist and that of the rapist conqueror seem to coincide, making of tourism an imperialistic activity with sexual undertones. The image of the Casbah trapped by the snake-like European parts of Algiers is also quite powerful. The European parts of the city form a serpent of buildings around the Casbah, an image of French colonization based on biblical imagery. 'European' and 'power' are forever linked to the guilt of colonization. Growing up, the conqueror's identity seems to colonize the Algerian part of Cardinal's being, through the education delivered by the family and by society.

Religious practices are pointed out by Cardinal as particularly powerful tools to manipulate young minds:

> La première communion était un tournant dans notre vie. C'était la fin de l'enfance, l'entrée dans l'adolescence. Après, ce n'était plus pareil. Après ma première communion, je suis devenue plus française.
> (The first Holy Communion was a turning point in our lives. It was the end of childhood, the entry into adolescence. After that, things were no longer the same. After my first Holy Communion, I became more French)[45]

The ritual of the first Holy Communion marks a passage out of childhood. Thus, becoming more French after it has taken place indicates that Frenchness and childhood are opposites. Leaving childhood behind creates a great deal of tension around the young girl's body. Patrice J. Proulx comments on the function of the female body: "Inscribed in the text is an implicit convergence of the protagonist's body and Algeria. The body, then, emblematizes the lost country, both in a physical and in a spiritual sense."[46] The

---

beating hearts and, unconsciously, the impression of committing an act of violence / rape – tourists in our own city. I think that while we were climbing up or rushing down the alleys of the Casbah, which smelled of spices and the sewer, we knew that we were the heirs of the victorious conquerors.

[44] Cairns, "Roots and Alienation in Marie Cardinal's *Au pays de mes racines*," 351.

[45] Cardinal, *Au pays de mes racines*, 59.

[46] Patrice J. Proulx, "Representations of Cultural and Geographical Displacement in Marie Cardinal," *Centennial Review* 42.3 (1998): 529.

female body on its way to adulthood is lost for the physical pleasures of childhood, associated with Algeria, and imprisoned in a paralyzing set of moral rules representing France. During the preparations for the ceremony, the message transmitted is that of purity:

> Intactes, nous devions être intactes, propres, nettes, dans nos pensées et dans nos corps. Sur nous reposait l'avenir de la pureté de notre peuple et de la catholicité. C'était lourd.
> (Intact, we had to be intact, clean, neat, in our thoughts and in our bodies. On us depended the future of the purity of our people and of catholicity. It was a heavy burden)[47]

The stereotypical image of the woman as the defender of moral values is clearly attached to this religious upbringing. Built on the misconception that the woman has no sexuality of her own and that she therefore needs to help the man control his animal instincts, this idea in some ways seems to express an admiration for women as morally superior creatures, when it actually reduces the woman to a Madonna-like receptacle of moral rules. Becoming a woman is associated with becoming French, and the combination of the two implies a need to defend people and religion, as well as one's own body. In *Au pays de mes racines*, as Angelfors states when analyzing *The Words to Say It,*

> Le but du 'dressage' étant d'intégrer la jeune fille dans une société basée sur la hiérarchie entre Français et Arabes, entre hommes et femmes, la transgression sexuelle et culturelle qu'on avait tolérée chez l'enfant se trouve donc sévèrement réprimée à partir de l'adolescence.
> (The goal of the 'training' is to integrate the young girl into a society based on the hierarchy between French and Arabs, between men and women. The sexual and cultural transgression that had been tolerated in the child is thus severely punished from adolescence onwards)[48]

Embracing her sexuality and associating with the Algerian becomes impossible for the young girl. Just as the female Algerian clothing customs seem to give more freedom to the woman's body than the French, there is a

---

[47] Cardinal, *Au pays de mes racines*, 60.
[48] Angelfors, *La Double Conscience*, 173.

surprisingly strong connection between Algeria and a certain sensuality/
sexuality and freedom, where France is the repressive power imposed upon
the young girl.

This way of educating children is characterized as brainwashing by
Cardinal, who writes: "Le lavage de cervelle ne se fait pas que dans les
camps de redressement, il se fait aussi dans les familles, et il n'en est pas
moins estropiant" (Brainwashing isn't only done in reformatory camps, it is
also done in families, and it is no less crippling).[49] By juxtaposing the
family and the reformatory or the prison camps, Cardinal establishes a connection between the two, indicating that families can be just as harmful and
violent as harsh disciplinary action in a different setting. "Cardinal's narrator belongs to the French land-owning bourgeoisie whose stance toward
the Algerian Arabs was benevolent paternalism laced with Catholic missionary zeal," Lionnet writes, about *The Words to Say It*.[50] This characterization of the family also pinpoints the ingredients of the educational
environment described in *Au pays de mes racines*. The idea of paternalism
and Catholicism is also linked to the education of children. Cardinal goes
on to explain:

> A dix-huit ans, ma conversion était 'presque' parfaite. Elle ne s'est
> pas opérée dans le but d'être différente des Arabes, non, elle s'est
> perversement opérée dans le but de devenir une bonne chrétienne,
> une bonne Française et une dame.
> (At eighteen, my conversion was 'almost' perfect. It had not been
> performed with the aim of being different from the Arabs, no, it was
> perversely performed with the aim of becoming a good Christian, a
> good French woman and a lady)[51]

Hence, being French also entails being Catholic and a lady persuaded of her
superiority. The daughter needs to estrange herself from the Arab community in order to be a part of the paternalistic missionary society of her
family. Strong words are used to describe this phenomenon, this metamor-
phosis. It is compared to mutilation and conversion. Body and religion are
intertwined in a complex structure and Cardinal seems to be saying that

---

[49] Cardinal, *Au pays de mes racines*, 32.
[50] Lionnet, *Autobiographical Voices: Race, Gender, Self-Portraiture*, 193.
[51] Cardinal, *Au pays de mes racines*, 32.

she, as a *pied-noir*, wasn't born French, but was forced to become so, and
that this created a void within her.

Being French is often associated with reduction and confinement. When
suffering from writer's block, Cardinal describes the experience in the following manner:

> Impression d'être dans une prison de laquelle je ne sortirai que
> lorsque j'aurai fini ce livre. Impression que j'ai perdu des maillons
> de ma vie, certaines clefs. Impression que je me suis trop francisée,
> que j'ai oublié quelque chose, quoi?
>
> (A feeling of being in a prison which I will not leave before I have
> finished this book. A feeling that I have lost some links in my life,
> certain keys. A feeling that I have become too French, that I have
> forgotten something, what?)[52]

The vocabulary used to convey these impressions (prison, loss, links in a
chain, keys, forgetting) has negative associations, and among them the
word describing the process of becoming too French tells us that being
French equals lack of freedom, unity, comprehension, creativity, and
memory. Becoming too French is an obstacle to creation, to writing, to
living in the world of the writer. In her study of Cardinal's *The Words to
Say it*, Lionnet writes: "Claiming a cultural background that reaches far
beyond the confines of France's *hexagone*, [Cardinal returns] to [her] colonial roots to find sources of creativity."[53] Angelfors points out that the trip
to Algeria in *Au pays de mes racines*, signifying the re-connection with the
mother-earth, is a way out of the writer's block, a strategy to renew the
capacity to create, to write, thus showing that the primitive mother and
writing are intimately connected to one another.[54] Lionnet describes Cardinal's childhood as split between two maternal orders: "a mothering of sorts
by the natural environment and the nonwhites who are part of [her] daily
life, in the absence of a truly nurturing biological mother."[55] Through the
association between the biological mother and France, one can conclude
that Frenchness also impedes the creative processes. This Frenchness is a
result of education, hence it is opposed to creativity: "Je me suis laissée en-

---

[52] Cardinal, *Au pays de mes racines*, 84.
[53] Lionnet, *Autobiographical Voices: Race, Gender, Self-Portraiture*, 191.
[54] Angelfors, *La Double Conscience*, 190.
[55] Lionnet, *Autobiographical Voices: Race, Gender, Self-Portraiture*, 193.

vahir par la mauvaise herbe de la science étrangère et maintenant j'étouffe"
(I have let myself be invaded by the weeds of foreign science and now I
suffocate).[56] Science adapted to French standards invades her as weeds take
over plantations, suffocating the original plants. When compared to the
previously analyzed images using weeds, the representational patterns are
in a sense reversed, since the weeds are here associated with colonial power
and imperialism. The cultivated soil represents the Algerian part of the narrator, linked back to the family farm and the cultivation of the land. The
weeds represent the bad seeds brought there through contact with the
French, which then, through a play on words, is deprived of its status of
Culture. Cultivating the land is associated with the Algerian context as if
colonization had never brought about the *pied-noir* settlements, and the narrator's presence there and her association with the land is original and pure.
The identification between self and land can be detected in the vocabulary
of invasion and otherness ('envahir' and 'étrangère'), making of the narrator the colonized land of Algeria.

Becoming French puts an end to being/feeling Algerian, and one expression of this transformation is losing the command of the Arabic language. Cardinal explains:

> En devenant adolescente j'avais perdu le goût des vacances à la
> ferme, je préférais les passer en France ou sur les plages où nous
> nous retrouvions entre jeunes Français. Mes amis étaient tous fran-
> çais. Dans mon collège il n'y avait que des Françaises, à l'université
> il n'y avait que des Français.
> (When becoming an adolescent I lost the taste for holidays on the
> farm, I preferred spending them in France or on the beach where I
> used to meet other young French people. My friends were all
> French. In my high school there were only French girls, at the uni-
> versity there were only French students)[57]

The segregated society that Cardinal describes here is an obstacle to her
continued practice of Arabic, the on-going brainwashing creating the feeling that putting a distance between herself and the Arab community, inte-
grating herself in the French community, is what she actually wants. The
French, previously considered Other, is now what she associates with.

---

[56] Cardinal, *Au pays de mes racines*, 37.
[57] *Au pays de mes racines*, 81.

From *pied-noir* firmly rooted in the Algerian soil, her identity shifts to
French. Speaking Arabic is associated with childhood, being French with
becoming a young woman. An interesting episode which illustrates this
shift is when the young woman is involved in a car accident and starts to
speak Arabic to a man coming to her rescue, without realizing at first that
this is what she is doing. It is the little girl she once was who speaks Arabic,
she explains. Understanding this, she suddenly cannot speak Arabic any-
more. She shortly thereafter discovers that the accident has ripped her dress
apart and that she is half-naked. Covering herself up, she describes how the
little girl disappears and how she becomes "une jeune Française digne,
effarouchée, face à un bicot sauvage et mal dégrossi" (a young French girl,
dignified, frightened, facing an uncivilized and unrefined Arab).[58] She fears
rape, but instead the man gets help from "un colon français bien vociférant,
bien vulgaire" (a very vulgar, vociferous French colonist).[59] Being French
and a young woman is associated with fear, it means fearing rape from an
Arab, but not from a *pied-noir*, regardless of their behaviour. In Cairns'
reading, there is a "glaring contrast between the Arab's commendable
behaviour and the boorish sexism of the 'colon français'." She asserts:
"The initial trust for the Arab was that of a child not yet contaminated by
apprehension of his possibly 'sinful' motives, not yet alienated by Chris-
tianity from people of 'Other' races and creeds."[60] Becoming French, then,
is adopting a racist and xenophobic attitude because of religious practices.
It seems important to point out, however, that the 'sinful motives' are
focusing on the young woman's body. The body of the young woman
which needs to be protected and controlled is incompatible with the Algerian part of her identity, separates her from her childhood self, and deprives
her of the Arabic language. In Angelfors' analysis of *The Words to Say It*,
she establishes that the split identity of the narrator is based on a series of
contradictory elements. On the one side, Angelfors lists 'masculine'/Arab
identity, colonized, Algeria, mother-nature, body, blood/biological *'règles'*[61]
and life, and, on the other, 'feminine'/French identity, colonizer, France,
mother-culture, spirit, silence/cultural *'règles'* and death. 'Body' in this

---

[58] Cardinal, *Au pays de mes racines*, 82.

[59] *Au pays de mes racines*, 82.

[60] Cairns, "Roots and Alienation in Marie Cardinal's *Au pays de mes racines*," 349.

[61] Angelfors makes quite productive use of the word "règles," which signifies both
menstrual bleeding and rules.

system is associated with bodily pleasure and sensuality, inscribed in the Algerian context. At the same time, the French identity is deprived of the body, submitted to the spirit. Both of these affirmations are to a large extent true also for the image of France transmitted in *Au pays de mes racines*. When I argue here that the body is linked to the French, it is not the body in harmony and interaction with the world as in the sensual Algerian childhood, but the body that becomes a problem, a reason for fear. In fact, it may be more appropriate to speak not of the body itself, but of the conception of it. The narrator of *The Words to Say It* is caught between two identities, as Angelfors points out. One is perceived as authentic, the other as imposed by society through the mother.[62] In my analysis of *Au pays de mes racines*, the same goes for the conception of the body, free in the Algerian setting, imprisoned in the French. As Angelfors emphasizes, in *The Words to Say It* Cardinal considers that the vulnerability of the woman's body could be seen as the point of origin of a fear common to all women, transmitted from mother to daughter.[63] This fear also informs the upbringing of the young woman described in *Au pays de mes racines*. The French woman is, in this episode of *Au pays de mes racines*, reduced to her vulnerable body, which is unspeakable for Cardinal in the Arabic language.

V

The female body is actually a place where French and Algerian attitudes can be said to coincide, at least in part. Cardinal evokes the traditional Algerian and Muslim wedding ritual she encounters as a child when Zorah, a friend from the childhood farm, is married off to a much older man at the age of thirteen. The little girl watches through the window how the newly wed husband goes into Zorah's room and how, when he leaves the room a while later, the family comes out after him, exposing the bloodstained sheets. Her reaction is rendered by incomplete sentences, expressing her state of shock:

> Mal dans le ventre. Mal dans le ventre. Quitter la fenêtre. Me lover dans mon lit. Me boucher les oreilles. Dormir.

---

[62] Angelfors, *La Double Conscience*, 188.
[63] *La Double Conscience*, 186.

(Pain in the stomach/womb. Pain in the stomach/womb. Leave the window. Roll up in my bed. Put my fingers in my ears. Sleep)[64]

This whole passage is narrated in connection with the description of the first Holy Communion when the young girls are prepared for their future life as women who respect religion and traditional morality. The importance and role of the female body are defined by the idea of virginity:

> Jamais il n'était question directement de la virginité de nos corps et, en même temps, il n'était question que de ça [...] Virginité précaire faisant l'objet de toutes les convoitises, de tous les vices, et qu'il fallait défendre coûte que coûte pour un avenir d'amours sublimes et d'enfants splendides.
> (It was never directly about the virginity of our bodies, and at the same time, it was only about that [...] Precarious virginity which was the object of all covetousness, of all vices, and that had to be defended at all costs for a future of sublime love and splendid children)[65]

The relation between girls and boys, men and women, evolves around this idea of virginity. This is where the differences between French and Algerian attitudes tend to disappear, when Cardinal explains:

> Bouleversement: je découvrais que chez les Français aussi le mariage pouvait être une sauvagerie.
> Depuis les noces de Zorah, à la ferme, je savais que les Arabes n'étaient pas comme nous, qu'ils avaient un côté bestial. Pendant la retraite de ma première communion j'ai su que nous n'étions pas mieux. Plus hypocrites, c'est tout.[66]

Cardinal seems to be saying that cultural difference is in some ways erased when it comes to being a woman, since she is always subordinate to man, a victim of male sexuality. Of course, Cardinal does evoke the differences in

---

[64] Cardinal, *Au pays de mes racines*, 65.

[65] *Au pays de mes racines*, 60–61.

[66] *Au pays de mes racines*, 61. Upheaval: I discovered that also among the French marriage could be savagery. Since Zora's wedding at the farm, I knew that the Arabs weren't like us, that they had a beastly side. During the retreat of my first Holy Communion I learned that we weren't any better. More hypocritical, that's all.

education and upbringing that separate her from the Algerian girlfriends of
her childhood:

> J'ai fait des études. Baccalauréat. Licence de philosophie. Diplôme
> d'études supérieures. Préparation à l'agrégation... Et mes anciens
> copains de la ferme, que deviendront-ils? Les filles, dès leur puberté,
> seront séquestrées. Elles ne devront plus être vues des hommes.
> Toutes jeunes elles seront mariées et passeront du ghetto de la *raïma*
> de leur mère au ghetto de la *raïma* de leur belle-mère.[67]

She goes on to describe how the lives of these young women will, in all
important details, be repetitions of the lives of women living before them.

The situation of women in the Algeria she visits as an adult is also described. Cardinal's own experience of travelling in the country is evoked:

> Toujours les regards des hommes sur nous comme si nous étions de
> la marchandise ambulante qui se juge, se jauge, s'évalue. Toutes ces
> mouches sur nous, sans arrêt, collantes, agaçantes, impression de
> n'avoir aucune liberté. Impossibilité d'exister dehors [...] L'espace
> vital se réduit considérablement pour une femme ici.
> (Always the gaze of the men upon us as if we were walking mer-
> chandise that is judged, measured, evaluated. All these flies upon us,
> continuously, sticky, annoying, the impression of having no liberty.
> Impossibility of existing outdoors. [...] The vital space is considera-
> bly reduced for a woman here)[68]

Being French and being a woman, especially when in Algeria, means that
what is considered normal behaviour in Europe, in France, provokes very
strong reactions. In this context, walking in the street is provocative and
entails being stared at by men, being submitted to "the oppressive power of
the unfettered male gaze," as Cairns puts it.[69] The comparison between the
male gaze and flies could be linked to the previously analyzed image of the

---

[67] Cardinal, *Au pays de mes racines*, 33. I have studied. High school graduation.
Bachelor's Degree in philosophy. University diploma. Preparations for the Agregation...
And my old friends from the farm, what will become of them? The girls, from puberty
onwards, will be sequestrated. They should no longer be seen by men. Very young they
will be married off and will pass from the ghetto of the *raïma* of their mother to the
ghetto of the *raïma* of their mother-in-law.

[68] *Au pays de mes racines*, 171.

[69] Cairns, "Roots and Alienation in Marie Cardinal's *Au pays de mes racines*," 355.

French as having difficulties putting up with flies as well as the Algerians. Thus, French women would have more difficulty being reduced to objects under the eyes of men. Being a French woman thus means challenging the norms and exposing yourself to unpleasant experiences. Claiming an existence outside of the home and feeling trapped in a reduced space is also being French. Being a Frenchwoman is being a feminist.

This feminism reveals itself clearly when Cardinal, reading the newspaper, encounters the views of an Algerian woman who claims that colonization is the reason why Algerian women have a hard time making themselves heard in society. Cardinal comments:

> Quelle chance de pouvoir encore croire que l'oppresseur c'est l'étranger et qu'il suffit de le chasser pour que ça aille mieux du côté des femmes! Ça m'a laissée rêveuse. Voilà bientôt dix-huit ans que les oppresseurs sont partis et cette brave dame va bientôt se rendre compte de ce que c'est que la condition féminine.[70]

What Cardinal seems to say is that women are trapped in the solidarity they feel towards the men of their country, of their class, of their culture, and that they need to focus more on the oppression imposed by these men. Women will always be oppressed so long as they do not unite across borders, nations, countries, cultures, ethnicities, languages, and classes. The echo from Simone de Beauvoir, the French feminist by definition, is loud and clear.[71] Angelfors' study shows that Cardinal's view of oppression in earlier works is based on class rather than gender, but she also acknowledges that the conception of the relation between men and women is more radical in *Au pays de mes racines*,[72] quoting the first two sentences of the following passage from the text:

---

[70] Cardinal, *Au pays de mes racines*, 119. What good fortune it is to still be able to believe that the oppressors are the foreigners and that throwing them out is enough to make things better for women! That had me dreaming. It was almost eighteen years ago that the oppressors left and this good lady will soon realize what the condition of women means.

[71] Simone de Beauvoir, *Le Deuxième Sexe* (Paris: Gallimard, 1949). See also Carolyn A. Durham, who explores the possible influence of Beauvoir's *La Femme rompue* on Cardinal's *Une Vie pour deux*: Durham, "Patterns of Influence: Simone de Beauvoir and Marie Cardinal," *French Review* 60.3 (1987): 342–48.

[72] Angelfors, *La Double Conscience*, 216.

Je ne peux pas me résigner à accepter l'exploitation sous quelque forme que ce soit. Être consciente d'être une femme c'est vivre la plus profonde révolte, c'est aller au-delà de la lutte des classes puisque les femmes de toutes les classes sont exploitées. Je vis dans cette révolte. Au lieu de continuer à se gargariser avec les grands mots et les grandes idéologies qui font et défont des colons et des colonisés, cela avec une constance désespérante et au rythme inhumain d'une économie criminelle, pourquoi ne pas se mettre à parler du pouvoir?[73]

If "French" and "power" are associated when the Algiers of the French era is concerned, as was established in a previous section (IV) of this essay, being French and a woman seems to complicate the relation to power. Frenchness must be given a gendered dimension in order to convey all the possible incarnation of what is French. Introducing feminism into the discussion on how Africa, in the form of a *pied-noir* writer, represents Europe, adds a twist. Cardinal gives voice to Africa, a particular version of Africa. A *pied-noir*, female, feminist intellectual offers her view of France and of Frenchness, from within as well as from the outside. As Cardinal puts it: "Double culture, double liberté pourrait-on coire, mais c'est le contraire" (Double culture, double liberty one might think, but it is the opposite).[74] True to the double vision, she also expresses the opposite:

Être née à la colonie dans une famille de colons est un fait lourd à porter; et pourtant, être une créole est une joie, une pétillance en moi. Sans arrêt la terre et la tête, le corps et l'esprit, se battent et s'unissent dans des mêlées épuisantes. J'enfonce des portes ouvertes, tout cela est vrai pour n'importe qui, ces conflits ou ces accordailles sont le meilleur de nos vies, sa cannelle ou son poivre. Mais quand la culture est double et doubles aussi les géographies et les histoires, l'équilibre est constamment en péril, il y a peu de repos.[75]

---

[73] Cardinal, *Au pays de mes racines*, 183. I cannot resign myself to accept exploitation in any shape. Being conscious of being a woman is to live the most profound revolt, it is going beyond the class struggle since women of all classes are exploited. I live in this revolt. Instead of continuing to swallow whole the big words and the big ideologies that do and undo the colonists and the colonized, and this with an appalling constancy and with the inhuman rhythm of a criminal economy, why not start talking about power?

[74] Cardinal, *Au pays de mes racines*, 101.

[75] *Au pays de mes racines*, 23–24. To be born in the colonies in a family of colonists is a heavy burden to carry ; and yet to be a creole is a joy, a sparkling in me. The land

When Pat Duffy states that Cardinal's text points to a positive view of "cultural duality" and that "for Cardinal it is Algerian culture that enriches," one could argue that Cardinal sets up Algeria and not France as the original, and Frenchness as something that initially destroys the harmony of the Algerian, even though the final result may be enrichment.[76] Just as Cardinal points to the thrill of creoleness and the constant movement it involves, one can say that the image of France and Frenchness given by Cardinal gains in interest precisely because it is incessantly moving from the African point of view to the European, showing how both positions inform the representation when Africa is writing Europe.

VI

Marie Cardinal as the African representative writing Europe employs numerous strategies in order to convey the double perspective of inside and outside. Contrasting images of Africa and Europe serve as a nuanced way of expressing not only what each place and culture is like, but also how the differences create a split in the characters belonging to both. Cardinal evokes the European way of life, her relation to French geography, history, and religion, the use of language and the conception of the body in the French context. These contrasting images are not constructed as equal, but there is a strong feeling of discomfort associated with everything French, especially in comparison to anything Algerian. Africa thus writes Europe as a strange and exotic place which cannot compete with the African homeland for the narrator's heart.

The vision of France through the eyes of the pupil at the colonial school that the narrator once was conveys the same image of strangeness as the contrasting images. What is striking here is the fact that there are not many corresponding images of Africa transmitted through the colonial school. Only the Arab enemies of the crusaders are depicted in textbooks; the members of the *pied-noir* community are nowhere to be found.

---

and the head, the body and the spirit fight and unite continuously in exhausting conflicts. I flog dead horses, this is true for anybody, these conflicts or these agreements are the best of our lives, its' cinnamon or its' pepper. But when the culture is double and double also the geographies and the histories, the balance is constantly in danger, there is little rest.

[76] Pat Duffy, "Realigning Cultural Perspectives: Marie Cardinal and Camara Laye," *French Cultural Studies* 12.1 (2001): 19.

The image of Europe is always built on hierarchical patterns where France, regardless of the context, is placed above Algeria. Based on the notions of good and evil, of awareness of the sacred, on the idea of war and conquest, the hierarchy places the French not only above the Algerian Arab but also above the *pied-noir*, depicted as a naive admirer of France, a devoted lover with lots of guts but no brain. Europe exploits not only the native inhabitants of Algeria but also her own people, who seem somehow inferior, as if the contact with the colonized has rubbed off some of the inferiority the French see in them. Africa, in Cardinal's words as *pied-noir* representative, writes Europe as a colonizer with a double frame of colonization.

At the same time, there is a shift in Cardinal's life story, placed around the time of the first Holy Communion, where she goes from identifying with Algeria to identifying with France. France is here written as a suffocating, confining state of being that the child is programmed to embrace, leaving the more harmonious Algerian state of childhood behind and moving into adulthood. Instead of writing France as liberation and access to a culture of higher standing, which would be the normative view of becoming an adult in this context, Cardinal shows the way in which unbecoming African and becoming French is, in her view, synonymous with loss. The educational methods used by the families to attain the desired Frenchness are described as brainwashing and the training of wild animals into pseudo-animals performing circus acts on command. There is a fragility in this identity-building, as the pursued ideal is practically unattainable for the *pieds-noirs*, at least in the eyes of the French.

The last lens through which Cardinal looks at Europe as represented by the French is that of feminism. While reflecting on what it means to be a woman in the split context of the *pied-noir*, Cardinal points to both differences and similarities between womanhood in the Algerian and in the French paradigm. She seems to come to the conclusion that being French and a woman is also being a feminist and thus provocative in the eyes of the Africa she may no longer claim to belong to after twenty-four years of absence. While displaying her critical view on the lack of solidarity between women from different backgrounds in a postcolonial context, Cardinal is also writing Europe through her use of European feminism from a *pied-noir* perspective, writing Europe from the outside as well as the inside. Cardinal also writes Europe as an African when she explores the notion of her double identity, since the *pied-noir* perspective of being both/neither

African and/nor European mirrors present-day European identities at the intersection of gender and ethnicity.

WORKS CITED

Angelfors, Christina. *La Double Conscience: La prise de conscience féminine chez Colette, Simone de Beauvoir et Marie Cardinal* (Lund: Lund UP, 1989).

Beauvoir, Simone de. *Le Deuxième sexe* (Paris: Gallimard, 1949)

Cairns, Lucille. "Roots and Alienation in Marie Cardinal's *Au pays de mes racines*," *Forum for Modern Language Studies* 29.4 (1993): 346–58.

Cardinal, Marie. *Au pays de mes racines, suivi de Au pays de Moussia par Bénédicte Ronfard* (Paris: Grasset & Fasquelle, 1980).

———. *The Words to Say It* (London: Women's Press, 1983).

Duffy, Pat. "Realigning Cultural Perspectives: Marie Cardinal and Camara Laye," *French Cultural Studies* 12.1 (2001): 5–21.

Durham, Carolyn A. "Patterns of Influence: Simone de Beauvoir and Marie Cardinal," *French Review* 60.3 (1987): 342–48.

Glissant, Édouard. *Le Discours antillais* (Paris: Gallimard, 1981).

Ha, Marie–Paule. "Outre-mer/autre mère: Cardinal and Algeria," *Romance Notes* 36.3 (1996): 315–23.

Lionnet, Françoise. *Autobiographical Voices: Race, Gender, Self-Portraiture* (Ithaca NY: Cornell UP, 1989).

Proulx, Patrice J. "Representations of Cultural and Geographical Displacement in Marie Cardinal," *Centennial Review* 42.3 (1998): 527–38.

◁▷

From Heterotopia to Home

– ◇ – The University and the Politics of Postcoloniality
in Tayeb Salih's *Season of Migration to the North*
and Leila Aboulela's *The Translator*

ALEXANDRA W. SCHULTHEIS

I

T AYEB SALIH'S *Season of Migration to the North* and Leila
Aboulela's *The Translator* together address a century of Sudanese
colonial and postcolonial history, centering on the struggle to reconcile the religious and educational backgrounds of the elite with the
demands of postcolonial modernity. From the end of the Mahdiyah in
1898,[1] through Sudan's independence from Britain in 1956, and finally to
the islamization policies of the 1990s, the three central characters of the
novels wrestle with tension between their Western educations and the
religious and gendered codes governing daily life in colonial and postcolonial Sudan. For Salih's two main characters, the unnamed narrator and
Mustafa Sa'eed, as well as Aboulela's Sammar, experiences at British universities both shape and challenge their identities as modern, Islamic,
Sudanese in an increasingly globalized world. In this essay, I trace the
parallel between the central characters' engagement with the British university and the university's accommodation to colonial and neocolonial demands. In both processes charted by these novels, the university plays a key

---

[1] The Mahdiyah is often described as the first Sudanese national government, defined
by the imposition of Islamic law and jihad against British and Egyptian colonialism.
Mustafa Sa'eed's birth corresponds to the Mahdist defeat in 1898 by Kitchener's forces.

role in the failure of postcolonial nationalism and the elision of alternative, non-imperializing narratives of modernity.

Season of Migration to the North (1969) opens with the following description of the anonymous narrator's return to Sudan after seven years of study in England. Underscoring the novelists' common concerns, Aboulela presents the quotation in the form below (with ellipses) as the epigraph for Part Two of *The Translator* (1999) when Sammar returns home from Aberdeen, Scotland:

> [...] the fog cleared and I awoke, on the second day of my arrival, in my familiar bed in the room whose walls had witnessed the trivial incidents of my life in childhood and the onset of adolescence [...] I heard the cooing of the turtle-dove, and I looked through the window at the palm tree standing in the courtyard of our house [...] I looked at its strong straight trunk, at its roots that strike down to the ground, at the green branches hanging down loosely over its top, and I experienced a feeling of assurance. I felt not like a storm-swept feather but like that palm tree, a being with a background, with roots.[2]

The metaphor invoked by Salih and Aboulela contrasts the rooted palm with the vicissitudes or storminess of foreign experience, suggesting the timelessness and ahistoricism of 'home' as refuge from the flow of History abroad. The manichaean logic of the metaphor (tradition/modernity, Africa/Europe, stasis/flow) deteriorates, however, as the choices and places the characters encounter are endowed with socio-political context. Returning to Sudan for these characters ostensibly means returning home with advanced training necessary to contribute to the development of the postcolonial nation, whose modernity seemingly depends upon a utopian melding of tradition and 'progress'; yet the novels ultimately reject that narrative as the loyalty of the three protagonists to the nation diminishes. The British university figures in the novels not only as a site of an imperializing, orientalist production of the Other in a Saidian sense but also of self-invention for its African attendees. It is thus pivotal in the characters' understanding of the complex relationship between ex-colony and imperial centre, as not simply

---

[2] Tayeb Salih, *Season of Migration to the North*, tr. Denys Johnson–Davies (Portsmouth NH: Heinemann, 1969): 1–2, quoted in Leila Aboulela, *The Translator* (Edinburgh: Polygon, 1999): 121.

one between margin and centre, as well as their own choices within that relationship.

In her reading of *Season of Migration*, Laura Rice turns to Michel Foucault's concept of heterotopia as a way of capturing these complexities because of the ways in which heterotopia intervenes in dualistic narratives of margin and centre. As Rice notes, heterotopia destabilizes the "reality/utopia dyad" and "foreground[s] the representational foundation upon which we construct what we commonly think of as reality."[3] In "Of Other Spaces," Foucault, writing from an explicitly European perspective, argues that we in the West can best understand the relations governing our current historical epoch through the heterotopias that reflect to/upon the ostensibly 'real' its potential and failures.[4] He concludes with the suggestion that colonies might function as exemplary heterotopias of compensation whose "role is to create a space that is other, another real space, as perfect, as meticulous, as well arranged as ours is messy, ill constructed and jumbled."[5] As a space that produces both "mythic and real contestation of the space in which we live,"[6] heterotopia offers a reflected image of ruling relations of power that is also an imagined projection. We might expect the distance between the (ex-)colony and the imperial centre, then, to reveal the contours of global relations of ruling for many of the world's citizens. Rice focuses her analysis on Sa'eed's reconstructed English room as a heterotopia which reveals him as at once "constituted by the colonizer's ideology" and a "mirror held up to reveal" that ideology. The narrator, in looking at the same mirror, sees both himself in Sa'eed and the failures of home as either "the certainties of positivism [or…] the routines of tradition."[7] Leaving aside Foucault's assumption of a seemingly idealized imperial perspective on the prospects of colonial planning and execution

---

[3] Laura Rice, "Of Heterotopias and Ethnoscapes: The Production of Space in Postcolonial North Africa," *Critical Matrix* 14 (30 September 2003): 36–75. Online: http://ez.hamilton.edu:2048/login?url=http://proquest.umi.com/pqdweb?did=671854121&sid=1&Fmt=3&clientid=5446&RQT=309&VName=PQD: 3 (accessed 20 March 2006).

[4] Michel Foucault, "Of Other Spaces," tr. Jay Miskowicc, *Diacritics* 16.1 (Spring 1986): 22–27. The essay was drawn from a lecture Foucault gave in 1967. Although never reviewed for publication by Foucault, it was first published in French in 1984, just before his death.

[5] Foucault, "Of Other Spaces," 27.

[6] "Of Other Spaces," 24.

[7] Rice, "Of Heterotopias and Ethnoscapes," 4, 7.

and in contrast to Rice's analysis of Sa'eed's private space, I wish to examine the uses and transformations of the university as heterotopia in both *Season of Migration* and *The Translator*. The university would seem to be an exemplary heterotopia in Foucault's terms because of the way in which it both reflects dominant ideologies and ideally offers some critical distance from them. The university in the novels serves as a key both to imperial expansion and to individual agency, yet does so from the postcolonial subject's rather than the colonizer's perspective. This shift from an imperial to a postcolonial viewpoint reverses Foucault's terms, rendering the university and its British setting the heterotopic mirror of the space in which the elite operate in the postcolonial nation as well as the European society of which these foreign-born students are not quite a part. The novels effect a further transvaluation of these terms by tracing the gradual transformation of the heterotopic space into home, and, to a greater or lesser extent, the characters' simultaneous rejection of postcolonial national identity in favour of the rewards offered by the European university.

This transformation, mapped through three generations of elite Sudanese in the novels, overlaps with that of the university described eloquently by Bill Reading in *The University in Ruins*. Outlining the changing social function of the university through the shift in official academic rhetoric from celebrating its "national cultural mission" to a corporate model of "excellence," Reading argues that the European and American university has replaced its traditional national function with one dedicated to the reproduction of capital across national borders.[8] Thus, I argue below that *Season of Migration*'s central narrator and Sammar elucidate ways in which the European university, as a central institution in contemporary global economics and the power structures they serve, increasingly challenges the feasibility of alternative postcolonial modernities in the novels.

Foucault describes heterotopia as a mirror capable of simultaneously reflecting multiple realities, underscoring one's participation in and (in the space between the gaze and the reflection) distance from what counts as real. The mirror privileges representation over 'reality' or ordinary existence and, thus, the possibility of invention and fluidity over an ostensible fixity. As "counter-sites, a kind of effectively enacted utopia in which the real sites, all the other real sites that can be found within the culture, are

---

[8] Bill Reading, *The University in Ruins* (Cambridge M A : Harvard U P, 1996): 13.

simultaneously represented, contested, and inverted,"[9] universities serve as exemplary heterotopias to and within modern life. Functioning in theory as banks of knowledge and gatekeepers to professional status, universities meet Foucault's criteria for heterotopias in several key areas: they provide limited access to society's governing codes; various departments provide competing, even conflicting approaches to understanding past and present, while skill components ensure that only the initiated will gain the most profit from and influence over the future; and their libraries and research centres claim deep reservoirs of knowledge in time.[10] For those studying in their home nation, university attendance may range from a rite of passage central to maintaining a privileged social position to a rare opportunity to advance. In either case, despite its rhetorical claims as a democratic social space dedicated to building 'knowledge', universities, whether aiming at the production of national culture or at a corporate model of excellence, are intimately tied to the national bourgeoisie and the continuation of prevailing socio-economic structures. For immigrants from less developed nations, universities would appear to offer unparalleled access to a wider, international world of privilege and influence, access often granted with the caveat or assumption that one will return home to share the benefits with one's own citizenry (even though attendance at a Western/Northern university already signals one's exceptionalism or membership in a national elite, one's distance from the ordinary existence of one's fellow citizens).

We might expect, given Said's foundational study of the university as an academic and corporate institution whose development of orientalism both served the aims of empire and reflected more keenly Western desires than Asian, Middle Eastern, or 'Other' realities, that colonial and postcolonial subjects would find themselves alienated in attendance at such institutions. Indeed, many characters, especially women, in contemporary African fiction manifest such alienation both abroad and once they return home. Esi, in Ama Ata Aidoo's *Changes*, cites tranquilizers as the best cure for racist and sexist professors as well as academic stress in England:

> Like any member of the late-twentieth-century African or other world female élite and neo-élite, she had always known of tranquillisers. At least since she was at the university. After all, you were supposed to become aware from your first year on campus that just

---

[9] Foucault, "Of Other Spaces," 24.
[10] "Of Other Spaces," 25–26.

about everything in this life ruined nerves: ... not knowing how to handle male-chauvinist lecturers who didn't even make the effort to read your essays properly because you were a woman; wanting to be a nuclear physicist but everyone telling you it's much safer to go into teaching because, you know, isn't that too much for a woman?... and wouldn't that be too exotic anyway for Africa?[11]

Teenage Nyasha, in Tsitsi Dangarembga's *Nervous Conditions*, also comments upon the lessons of discrimination "she had learnt first-hand in England" when white Rhodesian missionaries sponsored her parents for graduate degrees in England; while the often violent attempts of her father, Babamukuru, to instil discipline and maintain propriety in his family point to sublimated anger over his patronage and the precariousness of the position it garnered him back in Rhodesia.[12] Even Aboulela's Sudanese student, Shadia, from the prize-winning short story "The Museum," describes herself as "someone tossed around by monstrous waves" at the beginning of graduate school.[13] Shadia and the other foreign students trade stories about "a Nigerian [who] on this very same course committed suicide" and the racist attacks in the city that make their families afraid to go outside.[14] These characters also find themselves outside of the cultures they once knew: Nyasha calls herself a "hybrid" who is neither fully Shona nor English;[15] Esi cannot negotiate prevailing gender codes of conduct regulating personal relationships, and ends up at once married to a polygamist and alone; and Shadia finds herself on the phone with her fiancé, "listen[ing] to the Khartoum gossip as if listening to a radio play."[16] In these instances, attending a Western university which initially appears as an unparalleled opportunity, becomes a trial to survive, and ultimately leaves one estranged culturally and financially (because of his/her comparative wealth) from family and community back home. The experience renders both Europe

---

[11] Ama Ata Aidoo, *Changes: A Love Story* (New York: Feminist Press, 1993), 143–44.

[12] Tsitsi Dangarembga, *Nervous Conditions* (New York: Seal, 1996): 63, 114–15.

[13] Leila Aboulela, "The Museum," in Aboulela, *Coloured Lights* (Edinburgh: Polygon, 2001): 88.

[14] Aboulela, "The Museum," 88, 89.

[15] Dangarembga, *Nervous Conditions*, 78.

[16] Aboulela, "The Museum," 92.

and Africa uncanny, or 'unhomely' in Bhabha's reading of Freud,[17] as the characters find themselves doubly alienated. As Bhabha writes:

> Culture [which I read here in terms of the university] is *heimlich*, with its disciplinary generalizations, its mimetic narratives, its homologous empty time, its seriality, its progress, its customs and coherence. But cultural authority is also un*heimlich*, for to be distinctive, significatory, influential and identifiable, it has to be translated, disseminated, differentiated, interdisciplinary, intertextual, international, inter-racial.[18]

The characters cited above find themselves caught in the "time of a colonial paradox,"[19] a paradox I also want to read spatially here. Neither home nor away, they find themselves in a no-place between the university training-ground and their nation of origin.

Such reactions may be predictable if the university's traditional mission, as Reading argues, is "to train citizen subjects" and "legitimate[e] national culture" as well as to provide a "microcosm of the pure form of the public sphere."[20] Colonial and ex-colonial subjects face the difficult prospect of reconciling the benefits of university learning with concomitant lessons of their own supposed national (and racial) inferiority. As Nancy Fraser and Bruce Robbins, among others, have shown, the ideal public sphere, even in theory, exists only for a potentially imperializing, bourgeois, male subject, thereby relegating the colonial or ex-colonial African student to a hetero-topic no-place where, in Foucault's terms, "I see myself where I am not [...] and] I discover my absence from the place where I am."[21] Those like Esi or Salih's narrator who return to work in the postcolonial bureaucracy are strikingly silent about the national goals of their work, suggesting that either their own training or national planning remains co-opted by neocolonial power-structures and/or the demands of global capitalism. Esi's work as a statistician is seemingly an end unto itself, without application or purpose, as she describes her work: "how much I put into my job [...]

---

[17] Homi K. Bhabha, *The Location of Culture* (New York: Routledge, 1994): 10, 136.
[18] Bhabha, *The Location of Culture*, 136–37.
[19] *The Location of Culture*, 137.
[20] Reading, *The University in Ruins*, 14, 20.
[21] Foucault, "Of Other Spaces," 24.

sometimes I even take home data to analyse!"[22] Even *Season*'s narrator's friend comments that civil servants in the Department of Education "waste time in conferences and poppycock" and demands: "What's the use in our having one of us in the government when you're not doing anything?"[23]

The characters' engagement with the university marks the distance and time between Africa and Europe as the site of a violent irruption of modernity. This distance is not between timeless peasant life in a rural African village vs. that of the bourgeoisie in a modern British metropolis: Sa'eed came from just south of Khartoum and was educated in Cairo at an early age; the narrator lives and works in Khartoum, returning only periodically to the village; and Sammar was born in Britain and rejoined the life of the Khartoum elite at the age of seven.[24] Rather, the temporal and spatial distance is between the dominance of our current stage of transnational, flexible, corporate capitalism, promulgated by the university, and the needs of the postcolonial nation. As Saree Makdisi argues in two excellent essays on the relationship of *Season of Migration* to Arab modernism (as a literary "tendency"),[25] the violence of modernity comes from the double alienation occasioned by the failure to integrate timeless Arab traditionalism with modernization-as-europeanization into a singular narrative. Makdisi reads *Season of Migration* against the background of the *Nahda* or 'renaissance' of the nineteenth century which "culminated in the movements of Arab

---

[22] Aidoo, *Changes*, 50.

[23] Salih, *Season of Migration*, 118.

[24] Their educational backgrounds reflect that of their authors, as Salih took a degree in International Relations from the University of London and Aboulela, the daughter of Sudan's first female demographer, who was also a university professor, earned hers in statistics at the London School of Economics. Citing her return to England as an adult as an opportunity to practise a stricter form of Islam, Aboulela notes: "I grew up in a very westernized environment and went to a private, American school. But my personality was shy and quiet and I wanted to wear the hijab but didn't have the courage, as I knew my friends would talk me out of it [... Back in London in 1989] I felt very free to wear the hijab." Quoted in Anita Sethi, "Keeping the Faith: Award-winning novelist Leila Aboulela tells Anita Sethi why her religious identity is more important to her than her nationality," *The Guardian* (5 June 2005): online http://books.guardian.co.uk/print /0,3858,52085551-99930,00.html (accessed 12 February 2006).

[25] Saree S. Makdisi, "'Postcolonial' Literature in a Neocolonial World: Modern Arabic Culture and the End of Modernity," *boundary 2* 22.1 (Spring 1995): 96.

nationalism."[26] Citing the influence of the Arab scholar Rifaah al-Tahtawi on this cultural and political movement, Makdisi notes that the dominant view of Arab modernity links "social, cultural, and religious traditionalism" with "the adoption of certain 'modern' principles, especially in science, technology, and economy" that are associated with Europe.[27] Such thinking renders the past at once ahistorical and inaccessible and the future "always already displaced and deferred."[28] Makdisi argues that *Season of Migration*, in its treatment of gender and its narrative form (combining influences of European modernism and the Arab oral tradition of *hakawati*),[29] works both politically and aesthetically to interrogate the effects of the *Nahda*, thereby creating the opportunity for alternative narratives of the modern present:[30]

> The tendency that I am calling here Arab 'modernism' contests the *political* as well as the narrative strategies hitherto put into practice in the Arab world, strategies based on narrowly conceived nationalism, on teleology, on a unilinear sense of history, and on modernity as defined either by capitalist institutions or socialist revolutions that *both* hold open the promise of what turns out to be perpetually deferred happiness. And hence it stakes its claims both in opposition to the West *as well as* to the various Arab states as they actually exist.[31]

Makdisi's subtle analysis illuminates how the narrative ambiguities of *Season of Migration* create the potential for the imagining of an alternative present, although that potential seems curiously linked to the ultimate failure, in Makdisi's reading, of the "migration" of the title. If, as he argues, the final scene in which the narrator struggles at a bend in the Nile to reach an undetermined shore (he is disoriented, the bend in the river has made its consistent northward flow unreadable, and he calls out for help as he risks drowning) represents a "quest" or "migration" that never takes place, then we might find in *The Translator* one possible completion of that journey.

---

[26] Saree S. Makdisi, "The Empire Renarrated: *Season of Migration to the North* and the Reinvention of the Present," *Critical Inquiry* 18 (Summer 1992): 806, n4.

[27] Makdisi, "The Empire Renarrated," 807.

[28] Makdisi, "'Postcolonial' Literature in a Neocolonial World," 90.

[29] "The Empire Renarrated," 814.

[30] "'Postcolonial' Literature in a Neocolonial World," 87.

[31] "'Postcolonial' Literature in a Neocolonial World," 86 (emphasis in the original).

Thus, I wish to focus this argument about modernity on the university, the site that binds these characters to one another and to Europe, and extend it to *The Translator*. The more recent novel consciously invokes *Season of Migration*, brings its historical context more closely into the present, and offers a conclusion to the narrative of migrancy. The potential for redirecting the present that Makdisi finds in *Season of Migration* disappears in *The Translator*, as Aboulela uses the romance genre not to grapple with the disorientiations of the uncanny – in Bhabha's terms, to "speak to the 'unhomely' condition of the modern world"[32] or to expose the "awkward, ambivalent, unwelcome truth of empire's lie"[33] – but to assuage its discomforts through a return to what is seemingly *heimlich*.

II

Although *Season of Migration to the North* loosely covers the period from 1898 to the early years of independence in the late 1950s and 1960s, the central narrative takes place around independence in the waning years of the university's traditional function. The novel presents two generations of Sudanese intellectuals educated abroad. Mustafa Sa'eed, the colonized genius whose life spans colonial rule, was born when the British consolidated their power in 1898, left Sudan at fifteen to study in Cairo, went to London after World War I to study economics, and returned to Sudan, only to vanish around independence in 1956. His often mirrored double, alter ego, and metaphorical son, the central narrator, studied "the life of an obscure English poet" at university and then returned home to work for the newly independent civil service, first as an instructor in pre-Islamic literature and then as a bureaucrat in the Department of Education. The two men represent two distinct bids for national unity, central to the success of any national liberation movement and newly independent nation-state, as well as the failures occasioned in both cases by the comprador elite.

Sa'eed's background – as the son of an Arab from the north and a slave from the south – establishes him as a potential representative of national cohesion, though his legacy is one of colonial acquiescence rather than resistance. According to various reports of his background and whereabouts, his father's tribe worked against the Mahdiyah and then on behalf

---

[32] Bhabha, *The Location of Culture*, 11.
[33] *The Location of Culture*, 138.

of "Kitchener's army when he reconquered the Sudan."[34] Others noted that Sa'eed's own remarkable facility with the English language secured him high posts in the colonial administration, the nickname "black Englishman" by his peers, and the dubious honour of being "the first Sudanese to marry an Englishwoman, in fact he was the first to marry a European of any kind."[35] These supposed triumphs appear in ambiguous context, as one of the speakers, a retired civil servant himself, describes them within a critique of British colonial and neocolonial influence:

> The English District Commissioner was a god who had a free hand over an area larger than the whole British Isles and lived in an enormous palace full of servants and guarded by troops. They would employ us, the junior government officials who were natives of the country to bring in the taxes. The people would grumble and complain to the English Commissioner, and naturally it was the English Commissioner who was indulgent and showed mercy. And in this way they sowed hatred in the hearts of the people for us, their kinsmen, and love for the colonizers, the intruders. Mark these words of mine, my son. Has not the country become independent? Have we not become free men in our own country? Be sure, though that they will direct our affairs from afar. This is because they have left behind them people who think as they do. They showed favour to the nonentities – and it was such people that occupied the highest positions in the days of the English.[36]

Multiple ambiguities mark this passage. Sa'eed, with his academic strengths and low social status, is both remarkable and a 'nobody'. In the eyes of a participant in the bureaucracy, Sa'eed *should* have been an exemplary colleague, even though the speaker remains critical of the colonial administration itself. Moreover, by addressing the narrator colloquially as "my son," he echoes persistent questions in the text about the narrator's relationship to Sa'eed and insinuates that the narrator, too, furthers a neocolonial agenda. While the different accounts of Sa'eed's accomplishments consistently attest to his extraordinary intellect and promise, what is at stake in the application of that intellect and promise varies with the context. Whereas, within Sudan, Sa'eed's background and

---

[34] Salih, *Season of Migration*, 54.
[35] *Season of Migration*, 55–56.
[36] *Season of Migration*, 53–54.

early government work make him "part of the problem" facing the soon-to-be-independent nation, he is a figure of resistance and revenge earlier in Britain (in the central drama of the novel), and finally a well-respected if somewhat estranged member of a farming community in Sudan on the verge of independence.

Brian Gibson ably summarizes the focus most critics have placed on the novel's "colonial politics, from Mustafa Sa'eed's adoption of an Oriental persona to his conquests of Englishwomen in order to avenge the ways in which the South/East has been penetrated and possessed by the North/West."[37] This focus on Sa'eed's thirty-odd years in Britain corresponds to the dramatic tension of the novel – Sa'eed's seduction of English women, their deaths that follow, and his subsequent imprisonment for his English wife's murder, yet neglects the ways in which he represents shifting, conflicting positions *vis-à-vis* (neo)colonial rule. As noted above, the older comprador elite within Sudan admire Sa'eed as one of the best and brightest among them even when they attest somewhat ruefully to their own collaboration with colonial rule and his work on behalf of the British. In the present tense of the novel, we meet Sa'eed through the narrator, a member of the next generation of the Western-educated elite (his respectful title, "Effendi" or "Sir," signifies his status as both an educated man and a high-level civil servant), who is introduced to Sa'eed the farmer upon returning to his home village from study abroad and work in Khartoum.

The narrator, as noted in the initial quotation from the novel, views his return home in romanticized terms of timeless cultural values, natural growth as opposed to technological change, and family and community bonds rather than individual autonomy. Uncovering Sa'eed's background reminds the narrator of the uncanny moment of modernity and its incompatibility with his nostalgic view of rural life, of how his own education estranges him from the village. As a regular worshipper at the mosque, hardworking farmer, educated member of the agricultural committee, and dedicated husband, father, and neighbour, Sa'eed has defined a place for himself in the village that the narrator, despite his birth there, now lacks. To the extent that Sa'eed succeeds in "yoking the itinerant metropolitan intellectual tutored in the very heart of British colonial domination into common cause with the rural peasantry," the goal to which the narrator aspires,

---

[37] Brian Gibson, "An Island Unto Himself? Masculinity in *Season of Migration to the North*," *Jouvert* 7.1 (2002): online (accessed 10 April 2003).

Sa'eed represents a possible future for Sudanese nationalism.[38] At the same time, the narrator, who shares Sa'eed's intellectualism and fluency in English, doubts this representation and, after hearing Sa'eed recite English poetry, demands threateningly: "'It's clear you're someone other than the person you claim to be,' I said to him. 'Wouldn't it be better if you told me the truth?'"[39]

Sa'eed reveals his seductions in London, including the sexualized murder of Jean Morris, partly in conversation with the narrator and partly through the clues left, Bluebeard-fashion, in the locked English library/ living room he has constructed alongside his home. The narrative proceeds disjointedly through various times and spaces: Sa'eed's house, where he tells his story over tea, the English room that the narrator enters once Sa'eed disappears (he has presumably drowned in one of the periodic floodings of the Nile, though the text takes great care to inform us of his prodigious swimming abilities and wanderlust), and the lecture halls, courtroom, and bedrooms of England of Sa'eed's triumphs and crimes. As Gayatri Spivak notes in her reading of the novel, the disjunctures of the narrative structure, including in the English room when, "without the plausibility of obvious flashback, the dead Mustafa Sa'eed's narrative voice resumes unexpectedly, telling the story of the murder of a white woman, his previous wife, as the successful completion of an act of sex" (63), document "the violence of the encounter with 'modernity'."[40] She emphasizes that the "a-chrony" of the narration "keeps the event's status narratologically undecidable."[41]

The critics Robert Spencer and Laura Rice, as noted earlier, adroitly read the English room as a heterotopia in which "the condensed and repressed narrative of [the narrator's] community is chronicled."[42] Upon entering this private space and seeing the trappings of Sa'eed's "ideal of an enlightened British self,"[43] including his English-language Qur'an, canonical texts of Western culture from Plato to Shakespeare to Freud, and Sa'eed's own

---

[38] Robert Spencer, "'This Zone of Occult Instability': The Utopian Promise of the African Novel in the Era of Decolonisation," *New Formations* 47 (Summer 2002), 72–73.

[39] Salih, *Season of Migration*, 15.

[40] Gayatri Spivak, *Death of a Discipline* (New York: Columbia UP, 2003): 63.

[41] Spivak, *Death of a Discipline*, 64.

[42] Spencer, "'This Zone of Occult Instability'," 74.

[43] Rice, "Of Heterotopias and Ethnoscapes," 6.

anti-imperialist writings, the narrator terms it "A graveyard. A mausoleum. An insane idea. A prison. A huge joke. A treasure chamber"[44] – all forms of heterotopia; the room reflects the intertwining of colonial and sexual politics that Sa'eed recognized and utilized while abroad and that the narrator is forced to come to terms with in his native village. The narrative function of the room parallels that of Sa'eed's interlocking realms of the lecture hall, courtroom, and bedroom in England.

Recognizing the incompatibility of his "icy" (read: 'Northern') intellect and black skin at the university, Sa'eed exacts a personal revenge for colonialism through his deployment of orientalist tropes to seduce white women (particularly the daughters of civil servants and retired military officers):

> My bedroom was a graveyard that looked onto a garden; its curtains were pink and had been chosen with care, the carpeting was of a warm greenness, the bed spacious, with swansdown cushions.
> There were small electric lights, red, blue, and violet, placed in certain corners; on the walls were large mirrors, so that when I slept with a woman it was as if I slept with a whole harem simultaneously.
> The room was heavy with the smell of burning sandalwood and incense, and in the bathroom were pungent Eastern perfumes, lotions, unguents, powders, and pills.
> My bedroom was like an operating theatre in a hospital.[45]

Orientalist trappings serve clinical aims as Sa'eed entices women into his bedroom, only to assert the dominance over them that he, as a colonized African, lacks in other spheres. By giving the colonizers and their daughters what they desire, he ensures his success among them, elucidates the power dynamics of orientalism through the fields of law, economics, and sexual relations, and finally guarantees a measure of liberal sympathy that ultimately saves him from hanging for Jean Morris's murder. As his defence lawyer argues, "Mustafa Sa'eed, gentlemen of the jury, is a noble person whose mind was able to absorb Western civilization but it broke his heart."[46] This racism persists uncannily alongside a view of the university

---

[44] Salih, *Season of Migration*, 137–38.
[45] *Season of Migration*, 31.
[46] *Season of Migration*, 33.

as ideally a neutral space. Discussing Sa'eed's illustrious reputation with the narrator and another Western-educated Sudanese professor, an English-man who followed Sa'eed at Oxford and now works in the Ministry of Finance critiques Sa'eed's promotion of leftist economics as politics rather than scholarship, concluding:

> If only he had stuck to academic studies he'd have found real friends of all nationalities, and you'd have heard of him here. He would certainly have returned and benefited with his knowledge this coun-try in which superstitions hold sway. And here you are now believ-ing in superstitions of a new sort: the superstition of industrializa-tion, the superstition of nationalization, the superstition of Arab unity, the superstition of African unity. Like children you believe [...]. Through facts, figures, and statistics you can accept your reality, live together with it, and attempt to bring about changes within the limits of your potentialities.[47]

Although the narrator recognizes the Englishman's faith in pure economics as "the superstition of statistics,"[48] he nonetheless remains caught in the conundrum of reconciling his own Western training with a workable pro-gramme of Sudanese modernity and postcolonial nationalism. For the Englishman, working for the Ministry of Finance need not correspond to a viable nationalist programme, while the narrator faces the problem of "na-tionalism as a rhetorical alibi for the comprador middle class."[49]

The narrator unwittingly reveals the incompatibility of Western and rural Sudanese perspectives, eventually recognizing his own complicity in their disjuncture as he sees himself within Sa'eed's mysterious room. Sensing "once again there was that feeling that the ordinary things before one's very eyes were becoming unordinary"[50] whenever he faces the rumours, reflec-tions, and intimations of Sa'eed's life, the narrator is unnerved by the dis-ruptive presence of the uncanny: of his and Sa'eed's discomfiting parallels and of the fissures between the narrator's idealization of village life and his critical view of the gender dynamics that help sustain it. As Spencer argues,

---

[47] Salih, *Season of Migration*, 59.
[48] *Season of Migration*, 60.
[49] Spencer, "'This Zone of Occult Instability'," 75.
[50] *Season of Migration*, 51.

[the narrator's] too cosy identification with the collective upon his
return is purchased at the price of a repression of the myriad patriarchal and myopic habits that characterize that community and
which his role as intellectual might contribute to ameliorating.[51]

The twice-displaced reflection of colonial and sexual politics in the English
room and Sa'eed's British "emplacements" (Foucault) interrupt the process
of repression that Spencer cites above. Heterotopia produces and reflects
the uncanny in the sense of the "defamiliarization of familiar space,"[52]
rendering ordinary existence's ideological structures visible to scrutiny.
Like Bhabha, Spivak welcomes the potential the uncanny represents to dis-
close the rifts in ostensibly seemless narratives of reality. For her, the presence of the uncanny makes possible the embrace of radical alterity between
oneself and others, in "an inexhaustible taxonomy of names, including but
not identical with the whole range of human universals."[53] I follow her turn
to gender as "a critical instrument rather than something to be factored in in
special cases"[54] to welcome the presence of the uncanny as well as a com-
monalty produced through the acknowledgment of radical alterity that the
uncanny may foster. The violence of modernity for Sa'eed and the narrator
then comes to the fore in the gendering of colonial and postcolonial
politics. Whereas Spivak finds promise of overcoming that violence in the
blunt speech of and wailing of the older generation of village women –
voices that disrupt the gendered binary 'logic' of tradition and women
versus modernity and men and point to other possible articulations of modernity – I want to focus here on the ways in which the ambiguities of the
narrative underscore Sa'eed and the narrator's failures in this regard from a
postcolonial standpoint.

     For Sa'eed in England, transforming himself into Othello, the Arab-
African, teller of stories, teller of lies, allows him to reverse the effects of
colonial power even though he operates within its familiar discursive realm.
His response to the violence of colonialism is to reverse the gendered terms
in which it frequently operates while perpetuating violence himself (and, as
Makdisi notes, incurring violence as he "willingly becom[es] for his vic-

---

[51] Spencer, "'This Zone of Occult Instability'," 73.
[52] Spivak, *Death of a Discipline*, 77.
[53] *Death of a Discipline*, 73.
[54] *Death of a Discipline*, 74.

tims the incarnation of the great Orientalist myth-fantasy"[55]). He over-
comes alienation from Britain and the failure of the university as an idealized public sphere by at once empowering himself through Orientalist
tropes and revealing the inconsistencies of their ideological foundations. As
the courtroom scenes reveal, Sa'eed is certainly guilty of murder, but who
is guilty of perpetuating orientalism for imperial ends?

For the narrator, anticipating the demands of postcoloniality, the situation is more complex. Upon Sa'eed's disappearance during the flood, the
narrator becomes the guardian of his property, his wife, Hosna, and their
two sons. When the lecherous patriarch Wad Rayyes announces his desire
to wed the undesiring Hosna, the narrator, with characteristic lack of will-
power, refuses to save her by taking her as his second wife (though she asks
him to and implies that she could be his wife in name only). Although this
resolution would conform to village norms, it conflicts with the narrator's
rejection of polygamy – a rejection strengthened by his education abroad.
His estrangement from the village becomes apparent when Wad Rayyes
rapes Hosna after their marriage. Hosna makes good on her promise to kill
him and then herself, and the narrator, at work in Khartoum during the
tragedy, cannot get even his grandfather or best friend to tell him what has
happened once he returns home. The narrative moves disjointedly from the
narrator's finally learning of the tragedy and admitting his own love for
Hosna to the scene of his entry into Sa'eed's world/room (which concludes
with Sa'eed's ghostly telling of his murder of Jean Morris), to the narrator's
decision, "I had to do something."[56] Following once more Sa'eed's path,
the narrator goes to the river and, "resolved to make the northern shore,"
finds himself "half-way between north and south" when the water over-
takes him and he fears he will drown.[57] Acquiescing to the current pushing
him back to the southern shore, he "decides" to "choose life [...] because
there are a few people I want to stay with for the longest possible time and
because I have duties to discharge."[58] Given his persistent failure to attend
to the gender dynamics of the village or to reconcile his nostalgia for traditional village life with his modern sensibilities, as well as his emulation of
his grandfather and his duties toward Hosna and Sa'eed's two sons, it is

---

[55] Makdisi, "The Empire Renarrated," 812.
[56] Salih, *Season of Migration*, 166.
[57] *Season of Migration*, 167.
[58] *Season of Migration*, 168.

difficult to read the narrator's conclusion as productive in the terms Spivak outlines. Spivak, as noted above, locates this productive potential in the women's speech. The novel, however, returns to its central narrator's story. While he apparently stays in Sudan, he remains suspended between the village whose patriarchal norms sanctioning the polygamy he rejects and the England and Khartoum he repeatedly fails to narrate. He identifies with a masculine realm defined by his grandfather, guardianship of the two boys, and the "dear sirs" and "gentlemen" to whom he addresses the narrative; at the same time, he continually misreads and ultimately fails women. We see this when he says he hears a "cry of pleasure" from Wad Rayyes's house, when we learn later that his eldest wife says "Good riddance!" at Wad Rayyes's death, and when he refuses to respond to Hosna's pleas for his help.[59] Sa'eed, on the other hand, if his oft-mentioned swimming prowess proved reliable, forsakes the postcolonial nation entirely for the ostensible rewards his intellect and black masculinity garner in Europe, rewards dependent upon some form of continuation of orientalist ideology.

III

From independence in 1956 to 1999, when *The Translator* was published, Sudanese nationalism was troubled by frequent coups and persistent civil war. The June 1989 coup by the National Islamic Front, which had won elections but was denied power by the secular military, initiated a nationalism based upon a policy of islamization and construction of an Islamic nation, the *umma*. This development corresponded to economic policies that encouraged growth of the Islamic bourgeoisie (as opposed to that of the predominantly Christian communities of the south), the imposition of

---

[59] Salih, *Season of Migration*, 47, 128. Brian Gibson reads the narrator at the end as having rejected "ego-driven maleness represented by Mustafa and Wad" and the "conservative, pious masculinity of his grandfather" in favour of "a more human community" epitomized briefly in the novel by the Bedouins (Gibson, "An Island Unto Himself"). This reading productively complicates the reading of gender in the novel as more than just binaristic, however, it neglects the extent to which the Bedouin scene is masculinized and idealized, like the early scenes in the village. The crisis in masculinity that Gibson foregrounds reveals to me not so much a turn toward some form of humanism as, in Spencer's words, "the dawning obsolescence of the nationalist programme," or the failure of Effendi's existing models of identity to align with or contribute to a viable nationalism (Spencer, "'The Zone of Occult Instability'," 75).

shari'a, and changing emigration patterns. Salma Ahmed Nageeb argues that "construction of the *umma* [...] is a model of nation-state building that underlines a discontinuity between 'state Islam' and 'popular Islam' or the existing cultures and ways of life."[60] *The Translator*, which takes places mostly during the 1980s and 1990s in both Aberdeen and Khartoum, obliquely references this religious and political context along with that of the first Gulf War, as Sammar holds fast to Islamic traditions while rejecting life in Sudan. More recent political events such as the genocide in Darfur, the 9/11 tragedies, and US- and British-led war in the Middle East (and the anti-Islamic rhetoric that attends it) complicate readings of the novel today. Aboulela, writing after the first Gulf War, proposes an Islamic humanism and marriage between North and South that seems problematic today, not because cultural reconciliations are not possible but because of the intense debate surrounding the terms that frame it. Echoing *Jane Eyre*'s romantic conclusion, as well as Jean Rhys's anticolonial rejoinder in *Wide Sargasso Sea*, *The Translator* details the developing relationship between a young, widowed Sudanese translator, Sammar, and the older "Middle Eastern historian and lecturer in Third World Politics,"[61] Rae Isles, for whom she works at the university in Aberdeen. Their relationship appears doomed by Sammar's religious convictions, which would prevent her from marrying a non-Muslim, Rae's avowed secularism, and the potentially negative career effects of his liberal politics and investment in Sammar. More like the story of Jane than of Rhys's Antoinette, Sammar's concludes happily when Rae converts, formally proposes to Sammar in Sudan, trades authoring monographs for textbooks, and the couple head back to Aberdeen.[62] The novel constructs their common ground through religion and professionalism, leaving aside the potential 'problem' of national identity or broader *umma*.

In a 2005 interview to promote her second novel, *Minaret*, Aboulela discusses her grounding in religious rather than national identity: "I can carry [religion] with me wherever I go, whereas the other things can easily be

---

[60] Salma Ahmed Nageeb, *New Spaces and Old Frontiers: Women, Social Space, and Islamization in Sudan* (New York: Lexington, 2004): 18.

[61] Aboulela, *The Translator*, 5.

[62] For a slightly longer discussion of parallels between *The Translator* and *Jane Eyre*, see John A. Stotesbury, "Genre and Islam in Recent Anglophone Romantic Fiction," in *Refracting the Canon in Contemporary British Literature and Film*, ed. Susan Onega & Christian Gutleben (New York: Rodopi, 2004): 69–82.

taken away from me."[63] Critical work on *The Translator* adheres to this claim. Calling *The Translator* a *"Scottish* novel" (emphasis in the original), John A. Stotesbury finds that "while Sammar's soul remains embedded – rooted – in Islam, her heart remains in Scotland."[64] The strength of her faith, moreover, argues Geoffrey Nash, becomes a site of feminized resistance to "the frustrations of a dysfunctional Muslim African polity as well as marginalization in an empty Western metropolis."[65] In these readings, Aboulela's appropriation of conventions of Western romance defines a sphere in which the heroine's Islamic identity can reach fruition in marriage as well as serve as an antidote to what she has elsewhere called the West's "abundance mixed with emptiness, an abundance without blessing."[66]

Central to both the reviewers' and Aboulela's own invocation of the productive uses of the romance genre is a valuing of the familiar, knowing, comforting conclusions it ostensibly offers, the promise of culture as *heimlich*. Rather than identify such gains achieved through romance (as genre and in relationships between a non-Western, Islamic woman and a white, Western man), I would like to explore the productive potential of the uncanny in the spaces the characters inhabit. This approach demands a reading against the conventional gendered dynamics and structural codes of romance fiction, suggesting that in their failure, in terms of the genre, rather than their success we might find ways of living *with* radical alterity. In place of the rural image of the rooted tree that Salih offers, *The Translator* opens in the Winter Garden of Duthie Park, initially planted by Miss World 1979 and containing an arboretum and flora specimens from around the world. This transnational space underscores the power of the collector to create pleasure at home from environments abroad, and thus the lasting effects of colonial power. For Sammar and Rae, meeting alone together for the first time, it is also a site re-imagining the Other within and against the guise of the familiar. As they talk on a bench in the room that "was meant to give the impression of a desert," with "cacti [...] like rows of aliens in shades of green, of different heights, standing still, listening," the sense of

---

[63] Sethi, "Keep the Faith."

[64] Stotesbury, "Genre and Islam in Recent Anglophone Romantic Fiction," 73, 77.

[65] Geoffrey Nash, "Re-Siting Religion and Creating Feminised Space in the Fiction of Ahdaf Soueif and Leila Aboulela," *Wasafiri* 35 (Spring 2002): 28–29.

[66] Leila Aboulela, "Moving Away From Accuracy," *Alif: Journal of Contemporary Poetics* 22 (1 January 2002), online: 198.

foreboding is ameliorated by Sammar's transformation of Winter Park into the deserts of Sudan.[67] Translating her name for Rae, she explains: "It means conversations with friends, late at night. It's what the desert nomads liked to do, talk leisurely by the light of the moon, when it was no longer so hot and the day's work was over."[68] This early scene defines the central question of the novel: given that the idealized communal Bedouin world (another version of the idealized past that Makdisi identified as ultimately alienating in his argument regarding the *Nahda*) has evidently passed (it was what the nomads "*liked* to do"), will Sammar be able to re-create some version of that intimacy in Aberdeen? She consistently gauges the potential of their intimacy against its possible interruption by the uncanny, finding repeatedly that "she had never said anything that surprised him before [and] she wanted it always to be like that."[69] If, as Homi Bhabha argues, "the un-homely moment relates the traumatic ambivalences of a personal, psychic history to the wider disjunctures of political existence,"[70] we should be wary of romantic conclusions based on the denial of the uncanny. Indeed, despite the seemingly happy ending, the novel details the extent to which both the British university and the Sudanese elite reject its Islamic humanist claims.

In privileging the role of the translator within the genre of romance, Aboulela combines faith and love to suggest that Sammar, in helping to bring Rae to Islam, is successful within "the freedom of faithful reproduction and, in its service, fidelity to the word."[71] In this dream of perfect translation of the sacred, "just as, in the original, language and revelation are one without any tension, so that translation must be one with the original [...] in which literalness and freedom are united."[72] As Sammar tells Rae: "Allah tells us in the Qur'an, reminds us again and again, these verses are not the words of a poet, they are Divine revelation, certain truth."[73] My

---

[67] Aboulela, *The Translator*, 4.

[68] *The Translator*, 5.

[69] *The Translator*, 6.

[70] Bhabha, *The Location of Culture*, 11.

[71] Walter Benjamin, "The Task of the Translator: An Introduction to the Translation of Baudelaire's *Tableaux Parisiens*" ("Die Aufgabe des Übersetzers," 1923), tr. Harry Zohn (1968), in *The Translation Studies Reader*, ed. Lawrence Venuti (New York: Routledge, 2000): 20.

[72] Benjamin, "The Task of the Translator," 23.

[73] Aboulela, *The Translator*, 112.

reading of the productive potential of the novel corresponds to Paul de Man's rereading of Walter Benjamin's "The Task of the Translator":

> We think we are at ease in our own language, we feel a coziness, a familiarity, a shelter in the language we call our own, in which we think that we are not alienated. What the translation reveals is that this alienation is at its strongest in our relation to our own original language, that the original language within which we are engaged is disarticulated in a way which imposes upon us a particular aliena-tion, a particular suffering.[74]

Reading against the idealized claims of romance and translation, in other words, enables the uncanny to emerge at the moment of alienation to identi-fy the relations of ruling that shape conditions of ordinary existence at the British university and in Sudan. The happy conclusion of *The Translator* in marriage and in Scotland, with Sudan reduced to a tourist destination, fits the expectations of both genre and translation; however, that conclusion masks the failure of Sudanese postcoloniality upon which it depends. Inter-estingly, although Rae recognizes early on that "translations don't do [the Qur'an] justice,"[75] the novel leaves the problem of translation aside in validating his authentic conversion, even though he has not become fluent in Arabic.

Sammar arrives in Aberdeen as a member of a generation of migrants driven by economic rather than humanitarian interests. Accompanying her husband, who is attending medical school, she fits the dominant class of migrants surveyed by Rogaia Mustafa Abusharaf.[76] Out of 300 migrants surveyed, Abusharaf found that 92 percent were Muslims, 92 percent from the north (rather than the predominantly Christian south that has lacked economic opportunities and suffered more human rights violations since the islamization policies were initiated). Most migrated for education and economic opportunities, and most came from the best-educated segment of the home population.[77] These numbers correspond broadly to the global

---

[74] Paul de Man, "Conclusions: Walter Benjamin's 'The Task of the Translator'," in *The Resistance to Theory* (Minneapolis: U of Minnesota P, 1986): 84.

[75] Aboulela, *The Translator*, 112.

[76] Abusharaf surveyed North American migrants from 1992–98, and I am assuming the percentages would be roughly comparable to Britain.

[77] Rogaia Mustafa Abusharaf, *Wanderings: Sudanese Migrants and Exiles in North America* (Ithaca NY: Cornell UP, 2002): 8–9.

survey of foreign students in the world conducted by UNESCO and reported by Reading in *The University in Ruins*, which attests to the growth of economic migrancy and consumerism in higher education.[78] Reading concludes that "the personal and cultural costs of migration are immense, yet what is clear is that the economic pressure to migration in a global market is rendering the labor force more flexible and adaptable to capital at the direct expense of the integrity of the nation-state as a cultural formation."[79]

For Sammar, those costs include the loss of her husband, Tarig, and son, Amir (her husband was killed in a car accident and, in her grief, she sent her son back to Khartoum for her mother-in-law to raise), and numb existence in a heterotopia of the university and her sterile apartment. Belonging neither in Sudan nor in Britain, she seems closest to sharing this liminal space with Rae's secretary, Yasmin, who, despite being raised in Britain by first-generation Pakistani immigrants and being extremely knowledgeable about the social services provided by the state, "had a habit of making general statements starting with 'we', where 'we' meant the whole of the Third World and its people."[80] Although Yasmin has a political savvy and sense of injustice Sammar apparently lacks, she and her husband, who works "some of the time on the oilrigs off-shore,"[81] are active participants in the production and circulation of global capital, such that their identities are shaped more by their roles as consumers and corporate laborers than by national belonging, thereby exacerbating the "hollowing out of [their] political subjectivity."[82]

While Yasmin exists in a contradictory relation to the political and economic forces of global capitalism, Sammar lives in a political no-place, "in a room with nothing on the wall, nothing personal, no photographs, no books; just like a hospital room [...]. Four years in a hospital room she had made for herself."[83] Her heterotopic apartment echoes the failed promise of medical training for Tarig, a failure made explicit when his body is brought there, among his colleagues, after the accident. The apartment also contrasts with the hospital as a site of healing for the asthmatic Rae and, final-

---

[78] Reading, *The University in Ruins*, 48-4-9.
[79] *The University in Ruins*, 48.
[80] Aboulela, *The Translator*, 10.
[81] *The Translator*, 10.
[82] Reading, *The University in Ruins*, 48.
[83] Aboulela, *The Translator*, 14.

ly, with Rae's house, which Sammar terms "a real home."[84] Caught between the resonances of the hospital-as-home for the two men, Sammar
finds herself literally and figuratively on the stairwell. In one of several pas-
sages in which Sammar uses the stairway phone to call Rae, she muses,
"Where was she now, which country? What year? She climbed the stairs
into a hallucination in which the world had swung around. Home and the
past had come here and balanced just for her."[85]

The transformation of heterotopia into home, while facilitated by contact
with Rae, is initially deferred in the novel by competing claims of university politics and Sammar's faith. Far from being an idealized public sphere
of knowledge and dialogue, the university Aboulela details is notable for its
awkward moments, petty politics, superficial tolerance of difference, and
false claims of objectivity. Rae, whose too-liberal book on the *Illusion of an
Islamic Threat* wins him favourable reviews but declining political capital,
is passed over for a consultancy on an anti-terrorist programme, his under-
graduates fail to attend his lectures, and his health problems intrude on his
teaching schedule. His doctoral student, Diane, when not avoiding him in
her embarrassment at getting behind in her work, childishly mimics his
inquiries and complains about his grading. The other office staff gossip
about Rae's health, his work, and his relationships. Students and faculty,
meanwhile, vehemently attest to their liberalism and multicultural leanings.
Sammar remembers, for instance, Jennifer, the head of the Languages department, calling her in for a meeting during the first Gulf War "when suddenly everyone became aware that Sammar was Muslim": "Jennifer said,
'My boyfriend is Nigerian,' and paused as if that statement had a deeper
meaning she wanted Sammar to grasp [...]. Jennifer talked away fresh and
brisk, reassuring her of how broad-minded and tolerant she was, not like so
many people. 'For example,' Jennifer said, 'I have no problem at all with
the way you dress'."[86]

The hypocrisies of the university, where success seems measured in outside contracts and requests for commentary from prominent media outlets,
become more poignant and telling than caustically funny when they
impinge upon Sammar and Rae's relationship. The central impasse of the
romance emerges as a conflict between secular (ostensibly objective)

---

[84] Aboulela, *The Translator*, 14.
[85] *The Translator*, 36.
[86] *The Translator*, 88–89.

knowledge and religious conviction. When Sammar asks Rae to convert so that they may marry, he explains:

> "It's not in me to be religious [...]. I studied Islam for the politics of the Middle East. I did not study it for myself [...].I believed the best that I could do, what I owed a people and a place that had deep meaning for me, was to be objective, detached."[87]

This 'reasoned' explanation relegates Sammar to the place "where his students sat, on that same armchair, panicking about their exams, their financial difficulties, on the edge of dropping out" and precipitates her anguished departure for Khartoum.[88]

In the context of the romance novel, this scene defines "the series of obstacles in the form of 'social or psychological barriers' that need to be overcome for [the popular heroine's] quest to be resolved satisfactorily in marriage,"[89] in this case the need for them to meet as equals and for Rae to reconcile the demands of faith and objectivity. More productively, however, we might read this scene for its depiction of the limitations of Western academic discourse in addressing issues of faith and the modern communities they might engender. "The problem is," in Dipesh Chakrabarty's words, that "we do not have analytical categories in academic discourse that do justice to the real, everyday and multiple 'connections' we have to what we, in becoming modern, have come to see as 'non-rational'."[90] The argument between Rae and Sammar that temporarily suspends their relationship portends a broader problem of the presence of religion in the university, of the failure of academic discourse (and, in the second section of the novel, of the postcolonial state) to reconcile identifications based on faith with those of modernity.

Back in Sudan, Sammar witnesses at first hand the limitations of the government: power failures that repeatedly stop the characters' fans, computers and VCRs, water cuts, "rubble-strewn" streets, job shortages, low

---

[87] Aboulela, *The Translator*, 113–14.

[88] *The Translator*, 114.

[89] Stotesbury, "Genre and Islam in Recent Anglophone Romance Fiction," 71.

[90] Dipesh Chakrabarty, "Radical Histories and the Question of Enlightenment Rationalism: Some Recent Critiques of Subaltern Studies," in *Mapping Subaltern Studies and the Postcolonial*, ed. Vinayak Chaturvedi (London & New York: Verso, 2000): 262.

pay, poor schools, and book shortages.[91] Signalling the discontents of the elite, relatives and friends regularly "curse the government, the electricity company, life itself" and berate her for abandoning her opportunities in Britain.[92] Nageeb writes that the "Islamist state increasingly polices spaces in order to [...] ensure the production of 'Islamic citizen,' a process of Islamization, corresponding to 'nationalization' that tends to erode other forms of local subjectivity, identities." This policing, ironically, produces a de-territorialization as the elite increasingly consume television and internet images of the West.[93] Writing after the 1992 General Education Act, which provides for the "Islamization of knowledge," including at the university level, Aboulela avoids direct mention of politics, but notes the humiliation of the women in her literacy classes, whose "reading syllabus was set by a government commission and [for whom] because of the shortage of books, children's school books were used,"[94] as well as her relatives urging her to take her son back to Britain for his education: "You don't know how the schools here have become."[95]

The centrality of gender in the work of building the *umma* is manifested in the distance between the islamization of social space – for instance, as legislated by the Public Order Act of 1991 that "defines appropriate Islamic conduct at the public level and addresses appearance, particularly that of women, and public interaction"[96] – and the depoliticized Islam that Sammar invokes in trying to make Khartoum seem like home. Challenged by the inheritance laws that limit her ownership of the house (after Tarig's death, the house belongs to Sammar, her mother-in-law, and Amir, with Amir owning the majority share) and codes of marriage and family life that leave her at the mercy of her mother-in-law's spite and bitterness over Tarig's death, Sammar seems relegated to a lonely life as a single woman in a feminized domestic sphere. Rae saves her from this 'fate' by following traditional codes of conduct. He has his Arab friend write to her in Arabic with a formal marriage proposal and news of Rae's conversion, writes himself in English, then comes to meet her family and bring her back to

---

[91] Aboulela, *The Translator*, 133.
[92] *The Translator*, 131.
[93] Nageeb, *New Spaces and Old Frontiers*, 32.
[94] Aboulela, *The Translator*, 152.
[95] *The Translator*, 137.
[96] Nageeb, *New Spaces and Old Frontiers*, 19.

Aberdeen, noting: "I wanted to do everything properly."[97] Sammar jokes, "If I was someone else [...] I would tell you now, I don't want to go back with you, I don't want to leave my family, I love my country too much." Rae is not worried by this potential derailment of his proposal, responding knowingly: "You're not someone else."[98]

Not only does Rae's conversion, whose potential Yasmin described earlier in the novel as "professional suicide,"[99] allow Sammar and Amir to reclaim Britain as home, it is purchased at a price set by the university. Referring obliquely to the way their relationship undermines his professional standing (already in jeopardy because of his liberalism) as an expert on the Middle East, he notes:

> "I am writing a textbook, an introduction to the politics of North Africa. I've decided it's time for me to write a textbook and not concentrate so much on analysing current affairs."[100]

It is worth noting the value university assessment might place on such a project: the more widely adopted the textbook the better, above potentially controversial monographs with more limited audiences/consumers.

Wittingly or unwittingly, Aboulela places Rae's professional transformation in the context of its orientalist roots (and routes) while insisting on his ability to attend both to religious conviction and to scholarly demands of objectivity. Asking Sammar about visiting Umdurman, the burial place of the saints, he remembers his father showing him old maps "on which Eritrea and Palestine existed" when he was a child: "I used to see the name Umdurman, written near the blue line of the Nile. I would say Umdurman to myself, over and over again, liking the sound of it."[101] Deciding they will visit the old houses, camel market, and saints' graves before they leave, Rae and Sammar forgo the electricity failures and hotel rats of Khartoum for one last nostalgic look at premodern and precolonial Sudan before returning to Aberdeen. There, her skills as *his* translator are presumably no longer needed, although she no doubt has more professional opportunities than in Sudan, and his position in the contemporary university has been

---

[97] Aboulela, *The Translator*, 177.
[98] *The Translator*, 179.
[99] *The Translator*, 20.
[100] *The Translator*, 176.
[101] *The Translator*, 182.

secured. He appears ready to educate the next generation of the transnational elite in the demands of global capital and its (neo)colonial under-
pinnings. Acceding to Rae's romantic view of the past, one that dovetails
with her invocations of the lost world of the Bedouin, Sammar completes
the journey from Sudan to Britain that was at least begun by Mustafa
Sa'eed. Significantly, his birth coincided, as Makdisi reminds us, with "the
year the bloody defeat of the Mahdist forces by Kitchener's army in the
battle of Omdurman, which signaled the final collapse of Sudanese resistance to British encroachment."[102]

IV

The critique offered here of the university and the possibility of translation
is not, in this reading, wholly lamentable, as these conditions necessitate a
renewed commitment to one's ethical responsibility for the radical Other,
for irreducible alterity. As Robert Eagleston writes,

> We are each responsible for those we do not, cannot, and could not
> understand [...].
>   Does this mean that we should not translate? No. But it does
> mean that we have ethical grounds to be even more suspicious of the
> idea of translation and the way in which it relates to communities:
> 'what I translate is upset by the way I translate.'[103]

The Translator invites such questioning into the possible nature of community and conversation based upon alterity that emerges through the uncanny, rather than familiarity and homeliness, because of the way in which
it foregrounds the uncanny in its rendering of romance. Both *Season of
Migration* and *The Translator* outline the absence of alternative modernities that might find support in communities between a Bedouin-inspired
past and the comprador elite at home and abroad. We are left with the
questions Simon Gikandi raises at the end of his essay on "Globalization
and the Claims of Postcoloniality" about whether to read works such as
these Anglo-Sudanese novels (*Season to Migration* was originally written

---

[102] Makdisi, "Empire Renarrated," 811.

[103] Robert Eagleston, "Levinas, Translation, and Ethics," in *Nations, Language and
the Ethics of Translation*, ed. Sandra Bermann & Michael Wood (Princeton NJ: Princeton UP, 2005): 137.

in Arabic, while *The Translator* is an anglophone text) as "powerful signs of global culture" or whether "globality has become a supplement, or even alibi, for prior categories of national culture such as Englishness."[104] One wonders, too, about their reception in Sudan. Those of us who continue to make our living in the university, where the commitment to 'excellence' is often measured by the external funding we win, face the challenge of sly translation: of teaching and reading for the presence of the uncanny that disrupts neat equations of cultural authenticity, linguistic fixity, and economic and political power and suggests other foundations for modernity.

WORKS CITED

Aboulela, Leila. "Moving Away From Accuracy," *Alif: Journal of Contemporary Poetics* 22 (1 January 2002), online: 198–208.

——. "The Museum," in Aboulela, *Coloured Lights* (Edinburgh: Polygon, 2001): 87–106.

——. *The Translator* (Edinburgh: Polygon, 1999).

Abusharaf, Rogaia Mustafa. *Wanderings: Sudanese Migrants and Exiles in North America* (Ithaca NY: Cornell UP, 2002).

Aidoo, Ama Ata. *Changes: A Love Story* (New York: Feminist Press, 1993).

Benjamin, Walter. "The Task of the Translator: An Introduction to the Iranslation of Baudelaire's *Tableaux Parisiens*" ("Die Aufgabe des Übersetzers," 1923), tr. Harry Zohn (1968), in *The Translation Studies Reader*, ed. Lawrence Venuti (New York: Routledge, 2000): 15–25.

Bhabha, Homi K. *The Location of Culture* (New York: Routledge, 1994).

Chakrabarty, Dipesh. "Radical Histories and the Question of Enlightenment Rationalism: Some Recent Critiques of Subaltern Studies," in *Mapping Subaltern Studies and the Postcolonial*, ed. Vinayak Chaturvedi (London & New York: Verso, 2000): 256–80.

Dangarembga, Tsitsi. *Nervous Conditions* (New York: Seal, 1996).

De Man, Paul. "Conclusions: Walter Benjamin's 'The Task of the Translator'," in de Man, *The Resistance to Theory* (Minneapolis: U of Minnesota P, 1986): 73–105.

Eagleston, Robert. "Levinas, Translation, and Ethics," in *Nation, Language and the Ethics of Translation*, ed. Sandra Bermann & Michael Wood (Princeton NJ: Princeton UP, 2005): 127–138.

Foucault, Michel. "Of Other Spaces," tr. Jay Miskowicc, *Diacritics* 16.1 (Spring 1986): 22–27.

---

[104] Simon Gikandi, "Globalization and the Claims of Postcoloniality," in *Postcolonialisms: An Anthology of Cultural Theory and Criticism*, ed. Guarav Desai & Supriya Nair (New Brunswick NJ: Rutgers UP, 2005): 631.

Fraser, Nancy. "Rethinking the Public Sphere: A Contribution to the Critique of Actually Existing Democracy," in *The Phantom Public Sphere*, ed. & intro. Bruce Robbins (Minneapolis: U of Minnesota P, 1993): 1–32.

Gibson, Brian. "An Island Unto Himself? Masculinity in *Season of Migration to the North*," *Jouvert* 7.1 (2002): online [accessed 10 April 2003].

Gikandi, Simon. "Globalization and the Claims of Postcoloniality," in *Postcolonialisms: An Anthology of Cultural Theory and Criticism*, ed. Gaurav Desai & Supriya Nair (New Brunswick NJ: Rutgers UP, 2005): 608–34.

Makdisi, Saree S. "The Empire Renarrated: *Season of Migration to the North* and the Reinvention of the Present," *Critical Inquiry* 18 (Summer 1992): 804–20.

——. "'Postcolonial' Literature in a Neocolonial World: Modern Arabic Culture and the End of Modernity," *boundary 2* 22.1 (Spring 1995): 85–115.

Nageeb, Salma Ahmed. *New Spaces and Old Frontiers: Women, Social Space, and Islamization in Sudan* (New York: Lexington, 2004).

Nash, Geoffrey. "Re-Siting Religion and Creating Feminised Space in the Fiction of Ahdaf Soueif and Leila Aboulela," *Wasafiri* 35 (Spring 2002): 28–31.

Reading, Bill. *The University in Ruins* (Cambridge MA: Harvard UP, 1996).

Rice, Laura. "Of Heterotopias and Ethnocscapes: The Production of Space in Postcolonial North Africa," *Critical Matrix* 14 (Fall 2003): online 36–75, http://ez .hamilton.edu:2048/login?url=http://proquest.umi.com/pqdweb?did=671854121& sid=1&Fmt=3&clientid=5446&RQT=309&VName=PQD (accessed 3/20/2006).

Robbins, Bruce, ed. & intro. *The Phantom Public Sphere* (Minneapolis: U of Minnesota P, 1993).

Said, Edward W. *Orientalism* (New York: Vintage, 1979).

Salih, Tayeb. *Season of Migration to the North*, tr. Denys Johnson–Davies (Portsmouth NH: Heinemann, 1969).

Sethi, Anita. "Keep the Faith: Award-winning novelist Leila Aboulela tells Anita Sethi why her religious identity is more important to her than her nationality," *The Guardian* (5 June 2005): online http://books.guardian.co.uk/print/0,3858,5208 5551-99930,00.html (accessed 12 February 2006).

Spencer, Robert. "'This Zone of Occult Instability': The Utopian Promise of the African Novel in the Era of Decolonisation," *New Formations* 47 (Summer 2002): 69–86.

Spivak, Gayatri Chakravorty. *Death of a Discipline* (New York: Columbia UP, 2003).

Stotesbury, John A. "Genre and Islam in Recent Anglophone Romantic Fiction," in *Refracting the Canon in Contemporary British Literature and Film*, ed. Susana Onega & Christian Gutleben (Amsterdam & New York: Rodopi, 2004): 69–82.

‹›

Refusing to Speak as a Victim

– ‹› – Agency and the *arrivant*
in Abdulrazak Gurnah's Novel *By the Sea*

MARIA OLAUSSEN

I

I N ABDULRAZAK GURNAH'S NOVEL *By the Sea*, Saleh Omar,
an elderly man from Zanzibar, arrives in England with the conviction
that he should pretend that he does not speak English. He carries with
him a casket of incense, *ud-al-qamari*, as a token of his connection to the
past, and in his story he allows this casket to carry the significance of his
identity into his new place rather than the usual name, passport, and language. His passport, and therefore also his name, belong to a deceased man,
Rajab Shaaban Mahmud. Significantly enough, he is obliged to leave his
casket at the customs, and he is admitted into Britain only after having
uttered the words "refugee, asylum."

Arrival and exile in Europe is a common theme in Abdulrazak Gurnah's
fiction. This theme is often placed against the backdrop of the history of
Zanzibar, emphasizing the history of travel and migration which brought
together African peoples and Indian merchants under both Arab rulers and
European colonial authorities. *By the Sea* is his sixth novel and it continues
to explore the theme of exile in Europe. It is therefore not set against a
particular, ethnically homogeneous homeland, but forms part of the ongoing exploration of how identities and cultures are formed and develop.
The protagonists of Gurnah's novels are often men who, in their confrontation with radical changes in society or through their experience of exile,
find that definitions and ideals of masculinity change. Complex relation-

ships between men, family feuds and estranged relations are found in most
of Gurnah's novels.

The novel *By the Sea* involves two character–narrators, Saleh Omar and
Latif Mahmud, who, to varying degrees, both come to experience themselves as recipients of European benevolence. They share a story of the past
in Zanzibar, but have both come to live in Britain. Latif Mahmud also lived
in East Germany. The definition of Europe in this narrative is thus shaped
by the opposition between the old life and the new life, as well as by the
attempts at finding new forms for the story of the past. This story is framed
primarily as a way for the narrators to come to terms with their different
experiences of the past, a way to reach some kind of understanding and
reconciliation. It is, however, not told as a way of communicating with their
new surroundings in Britain.

In this encounter with Europe, Saleh Omar finds that his admittance is
possible only by accepting a predetermined relationship between himself as
a help-seeking stranger and Europe defined as helper. The production of
Europe in this novel can be read as a critique of an unquestioning acceptance of the relation between victim and helper, as well as a wish to
articulate the complexities of this relation. In a discussion about human
rights, Gayatri Spivak points out that the word 'rights' in this context "acquires verbal meaning by its contiguity with the word *wrongs*. The verb *to
right* cannot be used intransitively on this level of abstraction."[1] Spivak
further argues:

> 'Human Rights' is not only about having or claiming a right or a set
> of rights; it is also about righting wrongs, about being the dispenser
> of these rights. The idea of human rights, in other words, may carry
> within itself the agenda of a kind of social Darwinism – the fittest
> must shoulder the burden of righting the wrongs of the unfit – and
> the possibility of an alibi.[2]

What is central to Spivak's stand on this issue, however, is what she calls
the "enabling violation"; the righting of wrongs must take place even in the
face of this violation. Spivak's concern here is to point to what she calls an
"epistemic discontinuity" between human-rights advocates and those whom

---

[1] Gayatri Chakravorty Spivak, "Use and Abuse of Human Rights," *boundary* 2 32.1
(2005): 523.
[2] Spivak, "Use and Abuse of Human Rights," 523.

they protect.[3] This discontinuity determines a situation where "the reasonable righting of wrongs is inevitably the manifest destiny of groups [...] that remain poised to right them; and that, among the receiving groups, wrongs will inevitably proliferate with unsurprising regularity."[4] In the novel *By the Sea*, this dichotomy between "the fit" and "the unfit" is brought out in a context which serves to highlight and problematize the definition of Europe as protector and helper.

Despite this focus on Europe, the narrative is structured around the two narrators' complex and intertwined experience of the past in Zanzibar. The first narrator, Saleh Omar, is known as Rajab Shaaban Mahmud, the name of a deceased person whose passport and identity he was able to obtain for the purpose of fleeing to Britain. Throughout the narrative, the curious past connections between the deceased and the narrator are revealed. Saleh Omar was a successful businessman in Zanzibar, who obtained the house of Rajab Shaaban Mahmud through a complicated business deal. At the centre of this deal is one of the merchants from the Gulf, Uncle Hussein, who took advantage of the late Rajab Shaaban Mahmud and his family. The story of the past is told also from the perspective of the second narrator, Latif Mahmud, who happens to be the son of the late Rajab Shaaban Mahmud. This story reveals that the deceased was an alcoholic, a disgrace to his family, and ultimately unable to keep a roof over their heads. His wife was the mistress of a powerful politician, and it is her intervention that leads to the destruction of Saleh Omar's business in Zanzibar, and ultimately to his imprisonment and exile. It is in the act of fleeing that Saleh Omar takes the name of Rajab Shaaban Mahmud, the name of a victim, of a man who is not respected and who does not live up to ideals of masculinity in the form of a provider. In taking the name Rajab Shaaban Mahmud, Saleh Omar changes places with himself, occupying the position of his own victim. It is also significant that neither the process through which he comes to own Rajab Shaaban Mahmud's house nor the taking of the name occurs with any form of premeditation. It is, rather, the result of passivity and circumstance.

Gurnah's novels have constituted a problem for critics who look for expressions of a particular ethnic or migrant identity. Simon Lewis has discussed the novels of Gurnah and the Kenyan-Canadian author M.G. Vassanji,

---

[3] Spivak, "Use and Abuse of Human Rights," 527.
[4] "Use and Abuse of Human Rights," 530.

and concludes that these novelists are hard to place in terms of national literary traditions. He then asks himself:

> Under such circumstances, when individual identity, or subject for-
> mation, appears problematic, what happens to political agency?
> What kind of imagined communities do Gurnah and Vassanji affili-
> ate themselves with?[5]

He concludes that "their stories can oppose the narrative authority of European definitiveness not by speaking in a different tongue [...] but by undercutting narrative assumptions in other ways."[6] One assumption that is undercut through this refusal to produce literary subjects in the form of representatives for particular ethnic groups is the idea of a direct relation between the subject of literature and particular ethnic identities. The responsibility of the author and the reader is, in this assumption, seen as linked to their ethnic or national identity or to the political position they take on behalf of such groups. If the process of interpellation, whereby the subject comes into being as an individual within existing discursive contexts, is itself the object of scrutiny, the study of literary texts is not primarily about seeing characters as representatives of particular ethnic groups. It could, rather, focus on the process of interpellation itself and could open up to new ways of expressing human subjectivity. Derek Attridge's *The Singularity of Literature* argues for this understanding of textual instrumentality:

> A responsible textual instrumentality can rest only on readings that
> are themselves responsible, and there is currently a great danger that
> the works being invoked as keys to historical understanding or
> political progress will not be attended to with sufficient scrupulous-
> ness to allow them to complete (which will usually also be to com-
> plicate) the task they are called in to perform.[7]

'Singularity' is understood in the Derridean sense of absolute otherness, a position which resists the known and the general even when the text evokes

---

[5] Simon Lewis, "Impossible Domestic Situations: Questions of Identity and Nationalism in the Novels of Abdulrazak Gurnah and M.G. Vassanji," *Thamyris* 6.2 (Autumn 1999): 217.

[6] Lewis, "Impossible Domestic Situations," 224.

[7] Derek Attridge, *The Singularity of Literature* (London & New York: Routledge, 2004): 13.

generality. The function of literature is here to resist a construction of the authenticity of a predetermined Other, defined in terms of, for instance, gender, national identity or ethnicity.

In this reading, I want to pay attention to resistance, focusing on how the text articulates new ways of understanding human subjectivity through the ideas of European rescue and of the agency of the victim. The narrative stresses the importance of the discursive frame within which the victim articulates his own position, and shows how this position is gendered in rather complex and contradictory ways. In turning the focus to the representation of Europe, we find that the idea of rescue is closely tied up with how Europe comes to be defined as a space which marks the speaker as a stranger and an outsider. Derrida's concept of the *arrivant* can be used to discuss this aspect of the novel.

The question of speech and silence is also articulated on many levels. Here I will focus on the use Gurnah makes of Herman Melville's story "Bartleby, the Scrivener" and the significance of the refusal of agency for the question of subjectivity expressed in the novel. This issue comes to be closely related to how the subject of literature stands in relation to the constitution of identities and how the limits and possibilities of human identity are expressed. Literature of migration need not be read only as the expression of the experience of particular groups of migrants but could also be read as part of the ongoing interrogation of the meaning of Europe in the articulation of any subject-positions.

The representation of European rescue is also gendered, in the sense that the space offered to the outsider is framed as a domestic space, marked as distinct from the public space of influence and power. The asylum seekers are all men and their helpers are women. Saleh Omar's initial refusal to take up the position of a speaking subject is slowly undermined by a constellation in which he finds his place as the elderly 'father' of one of his helpers. The gendering of European rescue when it comes to asylum seekers needs to be placed in relation to the history of European expansion. In the influential essay "Can the Subaltern Speak?" Spivak argues:

> Imperialism's image as the establisher of the good society is marked
> by the espousal of the woman as *object* of protection from her own

kind. How should one examine the dissimulation of patriarchal strategy, which apparently grants the woman free choice as *subject*?[8]

The problem of agency and the freedom of the speaking subject take on
new dimensions when studied from the perspective of the gendering of the
helper–victim opposition.

II

In Gurnah's novel, Europe is potentially a space for new beginnings. The
character–narrators arrive as strangers and are thus seen as traversing a
boundary into something that could hold different and hitherto unknown
possibilities. Derrida's concept of the *arrivant* can be used when trying to
understand how this crossing into the new space is represented. Two episodes in the novel are particularly important here – these concern Latif
Mahmud and his encounter with the family of his pen-pal in East Germany,
and the significance of the casket of incense, *ud-al-qamari*, at the arrival of
Hussein the trader to Zanzibar and, later, at the arrival of Saleh Omar in
Britain.

When Latif Mahmud arrives in Dresden, he contacts his pen-pal, Elleke,
whom he naturally believes to be a woman. They make arrangements to
meet, and only then does he find out that he has been corresponding with
Jan, a young man who lives with his mother, named Elleke. Their encounter is dominated by what initially seems a rather mundane problem of wearing the wrong shoes for the European winter. Latif Mahmud's feet are
bleeding by the time they arrive at the flat: "There I stood then, bleeding on
the doormat outside Jan's mother's flat, my feet so numb that I had not
noticed a gash on my foot."[9] The narrative continues with a detailed description of the arrangements that have to be made in order to clean up the
wound, as well as of the ensuing sense of embarrassment experienced by
Latif Mahmud. There is, however, a surprising new element in this encounter when Elleke starts washing his feet:

---

[8] Gayatri Chakravorty Spivak, "Can the Subaltern Speak?" in *Marxism and the Interpretation of Culture*, ed. Cary Nelson & Lawrence Grossberg (Urbana: U of Illinois P,
1988): 299.

[9] Abdulrazak Gurnah, *By the Sea* (London: Bloomsbury, 2002): 126. Further page
references are in the main text.

She tore another rag into strips and dressed my wound, smiling and squatting on her heels when it was all done.

"I thought I would meet you, although I didn't know it would be you," she said.

I didn't understand what she meant, and must have frowned, but I did understand something, that she was expressing a desire which I fulfilled in some surprising way, something she had wished for and it turned out to be me. I thought I would meet you, although I didn't know it would be you. It sounds reasonable in a strange sort of way. (127)

Elleke explains herself by referring to Odysseus' homecoming, where he was recognized by an old woman by the scar on his foot. "Every great hero or prince was breast-fed by a tired old woman who sits neglected by the ashes of the royal hearth" (127). Instead of identifying with Penelope as the woman who sits waiting, Elleke chooses to take on the role of Euryclea, a servant, in relation to Latif Mahmud, a young man whom she has just met.

In *Aporias*, Derrida introduces the concept of the *arrivant* within the framework of a rhetoric of borders which includes questions about the meaning of identities as well as the connections between identities and place.

I am talking about the absolute *arrivant*, who is not even a guest. He surprises the host – who is not yet a host or an inviting power – enough to call into question, to the point of annihilating or rendering indeterminate, all the distinctive signs of a prior identity, beginning with the very border that delineated a legitimate home and assured lineage, names and language, nations, families and genealogies. The absolute *arrivant* does not yet have a name or an identity. It is not an invader or an occupier, nor is it a colonizer, even if it can also become one. This is why I call it simply the *arrivant*, and not someone or something that arrives, a subject, a person, an individual, or a living thing, even less one of the migrants I just mentioned.[10]

Elleke's questions point to a wish to redefine the event which brought the bleeding Latif Mahmud to her doorstep. Her questions revise the issue of his identity away from the predetermined relation of a European–non-Euro-

---

[10] Jacques Derrida, *Aporias*, tr. Thomas Dutoit ("Apories: Mourir – S'attendre aux limites de la vérité"), in *Le Passage des frontières: Autour du travail de Jacques Derrida* (1993, tr. Stanford C A: Stanford U P, 1993): 34.

pean opposition to an altogether new way of conceiving of who he is and
why he arrives. This is ultimately an expression of the wish to enter the
world anew with a different history and a different trajectory of belonging.
In Derrida's discussion, this possibility is expressed not through the rhetoric of traversal and arrival but through the idea of receiving the wholly
Other: "the one who invites and receives truly begins by receiving hospitality from the guest to whom he thinks he is giving hospitality. It is as if in
truth he were received by the one he thinks he is receiving. Wouldn't the
consequences of this be infinite? What does receiving amount to?"[11]

Elleke's encounter with Latif Mahmud leads her to revisit her past and to
trace the trajectory of her own identity through a reconnection with the history of European expansion as well as with European history. She places
their encounter within the story of Odysseus and introduces the element of
the waiting woman, thereby granting him, the stranger, the position of the
returning hero. What is significant in this encounter between Latif Mahmud
and Elleke is the fact that she has no preconceived idea of what he is or
why he has come. This sense of openness to the stranger is preserved in
spite of the apparently well-known realities of his arrival in the GDR and
the circumstances surrounding the history of his correspondence with Jan.
The encounter gives Elleke the opportunity to talk about her past as a colonial land-owner in Kenya. This story is now told as part of the history of
Europe, where the efforts of Elleke's parents to "get away from Europe and
its wars" are finally shown to be in vain. Elleke connects this failure to the
inability of the Europeans in Kenya to come to terms with their situation in
ways other than by dominating those around them:

> My father was fond of saying that our superiority over the natives
> was only possible with their consent. All Europeans had to observe
> the thin line beyond which the mysterious moral authority over the
> native would vanish, and we would have to torture and murder to
> regain it. Poor Papa, he didn't think that it was the torture and mur-
> der that were committed in our name which gave us that authority in
> the first place. (132)

The subsequent history of Elleke's family is caught up with the history of
Nazi Germany, the displacement and expulsion of Germans, the bombing
of Dresden, and the division of Germany in 1949. This history is first and

---

[11] Derrida, *Aporias*, 10.

foremost a history of borders and divisions, with an awareness of how these borders and divisions are easily redrawn and challenged. European identity is here revealed to be both elusive and a result of contested power-structures.

The encounter between Elleke, Jan, and Latif, significantly, also leads to new border crossings when Elleke encourages Jan and Latif to travel, and, without the knowledge of Latif, to flee the GDR for the West. The *arrivant* thus involves Elleke and Jan in a process which does not revolve around the identity of the *arrivant* but, rather, constitutes a starting-point for revisiting the past as well as for moving on to a wholly unexpected future:

> As long as the waiting can only be directed toward some other and toward some *arrivant*, one can and must wait for something else, hence expect some other – as when one is said to expect that some-thing will happen or that some other will arrive.[12]

Latif Mahmud's function as an *arrivant* in relation to Elleke and Jan must be viewed within the context of their ability to trace their own precarious identification with European history, both as colonizers and as displaced persons. Saleh Omar, by contrast, is received as someone already predeter-mined by the circumstances of his arrival. Interestingly enough, the first case involves communication and openness on the part of the *arrivant*, whereas the second instance involves silence. The most important element of Latif Mahmud's encounter with Elleke and Jan involves the awareness of the history of European expansion and its consequences for the colo-nized. In Saleh Omar's case, the European helpers have defined his needs and taken action on his behalf even before they are able to talk to him. They do this, however, with reference only to the circumstances in Africa, not with any awareness of their own connections to that history.

Saleh Omar's arrival in Britain can most fruitfully be read as part of a much older history of travel and of arrival, most significantly that of the Persian and Arabic traders arriving in Zanzibar. One of the most important events connecting the stories of the two narrator–protagonists in *By the Sea* concerns the Persian trader Hussein and his involvement with Rajab Shaa-ban Mahmud's family, and ultimately the destruction that he brings to that family. In Saleh Omar's story, the connection between his own arrival in Europe and the story of the trader Hussein's travels is created through the

---

[12] Derrida, *Aporias*, 65.

significance of the casket of incense that Saleh Omar carries with him from
Zanzibar. Saleh Omar is clear about the fact that neither his stolen passport
nor his refusal to speak English will ultimately keep the immigration
officials from finding out what they want. He does, however, regard his belongings as something more valid that the misleading and missing documents that he presents on arrival: "I imagine there would be pleasure too in
having an assured grasp of the secret codes that reveal what people seek to
hide, a hermeneutics of baggage that is like following an archeological trail
or examining lines on a shipping map" (7).

The hermeneutics of the casket of incense is what opens up the possibility of a different story from the one that the immigration officer Kevin
Edelman had already prepared himself for. In this respect, the *ud-al qamari*
is what signals a continuation of the story of the past and at the same time
opens up the possibility of the wholly unexpected.

> It was not my life that lay spread there, just what I had selected as
> signals of a story I hoped to convey. Kevin Edelman opened the
> casket and started with surprise at its contents. Perhaps he had ex-
> pected jewellery or something valuable. Drugs. "What's this?" he
> asked, then carefully sniffed the open casket. It was hardly neces-
> sary, as the little room had filled with glorious perfume as soon as
> he opened the box. (8)

This glorious perfume creates a link with the past, in which Saleh Omar
and Latif Mahmud's stories are connected through their respective dealings
with the trader Hussein. In this way, the incense comes to stand for a process of signification which ultimately undermines the life and identity of
both protagonists. It is also important to note that the *ud-al-qamari* does not
originate in Zanzibar but arrives with the Persian trader Hussein. Hussein,
in turn, received the incense from his father, who purchased a large con-
signment in Bangkok, and who was able to explain that "ud-al-qamari, the
wood of the moon, was a corruption of ud-al-qimari, the wood of the
Khmers" (29).

The casket of incense that comes to stand for the most reliable connection to the past among Saleh Omar's belongings is thus revealed to contain
a long and complicated history and a genealogy which has been corrupted
along the way. What is even more important is the fact that the trader
Hussein brings a great deal of devastation into the lives of the protagonists
and also creates great enmity between their families. This does not in any

way reduce the quality of the incense. On the contrary, it seems as if the casket can fulfil the function of a connection to the past in Zanzibar, "the casket which I had brought with me as all the luggage from a life departed, the provisions of my after-life" (31), together with its associations of travel and movement: "I thought I could catch the odour of the fantasy of those distant places in the dense body of that perfume, although that was only because Hussein had bound the two things together for me with his stories, and I had surrendered to both so completely" (30).

The value of the casket for Saleh Omar does not lie in its connection to Zanzibar in the sense that it would form part of a culture of home and belonging. It derives its value from the fantasies associated with the trader's stories of places beyond Zanzibar. The trader Hussein and the immigration official Kevin Edelman are juxtaposed in the scene depicting Saleh Omar's arrival. They are revealed as opposites in the way they deal with the casket of incense as well as in their attitudes towards place and belonging:

> He [Hussein] gave me the casket as a gift, the casket Kevin Edelman plundered from me, and with it the last of the ud-al-qamari Hussein and his father bought in Bangkok the year before the war. [...] Kevin Edelman, the bawab of Europe, and the gatekeeper to the orchards in the family courtyard, the same gate which had released the hordes that went out to consume the world and to which we have come sliming up to beg admittance. Refugee. Asylum-seeker. Mercy. (31)

The casket of incense is thus both a gift and a sign of the *arrivant*. Both Hussein and Kevin Edelman are revealed as self-seeking in their relation to the *ud-al-qamari*. Hussein uses it while bargaining for a table he wants in Saleh Omar's furniture shop and Kevin Edelman simply uses his power as immigration official to steal the casket from Saleh Omar without having any official warrant to do so. The fantasies of distant places connected with the perfume in Saleh Omar's imagination are left at the immigration desk when he enters Britain. The possibilities inherent in the idea of the *arrivant* are brought to an end precisely through the inability of those whom Saleh Omar encounters in Europe to imagine the wholly Other. In Derrida's definition of the *arrivant*, the preconceived borders are what reduces the *arrivant* to an identity among others. The challenge that the *arrivant* poses is, rather, the possibility of rethinking arrival as a way of reformulating the identity of the place itself as well as of existing borders. It also encompas-

ses the idea of seduction and the indeterminacy of outcome when responding to otherness. A total openness to the *arrivant* involves both risk and
possibility, since the outcome of the encounter is unknown.

III

The incident describing Saleh Omar's arrival in Britain and his encounter
with the immigration officer Kevin Edelman underlines the need to occupy
the position of a help-seeking stranger. The stance of passivity is taken to
an extreme by Saleh Omar's decision not to speak English:

> I had been told not to say anything, to pretend I could not speak any
> English. I was not sure why, but I know I would do as I was told be-
> cause the advice had a crafty ring to it, the kind of resourceful ruse
> the powerless would know. (5)

The only words he decides to utter are "refugee, asylum." Kevin Edelman's
position as both a gatekeeper and the son of Romanian refugees can be read
ironically, but it also functions to underline the ideas behind a common
European identity:

> "But my parents are European, they have a right, they are part of the
> family. [...] You don't belong here, you don't value any of the
> things we value, you haven't paid for them through generations, and
> we don't want you here." (12)

Here the family metaphor is used to denote the accumulation of wealth for
future generations, as well as a guarantee for the continuation of shared
values through an assumed common European identity. The wealth that
Kevin Edelman sees it is his duty to guard against strangers is here revealed
as the result of the work by generations of colonized people. The "we" that
Edelman uses to lay claim to this wealth is established on the basis of a
fiction of racial and familial identification. The narrator can therefore enter
only as a passive victim, not as a person who shares a common history with
the British.

In the description of the British in Zanzibar, Saleh Omar remembers
complex feelings of admiration for "their audacity in being there, such a
long way from home, calling the shots with such an appearance of assur-
ance, and for knowing so much about how to do the things that mattered:
curing diseases, flying aeroplanes, making movies" (17–18). But rather than

being allowed to claim a sense of identification with this knowledge, of establishing a "we" such as it was possible to establish from the margins of Europe, the narratives functioned to construct and maintain difference:

> In their books I read unflattering accounts of my history, and because they were unflattering, they seemed truer than the stories we told ourselves. I read about the diseases that tormented us, about the future that lay before us, about the world we lived in and our place in it. It was as if they had remade us, and in ways that we no longer had any recourse but to accept, so complete and well-fitting was the story they told about us. (18)

An important aspect of the difference constructed through these stories had to do with defining the reason and purpose for the presence of the British. "Then it would seem that the British had been doing us nothing but good compared to the brutalities we could visit on ourselves" (18). The idea of colonization as a rescue mission aimed mainly at improving the lives of colonized peoples can thus be seen as part of an agenda of mystifying European exploitation and cruelty. What is also significant here is that this idea of rescue leaves the protagonist without protection from the stories produced by the Europeans about himself. While admitting admiration for the achievements of the British, he is simultaneously also subscribing to their view of him as inferior and different. In contrast to Kevin Edelman, who is able to use the trope of family connections in order to mark himself as one of the inheritors of European achievement, Saleh Omar's relation to these achievements is that of the outsider who will benefit from them only as a recipient of European benevolence. It is in this context that the issue of speech and agency is connected to the idea of European rescue.

Saleh Omar's refusal to speak English on arrival is therefore significant in relation to the issue of interpellation, victimization, and agency. When he finally agrees to speak, he uses the words of Bartleby in Melville's "Bartleby, the Scrivener" from the 1850s. "I preferred not to," Saleh Omar says, in answer to the exasperated question by Rachel, the lawyer who has been appointed as his legal aid. Saleh Omar's silence has brought about a situation where he has been perceived as wholly dependent on the activities of his helpers, while fully able to understand and evaluate their efforts. The expression by Bartleby is a way of breaking that silence, and it also signals an effort to communicate with Rachel on an equal basis, as readers of a story.

Rachel does not respond in the way he expected her to, but is instead "un-ashamedly irritated" (65).

> So then I knew she did not know the story "Bartleby the Scrivener."
> The brick wall made me think of it as soon as I walked into the
> room, and I was certain that when I started to speak I would find a
> way to say that sentence, to see if the wall had made her think of it
> too. A beautiful story. (65)

In Latif Mahmud's narrative, the connection with the story is established when a colleague of Rachel's at the refugee council tells him the reason he is no longer needed as an interpreter. Referring to Saleh Omar, he tells Latif Mahmud:

> "A strange one, it appeared he could speak English all along but
> he preferred not to." The way the man inflected *preferred* made it
> sound as if he was quoting.
> "Preferred. Like Bartleby," I said, always eager to show off, to
> confirm my credentials as a teacher of literature.
> "I'll get Rachel to give you a call," he said, so I assumed he
> didn't know the story. (74–75)

The efforts at communication are thus in both cases directed from the Zanzibari immigrants towards their European 'helpers', but without effect. It does, however, create a curious alignment between the two men, Saleh Omar and Latif Mahmud, whose experience of exclusion is heightened through these incidents.

Herman Melville's story of Bartleby has received critical attention from philosophers such as Gilles Deleuze and Jacques Derrida, who have reflected on its contribution to the question of the relation between agency and language. It is a story narrated by a lawyer, concerning his experience with one of his employees, a copyist, who appears in his office and wants to be hired, but who turns out to be increasingly unwilling to perform the work expected of him. This unwillingness and ultimate resistance to all work he is asked to do is expressed through the response "I would prefer not to." The narrator tells us that the main reason he hired Bartleby was his appearance; he gave the impression of someone who could handle the work of examining the accuracy of a copy, a "very dull, wearisome, and lethargic affair."[13] It is, however, precisely this duty of examining the copy that Bartleby objects to through the expression "I would prefer not to." This refusal to examine the copy not only makes Bartleby less useful as an employee than the lawyer initially expected him to be. It also challenges the assumed power-relation between them, until finally it becomes evident that Bartleby is the one who determines the nature of their relationship. In the end, Bartleby uses the expression "I would prefer not to" in response to every request by his employer, including that of leaving the premises or providing any information about his life. The only "item of rumour"[14] concerning Bartleby's past life that the narrator is able to share with the reader is the report that Bartleby had been working on in a dead-letter office:

> "Dead letters! Does it not sound like dead men? Conceive a man by nature and misfortune prone to a pallid hopelessness, can any business seem more fitted to heighten it than that of continually handling these dead letters, and assorting them for the flames? For by the cart-load they are annually burned. Sometimes from out the folded paper the pale clerk takes a ring – the finger it was meant for, perhaps, moulders in the grave; a banknote sent in swiftest charity – he whom it would relieve, nor eats nor hungers any more; pardon for those who died despairing; hope for those who died unhoping; good tidings for those who died stifled by unrelieved calamities. On errands of life, these letters speed to death."[15]

When the narrator finds out that Bartleby has actually moved into his premises and treats him, the rightful owner, as an intruder, he describes his own actions in terms of "impotent rebellion,"[16] adding:

> Indeed, it was his wonderful mildness, chiefly, which not only disarmed me, but unmanned me, as it were. For I consider that one, for the time, is [a] sort of unmanned when he tranquilly permits his hired clerk to dictate to him, and order him away from his own premises.[17]

---

[13] Herman Melville, "Bartleby the Scrivener" (1853), in Melville, *Billy Budd and Other Stories* (Harmondsworth: Penguin, 1986): 12.

[14] Melville, "Bartleby the Scrivener," 46.

[15] "Bartleby the Scrivener," 46.

[16] "Bartleby the Scrivener," 21.

[17] "Bartleby the Scrivener," 21–22.

Through this choice of words, the narrator introduces a somewhat unexpected gendered dimension to the narrative by describing himself rather
than the passive Bartleby as "impotent" and "unmanned." In Jacques Derrida's reading of this story in *The Gift of Death*, the relation between the
lawyer/narrator and Bartleby is placed within the context of stories about
men: "father and son, of masculine figures, of hierarchies among men."[18]
Derrida relates it to Kierkegaard's reading of the Old Testament story of
Abraham's sacrifice of his son Isaac, where the question of speaking versus
silence is connected to the issue of singularity and responsibility. In the
words of Derrida, "as soon as one speaks, as soon as one enters the medium
of language, one loses that very singularity."[19] The question of responsibility is generally seen as connected with speech and action rather than with
secrets and silence.

> For common sense, just as for philosophical reasoning, the most
> widely shared belief is that responsibility is tied to the public and to
> the nonsecret, to the possibility and even the necessity of accounting
> for one's words and actions in front of others, of justifying and own-
> ing up to them. Here on the contrary it appears, just as necessarily,
> that the absolute responsibility of my actions, to the extent that such
> a responsibility remains mine, singularly so, something no one else
> can perform in my place, instead implies secrecy.[20]

What is remarkable about Bartleby's silence, however, is that he speaks
without committing himself to anything. As Derrida puts it,

> Bartleby's "I would prefer not to" takes on the responsibility of a re-
> sponse without response. It evokes the future without either predict-
> ing or promising; it utters nothing fixed, determinable, positive, or
> negative.[21]

This expression "I would prefer not to" thus functions as a possibility of
some future action or speech, something which cannot be realized quite yet
or in these present circumstances. "The silhouette of a content haunts this

---

[18] Jacques Derrida, *The Gift of Death* ("Donner la mort"), tr. David Wills in *L'éthique
du don* (Paris: Transition, 1992; tr. Chicago: U of Chicago P, 1995): 75.

[19] Derrida, *The Gift of Death*, 60.

[20] *The Gift of Death*, 60.

[21] *The Gift of Death*, 75.

response."[22] This reading is highly relevant to the way the expression functions in *By the Sea*. Here we have the narrator himself relating his arrival in Britain and accounting for his refusal to speak: i.e. refusing to speak as a victim. The story of the past shows how the subject is interpellated in relation to colonial powers, the Persian merchants and the corrupt politicians of early independence. The possibility of claiming a singularity beyond known identities, in this case the colonized Zanzibari, is here linked to the possibility of universality, of being admitted to the knowledge of how to fly aeroplanes, cure disease or make movies without necessarily having to claim the ethnic specificity of the British.

The refusal to speak as a victim is also relevant in the context of Saleh Omar's situation in Britain, where he suffers through the indignities of being talked about in his presence by his various helpers, who, despite his silence, find it quite easy to make decisions for him. Saleh Omar is brought to a bed-and-breakfast for asylum seekers run by a woman called Celia. He describes her as loud and bullying, with a "fussy and random motherliness" (51). She cannot be bothered to learn his name, or the name he uses, Shaaban Mahmud, deciding to call him Mr Showboat instead.

> "He mopes a bit at times," Celia said. "But I think that's because he doesn't understand everything we say. Do you, Mr Showboat? That's what I call him. It's our nickname for him. He doesn't mind, I've asked him." (62)

In the same way as Bartleby has the lawyer or the law speaking for him, Saleh Omar finds himself in a situation where his female helpers take up the fight both against the problems he is fleeing from and against the British immigration authorities: "playing on the same side, dancing to the same cha-cha-cha tune, us refugee redeemers in our holy frocks" (75).

> "We can't just say go back to your horrible country and get hurt, we're too busy with our own lives. If we can help them, I think we should. [...] It didn't use to be that there were so many in the country, but what can we do? We can't send them back to those horrible places. I don't know what we can do?" (54–55)

Gilles Deleuze's reading of Bartleby identifies two strategies inherent in the formula "I prefer not to." One strategy concerns language as reproduc-

---

[22] Derrida, *The Gift of Death*, 75.

tion, whereas the other refers to the function of speech-acts. According to Deleuze, Bartleby's refusal to copy refers to an act of resistance against the reproduction of words, but it also "stymies all speech acts, and at the same time, it makes Bartleby a pure outsider [*exclu*] to whom no social position can be attributed."[23]

> This is what the attorney glimpses with dread: all his hopes of bring-
> ing Bartleby back to reason are dashed because they rest on *a logic
> of presuppositions* according to which an employer "expects" to be
> obeyed, or a kind friend listened to, whereas Bartleby has invented a
> new logic, *a logic of preference*, which is enough to undermine the
> presuppositions of language as a whole[24]

Both of these functions of 'passive resistance' can be found in *By the Sea*. What the novel is presenting, therefore, is a dichotomy between the good victim and the bad victim. The good victim is identified with agency and speech, even with a type of refusal that could be construed as the social position of a rebel. The bad victim, conversely, is the one who refuses agency and also undermines the functions of speech-acts. It is significant that the novel opens and closes with the protagonist's reflections on the visits by Rachel. We are told that she is a nuisance and a disturbance be-cause of the way she might or might not turn up when she has announced that she will visit him. All suggestions that he could improve his situation by getting a telephone or by contacting her are dismissed with the words, "I refuse to have one" and "I have no urge to do so" (1). His encounters with Rachel are described as reflections on his own passivity. His refusals undermine all her efforts without offering anything tangible instead. Whereas her interest in him seems to emanate from her wish to be seen as a "refugee redeemer," he comes to see in her the daughter who died tragically at an early age in Zanzibar while he was imprisoned. This establishes a relationship between them within the parameters of the family metaphor in which he is now the elderly, somewhat difficult father of a caring daughter. At this stage, Saleh Omar revisits the story of Bartleby and suddenly changes his wording slightly, thereby indicating a changed relation to his situation and his helpers. In a conversation with Latif Mahmud about the

---

[23] Gilles Deleuze, *Essays Critical and Clinical*, tr. Daniel W. Smith & Michael A. Greco (*Critique et clinique*, 1993; tr. Minneapolis: U of Minnesota P, 1997): 77.

[24] Deleuze, *Essays Critical and Clinical*, 77.

need for a telephone, Saleh Omar decides to mark his wish to leave Bartleby's words behind:

> "I have no urge to do so," I said, and saw him smile. I thought I knew what he was thinking. He would have preferred me to say, *I prefer not to*. But I had been thinking of what Rachel said, and thought I would read "Bartleby" again before speaking his words as the utterings of an admired desperado. (244)

Towards the end of the narrative, Saleh Omar describes his visits to Latif Mahmud in London: "Then when I had seen enough, he would put me on the train and Rachel would meet me at the other end, as if I was a decrepit old father that they shared between them" (244).

III

When the narrative in *By the Sea* moves beyond the story of Bartleby, it encompasses a more explicitly gendered dimension. As Derrida points out in relation to both the story of Abraham and Isaac and that of Bartleby, they do not "make a single allusion to anything feminine whatsoever, even less to anything that could be construed as a figure of woman. Would the logic of sacrificial responsibility within the implacable universality of the law, of its law, be altered, inflected, attenuated, or displaced, if a woman were to intervene in some consequential manner?"[25] In *By the Sea*, we have at least two women intervening. Celia is described as "motherly," but in negative terms only. Rachel is the lost daughter who has now come back to him, and here the encounters are described with some self-irony directed at his own refusals. The idea of rescue inherent in European–African encounters is here seen in terms of female helpers and the recalcitrant male victim, where the encounters are described by using family as a metaphor. It is precisely through the initially unwanted female intervention that Saleh Omar moves away from the Bartleby position towards a desire to communicate by telling his version of the stories of the past. This relation between the victim position and agency is expressed through the way in which Saleh Omar makes use of the story of Bartleby in his new life in Europe. His ability to communicate is expressed through the story, but it is not intelligible to anyone but himself and his countryman, Latif Mahmud. He is able to discuss

---

[25] Derrida, *The Gift of Death*, 76.

the story of Bartleby with Rachel only when he has told her the meaning of
the sentence "I prefer not to." Rachel dislikes the story: "Too much self-
pity for her liking, all that nineteenth-century melodrama" (198). The story
also makes her see Bartleby as cruel, an abuser. In response to Rachel's
dismissal, Saleh Omar replies:

> "Perhaps you have lost tolerance for that desire for isolation which
> faith in a spirit's ambition made heroic. So the kind of self-mortify-
> ing retreat Bartleby undertakes only has meaning as a dangerous un-
> predictability. Especially since the story does not allow us to know
> what has brought Bartleby to this condition, does not allow us to
> have sympathy for him. It does not allow us to say, yes, yes, in this
> case we understand the meaning of such behaviour and we forgive
> it. The story only gives us this man, who says nothing about himself
> or about his past, appears to make no judgement or analysis, desires
> no reprieve or forgiveness from us, and only wishes to be left
> alone." (199)

The use of the story of Bartleby points to different ways in which the
issue of agency, the speaking subject, and the literary text might be understood. Gregg Lambert has identified three important possibilities for the
understanding of literary enunciation in the readings of Bartleby by Deleuze and Derrida. First, there is what he calls

> identification of literature with a certain absolute non-response,
> which could lead us to understand that the subject who 'speaks' in
> literature speaks in an absolutely original manner, which does not
> copy or reproduce or respond to the subject in social space, in-
> scribed in its rituals and conventions, in its ideological apparatus.[26]

The second instance of non-response concerns the relation between "the
subject in literature and the subjects of moral duty and respect."[27] According to Lambert, these readings suggest that the literary subject does not
arise from interpellation and instead absolutely eludes this ideological
mechanism. One should therefore be wary of "binding statements to interpellated subjects and known identities." The third possibility concerns what
Derrida calls 'the hyberbolic condition' of the subject (of enunciation).

---

[26] Gregg Lambert, "The Subject of Literature Between Derrida and Deleuze – Law or
Life?" *Angelaki* 5.2 (2000): 188.
[27] Lambert, "The Subject of Literature," 188.

Here the literary subject exceeds or emerges outside the 'calculated' identity of the moral or civil subject which indicates a space of literature as the space of *différance* between the closed, relatively determined, or calculated democracy and what Derrida calls the "democracy to come." [28]

The non-response by Saleh Omar as the narrator of *By the Sea* is suggestive of the wish to find a space where "the stories they told about us" no longer reverberate in the stories that he himself finally decides to tell: "I have time on my hands, I am in the hands of time, so I might as well account for myself" (2). The refusal to speak as a victim must thus be set in opposition to the encounter with Latif Mahmud when he decides to return to the story of the past. As Erik Falk shows in his reading of *By the Sea*, the curious connection between Saleh Omar and Latif Mahmud, established through the name Rajab Shaaban Mahmud, re-creates families along new lines of kinship structures.[29]

Latif Mahmud similarly refers to Bartleby within the context of the telling of their different versions of the story of the past. In his case, it is the painful story of his father, Rajab Shaaban Mahmud, an alcoholic who was imposed on by the Omani trader Hussein, who seduced both his son, Latif Mahmud's elder, much-admired brother, and his wife before he finally engaged him in a deal which caused him to lose his house to Saleh Omar. After the disappearance of Hussein, the father became a devout Muslim, while the mother became the mistress of an important politician. Latif Mahmud invokes the story of Bartleby in relation to his experience of his father's misfortune and is now confronting Saleh Omar with his version of the events. In this new context, when the son Latif Mahmud is confronting him Saleh Omar has taken on the identity of Rajab Shaaban Mahmud – the victim's position rather than that of the persecutor:

> I don't even know if I remember that day, but I remember the story.
> It was the story of my youth. When I read "Bartleby" for the first
> time I realised that that was how I thought of my father, resigned in
> his futility and you his persecutor. I learned to read the story diffe-
> rently later, to see that it was not all about resignation and futility,
> but the first time I saw him in it. You found the story moving. I
> remember you said that. Moving. Why didn't you find him moving?

---

[28] Lambert, "The Subject of Literature," 188.

[29] Erik Falk, *Subject and History in Selected Works by Abdulrazak Gurnah, Yvonne Vera, and David Dabydeen* (Karlstad: Karlstad University Studies, 2007)

My father. Did you find him moving? Do you mind me describing
you as his persecutor? I mean of course you must mind, but do you
find it annoying, improper, discourteous beyond bearing? (168–69)

When he discusses the story with Latif Mahmud, it gains significance
within the frame of the story of the past. It is this particular context, the
communication between the two men about their shared experience in Zanzibar, that moves Saleh Omar from his position of silence to the decision to
tell his story. The listener is not a European but someone from the past who
feels that he has been wronged. Saleh Omar says:

> I knew I would tell him. I needed to be shriven. Not to be forgiven
> or to be cleansed of my sins, which were ones of pettiness and
> vanity rather than wickedness, and whose consequences had already
> been steep for me and for others. Little could be done to lighten
> those sins, I needed to be shriven of the burden of events and stories
> which I have never been able to tell, and which by telling would
> fulfil the craving I feel to be listened to with understanding. He was
> my shriver, and I knew I would tell him what he had asked of me.
> Then after telling him, I would have found a good place to stop and
> tell him that even Shahrazad managed to get some rest every sun-
> rise. I was just pressing home my advantage, pretending greater
> reluctance than I really felt, to make sure he would go after I an-
> swered him. And he had spoken well about himself, and I did not
> wish to seem ungiving in return. So I made a pot of sweet black tea
> and resumed. (171)

Other stories mentioned in the narrative concern *Thousand and One
Nights*. Those stories suggest the opposite stance from the story of Bartleby, in that it is speech and storytelling rather than silence that becomes
aligned with survival. What is remarkable about the references to *Thousand
and One Nights*, however, is that they do not contain any discussion about
the power of storytelling but function only as a reference point for
discussions about castration of eunuchs. It is significant that this exchange
takes place between two Zanzibari men in Europe who share a history of
having been exploited by Persian traders and European colonial authorities
and who are finally forced to flee from the newly independent nation.

   This encounter, too, ends with a movement from Bartleby to *Thousand
and One Nights*. Omar Saleh recounts how Latif Mahmoud addresses him
and compares him to a jinn:

"I think I imagined you as a kind of relic, a metaphor of my
nativity, and that I would come and examine you while you sat still
and dissembling, fuming ineffectually like a jinn raised from infer-
nal depths. Do you mind me talking to you like this?"
      "If you have to," I said. "Which jinn do you have in mind?" [...]
      "Qamar Zaman," I said. "That story has the stillest, shiftiest jinn
in the whole *A Thousand and One Nights*. With a horn in the middle
of his forehead. My favourite jinn, an utter grotesque, which is how
you imagined me." (169–70)

The story about the past in Zanzibar is largely determined by this relation
between the two men and their need to justify their past behaviour in the
eyes of the other. The refusal of agency on the part of Saleh Omar appears
only in relation to his European helpers, and here, too, he is reluctantly
drawn into an arrangement which he describes in terms of a domestic situation. This theme of domesticity and of the family as trope for the immigrant
man in relation to Europe is a recurrent one in Gurnah's fiction, as is his
use of passive male characters reflecting on their own passivity in relation
to these European women. One way of interpreting this could be to look at
it as the racialized reversal of the standard Western dichotomy of the
female as passive and the male as active. The refusal of agency in the European context on the part of the immigrant man could then simply be interpreted as a refusal to be dominated by women. This interpretation reinfor-
ces the idea of Europe as a place where gender equality has been achieved
and of immigrant men as 'bad victims' because of their refusal to accept
women in positions of power. This would be a continuation of the idea of
the civilizing mission where Europe brings enlightenment to the rest of the
world, often against their will, but always in their own best interests.

Gurnah's novel expresses, in my view, a rather more complex idea of
European rescue. This idea is advanced both through the redefinition of
subjectivity and agency and through the metaphoric deployment of
domestic space. What is quite remarkable about both Saleh Omar's and
Latif Mahmud's narratives is that the experience of Europe in Europe is
restricted to personal encounters with helping women, and that these encounters are described in terms of family. The space within which Saleh
Omar is asked to exercise his subjectivity is thus restricted to the domestic.
The idea of Europe that emerges here is thus not one of powerful and
emancipated women, but of a restricted space in which women are given

the right to exercise some power, often in order to alleviate the harsh blows of the real authorities. European men are curiously absent in this narrative. One exception is the Romanian immigration official in Saleh Omar's narrative; another is the East German pen-friend in Latif's narrative, who all through their correspondence has been impersonating a woman.

The refusal of agency on the part of the immigrant man in Europe places the discussion about the speaking subject in the context of colonialist images of masculinity. In *Effeminism: The Economy of Colonial Desire,* Revathi Krishnaswami argues that the ideal manliness which emerged in Europe in the eighteenth century functioned not only to demarcate the ideal man in opposition to women but was also developed "through a systematic 'unmanning' of minorities within and foreigners without Europe."[30] The masculine ideal was used in the imperial project to justify European expansion and was given a scientific basis through the use of physiognomy, anthropology, and medicine. Modern masculinity was seen as an expression of a moral, physical, and cultural superiority which was set in opposition to supposedly physically and morally degenerate colonized people. In the case of India, the trope of effeminacy was developed to express the assumed "racial, physical, moral and cultural weakness" of the colonized.[31] Although Krishnaswami sees the development of European myths of manliness as closely linked to imperial rule, he nevertheless agrees with Ashis Nandy's argument, which sees Indian effeminacy and European manliness as separate ideals which were brought into close proximity through colonialism.[32] Mrinalini Sinha, by contrast, argues that it was the imperial encounter that formed notions of masculinity both in the metropolitan centres and among the colonized. Her analysis of particular administrative crises in British India during the late-nineteenth century shows how the construction of "the manly Englishman" and "the effeminate Bengali" were produced as constitutive of each other rather than as part of specific national cultures. Her study also shows that the political controversies were staged around issues of women's rights in which British men were seen as

---

[30] Revathi Krishnaswami, *Effeminism: The Economy of Colonial Desire* (Ann Arbor: U of Michigan P, 1998): 15.

[31] Krishnaswami, *Effeminism,* 25.

[32] Ashis Nandy, *The Intimate Enemy: Loss and Recovery of Self Under Colonialism* (New Delhi: Oxford UP, 1983).

protectors of both European and Indian women against Indian men.[33] As Lata Mani and Partha Chatterjee have shown,[34] colonial intervention in favour of Indian women resulted in a separation of the public and the private spheres which defined the private sphere as ethnic and subsequently limited the political influence of Indian men. Political influence by Indian men in the public sphere was discussed in terms of the consequences this would have for European women. At the same time, colonial women were able to use these controversies to step into a more public political arena with the paradoxical aim of arguing for the paternalistic protection of Indian and European women alike by European colonial authorities. As several feminist scholars have argued, the European woman here comes to occupy a contradictory position of both subordination in relation to male-dominated colonial powers and domination in relation to colonized men as well as colonized women. Modern European masculinity is thus created through the imperial project both in its opposition to racialized ideas of effeminacy and through the separation of the private and the public spheres. According to John Tosh, middle-class masculinity in the Victorian period is "constructed in three areas – home, work and all-male associations."[35] The importance of the domestic sphere for masculinity is gained through a specific relation to the home.

> To establish a home, to protect it, to provide for it, to control it, and to train its young aspirants to manhood, have usually been essential to a man's good standing with his peers.[36]

But masculinity is also characterized by the "privileged freedom to pass at will between the public and the private."[37]

What Gurnah's novel thus suggests by confining the immigrant man in Europe to a domestic sphere is that his agency, both in political terms and as a speaking subject, will be limited to the sphere of his 'ethnic identity'

---

[33] Mrinalini Sinha, *Colonial Masculinity: The "Manly Englishman" and the "Effeminate Bengali" in the Late Nineteenth Century* (Manchester: Manchester U P, 1995).

[34] Lata Mani, *Contentious Traditions: The Debate on Sati in Colonial India* (Berkeley: U of California P, 1998); Partha Chatterjee, *The Nation and Its Fragments: Colonial and Postcolonial Histories* (Princeton N J: Princeton U P, 1993).

[35] John Tosh, *A Man's Place: Masculinity and the Middle-Class Home in Victorian England* (New Haven C T & London: Yale U P, 1999): 2.

[36] Tosh, *A Man's Place*, 4.

[37] *A Man's Place*, 2.

and not move into the area of public political power. As long as he remains within this sphere he is encouraged to speak and to act, to be a 'good' victim either in the sense of speaking as an immigrant or in that of acting as a rebel. Saleh Omar enters Europe as Rajab Shaaban Mahmud, a man who was unable to live up to the ideal of the male as provider and head of the domestic space. The division between the fit and the unfit is here gendered in opposition to a particular understanding of European masculinity.

Conclusion

Europe emerges, in this narrative, as a constricting site. The possibilities for freedom and movement but also of danger, disappointment, and mistaken routes inherent in the concept of the *arrivant* are curtailed and compromised in the encounter with the European opposition between helpers and victims. Central here is Gayatri Spivak's insistence on a scrutiny of the structures which allow certain groups to emerge as helpers and others as victims. Those who take upon themselves the task of righting the wrongs suffered by others also align themselves with the powerful, those who can take care of themselves and therefore also of others. The division of the world into the fit and the unfit is intimately bound up with the discursive formation of 'Europe' through geographical expansion and scientific exploration. 'Europe' thus comes to designate both desirable expertise and scientific progress and the division between those who were entitled to this heritage and those who were excluded.

In the novel *By the Sea*, the precariousness of this idea of Europe is presented through the childhood experience of Saleh Omar, through the immigration officer Kevin Edelman's views of Europe as heritage, and through Latif Mahmud's encounters with Jan and Elleke in the GDR. The *arrivant* is able to emerge as a promise or possibility only in those cases in which European history is revealed from another side, as a history of war, displacement, and suffering where Europeans have been both victims and villains, and very much in need of help. The reference to European history in connection with the *arrivant* shows how unstable the construction of Europe is and how the process of exclusion continues. By receiving the *arrivant*, the receiving power becomes defined as such and assumes the risk of challenging the borders between those who belong and those who are excluded. As the *ud-al qamari* shows, this is no small matter. Here we have a casket that moves between continents and generations, bringing wealth and happiness but also misery and destitution. The element of seduction is keenly present in relation to the casket and "Uncle" Hussein. Significantly enough, it is Hussein's influence over Latif Mahmud's father as well as his seduction of the elder brother and the mother that work to the benefit of Saleh Omar. Hussein's desire for the coffee table makes the *ud-al-qamari* change hands and starts the process through which Saleh Omar ultimately is forced to flee Zanzibar. Latif Mahmud's encounter with Elleke, on the other hand, overturns the expected victim–helper opposition and reveals the shakiness of that binary. The European defence of human rights is here seen as part of a process of defining Europe as the heritage of the 'fit' in opposition to the 'unfit', those who are either excluded or at the receiving end of European pity and benevolence.

The central concern in Gurnah's novel turns on the definition of the stranger and the implications of receiving the stranger. This concern is extended to the literary text itself through the invocation of the waiting women in the *Odyssey* and of Bartleby and his refusal of agency. The literary text is grounded historically and materially in the specific opposition that has emerged between Europe and the African immigrant, but it moves beyond and challenges that opposition through its insistence on the singularity of the speaking subject in literature.

WORKS CITED

Attridge, Derek. *The Singularity of Literature* (London: Routledge, 2004).
Callahan, David. "Exchange, Bullies and Abuse in Abdulrazak Gurnah's *Paradise*," *World Literature Written in English* 38.2 (2000): 55–69.
Chatterjee, Partha. *The Nation and Its Fragments: Colonial and Postcolonial Histories* (Princeton NJ: Princeton UP, 1993).
Deleuze, Gilles. *Essays Critical and Clinical*, tr. Daniel W. Smith & Michael A. Greco (*Critique et clinique*, 1993; tr. Minneapolis: U of Minnesota P, 1997).
Derrida, Jacques. *Aporias*, tr. Thomas Dutoit ("Apories: Mourir – s'attendre aux limites de la vérité"), in *Le passage des frontiers: autour du travail de Jacques Derrida*, 1993; tr. Stanford CA: Stanford UP, 1993).
——. *The Gift of Death*, tr. David Wills ("Donner la mort"), in *L'éthique du don* (1992; tr. Chicago: U of Chicago P, 1995).
Falk, Erik. *Subject and History in Selected Works by Abdulrazak Gurnah, Yvonne Vera, and David Dabydeen* (Karlstad: Karlstad University Studies, 2007).
Gurnah, Abdulrazak. *By the Sea* (London: Bloomsbury, 2002).

Krishnaswami, Revathi. *Effeminism: The Economy of Colonial Desire* (Ann Arbor: U of Michigan P, 1998).

Lambert, Gregg. "The Subject of Literature Between Derrida and Deleuze – Law or Life?" *Angelaki* 5.2 (2000): 177–90.

Lewis, Simon. "Impossible Domestic Situations: Questions of Identity and Nationalism in the Novels of Abdulrazak Gurnah and M.G. Vassanji," *Thamyris* 6.2 (Autumn 1999): 215–29.

Mani, Lata. *Contentious Traditions: The Debate on Sati in Colonial India* (Berkeley: U of California P, 1998).

Melville, Herman. "Bartleby the Scrivener" (1853), in *Billy Budd and Other Stories* (Harmondsworth: Penguin, 1986): 5–46.

Nandy, Ashis. *The Intimate Enemy: Loss and Recovery of Self under Colonialism* (Delhi: Oxford UP, 1988).

Sinha, Mrinalini. *Colonial Masculinity: The "Manly Englishman" and the "Effeminate Bengali" in the Late Nineteenth Century* (Princeton NJ: Princeton UP, 1993).

Spivak, Gayatri Chakravorty. "Can the Subaltern Speak?" in *Marxism and the Interpretation of Culture*, ed. Cary Nelson & Lawrence Grossberg (Urbana: U of Illinois P, 1988): 271–313.

——. "Use and Abuse of Human Rights," *boundary 2* 32.1 (2005): 131–89.

Tosh, John. *A Man's Place: Masculinity and the Middle-Class Home in Victorian England* (New Haven CT & London: Yale UP, 1999).

❖

Refugee(s) Writing

– ◁▷ – Displacement in Contemporary
Narratives of Forced Migration

JOPI NYMAN

I

N CONTEMPORARY REPRESENTATIONS of forced migrancy,
the case of Africa is often emphasized. Media representations turn the
refugee problem into a spectacle where migrants attempt to reach
Europe in overloaded boats, often failing in the process. While the question
of forced migration is widely debated in the fields of sociology, political
science, and social work, postcolonial literary studies have hitherto paid
scant attention to refugee writing as a genre or mode of expression. The
aim of this essay is to carve out new ways of approaching the field of
refugee writing by addressing the experience and narrative representation
of African refugees and asylum seekers in contemporary Britain through a
discussion of a variety of literary texts they have produced. In my discussion of their often autobiographical stories, I will examine the various ways
in which refugees imagine themselves and their journeying to Britain.

The notion of refugee identity is addressed as a consequence of contemporary forced migration and defined as a category of identity in whose
formation dislocation and liminality play a major role. The materials under
study come from the three volumes of *Refugees Writing in Wales* edited by
Eric Ngalle Charles, Tom Cheesman, and Sylvie Hoffmann and published
by the non-profit publisher Hafan Books in Swansea between 2003 and

2005.[1] The narratives, poems, and stories collected in these three volumes, sharing the title *Refugees Writing in Wales*, directly address the refugee experience in Britain. The collections offer rare glimpses into the reality of asylum seekers in a deprived British city, where racial violence is a fact both in the streets and at schools. The third volume, indeed, is dedicated to the memory of Kalan Kawa Karim, "killed by a blow to the back of the neck in a cowardly, unprovoked, racially motivated attack, in the early hours of 6 September 2004 in the centre of Swansea."[2] The collections include narratives by refugees – and other writers – from all over the world, both adult and children, but in my essay the focus is on narratives written or produced by people of African origin.[3] It should be noted that not all of the contributors are necessarily professional authors, or even writers who write in English. Some of the narratives are tales and memoirs, others are based on oral stories. Rather than merely aesthetic contributions, they have personal and communal functions. As Tom Cheesman points out in his preface to the first volume,

> All attest to the double value of refugee writing: to work through personal traumas, and to communicate with the world as individuals, instead of as the faceless, bogus bugbear of much UK media and ignorant public opinion.[4]

Accordingly, I aim to show how these narratives produce refuge as a form of liminal identity where the refugee needs to cope with the dominant culture and resist its racist gaze. In so doing, I will discuss first the image of

---

[1] *Between a Mountain and a Sea: Refugees Writing in Wales*, ed. Eric Ngalle Charles, Tom Cheesman & Sylvie Hoffmann (Swansea: Hafan, 2003); *Nobody's Perfect: Refugees Writing in Wales*, vol. 2, ed. Eric Ngalle Charles, Tom Cheesman & Sylvie Hoffmann (Swansea: Hafan, 2004); *Soft Touch: Refugees Writing in Wales*, vol. 3, ed. Eric Ngalle Charles, Tom Cheesman & Sylvie Hoffmann (Swansea: Hafan, 2005). There are, naturally, other anthologies dealing with refugee writing such as *The Bend in the Road: Refugees Writing*, ed. Jennifer Langer (Nottingham: Five Leaves, 1997).

[2] Anon., Dedication, in *Soft Touch: Refugees Writing in Wales*, vol. 3, ed. Charles, Cheesman & Hoffmann, 1.

[3] In addition to African refugees, the volumes include contributions from refugees from such countries as Iran, Iraq, Chile, Albania and Pakistan.

[4] Tom Cheesman, "Preface," in *Between a Mountain and a Sea: Refugees Writing in Wales*, ed. Charles, Cheesman & Hoffmann, 7.

the homeland offered in these stories and then address their responses to the cultural spaces of Britain.

II

It has been argued that the twentieth century is the century of war and refugees, which can be seen in the high number of the uprooted all over the world. In his recent book on the topic, Phil Marfleet claims that while globalization argues for open trade and free mobility, it has also constructed "new physical and cultural barriers"[5] that exclude forced migrants. But who are these forced migrants being barred from entering the nation-states of Europe? The idea of the refugee is historically protean and contingent, regularly "redefined by politicians and officials."[6] Hence, the refugee is a construct, but one that carries remarkable political weight:

> Refugees are produced by a number of factors: economic, political, social, cultural and environmental. Their lives are shaped by formal political and legal structures, and by both official and popular ideas of nation and nationalism, citizen and alien, 'race' and ethnicity.[7]

These issues can be seen in the ways in which dominant Western discourses of politics, law, and the media define their topic, generating images and stereotypes of hordes of barbarians entering our lands. As Marfleet points out, the viewpoint advocated by Western states encourages us to think about refugees in this manner, not as individuals with particular histories; instead, they are represented as "rootless opportunists whose claims for asylum are illegitimate and whose presence threatens host societies."[8] To quote from an article by Abdulrazak Gurnah:

> The debate over asylum is twinned with a paranoid narrative of race, disguised and smuggled in as euphemisms about foreign lands and cultural integrity. The Anglo-Saxon species is once again rumoured

---

[5] Phil Marfleet, *Refugees in a Global Era* (Houndmills: Palgrave, 2006): 5.
[6] Marfleet, *Refugees in a Global Era*, 13.
[7] *Refugees in a Global Era*, 7.
[8] *Refugees in a Global Era*, 193.

to be on the verge of extinction, when a glance around the world
shows how successfully it has invaded and displaced others.[9]

Thus, to offer an alternative to such ideological visions, this essay approaches refugees and refugee identity from a perspective that takes into
account what Marfleet and other refugee-studies scholars consider to be the
central issue structuring the experience of forced migration – displacement.[10] In Marfleet's words,

> Displaced people have been forcibly separated from or [...] compel-
> led to abandon their resources [...]: material possessions; access to
> land, housing and employment; kin and communal relationships;
> and familiar languages, traditions and institutions – the whole com-
> plex of economic, political, socio-cultural and psychological ele-
> ments that make up the framework for existence of each and every
> human being.[11]

As the quotation shows, forced migration can be distinguished from the
notions of nomadism and exile often glorified in literary studies and critical
theory. Caren Kaplan, in her *Questions of Travel* (1996), shows that several
critics have sought to maintain the distinction between the refugee and the
exile because of their attraction to the myth of solitary creation.[12] For instance, in his famous essay "Reflections on Exile," Edward Said contrasts
the mass experience of the refugee with that of exile – "'exile' carries with
it, I think, a touch of solitude and spirituality"[13] – and also suggests that
only the latter experience is of significance, as the former is "without a tell-
able history."[14] Said's ideas are based on the modernist cult of the exilic
writer, a Conrad or a Joyce, whose creative process is triggered by the
"solitude" which allows him to see more clearly.

----

[9] Abdulrazak Gurnah, "Fear and Loathing," *The Guardian* (22 May 2001): online
http://www.guardian.co.uk/g2/story/0,,494415,00.html [accessed 4 May 2005].

[10] Marfleet, *Refugees in a Global Era*, 193–94.

[11] *Refugees in a Global Era*, 194.

[12] Caren Kaplan, *Questions of Travel: Postmodern Discourses of Displacement* (Durham NC & London: Duke UP, 1996).

[13] Edward W. Said, *Reflections on Exile and Other Essays* (2000; Cambridge MA:
Harvard UP, 2003): 181.

[14] Said, *Reflections on Exile and Other Essays*, 176.

It may be argued that an understanding of identity as diasporic and trans-national, as being linked to several national formations, is distinct from earlier approaches to exilic writing, often produced by the elite, artists and political dissenters, in metropolitan spaces. In such studies as Terry Eagle-ton's *Exiles and Emigrés: Studies in Modern Literature* (1970) and Andrew Gurr's *Writers in Exile: The Identity of Home in Modern Literature* (1981), the experience of exile and being cut-off from one's own culture is under-stood as liberating.[15] In analyzing twentieth-century literature in Britain by writers such as T.S. Eliot, James Joyce, and Joseph Conrad, Eagleton claims that "the great art of English literature" by "foreigners and émigrés" stems from the authors' "access to alternative cultures and traditions."[16] For Eagleton, creativity results from the conditions of exile and a felt uneasi-ness with dominant values:

> I am concerned not so much with the work of 'literal' expatriates but with the 'social' exiles: with the work of Englishmen who reveal most acutely the cultural limitations which [...] are closely related to the problem of the 'émigré'.[17]

Andrew Gurr, in his analysis of writers including Katherine Mansfield, V.S. Naipaul, and Ngũgĩ wa Thiong'o, writes about "the freedom of exile" provided by "the insight which distance gives."[18] In privileging an indivi-dual exile, the experiences of entire groups are not heard, yet the emer-gence of refugee writers shows that their histories can be told. As a genre or mode of expression, refugee writing appears different from that by migrant writers such as Salman Rushdie and Bharati Mukherjee, in whose fictions transitions from one culture to another appear much less problematical and patrolled than what is shown in refugee narratives.

In her critique of Said, Kaplan suggests that the deconstruction of these apparently binary categories, exile and refugee, should make it possible to recover the history and cultural expression of the displaced refugees:

---

[15] See Terry Eagleton, *Exiles and Émigrés: Studies in Modern Literature* (London: Chatto & Windus, 1970); Andrew Gurr, *Writers in Exile: The Identity of Home in Mod-ern Literature* (Brighton: Harvester, 1981).

[16] Eagleton, *Exiles and Émigrés*, 15.

[17] *Exiles and Émigrés*, 18.

[18] Gurr, *Writers in Exile*, 25.

Historicizing refugee experience might bring a previously invisible
category back from the wilderness of the margins of criticism and
literature, perhaps through the inclusive mantle of the term 'diaspora'.[19]

The notions of displacement and diaspora are, then, in a dialogic relationship with each other. While the former suggests a loss of familiar space and
the need to accommodate, the latter links the displaced with one another,
suggesting that diasporic identity may be related more to community and
shared history than to a particular place of origin. What this means is that
the communities constructed around the experience of forced migration
may be different from those of traditional diasporas: the diasporic identity
of a particular ethnic or national group may be replaced by transnational
alliances and communities where the alliances cut across binaries and the
politics of location in a counter-hegemonic manner.[20]

   However, refugee identity as an expression of displacement can be
understood as an identity in transit, moving from the original home to
refugee camps and centres, crossing borders legally and illegally. Such an
identity can be described as liminal, the term understood here in the sense
proposed by Victor Turner, in which the individual moves from a fixed
sense of self and location into a new, different position. Thus identity, to
use Turner's words, "becomes ambiguous, neither here nor there, betwixt
and between all fixed points of classification; he passes through a symbolic
domain that has few or none of the attributes of his past or coming state."[21]
This is, indeed, the effect of displacement, where the migrant is forced to
give up the familiar, not knowing what the future will provide.

   As I will show, this liminality, the status of being on the threshold, is
constructed in at least three ways: physically, symbolically, and spatially.
The physical dimension can be seen in the emphasis on border patrolling,
where nation-states seek to prohibit other bodies from entering their soil.
Narratives by refugees offer various illustrations of such processes of ex-

---

[19] Kaplan, *Questions of Travel*, 121.

[20] Inderpal Grewal & Caren Kaplan, "Introduction: Transnational Feminist Practices
and Questions of Postmodernity," in *Scattered Hegemonies: Postmodernity and Transnational Feminist Practices*, ed. Inderpal Grewal & Caren Kaplan (Minneapolis: U of
Minnesota P, 1994): 13.

[21] Victor Turner, *Dramas, Fields and Metaphors: Symbolic Action in Human Society*
(Ithaca NY: Cornell UP, 1974): 232.

clusion. The symbolic aspect of liminality is woven into the narratives of forced migration through the use of languages and images of confusion, where the sense of exile and exhaustion creates an uncanny sense of in-betweenness. As Linda Camino puts it, the refugee's liminality suggests that s/he is "caught between old and new surroundings."[22] The spatial element is present in the practices of journeying and, in particular, mapping the space(s) of forced migration. Thus the refugee identity is constructed through movement, and since the refugee is not at home, her/his location is dislocation in the space of the Other. My readings of the representation of forced migration will focus on questions of space and journeying. I will emphasize what meanings are given by refugees to the space entered, and how they are positioned by discourses of exclusion. In so doing, I wish to approach refugee identity not as one of victimization, seeking instead to discuss its discursive construction and the potential for meaning it has in contemporary culture.

III

In Britain, the increasingly visible presence of refugees has generated what Kundnani calls the "new popular racism,"[23] transmitted in the name of the nation as dominant images popularized in mainstream media (tabloids) and enacted in everyday racism.[24] Just as black British writing has openly challenged the racialized bias of the English literary canon, the counter-discursive work produced by refugees seeks to invalidate dominant stereotypes of refugees as opportunists. The narratives constantly pay attention to racism and the perceived image people have of refugees, which can be seen in the first stanza of the poem "I Feel like Nobody Here" by Maxson Sahr Kpakio, a journalist and refugee activist originally from Liberia:

I feel like nobody here, ashamed, like everybody
Hates me,
But they don't know me, they really

---

[22] Linda Camino, "Refugee Adolescents and Their Changing Identities," in *Reconstructing Lives, Recapturing Meaning: Refugee Identity, Gender, and Culture Change*, ed. Linda Camino & Ruth M. Krulfeld (Basel: Gordon & Breach, 1993): 30.

[23] Arun Kundnani, "In a Foreign Land: The New Popular Racism," *Race & Class* 43.2 (2001): 41.

[24] Kundnani, "In a Foreign Land: The New Popular Racism," 48–49.

Don't know who I am either,
Only they know what they read in the
Newspapers about me
And that is not me.[25]

By conflating the speaking "I" of the poem with the objectified and de-
humanized object of popular newspaper journalism, Kpakio successfully
conveys the frustration of a refugee and challenges dominant representations. The poem also shows the refugee as an individual, not as the name-
less victim of civil wars and famine, seeking entry into Europe, as stressed
in their media representations.

The refugee narratives provide a multifaceted picture of the journeying
of the forced migrant from the place of origin to Britain and their often hostile reception. The narratives can be divided into two major groups: texts
dealing with the reasons for and phases of the refugee experience; and texts
narrating their experiences in Britain. The first group includes texts dealing
with questions of politics, oppression, poverty, and lack of civil rights.
Some of the narratives underscore the pain of the migrant by offering
images of torture, war, and racism, but they also discuss such issues as
homesickness and nostalgia. The effects of political turmoil can be seen in
many narratives describing the situation in such countries as Congo, Sudan,
and Zimbabwe. For instance, in his "The First Fear," a short story set
amidst the raging rebel war in Congo–Kinshasa, Aimé Kongolo describes
the fate of Tourra, a politics professor, who is shown returning to Kivu, a
town in the eastern part of the Republic of Congo, after seven years of absence due to the civil war, thinking, as his old neighbour puts it, that he is
now able to "belong somewhere."[26] Regardless of the changes in the country, Tourra feels that the actions of the government are ineffective:

> The politics he was teaching showed that the government's beha-
> viour had not changed. In fact the situation in his country was
> deteriorating. People were disillusioned. Corruption and injustice
> were rife at all levels. The country was fertile for rebel troops.[27]

---

[25] Maxson Sahr Kpakio. "I Feel like Nobody Here," in *Between a Mountain and a
Sea: Refugees Writing in Wales*, ed. Charles, Cheesman & Hoffmann, 68.
[26] Aimé Kongolo, "The First Fear," in *Soft Touch: Refugees Writing in Wales*, vol. 3,
ed. Charles, Cheesman & Hoffmann, 39.
[27] Kongolo, "The First Fear," 39.

Upon hearing that the rebels are approaching the town, and not willing to join their army, he decides to escape but accidentally finds himself in the camp of the anti-government rebels, who kill him: "'Look, a new recruit! Welcome! Well, well! What disgrace! Our enemy is mistaken!' – this was the rebels' greeting to him, for Tourra did not belong."[28] The final lines of the story, emphasizing basic human rights and individual liberties, point to their universal character: "To be free in spirit is the destiny of every human being – the living should take this to heart! Free in soul and free in spirit!"[29] In a similar vein, the poem "Africa, Mother" by Aliou Keita from Mali stresses the need for peace and unity to solve problems of warfare and famine:

> Africa, my Africa, I am thinking of you
>
> It is time to get together
> To decide to work and to eat together
> To ban war and tribal fighting together
>
> [...]
>
> Peanuts, milk potatoes and yams will be plentiful
> after the rainy season
> I will unite the people and bring the produce to them
> To feed up my mother Africa[30]

Instead of focusing on the atrocities of civil war, some other texts foreground such issues as censorship and freedom of speech. The writings by the Sudanese writer Abdalla Bashir–Khairi deal with the absence of human rights in Sudan and underline the impact of censorship. The short story "The Text Committee" satirically describes the power of "the Tribunal Committee of Textual Rectification."[31] The task of this committee is to examine and censor all possible texts, and its chair, "a true maestro," has perfected his task:

---

[28] Kongolo, "The First Fear," 41.

[29] "The First Fear," 41.

[30] Aliou Keita, "Africa, Mother," in *Nobody's Perfect: Refugees Writing in Wales*, vol. 2, ed. Charles, Cheesman & Hoffmann, 63.

[31] Abdalla Bashir–Khairi, "The Text Committee," tr. Ibrahim Gafar, in *Nobody's Perfect: Refugees Writing in Wales*, vol. 2, ed. Charles, Cheesman & Hoffmann, 43.

> He assigned to himself, long ago, the task of writing the idealizing
> reports refusing permission for any text that fails to restrict itself to
> the literal precepts of the official dispensation.[32]

By describing the questions that they pose to writers, Bashir–Khairi points
to an atmosphere of paranoia and an inability to present a critique of the
state of affairs, as well as revealing the impossibility of voicing dissent in
such conditions. As the political is redefined as the linguistic, this silencing
is constructed as a form of grammatical and thus apparently objective work,
rather than as official censorship:

> To these oppressive adepts are due the poll-taxes of speech.
> Through them alone all texts must pass, and none may be correc-
> ted except by their committee.
>   They thunder that the writer of the play *The Cock of Al-Hajja
> Bhana* must spell the title differently. And they add, in an insinuat-
> ing tone: "What do you *really* mean by the cock of Al-Hajja Bahan,
> anyway? And *who* do you mean, eh?" Before he answers this ques-
> tion himself, the maestro says haughtily: "Leave the text with us to
> correct the linguistic errors with which it is no less than rife. Go and
> don't come back until we summon you!"[33]

The danger of dissent expressed through literature can be seen explicitly
in the poem "I Guarantee" by the Zimbabwean William G. Mbwembwe.
This poem presents a series of contrasts between the government's official
explanation of the state of affairs and the way in which they are experienced at the grassroots level.

> I can guarantee, the rate of crime is very low in Zimbabwe
> Everybody's into it, it's the norm
> I can guarantee, fuel is plenty-plus in Zimbabwe
> Always at a filling station at the other side of town.[34]

The poem culminates in lines telling of the danger of dissent: "I can
guarantee a long life in Zimbabwe / Just don't carry this poem with you."[35]

---

[32] Bashir–Khairi, "The Text Committee," 43.
[33] "The Text Committee," 43; emphasis in the original.
[34] William G. Mbwembwe, "I Guarantee," in "The Angelic Faces (Two Poems)," in
Soft Touch: Refugees Writing in Wales, vol. 3, ed. Charles, Cheesman & Hoffmann, 28.
[35] Mbwembwe, "I Guarantee," 28.

What these texts reveal is a lack of cultural rights and of the right to narrate in particular, the latter considered by Homi K. Bhabha to be a fundamental human right and central to the experience of migrants and minorities:

> The right to free thought and speech is fundamental to the right to narrate. [...] To protect the "right to narrate" is to protect a range of democratic imperatives: it assumes that there is an equitable access to those institutions – schools, universities, museums, libraries, theatres – that give you a sense of collective history and the means to turn those materials into a narrative of your own. Such an assured, empowered sense of "selfhood," the knowledge that to tell your story is to know that there is a "public culture" in which it will be heard and could be acted upon, depends upon the nations' guardianship of what Article 5 of the International Convention on Economic, Social and Political Rights defines as "the right to take part in cultural life."[36]

In discussing the absence of civil rights in their countries of origin, some authors rely on literary conventions such as the fairytale and allegory, through which they are able to approach the political problems of their country of origin in order to narrate their experience. This can be seen in such stories as "The Poet's Garden" by the Algerian author Soleïman Adel Guémar. The protagonist of this story, the poet, who lives "on the roof-terrace of a high-rise apartment block [...] in an old washroom, three metres by two," seeks to transform this desolate space "into a pretty little garden."[37] The story shows how he gradually constructs such a utopian space, "a garden as lovely as those of ancient Babylon,"[38] carrying soil to his terrace – "'A poet's whim!'"[39] However, after some years the existence of such a dissident place is suddenly reported to the government by Sidi-El-Hadj El-Thawri, who has just married his young daughter to an

---

[36] Homi K. Bhabha, "On Writing Rights," in *Globalizing Rights: The Oxford Amnesty Lectures 1999*, ed. Matthew J. Gibney (Oxford: Oxford UP, 2003): 180–81. See also David Huddart's insightful article on Bhabha and the notion of cultural rights: "Hybridity and Cultural Rights: Inventing Global Citizenship," in *Reconstructing Hybridity: Post-Colonial Studies in Transition*, ed. Joel Kuortti & Jopi Nyman (Amsterdam: Rodopi, 2007): 21–41.

[37] Soleïman Adel Guémar, "The Poets' Garden," in *Nobody's Perfect: Refugees Writing in Wales*, vol. 2, ed. Charles, Cheesman & Hoffmann, 78.

[38] Guémar, "The Poet's Garden," 78.

[39] "The Poet's Garden," 79.

elderly army officer. As the story pits the poet's fanciful creation against what roof gardens are really for ("It's for television aerials, or maybe for playing football or a bit of jogging"[40]), the allegory is revealed as dealing with fundamentalism and censorship. As a sign of this, the local business-men promise money for the person who manages to kill the poet, "to achieve this patriotic honour."[41] Unsurprisingly, the end of the story shows the mob entering his garden and throwing the poet to what appears to be his death. Yet his fall is never-ending and miraculous, suggesting that he is beyond their reach. What the story seems to suggest is that the power of words in transforming spaces and ideologies cannot be underestimated: the poet's work, his garden, is shown to be able to take men's thoughts away from murder and violence:

> The garden was sublime. There were flowers of every colour and every possible shape. Nothing like them had ever been seen. One by one, the poet's attackers turned away from the spectacle of his fall to admire the splendours of his garden.[42]

The final image of the story hints at a different future in which poets are not fools but have a major role to play: "And the young boys played at being the little poet."[43]

The poems by Soleïman Adel Guémar are not always allegorical. Rather, images of torture and lack of civil rights are central to his writing, testifying to his commitment to the principles of human rights. A harsh critique of their violation can be seen, for instance, in the series of poems named "State of Emergency (Six Poems)." "State of Emergency," the first poem in this series, opens with images of military violence and organized torture, and its ending shifts the focus from the individual to the nation. Subsequently, it suggests a more general sense of humiliation and links individual traumas to national ones:

> 1.
> army boots kicking my face in
> fingernails torn out one by one
> skull savaged by a drill

---

[40] Guémar, "The Poet's Garden," 80.
[41] "The Poet's Garden," 81.
[42] "The Poet's Garden," 82.
[43] "The Poet's Garden," 82.

militia-men at my bed
in shifts until morning
awaiting the order to slit my throat
avidly

[…]

4.
Algiers betrayed
ordered to the electrodes
adopts a posture
which is foetal[44]

The poetry of Guémar is particularly striking in its intertwined images of violence, torture, and political disappointment. While the above poem shows a body in pain, a human being humiliated, "Fire of Joy" discusses the poet's nation of origin through images of blood and death:

land bled dry
murdered unceasingly
will you ever give birth
to the child I'm expecting from you.[45]

As "Known Places" puts it, these landscapes of terror are burning with fire; they are full of "road[s]" where one can find "remains of bodies / swollen by heat / eaten by animals" and where is "the burned field / still smoking / here monsters passed."[46] To stress this sense of disappointment and the failure of democracy, "Illusions" speaks of our inability to learn from history. For Guémar, safety is a mere misapprehension, a temporary refuge before the next wave of oppressors marches in:

and we thought we were back together again
in a land of asylum
while others hiding in the border shadows

---

[44] Soleïman Adel Guémar, "State of Emergency (Six Poems)," in *Soft Touch: Refugees Writing in Wales*, vol. 3, ed. Charles, Cheesman & Hoffmann, 30–31.

[45] Soleïman Adel Guémar, "Fire of Joy," in "Eight Poems," in *Nobody's Perfect: Refugees Writing in Wales*, vol. 2, ed. Eric Ngalle Charles, Tom Cheesman & Sylvie Hoffmann (Swansea: Hafan Books, 2004): 65.

[46] Soleïman Adel Guémar, "Known Places," in "Eight Poems," in *Nobody's Perfect: Refugees Writing in Wales*, vol. 2, ed. Charles, Cheesman & Hoffmann, 67.

were already waxing their new boots
but you didn't know it yet

[…]

and when you thought you heard
their nearly new boots
resounding
on the smoking tarmac
it was already too late[47]

IV

While the volumes include writing by refugees of all ages and
backgrounds, the issues of race, racism, and prejudice as a part of their
experience of Britain are shared by many writers. As Rebekah F., aged 10,
writes in "Black is …," her contribution to the first volume:

> This is what they say:
> Black is evil,
> It is dark,
> The colour is dull.
>
> This is what they say:
> In black there's a spark,
> A spark that's nasty.
>
> These are words people say,
> And this makes them sad.
>
> Is it out of hate?
> or the colour of their skin?
> But white people here
> Have racism within.[48]

In narrating a dominant attitude towards the forced migrants, the poem
sadly expresses a general atmosphere of racial prejudice. However, a com-

---

[47] Soleïman Adel Guémar, "Illusions" in "Eight Poems," in *Nobody's Perfect: Refu-gees Writing in Wales*, vol. 2, ed. Charles, Cheesman & Hoffmann, 66.

[48] Rebekah F., "Black is …," in *Between a Mountain and a Sea: Refugees Writing in Wales*, ed. Charles, Cheesman & Hoffmann, 23.

plementary perspective to the experience of Rebekah, providing us with a glimpse of hope, can be found in the writings by the nine-year-old Alice Salomon Bowen, whose mother is mentioned as working at a community centre frequented by forced migrants. While the prose text "Let's Get Along" locates its speaker as "Alice. I'm only nine," it also shows her insistence on equality and understanding of difference: "Just because they are different doesn't mean they are bad or trying to hurt us in any way."[49] As her writings show, the British perspective is not entirely unfriendly. In the short poem "Friendship," she puts her call for friendship and equality in the following way:

> Friends of all COLOURS
> Friends of all NATIONS
> Friends of all CULTURES
> Friends of TODAY
> Friends of TOMORROW
> Friends FOREVER[50]

In these writings, Britain appears as a contradictory space. While it offers a future free from violence and oppression, it also shows racial prejudices and problems. The images of Britain offered in the narratives pinpoint the refugees' problematical moments of entry. In describing the refugees' responses to life in Swansea, the narratives render its atmosphere as one of racism and discrimination. This appears to be particularly striking in a set of poems, "Swansea Collage," a version of which can be found in each volume. These "collages," based on conversations and poems by mainly French-speaking African women, have been put together by Sylvie Hoffmann, one of the editors of the volumes. In short poems forming the collage, occasionally no longer than merely one or two lines, the refugee writes back, questions, and wonders about her dislocation in the newly entered host country, where she is often dismayed or outright frightened:

> The cars
> I am frightened
> The streets

---

[49] Alice Salomon Bowen, "Let's Get Along," in *Nobody's Perfect: Refugees Writing in Wales*, vol. 2, ed. Charles, Cheesman & Hoffmann, 20.

[50] Alice Salomon Bowen, "Friendship," in *Nobody's Perfect: Refugees Writing in Wales*, vol. 2, ed. Charles, Cheesman & Hoffmann, 20.

I am frightened
The sea
I am frightened
I am frightened for my children.[51]

Furthermore, "Behind the Facades" shows a refugee mapping the city, where each building looks like a church:

What is behind?
    Is this a church?
No, no… it's a school
    Is this a church?
No, no… it's an Indian restaurant
    Is this a church?
No, no… it's the old Swansea police station[52]

In these poems, issues of cultural difference are also foregrounded, suggesting that the refugee is in a state of liminality. While the speaker in "Clyne Gardens" wonders whether entry to the tranquil greenery of the park is free, the poem "White Man" comments on the pace of life in Europe: "Never has any time / Rushes everywhere."[53] Similarly, "The British" reveals that "They say 'sorry' but do they mean it?"[54] Through comments on the way of life, the refugee writes herself into the space but maintains her difference and her own distinct identity. This is clear in the following two poems, of which the first one, "At Home," contrasts home with Britain: "We get up with the sun / We go to bed with the sun / No one sends us an electricity bill at the end of the month."[55] The second poem inserts the refugee into a community which, while consisting of refugees, finds itself a space in Britain, as "Swansea Central Library" becomes a site of interaction and mutual friendship, a home away from home. Yet the poem also reveals that these women are deprived of their original home and community, and have only each other to send messages to: "We send each other e-mails round the computer table / A good meeting place / A safe

---

[51] Sylvie Hoffmann, comp., "Swansea Collage," in *Between a Mountain and a Sea: Refugees Writing in Wales*, ed. Charles, Cheesman & Hoffmann, 75.

[52] Hoffmann, comp., "Swansea Collage" (2003), 74.

[53] Hoffmann, comp., "Swansea Collage" (2003), 78.

[54] Hoffmann, comp., "Swansea Collage" (2003), 77.

[55] Hoffmann, comp., "Swansea Collage" (2003), 77.

haven."[56] A similar notion of a safe meeting-place can also be seen in the first collage, where the only place welcoming the migrant is a church: "Yes, this is a church / You can come in if you wish."[57]

While the tone of some poems is melancholy and even angry, humour provides occasional relief, as revealed in the response to the speaker of the poem "Kingsway Centre," where she is taking language classes: "How is your English coming along? / – 'I must'."[58] In the "Swansea Collage" published in the third volume, sardonic humour is present in practically all the texts, but especially in "Geography for Beginners," which takes the form of an exercise in a textbook:

> I am from Palestine. I don't want money. I have learned to live without money. Just show me, where can I sleep? Where can I sleep?
>
> I am from the Sudan ...
> (*Read again from after "Palestine" to the end*)
>
> I am from Congo–Kinshasa
> (*Repeat the exercise*)
>
> I am from Ethiopia
> (*Get the idea?*)[59]

The final instructions tell the learners that they should be able to complete the exercise on their own: "*Take a map of the world, pick a country at war – civil war or any other war – and you can practise this exercise in the comfort of your own home. If you need help, just ask anyone in the queue at the Welsh or Scottish or English Refugee Council.*"[60] In rewriting instructional discourse from the perspective of the refugee, the text not only mocks British ignorance about the political situation in non-Western countries but also shows how the migrant, by appropriating the textbook genre, undergoes a transformation from the one who is taught ("I must") to the one who teaches, from object to subject. As studies of refugees have

---

[56] Hoffmann, comp., "Swansea Collage" (2003), 77.

[57] Hoffmann, comp., "Swansea Collage" (2003), 74.

[58] Hoffmann, comp., "Swansea Collage" (2003), 78.

[59] Sylvie Hoffmann, comp., "Swansea Collage," in *Soft Touch: Refugees Writing in Wales*, vol. 3, ed. Charles, Cheesman & Hoffmann, 104; emphasis in the original.

[60] Hoffmann, comp., "Swansea Collage," 104; emphasis in the original.

shown, the reconstruction of identity plays a central role in the process of adaptation; this rewriting signifies their acquisition of an empowered identity. In the process of rewriting, Africa comes to write Britain and Europe.

The issues of home and not-home are emphasized in much exilic and diasporic writing, and the poems occasionally offer glimpses of what has been left behind. As Guémar puts it in a poem called "Exile," the migrant's longing for home is evoked easily and surprisingly:

> my country
> gives off a scent
> which calls you by your first name
> the moment you turn your back
>
> your heart squeezes
> as at your first embrace[61]

The only way, however, to reach this space is through memory and fantasy: "my lunar memory / has woven flying carpets."[62]

Yet the pull of home has been shown to be negotiated when the subject occupies a diasporic identity, where multilocationality replaces the privileging of the site of origin. What diasporic narratives highlight is homing desire, discussed by Avtar Brah as an alternative to fixed narratives of origin.[63] To quote Brah, *"Diasporic identities are at once local and global. They are networks of transnational identifications encompassing 'imagined' and 'encountered' communities."*[64] In constructing diasporic identity, the immigrant links herself not with one transnational community but with several, crossing national boundaries and accepting the possibility of a home other than the originary one. Such a process can be traced in the poetry of Eric Ngalle Charles, whose journeying has taken him from Cameroon to Russia and on to Swansea. In addition to conventional subjects such as love, Charles's poetry also reflects on his childhood and its (post)colonial character, and it also imagines Britain as a new home. In

---

[61] Soleïman Adel Guémar, "Exile," in "Eight Poems," in *Nobody's Perfect: Refugees Writing in Wales*, vol. 2, ed. Charles, Cheesman & Hoffmann, 70.

[62] Guémar, "Exile," 70.

[63] Avtar Brah, *Cartographies of Diaspora: Contesting Identities* (London: Routledge, 1996): 192–93.

[64] Brah, *Cartographies of Diaspora: Contesting Identities*, 196; emphasis in the original.

"My First Language," the presence of different languages links Africa to Wales, and points up the many layers of postcolonial and multilingual identity:

> I thought
> I am Portuguese,
> Never owning a plantation
> Of my own,
> Then I thought I am German,
> Then I realised
> The English kicked
> The kingdom out.
>
> They said
> I was French –
> Oh no, Marie! le bread!
>
> Thanks to the queen –
> Queen Victoria that is –
> I was given the name
> Charles.
> Rumours say he was the great.
> Maybe I'm a Mormon
> Tracking a family tree.[65]

In narrating different histories for himself, the speaker emphasizes the connections between Europe and colonized Africa, and their impact for today. The final words of the poem make this point clear:

> I know my language,
> Existing passively,
> As others came
> And others left,
> Surprised why
> I speak in tongues.[66]

---

[65] Eric Ngalle Charles, "My First Language," in "Five Poems," in *Between a Mountain and a Sea: Refugees Writing in Wales*, ed. Charles, Cheesman & Hoffmann, 29.

[66] Charles, "Five Poems," 30.

In another poem published in the same volume, Charles goes further in linking African and Welsh spaces with each other. "A Mountain and a Sea," a poem about "home-coming," can be seen as multilocational poetry where the features of the original home in Africa are rewritten onto a European landscape. In writing about the Welsh mountains, the poet links them with stories and images of his past and his cultural traditions:

> Her giant gaze
> Looking down at me
> Like Yomadene,
> The guardian,
> The mountain
> Where my grandmother
> Lived after her death.
> A mountain of broken hearts.
>
> That for my homecoming.[67]

To underline the transformation of identity, and its transnational links, the poem next imagines a strikingly pastoral Welsh image of "A shining mountain / where sheep grazed, / By which means / My heart rejoiced,"[68] which is followed with an explicit rebirth in Wales: "On a wet journey to Llandudno / Washing away pain and longing, / A re-born voice crying / Between a mountain and a sea."[69] The final lines are also suggestive of the possibility of making this space one's home:

> That for my home-coming,
>
> Between a mountain
> And a sea.[70]

Thus Charles's poem reinscribes home in the acquired space and landscape of Wales, yet this home embodies the migrant's memories of other homes beyond the sea. Such a process of home-building is described by Sara Ahmed et al. as a way of collecting fragments and other traces of a former

---

[67] Eric Ngalle Charles, "A Mountain and a Sea," in *Between a Mountain and a Sea: Refugees Writing in Wales*, ed. Charles, Cheesman & Hoffmann, 90.

[68] Charles, "A Mountain and a Sea," 91.

[69] "A Mountain and a Sea," 91.

[70] "A Mountain and a Sea," 91.

home: "Making home is about *creating* both pasts and futures through inhabiting the grounds of the present."[71] Hence, both the poetry of Charles and the images carved out in the different versions of "Swansea Collage" are attempts to negotiate dislocation which use writing as a means of making home in the space of the Other, where the presence of the refugee is on occasion barely tolerated. As shown in "In the Fish and Chips Shop," a poem in "Swansea Collage," "Broad smile: / – 'Are you on holidays?'"[72] Yet the innocent-sounding question by the smiling shop assistant is not necessarily welcoming: the "broad smile" may easily turn into coldness and hatred, should the answer to the question turn out to be an undesired one: i.e. one revealing that the alleged vacationer is an asylum seeker.

V

Not only do the images and stories in these volumes told by African refugees themselves offer insights into the problems encountered in their countries of origin but they also tell of processes of dislocation, exile, and cultural adaptation. In their emphasis on the problematics involved in forced migration – the traumas generated by civil-war atrocities and the racism encountered in Britain in particular – the narratives appear to foreground the negative experience of migrancy, and understandably so. Nevertheless, as I have shown, some refugee narratives also suggest the possibility of reconstructing home and identity in the context of Britain. While the figure of the forced migrant as such cannot be romanticized and posited as a privileged model of identity in the postcolonial world, its presence in the former centre shows that it cannot be evaded and easily transported.[73] The migrant, as Homi K. Bhabha has put it, is inhabiting

---

[71] Sara Ahmed, Claudia Castañeda, Anne–Marie Forter & Mimi Sheller, "Introduction: Uprootings/Regroundings: Questions of Home and Migration," in *Uprootings/Regroundings: Questions of Home and Migration*, ed. Sara Ahmed, Claudia Castañeda, Anne–Marie Fortier & Mimi Sheller (Oxford: Berg, 2003): 9; emphasis in the original.

[72] Hoffmann, comp., "Swansea Collage," 77.

[73] This can be seen in the recent emergence of a number of Black British novels dealing with refugees and their presence in English spaces. These include Abdulrazak Gurnah's *By the Sea* (2002), Caryl Phillips's *A Distant Shore* (2003), and Benjamin Zephaniah's *Refugee Boy* (2001).

the postcolonial space [that] is now "supplementary" to the metropolitan centre; it stands in a subaltern, adjunct relation that doesn't
aggrandize the *presence* of the West but redraws its frontiers in the
menacing, agonistic boundary of cultural difference that never quite
adds up, always less than one nation and double.[74]

As testified in refugee narratives, the frontiers of Europe are not closed but
permeable, and its shores not beyond the effects of global forces. As stories
of dis- *and* re-location, these narratives tell of the emergence of a new
phase in European culture, where global flows affect the national narratives
of formerly homogeneous nation-states and generate new forms of identity.

WORKS CITED

Ahmed, Sara, Claudia Castañeda, Anne–Marie Fortier & Mimi Sheller. "Introduction" to *Uprootings/Regroundings: Questions of Home and Migration*, ed. Ahmed, Castañeda, Fortier & Sheller (Oxford: Berg, 2003): 1–19.

Anon. Dedication, in *Between a Mountain and a Sea* (2003), ed. Charles, Cheesman & Hoffmann, 1.

Bashir–Khairi, Abdalla. "The Text Committee," tr. Ibrahim Gafar, ed. Tom Cheesman, in *Nobody's Perfect* (2004), ed. Charles, Cheesman & Hoffmann, 43–45.

Bhabha, Homi K. *The Location of Culture* (London: Routledge, 1994).

——. "On Writing Rights," in *Globalizing Rights: The Oxford Amnesty Lectures
1999*, ed. Matthew J. Gibney (Oxford: Oxford UP, 2003): 162–83.

Bowen, Alice Salomon. "Friendship," in *Nobody's Perfect* (2004), ed. Charles,
Cheesman & Hoffmann, 20.

——. "Let's Get Along," in *Nobody's Perfect* (2004), ed. Charles, Cheesman &
Hoffmann, 20.

Brah, Avtar. *Cartographies of Diaspora: Contesting Identities* (London: Routledge,
1996).

Camino, Linda. "Refugee Adolescents and Their Changing Identities," in *Reconstructing Lives, Recapturing Meaning: Refugee Identity, Gender, and Culture
Change*, ed. Linda Camino & Ruth M. Krulfeld (Basel: Gordon & Breach, 1993):
29–56.

Charles, Eric Ngalle. "Five Poems," in *Between a Mountain and a Sea* (2003), ed.
Charles, Cheesman & Hoffmann, 27–36.

——. "A Mountain and a Sea," in *Between a Mountain and a Sea* (2003), ed.
Charles, Cheesman & Hoffmann, 90–91.

---

[74] Homi K. Bhabha, *The Location of Culture* (London: Routledge, 1994): 168; emphasis in the original.

——, Tom Cheesman & Sylvie Hoffmann, ed. *Between a Mountain and a Sea: Refugees Writing in Wales* (Swansea: Hafan, 2003).

——. *Nobody's Perfect: Refugees Writing in Wales 2* (Swansea: Hafan, 2004).

——. *Soft Touch: Refugees Writing in Wales 3* (Swansea: Hafan, 2005).

Cheesman, Tom. "Preface," in *Between a Mountain and a Sea* (2003), ed. Charles, Cheesman & Hoffmann, 7–8.

Eagleton, Terry. *Exiles and Emigrés: Studies in Modern Literature* (London: Chatto & Windus, 1970).

F., Rebekah. "Black is …," in *Between a Mountain and a Sea* (2003), ed. Charles, Cheesman & Hoffmann, 23.

Grewal, Inderpal, & Caren Kaplan. "Introduction: Transnational Feminist Practices and Questions of Postmodernity," in *Scattered Hegemonies: Postmodernity and Transnational Feminist Practices*, ed. Grewal & Kaplan (Minneapolis: U of Minnesota P, 1994): 1–33.

Guémar, Soleïman Adel. "Eight Poems," in *Nobody's Perfect* (2004), ed. Charles, Cheesman & Hoffmann, 64–70.

——. "The Poet's Garden," in *Nobody's Perfect* (2004), ed. Charles, Cheesman & Hoffmann, 78–82.

——. "State of Emergency (Six Poems)," in *Soft Touch* (2005), ed. Charles, Cheesman & Hoffmann 30–34.

Gurnah, Abdulrazak. *By the Sea* (London: Bloomsbury 2002).

——. "Fear and Loathing." *The Guardian* (22 May 2001): online http://www.guardian.co.uk/g2/story/0,,494415,00.html [accessed 4 May 2005].

Gurr, Andrew. *Writers in Exile: The Identity of Home in Modern Literature* (Brighton: Harvester, 1981).

Hoffmann, Sylvie, comp. "Swansea Collage," in *Between a Mountain and a Sea* (2003), ed. Charles, Cheesman &Hoffmann, 74–81.

——. "Swansea Collage," in *Soft Touch* (2005), ed. Charles, Cheesman & Hoffmann, 102–109.

Huddart, David. "Hybridity and Cultural Rights: Inventing Global Citizenship," in *Reconstructing Hybridity: Post-Colonial Studies in Transition*, ed. Joel Kuortti & Jopi Nyman (Amsterdam: Rodopi, 2007): 21–41.

Kaplan, Caren. *Questions of Travel: Postmodern Discourses of Displacement* (Durham NC & London: Duke UP, 1996).

Keita, Aliou. "Africa, Mother," in *Nobody's Perfect* (2004), ed. Charles, Cheesman & Hoffmann, 63.

Kongolo, Aimé. "The First Fear," in *Soft Touch* (2005), ed. Charles, Cheesman & Hoffmann, 39–41.

Kpakio, Maxson Sahr. "I Feel like Nobody Here," in *Between a Mountain and a Sea* (2003), ed. Charles, Cheesman & Hoffmann, 68–69.

Kundnani, Arun. "In a Foreign Land: The New Popular Racism," *Race & Class* 43.2 (2001): 41–60.

Langer, Jennifer, ed. *The Bend in the Road: Refugees Writing* (Nottingham: Five Leaves, 1997).

Marfleet, Phil. *Refugees in a Global Era* (Houndmills: Palgrave, 2006).

Mbwembwe, William G. "I Guarantee," in "The Angelic Faces (Two Poems)," in *Soft Touch* (2005), ed. Charles, Cheesman & Hoffmann, 28–29.

Phillips, Caryl. *A Distant Shore* (London: Secker & Warburg, 2003).

Said, Edward W. *Reflections on Exile and Other Essays* (2000; Cambridge MA: Harvard UP, 2003).

Turner, Victor. *Dramas, Fields and Metaphors: Symbolic Action in Human Society* (Ithaca NY: Cornell UP, 1974).

Zephaniah, Benjamin. *Refugee Boy* (London: Bloomsbury, 2001).

⟨⟩

Notes on Contributors and Editors

◀▷

CHRISTINA ANGELFORS is an Associate Professor of French at Växjö University in Sweden. She holds a doctorate from the University of Lund, Sweden and has also studied at the Sorbonne. She is the author of *La Double Conscience: La prise de conscience féminine chez Colette, Simone de Beauvoir et Marie Cardinal* (1989). She has published extensively on the autobiographical writings of Simone de Beauvoir. Her recent research is focused on the African francophone writer Calixthe Beyala. She is a member of the international editorial board of *Nouvelles Questions Féministes* and the editor and translator of Luce Irigaray into Swedish.

GABEBA BADEROON received a doctorate from the University of Cape Town. She has held fellowships at the African Gender Institute, the Oxford Centre for Islamic Studies, and the University of Sheffield. Baderoon is the author of the poetry collections *The Dream in the Next Body* and *A Hundred Silences*. She teaches at Pennsylvania State University.

GEOFFREY V. DAVIS teaches anglophone postcolonial literature at the Universities of Aachen and Duisburg–Essen in Germany. His major fields of teaching and research are the literatures of South Africa, Australia, and Canada. His most recent publication is a co-edited volume entitled *Staging New Britain: Aspects of Black and South Asian British Theatre Practice* (Brussels, 2006). He is currently chair of the Association of Commonwealth Literature and Language Studies (ACLALS).

DOROTHY DRIVER is a Professor of English, Adelaide University, Australia, and an Emeritus Professor and Honorary Research Associate at the University of Cape Town. She publishes widely in gender studies in Southern African literature, and was one of the editors of *Women Writing Africa: The Southern Region*.

JOPI NYMAN is currently Professor of English at the University of Joensuu in Finland. His research interests cover British, American, and postcolonial literature and culture, and he is currently completing a full-length study on contemporary diasporic fictions. His chief publications include: *Men Alone: Masculinity, Individualism and Hard-Boiled Fiction* (1997), *Hard-Boiled Fiction and Dark Romanticism* (1998), *Under English Eyes: Constructions of Europe in Early Twentieth-Century British Fiction* (2000), *Postcolonial Animal Tale from Kipling to Coetzee* (2003), and *Imagining Englishness: Essays on the Representation of National Identity in Modern British Culture* (2005). He has also edited several collections of essays, most recently *Reconstructing Hybridity: Post-Colonial Studies in Transition* (2007), co-edited with Dr Joel Kuortti.

MARIA OLAUSSEN is Professor of English at Växjö University in Sweden. She holds a doctorate from Åbo Akademi University in Finland and has held fellowships at the University of Cape Town and Princeton University. Her publications include *Three Types of Feminist Criticism and Jean Rhys's "Wide Sargasso Sea"* (1992) and *Forceful Creation in Harsh Terrain: Place and Identity in Three Novels by Bessie Head* (1997). Her research interests include South African autobiography, feminist theory, whiteness and masculinity, and representations of intimacy in African women's writing.

ANN–SOFIE PERSSON earned her doctorate in French from the Ohio State University in 2001. Her dissertation, "Tracer l'enfance: Poétiques autobiographiques chez Maria Wine, Patrick Chamoiseau et Nathalie Sarraute," deals with autobiographical childhood narratives. Her recent research concentrates on the Guadeloupean writer Maryse Condé and her autobiographical images. Since 2001, she has been teaching French literature, comparative literature, and gender studies at the University of Linköping, Sweden.

JARMO PIKKUJÄMSÄ is a doctoral student in the Africa Department, School of Oriental and African Studies, at London University. His main research interests concern the contemporary African novel and Islam, migration, urbanization, and gender in literature. He has published on Ken Bugul and Peter Kimani.

WUMI RAJI is an Associate Professor of Drama at the Obafemi Awolowo University, Ilé-Ifè, Nigeria. He took a doctorate in African and Postcolonial Literatures at the University of Ibadan, Nigeria in 1995, specializing in anglophone African and African-American literatures and theatre. He has held fellowships and/or guest professorships at the University of Bayreuth, Germany, and the Technical University of Dresden, also in Germany, as well as at Växjö University, Sweden, and the University of Cambridge. His book *Transformative Imagination: Essays in African Postcolonial Literature and Culture* is forthcoming.

ALEXANDRA SCHULTHEIS is an Associate Professor of Postcolonial Literatures and Theory in the Department of English at the University of North Carolina at Greensboro. She is the author of *Regenerative Fictions: Postcolonialism, Psychoanalysis, and the Nation as Family* (2004). She has also published on Tibetan autobiography, contemporary postcolonial literature, and pedagogy Her research interests cover postcolonial literatures and theory, international human rights in literature and film, contemporary colonialisms, and alternative modernities. Her current research project concerns transnational human-rights narratives in contemporary Tibet.

◄►

Index

❮❯